THE ORIGIN OF PERSPECTIVE

HUBERT DAMISCH

THE ORIGIN OF PERSPECTIVE

translated by John Goodman

THE MIT PRESS

CAMBRIDGE, MASSACHUSETTS

LONDON, ENGLAND

English translation © 1994 by the Massachusetts Institute of Technology. Published with the assistance of the Getty Grant Program. Originally published in French under the title *L'Origine de la perspective*. © 1987 by Flammarion, Paris. Works by Picasso © by SPADEM.

Completion of this volume was made possible by assistance from the Center for Advanced Study in the Visual Arts of the National Gallery in Washington, where the author was a resident scholar in 1982–83. He would like to express his gratitude to its director, Henry Millon, as well as to the entire staff of CASVA.

The schematic drawings and graphic reconstructions are the work of Jean Blécon, architect CRHA.

This book was set in Garamond 3 by DEKR Corporation and was printed and bound in the United States of America.

Library of Congress Cataloging-in-Publication Data

Damisch, Hubert.
    [Origine de la perspective.   English]
    The origin of perspective / Hubert Damisch ; translated by John Goodman.
        p.   cm.
    Includes bibliographical references and index.
    ISBN 0-262-04139-1
    1. Perspective.   I. Title.
NC750.D3413   1994
701'.82—dc20
                                                        93-21895
                                                            CIP

for Meyer Shapiro

Contents

xi   Translator's Note

xiii   Preface

Part One THIS POINT ASSIGNED BY PERSPECTIVE

2   1   At the Crossroads
A threshold text. If history there be, of what is it the history? The notion of "symbolic form." Panofsky as a reader of Cassirer. Perspective and its various kinds. An index, not of value but of style. Perspective and *Weltanschauung*. Panofsky as Hercules . . . Symbolism in painting.

22   2   Perspective, a
            Thing of the Past?
Perspective is not a code. There are paradigms and paradigms. The "purpose" of so-called scientific perspective. Panofsky and the avant-garde in 1925. Merleau-Ponty and the watchword of a return to primitive thought. Wittgenstein: a new "sensation." Perspective as myth, or how to get rid of it. Space according to reason.

42   3   Knowledge
            and Truth
A period-specific phenomenon. The denigration of the signifier. Perspective and the moment of the *cogito*. The geometrical dimension of sight and the function of the lack. The question of the fixed point in the *âge classique*. Point of view and point of subject. Perspective meditation and the value of origin. Desargues and the perspectivists. The two perspectivisms. Pascal: the *mad* point.

Part Two THE PROTOTYPE

58   4   The Tradition   Brunelleschi the inventor of perspective? Alberti's dedicatory preface. Filarete's treatise. Manetti's *Vita*. Vasari.

74   5   The Question of the Origin   The invention of the rule. The origins of perspective and geometry. The meaning of history. Perspective in practice and theory. Knowledge and truth. The Brunelleschi demonstration. The textual tradition.

88   6   The Monstration   *Was der Fall ist*. The lost prototype. And as for the sky. Perspective and the built object. Perspective shows. The mirror demonstrates.

100   7   The Painting's Reasons   The square of the *quadro*. Windows and doors. The schism between the eye and the gaze. A matter of angle, distance, and point of view.

114   8   The View   The mirror stage of painting. *Imago*: the phase effect. The double designation of the point. The fissure. Infinity, an idea of "what's behind one's head." What is vision? It's me, as if I were there. A hole that's a stain. A lentil for a ducat. The two witnesses. The value of the autopsy. The "small" *braccia*. *E pareva che si vedessi 'l proprio vero.*

142   9   Geometry Made Real   The second experiment. The indiscretion of he who looks. The return of the denoted. A positivist notion of truth. The destruction of the painting. The question of infinity. An unprecedented idea.

156   10   The Renaissance and the Repetition of the Original   The inversion. The loss. Truth of painting, truth in painting. *E iscritto non si truova*. Brunelleschi, "inventor of the Renaissance"?

Part Three SUSPENDED REPRESENTATION

168   11   "Et anticho in prospettiva"   The *Città ideale* and the "Urbino perspectives." Inventories. Proof by context. *The Mandrake*. What is thinking?

198   12   Distancing Maneuvers   Evasive tactics. The tragic scene and the comic scene. The view (continued). Architectural reference. The theater and "flat" painting. Illusion and trompe l'oeil. Scenography. The case of set design. A long-established procedure.

236   13   The Reading at an Impasse   The descriptive illusion. Meaning and reference. What is describing? Reckoning with painting without being taken in by it. Poetry as precision. The representation's absence from its place. Perspective transfixed. Perspective and architecture. Sites of writing.

Contents

278   14 **To See Them, You Say, and Describe Them**   The need for finesse. Structuralism, without knowing it. Learning to count to three. A rule for description. Transformations. The invariability of the point. The sun in Baltimore. Absence makes for meaning. Shutters. The blank, the enigma.

314   15 *De prospectiva pingendi*   Epistemology of the group. The painting of reference. The prototype, again. Clouds in painting. Symmetries and automorphisms. Aberrations and curious perspectives. The hole. Transgressing the limits. Piero's demonstration. The genius of perspective. Ensigns in painting. The consistent angle.

374   16 **The Loci of the Subject**   The view (*tertio*). Diderot's telescope. Rotation/ostension. *Quasi per sino in infinito*. The subject holds by a thread. Serlio and the horizon of the theater. Relief, style, and idea. The theater of painting. The contradictor. Poetry and geometry. *Las Meninas*, once again. The geometry of the sentence.

449   Index

Translator's Note

A few remarks concerning specific translation problems. *Dispositif perspectif* is used frequently by Damisch; I was initially stumped by the elusive first word of this phrase (which can mean "setup" or "apparatus," with their concrete implications, or "disposition," with its more abstract and conceptual overtones), all the more so as its very slipperiness is one reason Damisch uses it consistently—though it is also intended to evoke Benveniste's phrase *dispositif d'énonciation* ("sentence structure," with a marked emphasis on the performative aspect of speech as opposed to writing). I have rendered it throughout as "perspective configuration."

Age classique is a term of historical periodization which has no precise equivalent in English, designating roughly the period falling between the Renaissance and the modern era centered in the "classic" seventeenth century; it has been left in the original French.

Représentation carries all the meanings of the parallel English term and then some: in French it also means "performance," in the sense of a theatrical presentation, and Damisch does his best to make this *double entendre* work for him in part III. Its very title is a pun on the word: *Représentation suspendue* can signify either "suspended representation" or "performance postponed," both of which are relevant and intended by Damisch. As a translator I had to choose between them and opted for the first, primary meaning. But the reader should bear in mind the theatrical reference of the word as it is used here.

I have tried to employ standard renderings of Lacanian terminology but have not made a fetish of consistency: *charnière*, for instance, is sometimes translated as "hinge," sometimes as "pivot." Similarly for terms drawn from the phenomenological tradition, notably the writings of Husserl and Merleau-Ponty: I consulted the English language editions of these works but departed from their locution when it seemed appropriate for reasons of context and/or sense. This was, in fact, my procedure with all the translated works, notably the Renaissance texts by Manetti and Filarete which exist in excellent bilingual critical editions: I have sometimes diverged from the renderings of their distinguished translators, always in the direction (I hope) of readings that are more literal, if less elegant, than theirs, in a way consistent with Damisch's stated goal of "close reading."

Thanks to James Elkins and Marvin Trachtenberg, who assisted me, respectively, with technical terms and bibliography; to Dana Andrus of The MIT Press for her fine editing; and to Damisch himself, who was helpful in clarifying several points relating to some of the book's more difficult passages. But there are bound to be errors in any translation of a work of this intellectual breadth and density; egregious or not, all of them are mine.

J. G.

Preface

This book was born of impatience. A double impatience, traces of which will be felt here and there, for I have not wanted to remove all of them. First, I found it regrettable that subject matter as highly speculative as perspective—that used by painters, the *perspectiva artificialis* as opposed to traditional optics, both antique and medieval, the *perspectiva* said to be *naturalis*—had given rise only, apart from a few notable exceptions, to scholarly work that was often erudite (and for this reason alone precious, indispensable) but that failed to engage the relevant philosophical issues. I further observed that in different texts by different authors treating the question of perspective—if not perspective as a question—dogmatism, received ideas, prejudices, and, still worse, precipitate conclusions generally won out over the demands of knowledge and reflection. And this was all the more the case, in my judgment at least, when the analysis, or what passed for such, was in the service of a critical project that was clear-cut and radical.

But there is more. Such is indeed the heuristic power of the perspective configuration, and the value of it as a model for thought, that it continues to exercise its influence over the widest range of domains, while in the field of art any reference to so-called scientific perspective is taken to be an indication of archaism. This seems obvious enough when Michel Foucault refers to the compositional arrangement of *Las Meninas*, undermining and recasting its implications, reducing it to flatness, then by contrast restoring its three-dimensionality to illustrate retrospectively the workings of the system of representation that functioned as the bedrock of thought in the *âge classique*. The question becomes more complicated with Jacques Lacan, when he states that a painting (*tableau*) is "the relation through which the subject comes to find its bearings as such": while encouraged to do so in the service of perspective, we must take care not to confuse the subject here, which is the desiring subject, with the cartesian subject, the one that, in the historically defined moment of the *cogito*, gives itself out to be the correlative of science, in the modern sense of the word, while at the same time presupposing the unconscious—the index, from the start, of a split, a cleavage (Freud's *Spaltung*), and of the division experienced by the subject as a division between knowledge and truth.[1] I am amazed that although both of the texts in question have achieved the status of modern classics, these two treatments of the paradigm of perspective in contemporary theoretical writing have led to results diametrically opposed to those we might have had reason to expect. Foucault's discussion of *Las Meninas* and Lacan's digression on the scopic relation, despite their preliminary character (for preliminary is what they are), far from having cleared the way for more rigorous examination of an object of study which these publications presented in a new light, have remained undeveloped, at least in France, their only effect seemingly to have spawned a platitudinous discourse all the more discouraging because of its unjustifiable claims to theoretical legitimacy.

It would be overly fastidious to catalog here the imprecise definitions, the crude simplifications, not to mention the outright errors and misunderstandings, that are the stock in trade of those, their motives often suspect, who parrot formulations that no longer have even the merit of novelty. This tendency is especially pervasive in certain fields of inquiry that have only an indirect bearing on painting, for example, in studies of photography and film. A curious polemical debate took shape in these fields in Paris in the 1970s, fallout from which can still be observed today. Basing their arguments, as I myself did in 1963,[2] on the fact that the photographic box, and the camera which is its technical extension, function optically in a way wholly consistent with so-called one-point perspective (to such an extent that Delacroix could envision using photography as a means of producing the perspectival framework for his paintings), some maintained that photography and film disseminate spontaneously, and so to speak mechani-

---

1.   Cf. Jacques Lacan, "La Science et la vérité," *Écrits*, Paris, 1966, pp. 855–77 (not included in the English-language edition of *Écrits*).

2.   See Hubert Damisch, "Cinq notes pour une phénoménologie de l'image photographique," *L'Arc*, no. 21 (spring 1963, special photography issue), pp. 34–37; English trans., "Five Notes for a Phenomenology of the Photographic Image," in *Classic Essays on Photography*, ed. by Alan Trachtenberg, New Haven, 1980, pp. 287–90.

cally, bourgeois ideology (because perspective, having appeared at the dawn of the capitalist era, must of necessity be essentially "bourgeois"), while others (sometimes the same individuals) celebrated the pallid attempts of would-be experimental cinema to free itself from the "tyranny" of the single point of view and from the general constraints of perspective. Against which still others protested vigorously, citing perspective's scientific status as a means of defending it against accusations of its being an ideological tool. This debate is now an old story. But it has left copious traces behind it. It is frequently misclaimed that perspective, through the intermediary of the *camera oscura*, functions like ideology as understood by Marx.[3] While both of these, in the last analysis, rely on similar reasoning, the operation of perspective nonetheless differs from that of the *camera oscura* in two fundamental respects: first, it is not based on the play of shadows, but rather requires bright light if it is to produce its effect; second, it in no way dictates an upside-down reversal, only the simple possibility of turning the image from left to right, which poses an entirely different problem.

The assertion that the camera, by its very structure, exudes ideology can lead to two disparate interpretations. It is one thing to regard it, its mechanics, as an ideological contrivance. It is quite another to claim that it is such because it is regulated by the perspectival "code" and, through this, by an acquired ideology. In its capacity as a machine that is not intended to enhance vision (the camera is not a telescope) but rather to produce images, the apparatus must be regarded with suspicion, and we are encouraged to so regard it by the fact that the photographic process can only be carried out in darkness. If it has an ideological effect, this is not because at the back of the darkened chamber the image appears upside down: later steps in the process put this right, just as, according to Descartes, the "soul" is supposed to do for the image presented to it by the retina. No, this is because photography deceptively presents itself to us as a passive recording, an objective, because physical, reflection of the reality that is its ostensible material—and this with total disregard for the configuration by whose means it functions, which is effectively relegated to obscu-

---

3.   "If in all ideology men and their circumstances appear upside-down as in a *camera obscura*, this phenomenon arises just as much from their historical life-process as the inversion of objects on the retina does from their physical life-process," Karl Marx, *The German Ideology*, International Publishers, New York, 1970, p. 47.

rity, controlled as it is by a mechanism now so fully automated that we can use it without knowing anything about it.

It's all very well for some to maintain that the technical procedure in itself is neutral, and that if ideology there be, it should be sought in the message and not the code (thereby making it easier for us to grasp the interests shaping the project, itself ideological, of effecting a reduction of perspective to a straightforward graphic process, an enterprise that has been underway, as I will show, since the sixteenth century). This argument, supposing for a moment that it holds up, doesn't apply to the said technical procedure (or the said "code") decking itself out in stolen finery. Such an application might be proposed with regard to *perspectiva artificialis*, the only "scientific" thing about which would be its name. But this would create a double impasse, with regard to both the problems posed by reference, the resort to geometry as a rational foundation for *costruzione legittima*, and the mathematical support that was, historically speaking, a primary concern of painters' perspective, namely descriptive geometry and plane geometry. In other words, the debate cannot concern itself exclusively with the "basic apparatus" to the exclusion of the code in conformity with which the latter operates. The question of the semiotic status best assigned *perspectiva artificialis* remains entirely open, given that it lends itself to varied applications, any one of which could serve as the basis for a rule, or set of rules, sufficient to define a specific regime of representation. But even if it should be reduced to a "code," being nothing more than a conventional, partially arbitrary form of expression corresponding to a moment of representation, if not to that age which is said to be, par excellence, that of representation, ostensibly dominated by its structure—in other words, even if we grant that it has no existence, validity, signification, meaning, or pertinence that is not confined within strict chronological and historical parameters—such an assertion merits that we stop a moment to examine it more closely.

To claim that *perspectiva artificialis*, as it was constituted in the quattrocento, is a typical product of the bourgeois era is to beg the question. It is to give short shrift to the problem of antique perspective: although the ancients never elaborated a system of one-point perspective, the (late) examples of painted architectural decoration that survive at Pompeii and elsewhere suffice to demonstrate that their ability to reduce spatial relations to geometric measurements was relatively advanced. The same problem arises with the designation of *costruzione legittima* as "humanist." In my view it can be demonstrated that humanism (Tuscan or other) is irreconcilable with so-called central perspective, just as it is with the precise definition of the subject (*subject*, not Man) which is its corollary. Robert Klein has shown how Pomponius Gauricus, at the beginning of the sixteenth century, attempting to replace the rational, geometric perspective of quattrocento theorists with a perspective that he characterizes as "humanist," and whose primary concerns were with narratives.[4] A half-century later Vasari would complete the process of stripping *perspectiva artificialis* of its theoretical "aura," relegating it to the status of a straightforward technical procedure. To discuss perspective in terms of ideological critique is to foreclose all possibility of understanding its historical fortune, as well as the efforts of humanism, over almost a century, to bring it into conformity with its own standards, those—precisely—of ideology.

The eminently paradoxical status which is that of perspective considered as a cultural formation renders the historian's task particularly difficult, making him prone to all sorts of anachronisms. Thus, for example, it has been claimed that a new notion of space was put forward by Alberti—the same one, mathematical and idealist, for which Descartes would formulate a conceptual basis two centuries later, designating it as *extension*, conceived to be homogenous, continuous, and infinite. This is to forget that the geometry of the Greeks, to which the author of *Della pittura* consistently refers, was a finite geometry, one concerned not with space but with figures and bodies as described, or delineated, by their *boundaries*, whether these be circumscribing contours or the surfaces enclosing them, to use Alberti's own definition.[5] But it is not sufficient for the space within which perspective operates, which it in fact presupposes, to be posited as infinite: it must also be *centered*, which might appear to be a contradiction in terms.

4.   Robert Klein, "Pomponius Gauricus on Perspective," *Form and Meaning: Writings on the Renaissance and Modern Art*, Princeton, 1979, pp. 102–28.

5.   Cf, my *Théorie du nuage. Pour une histoire de la peinture*, Paris, 1972, p. 162. I should point out here that while the idea is regularly associated with the model proposed by Alberti, the notion of *costruzione legittima*, which supposedly originated with Leonardo da Vinci, only became current, in these terms, at the beginning of the twentieth century. Cf. Erwin Panofsky, "Das perspektivische Verfahren Leone Battista Albertis," *Kunstchronik*, vol. 16 (1915), pp. 504–16, and Samuel Edgerton, "Alberti's Perspective: A New Discovery and a New Evaluation," *Art Bulletin*, vol. 48 (1966), pp. 267–78.

It will be freely admitted that, like geometry, *perspectiva artificialis* was preoccupied from the start by the question of infinity. This is not to say that, from the beginning of the game, it rendered the image and the question of the "subject," as implied by the device, mutually indissoluble. And it is to go too far too fast, it is to move with undue haste to maintain, as does the prevailing lingo, that the modern age's conception of *representation* is rooted in this "umbilical knot." One could reach such a conclusion only after prolonged intellectual work, of a kind that is not identical with the elaboration, however rigorously and deliberately carried out, of the rules governing so-called central perspective: the nature, if not the structure, of the perspective paradigm is such that of necessity it imposed itself from the outset in its fully developed form, at the same time invoking an effort of conceptualization that supposedly preceded its integration into the mathematical order, whereas the reduction of perspective to a straightforward technical procedure would entail, by contrast, ideological relapses whose implications have yet to be fully grasped.

It follows that one must be quite naive to perceive, behind the will to subdue representation by means of the rational calculations which are at the origin of the perspectival project, the specter of Marx's "old enemy," merchandise. Quite naive or quite cynical: for such a discourse brings to mind others having to do with "bourgeois science" that are no longer considered respectable but that persist nonetheless, cunningly preparing themselves for an eventual return to the limelight. The attacks mounted against structuralism in the name of "history" are complicit with this ideological tendency, though they are also the result of quite different determinants. Of course the debate pitting a vision of things that is static, simultaneous, and ultimately spatial against one that is temporal, and thus dynamic, vibrant, even genetic, is an old one. This debate has not been ignored by modern science: one has only to consider the way Johannes Kepler, after having arrived at the metrical propositions governing the distribution of planets in the cosmos, proceeded to study the chronology of their movements, though he did this in hopes of confirming the existence of a universal architectonics.[6] It is nonetheless true that classical physics acknowledges the existence of time and space only in their abstract, quantifiable manifestations. "Time

---

6.   Cf. Gérard Simon, *Kepler astronome astrologue*, Paris, 1979, pp. 283ff.

sheds its qualitative, variable, flowing nature. It freezes into an exactly delimited, quantifiable continuum filled with quantifiable things . . . in short, it becomes space."[7] The same calculating genie is at work in art and the natural sciences, and its intervention leads to effects in those fields that are analogous, though not synchronous. But the mere observation that the preliminary formulation of a new ideational form called perspective preceded, by one or two centuries, what Edmund Husserl called the "Galilean mathematicization of nature" scarcely justifies our ascribing responsibility for it to an infrastructural determination. Unless we are to defer to a typically bourgeois conception of art, holding that it should adhere to the movement of "life" as closely as possible, avoiding all theory, if not all thought, as if it were the plague.

*

My admitted impatience with certain uses to which history has been put is certainly not meant to foreclose the possibility of analyzing works and texts in cultural terms, within the context of a history that, while not "total" or totalizing, is broadly conceived. A history that makes no claims to having the last word about anything, that is practiced under the express conditions that the very term naming the discipline is understood to be problematic, with nothing self-evident about it, and that the question of the different uses to which it lends itself, like that of its ultimate meaning, is to remain a constant reference point on the horizon of research, as well as the related question: If history there be, *of what* is it a history? With the result that history is most itself when it is taking the measure of something that partly eludes its grasp, necessitating a rethinking of the very notion of history.

One will not find here a history of perspective, nor of its discovery, nor of its rediscovery by the artists of the quattrocento. Works of this kind continue to appear, in large numbers and with variable results, though this production has become increasingly attenuated since the publication of the famous, and now venerable, text by Erwin Panofsky on *Perspective as Symbolic Form*, which even today, for better or worse, is a mandatory point of reference. But the truth is that all these works are open to the same criticism:

---

7.   Georg Lukács, *History and Class Consciousness*, English trans. by Rodney Livingstone, Cambridge, 1971, p. 90.

the historian thinks he can treat perspective as the product of a history that it is his task to reconstruct, as if it were a reality immediately accessible to him through art works and texts—an object of study, in short, that he thinks he has inherited, that is supposed to have been *given* him, such that its earliest manifestations, its more evolved ones, and finally its decline, disappearance, and destruction can be observed at leisure as in a laboratory. Two scenarios are made possible by this, both of which attest to the limits of cultural history. The first maintains that a mode of graphic representation such as perspective can only have an empirical origin, one linked to studio practice, and that *costruzione legittima* must have been preceded by a long series of tentative efforts, of periodic advances and retreats, before crystalliz- ing into the form that was subsequently theorized and codified. The second, precisely symmetrical to the first, would have us seek out the sources of *perspectiva artificialis* in erudition and theory, notably in antique and medi- eval optics—but has nothing to say that helps us grasp the exact nature of the causes entailing its decline, abandonment, and purported end in the early twentieth century. Unless we are to turn, again, to history, in a quasi- tautological move: if perspective has passed out of fashion, if its time has passed (after having shaped it, this time, in a very literal way), this is because it does not correspond to the look and requirements of our own.

Narratives of this kind are predicated on the existence of something called "history" that determines, in an almost Darwinian way, the fate of systems of thought and representation, of their birth as well as their death and replacement by others better adapted to the current needs of the spe- cies. This crude evolutionist notion of the emergence of cultural formations takes no account of the curiously paradoxical nature of those objects and structures I would call paradigmatic, which traverse history—or collide with it—because they function as so many models for thought, which is regu- lated by them, leaving their mark on the most diverse fields of endeavor, and remain resolutely unembarrassed (the history of science furnishes count- less proofs of this) by being declared "obsolete" if they can still be of use to it or advance its projects. Among these objects and structures, a catalog of which would be worth drawing up, perspective occupies a privileged posi- tion, for it embodies all the traits of a paradigm in the technical meaning of the word, a meaning—need I specify this?—that differs markedly from the slipshod one recently associated with the word in the field of the history of science, even implicitly contradicting it.

If by "paradigm" one understands a model used in declension or conjugation, then *costruzione legittima* fits this definition quite literally: its apparatus is characterized by the conjunction, the bringing together at a given point designated the "origin," of lines that measure the declension of figures, by establishing their relation to a shared horizon line, while simultaneously determining their conjugation on the plane. Clearly such a configuration functions syntactically. But this insight should not lead to neglect of its paradigmatic dimension. To each figure its place: at each point on the underlying checkerboard, if not within each of its squares, one figure and only one, among all those that are possible, can be situated—which brings us back to an order of combinations (or as Ferdinand de Saussure would say, "associations") that have no spatial extension. To be sure, declension and conjugation of figures within the perspective scene don't function in precisely the same way, but much theoretical work, beginning with that of Piero della Francesca, set out to impose on the *diminutio* strictly numerical rules of proportion entirely independent of all consideration of extension.[8] Without taking into consideration that, regarding the syntactical sequences deployed in this theater, the *costruzione legittima* proposes, in its very configuration, a formal apparatus which, with its viewpoint, vanishing point, and "distance point"—organizing itself as it does around the position of a "subject" taken to be the origin of the perspectival construction, the index of what is *here*, what *there*, and what *over there*—is equivalent to a network of spatial adverbs, if not personal pronouns: in other words, to what linguists call an "expressive apparatus" (*dispositif d'énonciation*, sometimes translated as "sentence structure").

Paradigm, from the Greek παραδείϰνθμι, "to show," "to exhibit," "to indicate," "to represent," "to compare": the hypothesis I intend to develop here, on the basis of an analysis, as rigorous as possible, of some of the procedures and operations that the perspective configuration (*dispositif*

---

8.   Cf. Rudolf Wittkower, "Brunelleschi and 'Proportion in Perspective,'" *Journal of the Warburg and Courtauld Institutes*, vol. 16 (1953), pp. 276–91; reprinted in R. W., *Idea and Image: Studies in the Italian Renaissance*, London, 1978.

perspectif) has fostered in practice as well as theory, would doubtless qualify for designation by the term used by Nicolas of Cusa[9] to indicate the resources a "model" can offer thought, whether it be understood in the Platonic sense of an idea of which the beings participating in it are the reflection, or rather in another, more strictly technical sense as a logical *artifact* that is something like the manifest essence of an object, real or ideal, which thought is attempting to comprehend. Perspective, as we shall see, shows, and even demonstrates. To such a point that the ascendency of the paradigm has made itself felt well beyond the borders of the regional domain within which it first made an impact (that of painting), and this without its having lost, to this day, any of its capacity to convey information or its power to attract.

*

It follows from the preceding that any treatment of perspective and its history must be predicated, from the very beginning, on the understanding that this history is by definition *plural*. As an object of knowledge, perspective is accessible to comprehension by means of a series of art works and texts, or discourses and experiences, of very different kinds that do not necessarily lend themselves to sustained reading and analysis, or to continuous narrative. This is why the most interesting publications on the subject, the ones animated and informed by genuine thought, are also the ones that, with no pretentions to providing a synthetic view of the whole, limit themselves to a single aspect of the problem: I have in mind, above all, the now classic book of Jurgis Baltrušaitis on anamorphosis and the work of Alessandro Parronchi on the initial experiments of Brunelleschi, as well as several studies in art history and the history of science to which I refer below. But the diversity of possible approaches only throws into higher relief the contradictions generated by the compartmentalization of knowledge, as well as the multiplicity of levels on which the paradigm can be observed to function. For the moment I will cite but a single example, one to which I will return further on. The treatise by Piero della Francesca, *De prospectiva pingendi*, lends itself to two radically divergent readings as well as to two

---

9. Nicolas of Cusa, *Le Profane, oeuvres choisies*, trans. into French by Maurice de Gandillac, Paris, 1942, p. 275.

opposing interpretations, depending upon whether one orients oneself in relation to the history of art or the history of science. With regard to the first, the limitations of the text are obvious: it seems as though Piero said nothing about painting, that his approach to perspective was singularly restricted and strictly deductive, completely unrelated to the actual practice of painters (notably his own), and couched in a language that none of the eminent specialists on this painter would hesitate to describe as archaic. If, on the other hand, one's point of departure is the history of mathematics, one cannot help but be struck by the extraordinary discourse that in many respects—beginning with the formulation of problems of spatial geometry in terms of plane geometry—seems to "anticipate" that of a geometry that would instruct itself using the example set by perspective before proceeding on to an advance (*relève*) in the conceptual order. That this air of novelty derives from the transposition into the painter's language of definitions that are the foundation of euclidean geometry, producing an effect that could be dubbed one of *translation* (in the etymological meaning of the word, the original model for which was established by Alberti), only makes it that much more remarkable: the painter's decision to adhere to a specialized discourse (*Parlo come pittore*, "I speak as a painter") paradoxically conferred on that discourse a significance it would have been impossible to anticipate, at least working within the conventional terms of the history of art and the history of science.

If I take Alberti's book—too often decried as that of a theorist completely removed from studio practice, more intent upon reducing perspective to a code that upon exploring the possibilities it seemed to offer painting—to be one of the fundamental texts of western culture, this is in part because it operates on several levels, with an unequaled mastery, and undertakes, in imitation of the paradigm that is its point of departure, to articulate several different histories. That is to say, one should not attempt, any more than with Piero's text, to analyze or interpret it in a univocal way. The same statement holds a fortiori for the myth of the origin of perspective as transmitted to us by tradition and for the entire body of work, whether practical or theoretical, made possible by Brunelleschi's experiments.

Thus my own project is not that of writing *a* history of perspective but rather, to appropriate a title used by Machiavelli, a set of "perspective stories," each of which aims at isolating one strand of the intricate network within which the paradigm is imbricated, trying to pursue it to its end, carefully noting points of intersection as well as boundary lines between discourses. "Stories," but which nonetheless will not be fables like those told by Pliny, if Alberti is to be believed, and which will have more to do with the "art of painting," the latter set out to build, working, as he says, with his own resources, *di nuovo*,[10] than with the history of art as it is usually practiced. Stories that address precisely painting's claim to a new kind of *truth*. Stories that in their variety, multiplicity, and difference set out not so much to determine what *perspectiva artificialis* was in a historical sense as to put it to work again, so to speak, in view of achieving a fuller understanding, from our retrospective viewpoint, of how useful a resource it has been for thought, now so intent upon being free of it. A warning to the reader: the pages that follow will have their share of trying passages and repetitions and will not be devoid of obscurity. In a mean-spirited review of the work of my friend Alessandro Parronchi, the author of one of the above-mentioned synthetic overviews felt comfortable asserting that current per-spective studies are excessively erudite and that the two virtues more neces-sary than ever in this field of study were clarity and brevity.[11] As regards these two catechismal virtues, I very much fear that pursuit of the one entails sacrifice of the other and that, as the prevailing platitudes demon-strate, simultaneous pursuit of both comes at a high price, namely the renunciation of thought. As for erudition, it can never be excessive if it manages to throw new light on texts and works of art, helping us to see them a bit more clearly and to more fully grasp the play of knowledge and truth.

WASHINGTON, September 1982
LE SKEUL, June 1984

---

10.   "Poi che non come Plinio recitamo storie ma di nuovo fabrichiamo une art di pittura . . .."
Leone-Battista Alberti, *Della pitture*, book II, ed. Luigi Malle, Florence, 1950, p. 78; English trans. by John R. Spencer, New Haven and London, 1956, p. 65.
11.   Samuel Y. Edgerton, review of Alessandro Parronchi, *Studi su la dolce prospettiva*, Milan, 1964, *Art Bulletin*, vol. 49 (1967), pp. 77–80. The remark is all the more cutting, given that Edgerton's own work is at its best when scholarship and erudition are most in evidence.

THE ORIGIN OF PERSPECTIVE

Demonstrate how nothing can be seen except through a small fissure

through which passes the atmosphere filled with images of objects

that cross in front of one another between the thick, opaque sides of

the said fissure. To this end, nothing immaterial can discern the

shape or color of an object, it being understood that a thick, opaque

instrument is necessary if, through its fissure, the images of objects

are to take on color and form.

LEONARDO DA VINCI, Codex Atlanticus, fol. 345 recto

Part One

THIS POINT ASSIGNED BY PERSPECTIVE

A threshold text.

If history there be, of what is it the history?

The notion of "symbolic form."

Panofsky as a reader of Cassirer.

Perspective and its various kinds.

An index, not of value but of style.

Perspective and *Weltanschauung*.

Panofsky as Hercules . . .

Symbolism in painting.

At the Crossroads

Anyone investigating perspective today, in its double capacities as object of knowledge and object of reflection, must negotiate territory that remains under the jurisdiction of a text that has attained classic status, one that still constitutes, more than half a century after its initial appearance, the inescapable horizon line and reference point for all inquiry concerning this object of study and all related matters, to say nothing of its theoretical and philosophical implications. And this is the case whether it is considered in a material sense, consistent with the way scholastics subjected objects to scientific scrutiny, or in a formal sense, regarding its conceptual framework.

One can pretend to have read it or affect to ignore it, like Pierre Francastel and John White (the latter ready to embrace the fantasy of curvilinear perspective, but without proposing any objective justification for this), or simply treat it as yet another citation in a bibliography whose considerable length will impress no one except fine minds who, while writing about it and adding their own names to the list, claim to see in perspective nothing more than an object of curiosity that's a bit obsolete or—to cite the paradoxical stance adopted by Robert Klein—an "inoffensive" discipline.[1] The consequences of such dodges and feints—misreading, or (much worse) the denial of that intellectual work of which perspective is simultaneously the occasion, the site, and the instrument—are sufficient to demonstrate that Panofsky's article on "Perspective as Symbolic Form," first published in the *Vorträge* of the Warburg Library for 1924–25 (and which resembles a lecture or summary, one to which the subsequent addition of an extensive set of notes gave a character that one might call labyrinthine, were

---

1. Klein, "Studies on Perspective in the Renaissance," *Form and Meaning,* op. cit., p. 129.

it not for the rigor of the argument), represents a kind of textual threshold that must be crossed before one can undertake—if such a project makes any sense—to "go beyond" it.[2]

To maintain, with Decio Gioseffi, that this celebrated text, however tainted it may be by multiple errors, has not so much clarified our ideas about perspective as intensified our confusion about them, and that it must now be considered, *from the historical point of view* (my emphasis), as an epistemological obstacle to be discarded,[3] this argument would seem to constitute another kind of dodge, though one that's subtler and better suited, to all appearances, to the demands asserted to be those of history and science. For to insist on the "scientific" character of perspective, and on the correspondence, entirely hypothetical, that might exist between vision of an object and that of its image in perspective, resolves none of the problems posed by the appearance, the *constitution*, in a given historical moment, of a form at least ideal, and—to be more precise—of a model of representation susceptible, in the fields of both art and science, to developments of a kind that might be qualified as *symbolic*—and this despite the fact that if they were founded upon rigorous demonstration, they would have been readily accepted. At that hinge (*charnière*) where nature and artifice, art and science, confront one another, the question of the status and functioning of the perspective paradigm remains completely open, as does that of the nature of its effect on the practice of painters and geometers, and even on the discourse of philosophers.

One always comes back to this question, and to the problem formulated by Émile Benveniste concerning language: If history there be, of *what* is it the history? Perspective's fortune in the study of art over the last century (apart from its impact on the history of painting) has largely resulted from the fact that it seemed to provide historians with a clearly

---

2.   Erwin Panofsky, "Die Perspektive als 'symbolische Form,'" *Vortrage des Bibliothek Warburg,* 1924–25, Leipzig–Berlin, 1927, pp. 258–330; reprinted in E. P., *Aufsätze zu Grundfragen des Kunstwissenschaft,* Berlin, 1964, pp. 99–167. English trans. by Christopher Wood, *Perspective as Symbolic Form,* New York, 1991.

3.   Decio Gioseffi, *Perspectiva artificialis. Per la Storia della prospettiva. Spigolature e appunti,* Trieste, 1957, pp. 6ff. Gioseffi's refusal to engage Panofsky's text was based on historical and theoretical considerations. A sign of the times, one that justifies the polemical tone I have adopted here: The refusal of theory, if not of all thought, has led certain historians (doubtless old before their time) to see it as nothing more than a "youthful folly." Cf. *infra,* chapter 12, p. 234, note 57.

defined object, one endowed with a formidable internal coherence and whose genesis and evolution they could easily study in terms distinct from, and more rigorous than, those used by them in studying "style"—though this last notion was cherished by them above all others, corresponding to analogous demands: the equivalent, if not of a specific language, at least of those verbal formations familiar to the linguist. The assignment to perspectival "form" of a symbolic value or function entailed certain difficulties with regard, precisely, to history, as is demonstrated, *a contrario,* by the transformations undergone by linguistics over the same period. To cite Benveniste once more, didn't Saussure's innovation consist in his making us aware that "language in itself does not admit of any historical dimension, that it consists of synchrony and structure, and that it functions only by virtue of its symbolic nature"?[4] Then what are we to say of science, if indeed this is nothing more than a well-constructed language, one enabling scientists to formulate questions eliciting answers couched in like terms? If perspective belongs to the symbolic order in one way or another, on either scientific or linguistic grounds, then does the statement Benveniste applied to language, and that a historian of science could well appropriate to his own ends, at least as regards mathematics, apply to it as well: "Time is not the agent of evolution, it is only its framework"?[5] Having come so far, we can no longer avoid the question: What if it were history, at least a certain kind of history, that functioned, with regard to perspective, as an epistemological obstacle?

This is one of the questions, and not the least, eluded by those currently dealing with perspective who choose to pay tribute to Panofsky only as a matter of convention, or who criticize him over such and such a point of fact or history, at the risk—to use Benveniste's terms once more—of "atomizing" their object of inquiry and conceiving of its evolution in mechanical terms. It is only too true that the author of "Perspective as Symbolic Form" blurred the distinction between vision and the optical process leading to the formation of an image on the internal, concave surface of

---

4. Émile Beveniste, "Tendances récentes en linguistique générale," *Problèmes de linguistique générale,* Paris, 1966, p. 5; "Recent Trends in General Linguistics," English trans. by Mary Elizabeth Meek, Coral Gables, 1971, p. 4.
5. Ibid.; English trans., p. 5.

des Geistes) and of deciding to what extent these forms do or do not constitute a system.[9]

For such is the central question around which, from the start, *The Philosophy of Symbolic Forms* is organized. And this question is of particular import to the theory of art, even though Cassirer applied his critique only to verbal thought and mythic thought, returning at the end of the work to a phenomenology of scientific knowledge, treating the form of "art" only incidentally, though he invokes it with some regularity. In accordance with one's predisposition to answer positively or negatively, one will be led to investigate whether some shared, constitutive element or principle is operative in the different "symbolic forms," on which basis it should be possible to think through their reciprocal configurations and articulations—the middle term having been found that facilitates extension of the work accomplished by transcendental philosophy to the totality of intellectual operations. Unless, that is, one abandons the notion of an encompassing unity, in which case the philosophy of the said forms would ultimately be reduced to a history clothing itself in the externals of a history of language, a history of religion and myth, or a history of art, as appropriate for each specific object.[10]

Cassirer thought he had found this element, this mediating principle, this middle term in what he called the "general function of symbolization": The philosophy of symbolic forms aims at nothing less than application of Leibniz's "universal characteristic," based on the idea that conceptual definition of any content whatever goes hand in hand with its stabilization in a *sign*, to the totality of symbolic activity, whether linguistically based or not. Were this project to prove successful, we would then have at our disposition "a kind of grammar of the symbolic function as such, which would encompass and generally help to define its special terms and idioms as we encounter them in language and art, in myth and religion."[11] Far from being a simple reflection, the *sign* is the instrument, as Benveniste would later put it, of a *re-production* that has meaning, that *makes*

---

9.   Cassirer, op.cit., vol. 1, introduction.

10.   Ibid.; English trans., p. 84.

11.   Ibid., p. 86.

sense, only insofar as it is subjected to a strict set of rules. As Cassirer asserts, the operation of the sign is indistinguishable from the very principle of consciousness, which implies that nothing can be posited by it that does not refer to something else, that does not need supplementary mediation. "Only in and through this *representation* does what we call the 'presence' of the content become possible."[12] It is still necessary, if one is to speak of *symbolism* as it is currently understood, for this representation, operating as it does like a kind of *mise en scene* or natural scenography—its signifying power being antecedent to the position of any specific sign—to be caught up in a network of relations that conforms to a principle of constitution, which in turn makes its mark on all its productions. In the last analysis the sole purpose of "symbolic forms," their sole *product,* is just this: *the conquest of the world as representation.*[13] "Thus language, myth, and art each constitutes an independent and characteristic structure, which does not achieve its value from an outward, transcendent existence that is somehow 'mirrored' in it. What gives each of these forms its meaning is that it builds up a peculiar and independent, self-contained world of meaning according to an inherent formative law of its own. Thus in all of them, as we have seen, a principle of objective formation is at work. They are modes of 'growing into being,' of *genesis es ousian,* as Plato called it."[14]

*

The import, within the framework of a philosophy of representation such as Cassirer's, of treating perspective as a "symbolic form" will be immediately apparent. Its operation seems to correspond perfectly to the function which is that of language, myth, and art, to say nothing of science: a function by no means specular, or passive, but rather constitutive, within the register of representation, of the order and even the meaning of things, first and foremost of the "world of objects." Including, as Cassirer insists, the synthetic function identifiable with the *I*: the "I" which in this capacity must be inscribed, from the beginning, within the "point of view," an idea that

---

12. Ibid., p. 98.
13. Ibid., vol. 3, p. 281.
14. Ibid., p. 383.

necessarily refers us back to that of the "subject" as well as to that of language and even, if Cassirer is to be believed, of the phonetic sign.[15] But this operation has meaning, once again, *makes* sense, only insofar as it conforms to a principle of constitution with its own specific rules. If man can learn to see an image in perspective, instead of seeing—in the words of Ludwig Klages—"a man drawn or painted in perspective" as animals do, as "nothing more than a piece of colored paper or canvas,"[16] this is because of what has already been said: "The conception of an aesthetic form in the sensible world is possible only because we ourselves created the fundamental elements of form. All understanding of spatial forms, for example, is ultimately bound up with this activity of their inner production and with the law governing this production."[17] Or, to cite Cassirer once more: "In each one of its freely projected signs the human [mind] apprehends the object and at the same time apprehends itself and its own formative law."[18]

While Cassirer may not have been fully aware of this, these statements have the merit of implicitly posing the question of the role of the symbolic in the realm of the imaginary. The very considerations that favor this assignation increase the difficulty of situating perspective within the symbolic order. Without going so far as to unequivocally identify it as a "symbolic form," thereby placing it on the same footing as art, with which it would then enter into competition—and would one then regard it as a simple "idiom," or as a singular form among all those in terms of which a plastic thought is realized, seeing it, along with Panofsky, as a manifestation of style, one that is itself incapable of bestowing value of any kind?[19]— it should be noted that in any case its range of application extends well beyond the field of art. To be sure, the notion of a unified space seemingly posited by certain paintings functions on a level quite distinct from that implied by the propositions of euclidian geometry: in the one case, space is apprehended qualitatively, intuitively; in the other, it is conceived as a rational, essentially metrical system. But the crucial consideration remains

---

15. Ibid., p. 91.
16. Ludwig Klages, *Ausdruckbewegung und Gestaltungskraft*, Leipzig, 1923, p. 198; cited by Cassirer, English trans., op.cit., vol. 3, p. 112.
17. Cassirer, op.cit., vol. 1, p. 88.
18. Ibid., p. 92.
19. "Allein wenn Perspektive kein Wertmoment ist, so ist sie doch ein Stilmoment . . . ." Panofsky, op. cit., p. 108; English trans., pp. 40–41.

the following: that a single network of lines can create an effect of depth that implies the negation, or—as the phenomenologists would put it—the *"néantization,"* of the plane onto which it is projected, to the gain of the image inscribed there, or it can be regarded as a figure of plane geometry, in accordance with the tenets laid down, long before Gérard Desargues, by Piero della Francesca in his *De prospectiva pingendi.* And this holds for countless perspectival sketches and studies: each is reducible to a principle of construction that can vary within certain parameters but that nonetheless conforms to a single design principle (the one designated by the term "perspective"), the same network of relations correlating, in the one case, with the realm of the imaginary and, in the other, with the realm of the concept. And it is just this that makes it difficult, if not impossible, where perspective is concerned, to establish a clear distinction between aesthetic determinations and logical ones. On this point, as on many others, we do well to heed Leonardo da Vinci, who observed that while perspective is the daughter of painting, she in turn demonstrates it.[20] And thanks to the considerable demonstrative power inhering in it, its effects were felt, as Panofsky saw very clearly, not only in painting but in science, especially geometry, upon which it had initially seemed to depend.

In truth, these questions do not seem to have interested Panofsky, whose intention was, as he says quite openly, "to extend Ernst Cassirer's felicitous term [i.e., 'symbolic form'] to the history of art."[21] The fact is, however, that, far from making reference to it from the start, he only introduces it after extended developments, supposedly based on psychophysiology, that directly contradict Cassirer's arguments because they take the retinal image, which has nothing to do with the symbolic order, to be the touchstone of perspective construction. And as for the definition he uses, which holds that perspective is one of those "symbolic forms" by means of which "intellectual meaning becomes so closely linked to a concrete sign as to be indistinguishable from it,"[22] it is sufficiently vague and generalized to

---

20. Cf. H. D., *Théorie du nuage,* pp. 215ff.

21. "Um Ernst Cassirer glücklich geprägten Terminus auch für di Kunstgeschichte nutzbar zu machen," Panofsky, loc. cit.

22. "Als eine jener 'symbolischen Formen' bezeichnet werden durch die ein geistiger Bedeutungsinhalt an ein konkretes sinnliches Zeichen geknüpft und diesem innerlich zugeeignet wird." Ibid.; cf. Cassirer, English trans., op.cit., vol. 1, p. 93.

justify any interpretation one would like. Perspective, a system of signs? Then it would have been necessary to specify what "use" such a system might be in this context, and whether it functions here in any way other than metaphorically. But to even pose this question would have made another approach to the problem necessary and inevitable: far from simply *applying* the notion of symbolic form to a field into which Cassirer himself had not ventured, as others in the same period tried to do with the concepts of psychoanalysis, it would have been necessary for Panofsky to conceive his investigation into perspective as a critical contribution to the philosophy of symbolic forms, without prejudging what the theoretical consequences of such an enterprise might be in his own domain, that of the history of art.

*

The precise moment chosen by Panofsky to introduce the notion of "symbolic form" into his text is not without its significance: it was carefully tied to a context, to his comparison of antique or "herringbone" perspective, in which orthogonals converge at several different points on a single vertical axis, with modern or "central" perspective, which conforms to the principle of a single vanishing point. Panofsky himself conceded that his analysis might seem to overemphasize purely mathematical aspects of the problem, at the expense of aesthetic ones and, to an even greater degree, those germane to the history of art; its great merit was to have acknowledged the extent of the difficulties inherent in any analysis, however tentative, or perspectival procedures as applied to any given period—difficulties that are *essential* and that cannot be fully explored without intensifying them still further, to such a point that one goes beyond the strictly comparative, relativist approach adopted by the author of *Perspective as Symbolic Form.* For the comparison between antique perspective and modern perspective, like the purportedly objective critique of *construzione legittima,* was meaningful for him only insofar as it led to reformulation of a question then preoccupying specialists: if history attests to the existence of several kinds of perspective none of which has a claim to absolute validity, the problem—again, an *essential* problem—is no longer simply that of discovering whether different periods or provinces of art knew perspective (perspective, or *a* perspective, the German language allows for some ambiguity here) but rather of determining *what* perspective they knew—which amounts to viewing perspective as a genus of which there are several different species.[23]

Panofsky did not address the first of these questions, ignoring those civilizations that seem to have been unfamiliar with perspective—at least with linear perspective—taking into consideration only those periods of western art that knew of it, or that *refused* it in a more or less deliberate and radical way: that refused it or *negated* it, in the dialectical sense of the word. Examples of this were early Christian art, which evidenced, in an almost tangible way, a destruction of the very idea of perspective,[24] and Romanesque art, in which its surviving vestiges were reduced to nought, though not without the establishment of a new relationship between elements brought together on the same plane that would evolve, eventually, into modern "systematic space" (*Systemraum*).[25] To say nothing of Byzantine art, in which light, in the form of gold or intense blue ground functioned, for the first time, as the very substance of the ideal realm.

The history of western perspective is thus construed as conforming to a crude Hegelian schema in which the moment of synthesis is itself subjected to teleological constraints, as is attested by the extended period of groping that—I am still summarizing Panofsky—led to the discovery, in image making, of the single vanishing point at the distant horizon of a checkerboard ground square perpendicular to the picture plane. But nothing in the analysis of the moment of "negation" provides us with an answer to the other question insinuating itself into his "history": Is it possible to have a figurative art that does not have perspective at its command in one form or another, however this might differ from our own conception of it? Or again, if the concept is to be broadened in this way, to avoid emptying it of all meaning: In the (supposed) absence of (some kind of) perspective, what "form" might take its place that would perform comparable symbolic functions, if it is true—as maintained by a compatriot of Cassirer and Panofsky, the sociologist Georg Simmel—that spatial relations are simultaneously the

---

23. "Und es ist in diesem Sinne für die einzelnen Kunstepochen und Kunstgebiete wesenbedeutsam, nicht nur ob sie Perspektive haben, sondern auch welche Perspektive sie haben." Panofsky, op. cit., p. 108; English trans., p. 41.
24. Ibid., p. 111; English trans., p. 47.
25. Ibid., pp. 112ff.; English trans., pp. 50ff.

condition and the expression of relations between individuals acting in history, whether real or imagined?[26]

With regard to medieval painting, Panofsky endorsed the prevalant idea that meaningful surface relations are reducible to a set of symbolic relations. But in what sense are these relations symbolic? In the sense that they proceed by convention, in opposition to the "natural" relations characteristic of an illusionist art that is fundamentally realist, like that of the Renaissance. The paradox here should be readily apparent: To the symbolic conception, linked to a denial of perspective, that prevails in medieval art is opposed the naturalist conception characteristic of the Renaissance. But given this opposition, how is it meaningful to qualify as "symbolic" the form to which the renaissant art is indebted, precisely, for its "naturalist," "realist" appearance? And is it a sufficient explanation of this seeming paradox to observe that in any case, and however "illusionist" it might be, perspective always includes some portion (a variable portion?) of convention, but not in such a way that we might classify and establish a hierarchical order among them? The form of perspective is not an index of value but of "style": Does this mean that it is only "symbolic" in accordance with a given stylistic moment and that there is never any perspective save in reference to a specific period? Does each moment of history have its own kind of perspective (supposing it has any at all), as each period has its own style?

Symbolic, the form known as "perspective"? Symbolic of *what*? The question might seem naive or crudely formulated, and it is. Nonetheless, it brings to the fore the inflection and even degeneration operated upon, in Panofsky's text and, even more, in the work of his epigones, a notion excluding, at least initially, all circumstantial determinants, including—first and foremost—determinants specific to a given period. Honesty compels us to state that the sections of Panofsky's text devoted to the genesis of the perspective construction with a single vanishing point offers a model of analysis as yet unsurpassed, one whose impact on subsequent criticism and analysis has not been as great as it should have been. It demonstrates, makes tangible, how art was able, in its own way, to serve as both site and instrument of an intellectual project casting doubt on the venerable Aristo-

---

26. Georg Simmel, *Soziologie*, Leipzig, 1908, p. 685; English trans., *The Sociology of Georg Simmel*, New York, 1950, p. 402

telian opposition between imagination and conceptual thought—the same thought of which perspective was a product but which it in turn furnished with new models, or tools, whose power is acknowledged in the conceptual realm as well as that of representation. The slow crystallization of the idea of spatial recession, over the course of a sequence of steps that in many instances were taken blindly—a process in which strictly graphic determinations were in a constant struggle with mathematical and logical ones—is a particularly telling example. As is that of the notion of planar intersection, paintings having been initially conceived in logical terms, as sections through material volume,[27] the idea of geometric *projection* having been formulated only later. These "histories," to say nothing of that—posing very different problems—of the "distance point," seem to complement and extend Cassirer's analyses nicely, and make an extremely important contribution to the "philosophy of symbolic forms" as well as to history, or better, to cultural anthropology, in the strongest and most radical meanings of these terms: never has the power accruing to the history of art when it dares run the risk of thought, and especially of questioning the very nature of "art" and of "history," been so apparent as on these pages.

*

Unfortunately, there is another strand of Panofsky's argument that is based on a misunderstanding—if not an outright denial—of Cassirer's critical project. If the philosophy of symbolic forms is not to be reduced to a history, specifically to the history of those particular forms that are language, myth, art, and science, then the question of their unity, tendentious at the very least, must be raised continually as a fundamental preoccupation of reason, in the expansive sense described above. Of their unity or, to put it better, of their mutual articulation. Nowhere is this question more pertinent than with regard to perspective—seeing as perspective arose simultaneously from the domains of art and science, of intuition and cognition. Trying to fathom how the ancient world could make do with a perspective in some sense layered, if not fragmented, the represented space being

---

27. Cf. on this point the admirable analyses of the miniature illustrating the *Office of the Dead* in the Turin-Milan Hours and of the *Virgin in the Church* in Berlin by Jan van Eyck, Panofsky, op.cit., pp. 119 and 152–54, notes 51 and 52; English trans., pp. 59–61 and 126–29, notes 51 and 52.

reduced to a simple composite (*Agregatraum*) as opposed to modern systematic space, Panofsky aptly observed that antique thought was not in a position to relate spatial properties to the common denominator of an encompassing substance, of a *quantum continuum*. As Max Jammer has demonstrated, Greek science and philosophy first conceived of space as discontinuous, because of local geometric variations (this can be observed in Plato), and later, in Aristotle, as anisotropic, because of the different orientations imposed on the substratum.[28] Such that Panofsky believed he could write that both "aesthetic space" and "theoretical space" recast perceptual space, though in different guises, in symbolic terms in one case and in logical terms in the other.[29]

The idea that antique perspective was a *response,* in the figurative register, to a notion of space conceived as a receptacle of bodies or a correlative of figures, this idea is perfectly acceptable so long as these are not referred (as Panofsky refers them) to a "view of space" or a "conception of the world" of which they would be, in their different ways, the expression[30] if not the *sign,* that word being understood in a way that has nothing to do with semiotics. Here one recognizes subtle derivations (*Raumanschauung, Weltvorstellung*) from the venerable notion of *Weltanschauung,* itself derived from Hegel's *Zeitgeist,* which had long since been accorded a place of honor in the project of *Geistesgeschichte* and was subsequently taken up and given a new credibility by Georg Lukács, in whose Hegelian brand of Marxism the notion of "world view" was relegitimized by replacing the spirit of a "people" (*Volksgeist*) with that of a "class,"[31] In 1923 the sociologist Karl Mannheim published an extended analysis of this notion intended for art historians, in the hope of providing them with conceptual models that were more sophisticated, and better suited to current intellectual trends, than those employed, in the wake of Wilhelm Dilthey, by Aloïs Riegl and

28.   Max Jammer, *Concept of Space: The History of Theories of Space in Physics,* preface by Albert Einstein, Cambridge, MA, 2d ed. 1970, p. 25.
29.   Panofsky, op.cit., p. 111; English trans., pp. 44–45.
30.   "So ist also die antike Perspektive der Ausdruck einter bestimmten Raumanschauung . . . und einer ebenso bestimmten Weltvorstellung." Ibid., p. 110; English trans., p. 43.
31.   Cf. Georg Lukács, *History and Class Consciousness,* op. cit. For a useful analysis of the Hegelian sources of *Kulturgeschichte,* cf. Ernst Gombrich, *In Search of Cultural History,* Oxford, 1969.

Antón Dvořák.[32] If we should want proof that Panofsky had read Mann-heim's article, we need not look very far: this article contains the initial formulation of the theory of the three levels of signification—objective, expressive, and documentary—which Panofsky would appropriate and trans-form, without citing his source, in the introduction to his *Studies in Iconol-ogy* of 1939. As always in such cases, this dissimulation should be taken as indexing a resistance, though one directed less against Mannheim than against Cassirer. For Panofsky, as a good art historian, was only too ready to conceptualize the relation between the different sectors of thought and human activity under the Nietzchean auspices of a *stylistic unity* correlating with the "genius" of a given period, with its *Weltanschauung* or, as Panofsky would put it during his American period, its "basic attitude." Readier, in any case, than he was to accept the idea, entailing a different set of prob-lems, of the possibility of competition between the various modes employed by the mind in its work of objectification. On the secondary, conventional level of signification, as on that of "symbolic values," the work of art should be considered, on its own terms, as the sign or symptom of "something else," the discovery of which is the goal of iconography.[33] Such that the symbolic functions just as color does for Sartre: nothing is ever "symbolic" save "of something." But conceived in such terms, analysis, however pene-trating its insights into the most intimate, and in part unconscious, opera-tions of culture, can only have a diagnostic value: that which seemed to be leading us toward semiology and a general theory of symbolism is thus reduced to a comparative study of sign systems.

To speak of a competition between the different symbolic forms of structures is also to admit the possibility of a struggle, of a collision, and of

---

32. Karl Mannheim, "Zur Interpretation der 'Weltanschauung,'" *Jahrbuch fur Kunstgeschichte*, vol. 15 (1921–22); English trans. in K. M., *Essays in the Sociology of Knowledge*, New York, 1952, pp. 32–83.

33. "When we try to understand it as a document of [the artist's] personality, or of the civiliza-tion of the Italian High Renaissance, or of a peculiar religious attitude, we deal with the work of art as a symptom of something else that expresses itself in a variety of other symptoms, and we interpret its compositional and iconographical features as more particularized evidence of this 'some-thing else.'" Panofsky, *Studies in Iconology. Humanistic Themes in the Art of the Renaissance*, New York, 1939, p. 8.

the eventuality of such a rivalry's producing fault lines, or at least fissures, in the culture of a given period which no amount of exegesis would be capable of patching up. If we retain a definition of culture as an organic, synchronous entity, each part of which is simultaneously an expression of the others as well as of the whole that contains them, we will find it difficult to understand how Euclidian geometry could have emerged within the context of Hellenic civilization, and, to an even greater extent, how it could have lent itself, after two thousand years, to transformation and ree-mergence (*relève*, the French rendering of the Hegelian term *Aufhebung*, usu-ally translated into English as "sublation") in a form that leads, by way of Descartes and Newton, to Kant's definition of space as the pure form of intuition, or—on the register of representation, the one that concerns us here—as *formal intuition*.[34] And this despite the fact, upon which Max Jam-mer insists, that Greek geometry never succeeded in constituting space as its proper object of study, remaining by the large confined to the plane.[35] But this was also true of Renaissance science, at least in its early stages. And it is somewhat abusive, from a historical point of view, to invoke, by way of Nicolas of Cusa and Giordano Bruno, the cartesian idea of extension as accounting for the invention, at the beginning of the fifteenth century, of *costruzione legittima*: as if the concept of homogeneous, unlimited extension had been, at such an early date, within the domain of the *representable*.[36] Besides the anachronism's being patent—to say nothing of the contradiction in terms, to which I will return subsequently, implied by the idea of a *continuum* that is infinite yet centered—it is far from clear that it sheds any light: for it could be that modern perspective initially conformed to the intellectual tradition of antiquity and that for a time was less concerned with space itself than it was with the bodies and figures for which it served

---

34. "Space represented as an object (as required by geometry), contains more than the mere form of intuition, namely, the *comprehension* of the manifold, which is given according to the form of sensibility, into a *perceptible* (intuitable) representation, so that the *form of intuition* gives the mani-fold only, while the *formal intuition* gives unity of representation." Emmanuel Kant, *Critique of Pure Reason*, English trans. by F. Max Muller, New York, 1966, p. 94. On the distinction between "form of intuition" and "formal intuition," cf. Martin Heidegger, *Interprétation phénoménologique de la critique de la raison pure de Kant*, French trans., Paris, 1982, pp. 135ff.

35. Jammer, loc. cit.

36. "In dem Bereich des Vorstellbaren." Panofsky, "Die Perspektive . . .," op. cit., p. 150, note 47; English trans., p.

as a recepticle, agreeing in every respect with the Aristotelian notion of an extension that is finite and differentiated, and consequently discontinuous.

If there are good reasons for opposing an "American" Panofsky, a humanist having come to terms with positivism, to a "German" Panofsky, tempted by theory and philosophy, care must still be taken not to place, in the years after Hamburg and his sojourn at the Warburg Institute, the great "Pan" (as he was nicknamed at Princeton), like Hercules,[37] at a crossroads obliging him to choose between history and philosophy. Even at Princeton, the company of Albert Einstein and Alexandre Koyré had an effect on his work and thought, as is attested by his essay on Galileo.[38] Far be it from me to maintain that *Perspective as Symbolic Form* was without import for his subsequent work: one need only point to the extended discussion of *perspectiva artificialis* in the introduction to the book on early Netherlandish painting, without doubt his masterpiece, as well as to *Renaissance and Renascences in Western Art*. But it is certainly not by chance, nor is it the effect of some ambient malignity, that his epigones have recognized in linear perspective the symbolic form par excellence *of* the Italian Renaissance, thereby voiding this notion of all theoretical and critical bite. If Cassirer's lesson is still relevant in our field, this is because it fosters scepticism toward a certain idea of symbolism, one that will condemn the history of art to a vegetative state for however long it persists in conceiving of itself as a "humanist" discipline (though let it be noted here that the meaning of this word in the context of the American university differs from the one having accrued to it in the European tradition). Through the question of the fixed point of the "subject," as Pélerin Viator would put it, perspective is given to our thought not only as a "form" bound up with an entire epistemological constellation, but—to turn the metaphor against itself, stripping it of all totalizing connotations—as a singular paradigmatic structure, one that is rife with paradoxes and that, in addition to being referenced to the real and the imaginary, is ruled by determinants that are, properly speaking, symbolic, in the precise Lacanian sense of this term. However many detours and subsidiary expeditions it may have prompted, the perspective paradigm is gov-

---

37. Erwin Panofsky, *Hercules am Scheidewege und andere antike Bildstoffe in der neueren Kunst*, Leipzig, Berlin, 1930.
38. Erwin Panofsky, *Galileo as a Critic of the Arts*, The Hague, 1954.

erned, in its regulated operation, by determinations and constraints of a structural order which as such are completely independent of both humanist culture and historical contingency. For it is a structural fact, if not a structural effect, that when man comes to terms with the symbolic order, his being is, from the very start, entirely absorbed in it, and produced by it, not as "man," but as *subject*. Today this strikes us as self-evident with regard to language, which can only be utilized if each speaker identifies himself as a "person," designating himself as an "I" and in turn positing himself as a "subject."[39] But with regard to painting? For a painting to be this configuration, this function Lacan says it is, through which the subject can get its bearings as such (*se repérer comme tel*), is the point designated by perspective, in this art, both necessary and sufficient?

---

39. Émile Benveniste, "La Nature des pronoms," *Problèmes de linguistique générale,* vol. 1, p. 254; English trans., pp. 219–20.

Perspective is not a code.

There are paradigms and paradigms.

The "purpose" of so-called scientific perspective.

Panofsky and the avant-garde in 1925.

Merleau-Ponty and the watchword of a return to primitive thought.

Wittgenstein: a new "sensation."

Perspective as myth, or how to get rid of it.

Space according to reason.

Perspective, a Thing of the Past?

To treat perspective under the rubric of symbolism is to enter into a dilemma, which Cassirer described perfectly and which can be reduced, as we have seen, to a choice between two hypotheses, one of which I would designate as strong and the other weak. Either the analysis will succeed in exposing the element or principle operative in the form of "perspective" as it does that of every other symbolic form—at which point it will have satisfied the demands of the project to establish a morphology or general grammar of the symbolic function, perspective being one of its components. Or it will fail—and focus should be shifted to a (regional, specialized) history that would retrace the genesis and evolution of this form and describe its successive manifestations, assessing their various cultural implications but never really confronting the question of the status of the form of "perspective" in the symbolic order.

At first glance the "strong" hypothesis (which is that of the *Philosophy of Symbolic Forms*) has against it, since we are dealing here with *perspectiva artificialis,* that it is difficult to see how the latter would be accessible to an analysis using the notion of the *sign,* rigorously construed. Although it managed, over an extended historical time frame, to appropriate for its graphic ends a set of objects essentially borrowed from architecture—aediculae, architectonic elements, colonnades, coffered ceilings, and vaults in recession, not to forget the pavement divided into squares that was the foundation of *costruzione legittima,* study of whose trace lines would eventually lead to the discovery of the vanishing point, according to Panofsky's argument—perspective is not a language, in Saussure's sense of a system of distinct signs that correspond to distinct ideas. But neither is it a code, at least not a numerical one, deploying a finite number of discrete elements. A brake and a guide for painting (*briglia e timone della pittura,* to cite

1 Raphael, *Ecstasy of Saint Cecilia*, ca. 1515–16. Bologna, Pinacoteca Nationale. Photo: Giraudon.

Leonardo[1]), of which she is the daughter but which she in turn demonstrates, perspective only has a generative function in some secondary sense. Its purpose is not to facilite the production of statements, of pictorial propositions. Its value is essentially reflexive and regulatory—which suffices to define a certain regime of painting, if not of representation. Thus there is no need to feign astonishment at the relatively small number of quattrocento works evincing strict perspectival construction; any more than to dwell on the fact that sixteenth-century painting seems to have veered away from the "exercises in perspective" dear to quattrocento artists, viewing them as the expression of a passing fashion. As a paradigm or regulatory structure, perspective is sometimes in operation precisely where one least expects it, where its intervention is least visible. If such is the case, it is because—as I've already suggested—the goal of *costruzione legittima* is not restricted to regulation of the diminution and conjugation of figures within the perspectival tableau; its function as a paradigm extends much further, or deeper, providing painters with a network of indexes that constitutes—I posit this hypothesis again—the equivalent of an expressive apparatus or sentence structure, one corresponding—in Cassirer's terms—to the symbolic element that is fundamental to the form of "perspective." Eventually the play of the paradigm makes itself felt through only a few coherent benchmarks (to which the notion of the sign is pertinent, but on another level and, if I may say, within a different perspective than that of the system, whose reversal, or relapse, it would represent), and eventually reference to the model assumes the deceptive character of, if not its repression or denial, then its explicit negation, which demands to be interpreted as such.

I will cite one among the many possible examples. Marisa Dalai has shown how the formal organization of the *Ecstasy of Saint Cecilia* by Raphael seems to have been devised so as, on the one hand, to impede any effect of depth suggested by the *vedute* between the heads of the figures, which open onto the surrounding landscape, and, on the other, to accommodate the foreshortened musical instruments scattered across the foreground: the compact mass of draped figures framing the saint creates a screen blocking all escape into the background, while the geometric construction of the objects

---

1. Leonardo da Vinci, Bibliothèque Nationale, ms. 2038, fol. 132 recto; cf. Jean-Paul Richter, *The Literary Works of Leonardo da Vinci*, 2d ed., London, 1939, vol. 1, p. 127.

does not conform to the constraints of any single viewpoint. A signal example of the *negation* of the paradigm to rhetorical purpose, namely representation of how the saint, to paraphrase Baldassare Castiglione, "having become
blind to terrestrial things, had eyes only for celestial ones."[2] But Cecilia
does not *see* the angel musicians appearing behind her on a gold cloud. She
hears them, whereas, according to conditions of presentation usually holding
for altar paintings, the high horizon line, the difference in scale between the
foreground objects and smaller angels, and even the breach cut into the
chromatic intensity of the deep blue sky should all contribute, whatever
Marisa Dalai may say, to an effect of a perspectival *da sotto in su,* one all the
more fully controlled for falling within the edges of a painting as opposed
to spreading over the expanse of a ceiling or cupola. The paradigm does not
cease to operate here; on the contrary, its double negation is equivalent to
an affirmation and corroborates Panofsky, who maintained that perspective
opened up an entire new realm for religious art, that of the "vision" as
understood in its most exalted sense, and which, though taking place
within the soul of the depicted personage, is made tangible to the viewer as
a disruption of prosaic space.[3]

*

"Paradigm": the word, as I've stated, can be a source of confusion, given
the ways it has been used in the history of science. If, like Thomas Kuhn,
one understands the term to designate a model of scientific practice which is
installed as normative at the beginning of a coherent tradition, as was the
case with Ptolomaic astronomy or Newtonian mechanics,[4] then there's nothing to prevent us from treating *perspectiva artificialis,* painter's perspective,
under an analogous rubric, without prejudicing its relations with the geometric optics of the ancients and *perspectiva naturalis* of the medieval period.
But if one understands by it no more than a constellation of ideas and
notions, of beliefs and prejudices that impose their law, in a given period,
on all production in the field of science and thought generally, as in that of

2.   Marisa Dalai, "La struttura compositiva e spaziale: una proposta di lettura," in *L'estasi di Santa
Cecilia di Raffaello da Urbino nella pinacoteca nationale di Bologna,* Bologna, 1983, pp. 105–17.
3.   Panofsky, "Die Perspektive als symbolische Form," op. cit., p. 126; English trans., p. 72. See
my *Théorie du nuage,* op. cit., part 2.
4.   Thomas S. Kuhn, *The Structure of Scientific Revolutions,* Chicago, 1970, pp. 10ff.

art, the temptation will be great to view *perspectiva artificialis* as only a conventional form of presentation perfectly suited to the times in which it was devised. Such that Samuel Edgerton could write, ignoring the fundamental question of the *Philosophy of Symbolic Forms* as well as Kuhn's real understanding of the notion of "paradigm," "the words 'convention' and 'symbolic form' signify only [as regards Renaissance linear perspective] that artists of that time sought out and practiced this construction in response to specific cultural demands within the Renaissance paradigm";[5] the same author assures us that the "mechanical structure" of this paradigm was finally determined by Newton, without evincing the slightest concern over the gap of three centuries separating the initial experiments of Brunelleshi from the articulation of the principles of Newtonian physics, not to mention the scientific revolution having transpired in the interim.

However crude it might be, the ultimately Hegelian approach adopted, as we've seen, by Panofsky enabled him to posit an analogous parallel between the history of *perspectiva artificialis* and that of other cultural formations, beginning with art, the field in which it first attracted attention through the creation of spectacular effects, but which manifestations simultaneously stimulated intellectual work incontainable within the bounds of any particular discipline. If a priori one considers a given civilization or culture to be an expressive totality, with each of its composite parts functioning as a kind of reduced matrix of the whole, the question of the systematic articulation of their diverse manifestations is resolved in advance. History—as too often happens even in contexts quite removed from the Hegelian tradition—can then take the place of "theory," it having only to produce the elements of the synthesis in accordance with which the period was organized, and this without reference to a "vision of the world" or any specific "mode of production."

The sign would here recover its cognitive rights to the extent that perspective construction could be considered the "sign" of an historical conjucture, which would find there its symbolic expression in the context of which it would have to be studied. As already noted, it's certainly not my intention to deny the relevance of a historical approach to the problem any

---

5. Samuel Edgerton, *The Renaissance Rediscovery of Linear Perspective,* New York, 1975, p. 162.

more than the interest of contextual studies (which presuppose, however disagreeable Edgerton might find this, a minimum of erudition as is evidenced by the chapters he himself devoted to contemporary developments in cartography as they relate to the translation, in early fifteenth century Florence, of Ptolemy's *Geography*[6]). But there is a great danger of treating perspective as just one object among others, if not as a simple product or effect, whereas it interests us here primarily as something that is *productive* of effects, insofar as its capacity, its power to inform extends well beyond the limits of the era in which it was born. Without any doubt, our period is much more massively "informed" by the perspective paradigm, thanks to photography, film, and now video, than was the fifteenth century, which could boast of very few "correct" perspective constructions. But evolutionism precludes our regarding these as anything more than simple survivors or archaic holdovers, even positively prohibiting us from thinking them in any other terms: when new ideas come to light, when new demands assert themselves to which a culture cannot respond in the terms already available to it, the "paradigm" should cede its place to another that is better adapted to them. If one holds that the theory of relativity signaled the fall of the reigning paradigm, the following conclusion is unavoidable: just as linear perspective provided the set of conventions best suited to that representation of "truth" prevalent in the Renaissance, "it is widely agreed [I am quoting Edgerton] that Cubism and its derivative forms in modern art are in the same way the proper pictorial means for representing the "truth" of the post-Einsteinian paradigm."[7]

Such a remark would make us smile, if it weren't so consistent with statements frequently made by cubism's epigones, with the partial exception that critical literature of the 1920s more often referred to so-called noneuclidean geometries than to the theory of relativity per se, which resisted fantastic translations into the visual order. Panofsky himself would later cede to this fashion of his period, of which "parallel chronologies" were the ultimate expression: in his great book on early Netherlandish painting, he went so far as to state that perspective construction "formalizes a conception of space which, in spite of all changes, underlies all postmedi-

---

6.   Ibid., chapters 7 and 8.
7.   Ibid., p. 162.

eval art up to, say, the *Demoiselles d'Avignon* by Picasso (1907), just as it underlies all postmedieval physics up to Einstein's theory of relativity (1905)."[8] Roland Barthes has described his bemused irritation at radio broadcasts proposing circumstantial connections of the kind "1789: convocation of the Estates General; departure of Necker; Concerto for Strings no. IV in C Minor by B. Galuppi," thereby suggesting to the general public the idea of a one-to-one correspondence between history and works of art.[9] But what are we to make then of a statement such as Panofsky's, which places the art of the Renaissance and the *âge classique* or the Baroque, and all modern science as well, from Galileo to Newton, from Desargues to Jean Poncelet, under the rubric of an aftermath, or—to use Panofsky's own term—of the prefix "post" (and, what's worse, as it's used in the term "postmedieval")?

It is not a matter of chance that studies of perspective enjoyed their greatest vogue at a moment in which it might have seemed that modern art had definitively turned away from it, as a result of its determination—as Malevitch put it—to "make paintings" rather than painting objects and "repeating nature," and the current revival of interest in it is symptomatic too. It is all the more remarkable to observe that in the heat of the battle for abstraction, in his discussion of it Panofsky chose to ignore something that his deliberately historicizing approach to the problem should have placed center stage, namely the rupture effected in the pictorial order by Cézanne. This would have entailed him, as a good neo-Kantian, to begin by undermining the pretense of so-called central perspective to restore an image of the objective world, showing its value to be entirely relative and strictly conjunctural, on the basis of pseudoscientific considerations borrowed form the physiology of vision, before dealing, in a note that must have been added to the final pages of his study very late, with avant-garde debates whose echoes reached him from Berlin or elsewhere, notably in an article by El Lissitzky published in 1925.[10] If we are to believe Lissitzky, antique

---

8. Erwin Panofsky, *Early Netherlandish Painting,* Cambridge, MA., 1953, vol. 1, p. 5.
9. Roland Barthes, "Histoire ou littérature," *Sur Racine,* Paris, 1963, p. 147; English trans. by Richard Howard, *On Racine,* New York, 1964, p. 153.
10. Panofsky, "Die Perspektive . . .," op. cit., p. 166, note 73; English trans., pp. 153–54. The article in question was published by El Lissitzky under the title "A. and Pangeometry," in the *Europa-Almanach* of Carl Einsten and Paul Westheim, Potsdam, 1925; cf. Sophie Lissitzky-Küppers, *El Lissitzky, Life, Letters, Texts,* London, 1968, pp. 348–54.

perspective limited and enclosed space, apprehending it, in conformity with the postulates of Euclid as a "rigid tri-dimensionality." Shattering one-point perspective into a thousand pieces, contemporary art, in its futurist guise, was said to have broken with this delimiting notion of space to arrive, under the banner of suprematism and neoplasticism, at representing intervals of depth not extensively, and by means of foreshortening, but—joining forces here with new ideas in psychology—*intensively* through the juxtaposition of colored fields of different values and tonalities. Though (like the author of the *prouns* himself) he said not a word about the problem posed by the resort, in paintings, to so-called axonometric perspective, in which the vanishing point is cast into the infinite, with "orthogonals" transformed into groups of parallel lines on the surface, Panofsky nonetheless observed that the way chosen by Lissitzky, the conquest of an "imaginary space" engendered by the rotation or balancing of mechanically manipulated volumes, was altogether consistent with a euclidean framework—as are today the optical deformations and transformations possible in electronic images, a fact that bears witness to the continuing productivity of two- and three-dimensional geometry, if not of perspective itself at the end of the century which began under the sign of the *Demoiselles d'Avignon* and the theory of relativity.

2   El Lissitzky, study for "Proun." Paris, Musée
National d'Art Moderne. Photo: Museum.

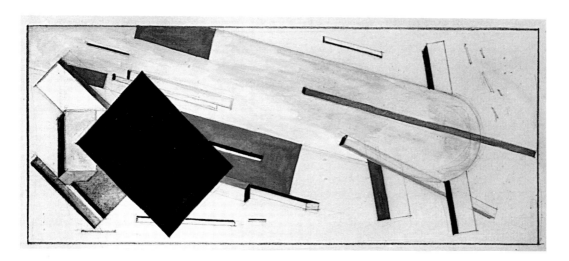

*

While Panofsky says nothing about Cézanne, it was contemplation of this painter's work that led a philosopher like Maurice Merleau-Ponty to question the nature of the ascendency of the perspectival apparatus over perception and to query the conditions in which painting might succeed in getting free of it so as to effect a return to the amorphous perceptive world that is its perpetual raw material, rather like philosophy as conceived by Husserl would do. The philosopher openly avowed that Panofsky's *Perspective as Symbolic Form* and the classic analysis of Cézanne's work by Fritz Novotny, *Cézanne and the End of Scientific Perspective,*[11] had influenced his own reflections in important respects. It was from Panofsky, as much as Novotny (Cézanne is another matter, one to which I will return subsequently), that he borrowed the idea of perspective as "cultural artifact." But in the "working notes" published by Claude Lefort as an appendix to the unfinished essay *The Visible and the Invisible,* the question of the means by which one might revert from a perception shaped by culture to a "crude," "primitive" perception is explicitly raised. And this question, cutting through the mirages of historicism and relativism, goes right to the heart of the problem: "Of what does information consist? By what act can it be unravelled?"[12]

The idea that perspective could *inform* perception, *orienting* it so completely that it shed its polymorphic character to become "euclidean," encourages one to think that the model's power could not be measured by the visible effects it has left in the field of art, any more than by its explicit impact in the realm of verbal discourse. It is perception itself, and not representations employing the means of art and discourse, that would be necessary to liberate from the rule of the perspective paradigm. Without doubt, any thesis according to which *culture informs perception in a way that allows us to say that culture is perceived* is circular, though it is advocated by any analyst pretending to acknowledge in a period's artistic production the expression of a vision of the world whose very concepts it would determine.

---

11. Fritz Novotny, *Cézanne und das Ende der wissenschaftlichen Perspektive,* Vienna, 1938 (untranslated).

12. "En quoi consiste l'information? Quel est l'acte par lequel on la défait?" Maurice Merleau-Ponty, *Le Visible et l'invisible,* Paris, 1964, p. 265; English trans. by Alphonso Lingis, Evanston, 1968, p. 212.

But in the case of perspective the *information* is not reducible to a historical given, nor to a stylistic trait. Certainly Merleau-Ponty was not disposed to admit that the privileged status of what he called "euclidean perception" was an effect derivative of "pregnance," in the sense used in the psychology of form and which expresses itself, as Jean Piaget asserted, as controlled compensation for the deformations to which perceptual structures are subject. In his eyes, as in those of Panofsky, whom he would have been among the first to read in France, the privileged status of linear perspective was far from absolute, but it still struck him as revelatory of the fashion in which perception misapprehended itself, to such a point that, whether termed "life," "natural perception," or the "savage mind," it is prone to put the immanent universe in its place, tending of itself toward autonomy, reducing the transcendent status claimed by the euclidean world for itself to that of one of its many aspects. *The key is in this idea that perception qua wild perception is of itself ignorant of itself, imperception,* tends of itself to see itself as an *act* and to forget itself as latent intentionality, as being at—." Or to put it another way (though, as Merleau-Ponty emphasized, this is another way of phrasing the "same problem"): "how every philosophy is language and nonetheless consists in rediscovering silence."[13]

*

I will not here address the question of what it might mean to speak of a "euclidean" perception, or of a vision "informed" by perspective, a perspective—I am still citing Merleau-Ponty—that would correspond to an "adult vision" as well as to "the invention of a world that is dominated and possessed, through and through, in an instantaneous synthesis":[14] a vision in the first person that is coherent, that evinces mastery, and that would imply as its condition the position of a subject that could eventually reclaim it for its own, as its own property, its own representation. I will only point out that those who, like Ernst Gombrich, dismiss this idea, see nothing contra-

---

13. *"La clé est dans cette idée que la perception est de soi ignorance de soi comme perception sauvage, imperception,* tend de soi à se voir comme *acte* et a s'oublier comme intentionalité latente, comme être a—"; "Comment toute philosophie est langage et consiste cependant à retrouver le silence." Ibid., pp. 266–67; English trans., p. 213.
14. Maurice Merleau-Ponty, "Le Langage indirect et les voix du silence," *Signes,* Paris, 1960, p. 63; English trans. by Richard C. McCleary, *Signs,* Evanston, 1964, p. 50.

dictory in conceiving of perception as an active process of selection, decoding, and anticipation.[15] Merleau-Ponty had no objection to this, provided one knew how to discern, beneath the information, the operation of language and its discriminating systems,[16] and took note of the fact that it is inherent in the perceived to be always already there, to be not the product of the act of perception but its reason[17]—as, in his view, the overarching project of philosophy should be to renew contact with the world as "significant being" (*sens d'être*) absolutely distinct from that which is represented.[18] In its capacity as the subject of a praxis, the subject of perspective appears to be bound up with a logocentric rationality by means of which the teleology of "natural light" is converted into an ideal entity, there where the perceiving subject demands, on the contrary, to be described "as a tacit, silent *Being-at* . . .—the *self* of perception as 'nobody,' like Ulysses, an anonymous one drowning in the world but who has yet to make his way through it. Nobody as imperception, evidence of nonpossession: it is precisely because one knows too well what one is dealing with that one has no need to posit it as ob-ject."[19]

Thus it is the *cogito* that we must persist in trying to "start over": this same *cogito* of which Lacan thought the perspective configuration offered an *analogon,* an imaginary version, if not a mute one. But it would be going too far to speak of a "tacit *cogito,*" a notion that is implicitly a contradiction in terms, as Merleau-Ponty himself noted, after Ludwig Wittgenstein.[20] It is the very question of subject and object, of transcendence, of intersubjectivity, of nature, that must be thought through anew. As Jacques Bouveresse has observed, this Husserlian project of reduction in many respects resembles that of Wittgentstein, who also posited the idea of a descriptive philosophy, of a phenomenology setting itself the task of destroying the cardinal concepts of metaphysics: "subject," "transcendental signified,"

---

15. Gombrich, *Art and Illusion,* op. cit., pp. 147–48.
16. Merleau-Ponty, *Le Visible et l'invisible,* op. cit., p. 254; English trans., p. 201.
17. Ibid., p. 272; English trans., p. 219.
18. Ibid., p. 306; English trans., p. 253.
19. ". . . comme *Etre-à* tacite, silencieux . . .—le *soi* de la perception comme 'personne,' au sens d'Ulysse, comme l'anonyme enfoui dans le monde et qui n'y a pas encore tracé son sillage. Personne comme imperception, evidence de non-possession: c'est justement parce qu'on sait trop bien de quoi il s'agit qu'on n'a pas besoin de le poser en ob-jet." Ibid., pp. 254–55; English trans., p. 201.
20. Ibid., pp. 229ff.; English trans., pp. 170–72.

"essence," etc. But Wittgentstein's horror of the pathos of initiation, of commencement, of origins, his view that any attempt to return to silence by means of language and philosophy was absurd, these suffice to make him the anti-Husserl par excellence.[21] In his view it is language, not the perceived, that is always already there: all statements (beginning with *cogito ergo sum*) should be comprehensible by others if the speaking subject (who is at one with what is spoken) himself understands it. Such that all "vision" should be sharable by others if the "subject" can see: there is no vision that is not accessible to some possible description or designation, as well as simultaneously ascribable to a given distance and a given point point of view as the very condition of vision. Just as there is no private property in language, there is none in perception: the very idea of a "perspective" contradicts such a notion. The problem then is how to distinguish that which is perceived from that which is represented. What we cannot speak about we must pass over in silence: but can't we try, if not to show it ("Don't look at my finger, look in the direction in which it is pointing"), at least to derive some sense of it, in such a way that language might articulate its silence, and discourse gain access to it?

Merleau-Ponty considered all of these objections, and more than once, as can be seen from his working notes. "Raw," "primitive" perception must be *invented*: it only remains to determine what role language is to play in this "invention." Wittgenstein maintained that the discovery of the "optic chamber" had led to a new way of speaking, a "new comparison," and, if one can *say* this, a "new sensation."[22] For our present purposes the question comes down to this: Must description necessarily resort to means that are those of representation, borrowing its forms, its metaphors? From the nonphilosophical place at which he believed we had arrived, Merleau-Ponty saw no possible way out other than to make a completely new start (the pathos denounced by Wittgenstein), to reject the instruments with which reflection and intuition had fitted themselves out, to install oneself "where they have not yet been distinguished, in experiences that have not yet been 'worked over,' that offer all at once, pell-mell, both 'subject' and

---

21.   Cf. Jacques Bouveresse, *Le Mythe de l'intériorité. Expérience, signification et langage privé chez Wittgenstein,* Paris, 1976, pp. iiiff.
22.   Ludwig Wittgenstein, *Philosophische Untersuchungen,* Oxford, 1953, para. 400; English trans. by G. E. M. Amscombe, *Philosophical Investigations,* New York, 1953, p. 121.

'object,' existence and essence."[23] Now, if there is any "experience" that philosophy has *worked over,* apparently to the point of satiety, it is surely that of representation in its perspectival guise. If this same philosophy should be reducible, as Wittgenstein believed, to a technique for analyzing concepts, it might seem as though such a reduction of the concept of "perspective" were already well advanced. But can we be so sure of this? Could it not be that having never been submitted to a proper philosophical critique, the perspective paradigm, as sometimes happens with texts, has acquired over time a kind of mythic power that is only reinforced by the uses to which it lends itself in contemporary philosophy?

*

I will take a single example, one that is now rather commonplace: the idea that perspective has become archaic, that its time has passed (painters' perspective, not that of architects and geometers, which is another story entirely), that the life cycle of classic representation has run its course. This is not a new idea. But it is significant that those artists and critics who were among the first to propose it based their argument on the cubist experiment and its immediate antecedents. I emphasize again that one of the basic tenets of the prevailing artistic discourse, and a commonplace of criticism, holds that the lesson of Cézanne (that of Seurat usually being passed over in silence) signaled the end of so-called scientific perspective and at the same time of an age, many would say the age par excellence, of representation. That does not prevent us from referring back, if not to Ghiberti, a least to Leonardo da Vinci, from finding in his *Treatise on Painting*—the first critical edition of which dates from the end of the nineteenth century—the premonitory symptoms of a critical trope that has scarcely changed since that time, one that holds that *costruzione legittima* reduces the viewing subject to a kind of cyclops, and obliges the eye to remain at one fixed, indivisible point—in other words, obliges it to adopt a stance that has nothing in common with the effective conditions of perception, any more than it does with the goals of painting, as properly understood.[24]

---

23. Merleau-Ponty, op. cit., p. 172; English trans., p. 130.
24. Cf. Martin Kemp, "Leonardo and the Visual Pyramid," *Journal of the Warburg and Courtauld Institutes,* vol. 11 (1977), pp. 128–49; the first critical edition of the *Codex Urbinas 1270* in the

3   Albrecht Dürer,
*Man Drawing a Reclining
Woman.* Print from the
*Unterweysung der Mes-
sung,* Nuremberg, 2d ed.,
1538. Photo: Biblio-
thèque Nationale, Paris.

A woodcut by Albrecht Dürer is frequently invoked as illustrating
the unbearable constraints entailed by these demands. And, in effect, it
shows an artist caught up in a veritable pillory as he draws the contours of a
(nude) model in front of him, gazing at her through a transparent, squared
screen, his eye immobile at the tip of a stiletto. But Dürer's image, far
from treating the operation of perspective (less preoccupied with the rationalization of vision than with the rationalization of representation), rather
describes the apparatus to which the painter should turn to facilitate
rational construction, to obtain a rendering that is perspectivally correct by
purely mechanical means in conformity with the principle of the *velum* posited by Alberti. In itself such an apparatus had no experimental value, as
opposed to the "gate" conceived by the same Dürer to demonstrate, in geometric terms, the point-by-point correspondence, in relation to a common
point of "origin," between the object and its projection onto an intersecting
plane. In the terms of Saussure one would say perspective was a *dense* system
(*un système serré*).[25] But the network, quite dense in fact, of constraints that
define it nonetheless provides the basis for a new kind of liberty illustrated
by another print, this one by Abraham Bosse, the friend and correspondent
of Desargues: here "perspectors" move at will over the terrain, each on his

Vatican was published by H. Ludwig in 1882–85. In 1910 Péladan brought out a very free,
approximate translation, which was the one read by Jacques Villon and his friends in the Puteaux
group, as well as by the epigones of cubism, notably Gleizes and Metzinger.
25.   Robert Godel, *Les Sources manuscrites du cours de linguistique générale de F. de Saussure,* Geneva,
1957, p. 29.

4   Abraham Bosse, *Les Perspecteurs.* Print from
the *Manière universelle de M. Desargues pour traiter
la perspective,* 1648. Photo: Bibliothèque Nationale,
Paris.

own, each directing his visual pyramid, its delimiting lines converging at
his eye, wherever he pleases. *Dove a mi paia, fermo uno punto*: "Where it suits
me, I make a point."[26]

*

Is the mythic status of such images in contemporary writing the result of
simple ignorance and misunderstanding: ignorance and misunderstanding of
what *perspectiva artificialis* really was in its time, leading to a miscomprehen-

---

26.   Alberti, *Della pittura,* book I, cited ed., p. 71; English trans., p. 56.

sion of its original context, of its historical roots? Panofsky saw quite clearly that the recent quarrels about perspective were not new ones and that there have been many, in the past, who would argue from the individual and subjective element it introduced into art to impugn it, while others, by contrast, declared its imposition of rigorous mathematical order to be intolerable. The fact that its operation can be viewed as affirming the reality principle or as expanding the sphere of the ego,[27] this ambiguity, this apparent contradiction, makes it easier for us to grasp how painters' perspective led to an ongoing investigation of the uses to which it could be put, into how it would best be employed. And how this could in turn imply the task, at once both historical and philosophical, or reopening this interrogation, of exposing its sources, recovering its beginnings, locating the traces of its development in the perspective configuration itself, as it was historically constituted; just as it could be taken to imply another task (without doubt a more tedious one), that of taking the precise measure of ongoing resistance to it.

But while even today perspective poses unresolved questions; while it is not merely a thing of the past; while it continues to inform, if not our perception, at least our discourse, our thought, and while one can conceive of the project of dispensing with it, or breaking it down, or—better yet—of deconstructing it, history will not be sufficient for such an undertaking, it won't provide us with this last word on the matter, and it can't even instruct us as to what we should understand "history" to mean. The same holds for perspective (that of painters) as holds, according to Merleau-Ponty, for philosophy and the work of art: "[It] is an object that can arouse more thoughts than are 'contained' in it (Can these be enumerated? Can one count up a language?), that retains a meaning outside of its historical context, that even *has* meaning only outside of that context."[28] The key phrase here is "that even *has*," namely a meaning that is its *own,* as opposed to being borrowed from the context. This is an assertion historians will have difficulty accepting, perhaps even declaring it to be incomprehensible. But if something like Merleau-Ponty's "sedimentary" or "vertical" history should be thinkable, and through it such things as the histories of art, philosophy,

27. Panofsky, "Die Perspektive . . .," op. cit., pp. 123–26; English trans., pp. 71–72.
28. Merleau-Ponty, *Le Visible et l'invisible,* op. cit., p. 253; English trans., p. 199.

and thought (to say nothing of the history of science, which imposes this idea on us, or better yet, which is the *realization* of this history), it must of necessity be predicated on such a position, and proceed in a way that does not preclude us from doing history, in the conventional meaning of this term, from going back further than Gottfried Leibniz, and even Descartes, in an attempt to discern the intentions of the "inventors" of perspective. And that leaves us free to exploit everything philology and erudition can teach us that might serve to advance our project of rejuvenating the perspectival experience, of "working it over," such that in the end—perhaps—we might have a better grasp of the meaning of "perspective"—and of "experience."

The phenomenological watchword of a return, beyond the objective being "historical truth" instituted by Descartes as the sole realm of legitimate scientific inquiry, to an "organic" or "primitive history" (*Urhistorie*[29]), this science of a pre-science, as Merleau-Ponty dubbed it, itself has a long history—as do contemporary calls for an art *brut*, untarnished by cultural determinations (though always produced by individuals of great cultural sophistication), and the validation of "primitive" thought forms because they purportedly accord more immediate access to a part of experience that our science has spurned, has allowed to lie fallow. As Jacques Bouveresse has written in discussing Wittgenstein, subjective space is no less "constructed" than objective space. It results from the addition of something, what Maria Reichenbach called a "subjective metric," to this latter space: "Visual space, which we are tempted to call 'primary,' can itself be interpreted as a second order construction erected on the foundation of physical space."[30] Jean Paulhan associated cubist painting with the idea of "space prior to reason" (*un espace d'avant les raisons*): a space of which, so to speak, we have no idea, "that falls on us without warning! A space in which we have no part, yet [whose existence] is incontestable! A space . . . felt by the heart, and which is not mediated by perspective—I mean by reflection, combination, arrangement, in short, by method and its reasons."[31] But the

---

29.   Ibid., p. 221; English trans., pp. 177–78.

30.   Bouveresse, op. cit., p. 334; cf. Hans Reichenbach, *Philosophie der Raum-Zeit-Lehre,* Berlin, Leipzig, 1928, p. 86; English trans. by Maria Reichenbach and John Freund, *The Philosophy of Space and Time,* New York, 1958, p. 83.

31.   Jean Paulhan, "La Peinture cubiste," *Oeuvres complètes,* Paris, 1966–70, vol. 5, p. 115.

fact that perspective must be challenged, that the attempt must be made to break it down, to deconstruct it, makes it clear that we are dealing, rather, with a space "after" or "according to reason" (*un espace d'après les raisons*). As for the other kind, nothing can be said about it without resorting to the—second order—resources of negation.

A period-specific phenomenon.

The denigration of the signifier.

Perspective and the moment of the *cogito*.

The geometrical dimension of sight and the function of the lack.

The question of the fixed point in the *âge classique*

Point of view and point of subject.

Perspectival meditation and the value of origin.

Desargues and the perspectivists.

The two perspectivisms.

Pascal: the mad point.

Knowledge and Truth

It bears repeating: if one were to deal only with painting, one would be forced to conclude that *perspectiva artificialis* had nothing like as significant an impact on western culture as is generally believed. If the treatises had been lost, and we thus found ourselves reduced to dealing exclusively with artifacts, our image of the art of the Renaissance and of the modern era would differ greatly from what it is today. In the context of this hypothetical state of affairs, the visual productions of the low countries might well have accrued a greater prestige for their apparent mastery of perspective than those of Italy, and this despite the fact that the Van Eyck brothers and their contemporaries had done nothing more than apply lessons learned from Sienese and Florentine artists of the trecento.[1] In the absence of explicit theory (which was lacking, precisely, in the northern countries, at least until Jean Pélerin, who limited himself to giving systematic coherence to a set of empirical procedures[2]), the subtle evocation of space in the *Madonna of Chancellor Rollin* and the *Arnolfini Wedding* might be regarded as evincing a developmental stage far more advanced than that ascribable to Italian *costruzione legittima* at the time. Conversely, the small number of works produced in quattrocento Italy in strict conformity with the principles of projection would be taken to indicate the distance that can separate theory from practice, and the evolution of sixteenth-century art as confirmation that the taste for perspective was but a period-specific phenomenon, no more than a stylistic quirk or a fashionable craze, and as such was likely to resurface from time to time.

---

1.   Panofsky, *Early Netherlandish Painting*, vol. 1, p. 9.
2.   Cf. Liliane Brion-Guerry, *Jean Pélerin Viator. Sa Place dans l'histoire de la perspective*, Paris, 1962.

But if anything can be described as a period-specific phenomenon, it is this version of history, which is quite prevalent today, and it must be analyzed in these terms. Renewing with the ideological project which was that of Vasari, it is far from innocent. To maintain that perspective served painting only by facilitating attractive games and astonishing spatial effects, the intention being to establish a distinction between two modalities—one practical and the other theoretical—of perspectival experience, as well as to displace its point of maximal impact; this is to imply that it was of greater consequence for philosophical thought and modern geometry than it was for art. Given the priorities currently prevailing within the art historical discipline, is it possible for us to conceive of a blurring of the boundaries between diverse areas of knowledge, and between art and science; is it possible for us to imagine that a single strand might figure in several of them, first passing through a field preoccupied with "theoretical" questions and subsequently wending its way into areas dominated by play and fable (as if play and fable could be treated as distinct from thought)? Can we posit to ourselves the image of such a fitful progress, can we conceptualize its possibility, without also inquiring into the status of perspective as a symbolic form, one whose history we could not undertake to write without transgressing disciplinary boundaries, given that this paradigm lends its quasi-magical aura (and its powers) to applications in the most diverse fields?

*

In his text Vasari treats perspective in a singular way: the author of the *Lives* consistently demotes it to the level of a simple technique, lavishing sarcasm on those who, like Uccello, devoted more time and effort to it than he deemed appropriate. Such a *denigration* of perspective (in the sense one can speak of a denigration of writing, of written characters, of the signifier in general) is surprising when one remembers that, a century earlier, painters had invoked their mastery of this new discipline as reinforcing their claim to a social status above that of artisans—to that of intellectuals. This becomes less baffling when we remind ourselves of the fault line, the irreparable fissure which the invention of *costruzione legittima* opened in "humanist" culture, the same culture of which it is held to be the product and the expression, whereas in fact it contradicts it—quite literally—in all key respects. Witness the analogy which Lacan emphasized (leaving himself just as open as Panofsky to charges of anachronism) between the reduction of "man" to an eye and this eye to a point, the fundamental move of *perspectiva artificialis,* and the crucial historical moment, decisive not only for human consciousness but for western science, of the institution of the cartesian subject: a subject that is anything but "humanist," as it is conceived to be strictly delineated by spatial and temporal coordinates (the instant being, in space, symmetrical to the point in time). Early research on perspective reveals an interest in vision whose relation to the *cogito,* itself a sort of geometral point, one cannot fail to *see* (according to Lacan).[3] But the symbolic dependence into which this analogy leads the cartesian subject also signals its limitations: according to this reading the perspective construction is nothing but an instrument of spatial orientation, one that has no bearing on vision. To convince oneself of this, one has only to read Denis Diderot's *Letter on the Blind for the Use of Those Who See*: there it is argued that someone born blind can grasp the idea of the distance separating things solely by means of touch, and so reconstruct geometral space for himself, much as Descartes represented dioptrics, the action of the eyes, as the conjugated action of two sticks. If "the geometral dimension of vision does not therefore exhaust what the field of vision as such offers us as the original subjectifying relation, far from it,"[4] does this imply one is reduced to appealing to anamorphosis, and to Dürer's inevitable gate, to complete it: that is to say—as we ought—to inscribing there the function of its lack?

If perspective is linked to vision, this is not in the capacity of informing it, or of proposing a model for it: those functions pertain to a geometral outlook in which it is certainly implicated but to which it cannot be reduced. And, contrary to what Michel Foucault claimed,[5] *perspectiva artificialis* does not imitate vision, any more than painting imitates space. It was devised as a means of visual presentation and has meaning only insofar as it participates in the order of the visible, thus appealing to the eye. Wittgenstein justly criticized Ernst Mach's attempt to represent in a draw-

3.   Jacques Lacan, *Le Séminaire XI, Les Quatre concepts fondmentaux de la psychanalyse,* Paris, 1973, p. 81; English trans. by Alan Sheridan, *The Four Fundamental Concepts of Psycho-analysis,* New York and London, 1978, p. 87. Cf. also "La Science et la vérté," *Écrits,* pp. 856ff.
4.   Ibid.
5.   Michel Foucault, *Les Mots et les choses,* Paris, 1966, p. 32; English trans., *The Order of Things,* New York, 1971, p. 17.

ing what the eye sees in specific conditions, beginning with the margins of the visual field, supposed to be blurry: it makes no sense for painting to use the means at its disposal to try to reinstate a visible image of the visual image because the painted image is itself given to vision, just like any other object in the visible world, and is thus governed by the rules of vision, with all the consequences that entails.[6] This explains why, as Lacan observed, the geometral dimension allows for a glimpse of how the subject is caught, maneuvered, captured inside the field of vision, and how painting can deliberately exploit it to captivate the "subject" in a relation of desire, but one that remains enigmatic ("What is the desire which is caught, fixed in the picture, but which also urges the artist to put something into operation?"[7]) That the place of the "subject" is not the geometral point defined by optic geometry, and that the same subject moves about within the painting, that it can be attracted and seduced by it, like Narcissus by his specular reflection, such is the very law of vision. In this respect the visible resembles the tangible: my hand can touch something only because it can itself be touched, and if vision, as Merleau-Ponty put it, following Descartes, is "a palpation of the gaze," it follows that the person who gazes must not be unfamiliar to the world upon which he looks: "From the moment I see, my vision must be doubled by a *complementary* vision, or another vision: myself seen from without as another would see me, installed in the midst of the visible, in the process of considering it from a certain spot."[8] The only difference in approach vis-à-vis things and paintings is that perspective—I will develop this point at length below—provides a means of staging this capture and of playing it out in a reflective mode.

Did not Leibniz say, in the language of his own time, that there is no point of view onto things, but that things and beings are themselves points of view, subject as such to exclusive rules determining that each one open onto the others only insofar as they converge, God being defined as the geometric aspect of all perspectives? An affirmation of a perspectivism one might call "classic," and whose formal apparatus guarantees the possi-

6. Ludwig Wittgenstein, *Philosophische Bemerkungen,* 1964, paragraph 213; English trans. by Raymond Hargreaves and Roger White, *Philosophical Remarks,* Chicago, 1975; cf. Bouveresse, op. cit., pp. 342ff.
7. Lacan, *Le Séminaire XI,* op. cit., p. 86; English trans., *Four Fundamental Concepts,* pp. 92–93.
8. Merleau-Ponty, op. cit., p. 177; English trans., p. 134.

bility of disengaging, of switching from one point of view to another, but against which Nietzsche protested, in the name of a radically different perspectivism: one in which the different points of view are anything but complementary, each one manifesting a divergence which he embraced, and which would correspond, according to Gilles Deleuze, from whom I take the remark, to an art more profound than that envisioned by Leibniz, an art capable of using difference as a means of communication.[9] That the perspective paradigm lends itself to these two contradictory interpretations, but not without the narcissism inherent in painting redoubling that of vision, will be one of the theses of this book. Another: that the notion of a "history of perspective" has no meaning except as it relates to the movement, constitutive of the paradigm as such, that continuously prompts a return to its own origins, logical as well as historical, and perhaps even mythic. If there is any aspect of perspective that is worth examining yet again, it is this movement, always resumed and always resumable, because always obstructed and of necessity destined to failure, there being no origin save one that is an *invention,* in all senses of the word.

*

These considerations take us rather far afield from the idea, somewhat simplistic and even figurative (in Pascal's sense), that one might be tempted to form of the operation of the perspective paradigm in the *âge classique,* and in the context of a science one would like to envision as constantly seeking to discover a point of view outside nature from which we might contemplate it unimpeded, all its mystery cleared away, with a single dominating gaze[10]—before Kant had established a point of orientation within the subject itself, in the place where knowledge resides, a development that put an end to the era in which perspective was held to be a model in perfect harmony with the idealist vision of the world, because this harmony derived more from its form than from its content. This would oblige us to return, despite ourselves, under the auspices of the *Weltanschauung,* to a critique of ideologies,

---

9.   Gilles Deleuze, *Logique du sens,* Paris, 1969, p. 203; English trans. by M. Lester and C. Stivale, *The Logic of Sense,* New York, 1990, pp. 173–74.
10.   Ilya Prigogine and Isabelle Stengers, *La Nouvelle alliance métamorphose de la science,* Paris, 1979, p. 23; English language ed., *Order out of Chaos: Man's New Dialogue with Nature,* Toronto and New York, 1984, p. 52.

if it were anything more than a fable, an unsatisfying one, and if the idea of the *point of view* were not (as philosophers and scientists realized soon after Descartes) separable from that of the "subject" imposed, due to a symbolic effect peculiar to language, by the first-person voice of the *cogito*.

As Michel Serres has shown, the question of the fixed point, or reference point, was a central preoccupation of the *âge classique*: such that it could be taken as the basic indicator of difference between various scientific and philosophical positions, as well as of their unity, of their deep-seated mutual complicity. In this sense (and in this sense only), the *cogito* can be regarded as the translation, itself in accordance with the cartesian ideal of world mastery, of a theme or methodical structure that recurs in all realms of knowledge and that lends itself to all manner of adjustments, translations, and transpositions. That this theme, this structure, constitutes, in its very form, a "vision of the world," so much is obvious. But the essential thing is that this form remains subject to demonstrative reason, such as that of geometry, and that its ideological content is of considerably less consequence than its rational architecture.[11]

This is not the place to enter into a detailed discussion of various aspects of the question of the fixed point in the physics, cosmology, and metaphysics of the *âge classique*. But I will take up two points made by Michel Serres which seem to me crucial in the context of my argument. As well as the troubling impact of the opening onto infinity on a notion of thought that is *polarized* in this way. In statics, as in cinetics and dynamics, the question of the fixed point allowed of no solution unless it was a *finite* question: it made no sense to look for the center of a revolving movement that was not completed, any more than to try to determine the point of equilibrium of a scale whose arms were of infinite length. Thus the opposition of the paired notions finitude/central point and infinity/decentering is a constant, one that permits us to distinguish between two methodological approaches, for example, between that of Kepler and the earlier ones of Nicolas of Cusa and Giordano Bruno. This observation is important for us, seeing as it suffices, as I've already hinted, to determine that the idea according to which the institution of central perspective would have corre-

---

11.   Michel Serres, *Le Système de Leibniz et ses modèles mathématiques*, Paris, 1968, p. 692.

lated with, if not presupposed, the mathematical definition of space as a homogeneous, infinite *continuum*, that this idea was, in the language of its time, a contradiction in terms. Space, if it is homogeneous, the world, if it is open (as Nicolas of Cusa and Giordano Bruno understood this, as well as in the direction of the infinitesimal), must be *decentered*: unless one proposes, with Pascal, that depolarized space is infinitely saturated with centers rather than being deprived of one, isotropism precluding all reference to a *naturally* privileged point of view. But for us to conceive the notion of an analytic space whose center is everywhere and nowhere, allowing of no origin save one that is arbitrary and peremptory, we must have nothing less than a revolution in the mathematical armature of knowledge; the infinitist geometry of Desargues must supplant the finite geometry of the Greeks, while computation of infinitely small quantities must become ubiquitous.[12]

The revolution spearheaded by Desargues has a particular interest for us. It is an indication of the considerable importance, for thought in the *âge classique,* of what Michel Serres has called "perspectival meditation." An importance as great, in his view, as that of infinitesimal calculus and dynamics. "Infinity carried the center off from us, yet seemed to restore it to us in a new guise."[13] In terms of geometry the aim of this revolution was nothing less than to allow for the centering of space in a way that did not preclude its infinite extension: "Euclidean geometry posits a homogeneous space in which all points are equivalent, in which all points are of no account, as regards spatial composition . . . The geometry of Desargues, by contrast, posits a space organized in relation to a point of view through which order is imposed on the random variety of the first. Here the point encompasses space and space encompasses the point, the word 'encompasses' being understood to embrace not only geometry, but vision and thought as well."[14] We can *see* immediately the implications following from the commodiousness of this notion of point of view: perspective posits a point "encompassing" space within a space that encompasses the point and that, insofar as it appeals to vision, is always already *thought.* The theorem of Desargues assimilating a bundle of parallel lines to a bundle of converging

---

12. Ibid., p. 649–50.
13. Ibid., p. 657.
14. Ibid., p. 693.

lines is coherent only in the context of projective geometry. But it is the work of perspectivists that led geometers to consider, as Kepler had already done,[15] systems of parallel lines as varieties of the system of converging lines whose point of convergence is situated at infinity.[16] This is confirmed by the title of the pamphlet published by Desargues in 1636, republished by Abraham Bosse at the end of his *Traité de perspective* (1647) and rescued from oblivion two centuries later by Poncelet, intended to provide specialists with a *Universal Method for Putting Real Objects or Objects for Which Specifications Are Available into Perspective, Such That Their Proportions, Measurements, and Distancing Are Correct, without Resort to any Point outside the Field in Question* (*Méthode universelle de mettre en perspective les objets réellement donnés ou en devis avec leurs proportions, mesures, éloignement, sans employer aucun point qui soit en dehors du champ de l'ouvrage*). Without resort to any point outside the field in question—in other words, without using a "distance point" as in the procedure handed down by Vignola but also without reference to a "point of view" in the trivial sense, one corresponding to the eye of a spectator positioned a set distance from the picture plane. This revolution was important; we must now try to determine whether it was totally without precedent in the theory and practice of perspective.

This question might seem of limited interest, if erudition, in the meaning acquired by the word (according to the *Robert* dictionary) at the end of the seventeenth century, namely knowledge based on the study of historical sources, documents, and texts, did not have the potential to upset received ideas concerning the role of the perspectival paradigm in the culture of its time. Michel Serres's account of how the question of the fixed point was transformed, in the seventeenth century, into that of the *point of view* confirms the importance of the work of perspective in this context. But it simultaneously imposes a definition of the notion of point of view according to which the value or function of the *origin* carries over every other, precluding further confusion of point of view and point of subject. Serres is right to emphasize the importance for Kepler—as obsessed by the quest for

---

15. Cf. Johannes Kepler, *Ad vitellionem paralipomena* (1604), pp. 93ff.: "*De coni sectionibus.*" On how Kepler came to consider a point in infinity as a special kind of finite point, cf. H. F. Baker, *Principles of Geometry*, Cambridge, 1929, vol. 1, p. 178.

16. Cf. Claude Tisseron, *Géométries affine, projective et euclidienne*, Paris, 1983, pp. 65–66, and, *infra*, chapter 16, pp. 386–87.

the center as he was repulsed by the idea of infinity—of the introduction of elliptical orbs: conical geometry assumes priority over spherical geometry, while meditation on the fixed point shifts its focus from the former's center to the latter's apex, by moving from the privileged point in the center of the configuration to a point of view from which the latter can be apprehended. [17] But the possibility, demonstrated by Pascal, of defining cones in projective terms, and of understanding their various sections, from single points to hyperbolas, as deriving from circles, this operation does not necessarily require that reference be made to any point exterior to the projective field that is the cone, since its apex becomes the privileged point from which one can perceive the correspondence between the original and its "metamorphoses" (to employ Leibniz' term). [18] In this way a split is consummated between the subject and "vision," which is itself caught up—as a point—in the set of transformations engendering the series of conical sections. And one need not resort to science to state that according to whether one's philosophical outlook privileges the geometry of the sphere, the cone, or the plane, the fixed point will be a center, a site, or an origin (that of the axes of the coordinates). [19] Which does not exclude the possibility of passing from the point of view of the subject to that of the eye (which, in painting, came to be known as the *vanishing point,* a phrase that nicely characterizes the opposition between a fixed point and its being pushed into infinity), by a kind of "shifting of gears" analogous to the linguistic one allowing us to change person, permitting us to pass from "I" to "you" or "he," and from the subject of a statement to that of the speaker.

*

We are still dealing with perspectival meditation as it would have been exercised by geometers, even though Desargues would willingly have placed himself on the terrain of the perspectivists. But the fact that it was by means of painting that perspective initially imposed itself as object and as an epistemological model for classic thought, this historical reality is not without consequences with regard to the latter, and to its genealogy. In the

---

17. Serres, op. cit., pp. 654–55.
18. Ibid., pp. 665–67.
19. Ibid., p. 657.

present context it obliges us to revisit this art, to reassess its premises and implications, as well as the conditions shaping the thought working through it. For the influence of the perspective paradigm over western thought, from Descartes and Pascal to Nietzsche and Wittgenstein (we might even trace it to back to Plato, necessitating a new approach to the problem of "ancient" perspective), has been remarkably powerful, and we can no longer make do with approximate, fantastic notions of what it is and how it has functioned.

The task incumbent upon us is of more than historical interest, and its importance extends well beyond the boundaries of the domain of philosophy. To say that our culture has been and continues to be shaped, informed, and programmed at bedrock level by the perspective paradigm is more than mere wordplay—though language requires that perspective not be an object like any other, because, metaphorically speaking, it has a bearing on the conditions determinant of all objectivity, of the perception of objects, from whatever angle or point view they might be considered, in relation to a horizon line and a set distance. Perspective has become so completely integrated into our knowledge, at the most implicit or unconscious level, that today we must turn to another kind of knowledge, erudite knowledge, and embark on an anamnestic project designed to recover it from the technological oblivion into which it has been plunged by ideology.

But is it sufficient for us to speak of *knowledge?* Louis Marin has revealed the key role, in Pascal and the Port-Royal *Logic,* of references to paintings and portraits, and to painting as a general model.[20] It would be worthwhile to expand the range of his investigation to the entirety of classic literature. Painting a manifestation of vanity? Its apologists have always known how to turn such arguments to advantage, just as philosophers of the *âge-classique* consistently proceeded from descriptions of a world deprived of a center to discovery of the fixed point.[21] The transition from the one discursive moment to the other corresponds to that in Pascal's *Pensées* in which, portraits being considered, the attention shifts from the question of resemblance to the process, the operation, on a feature-by-feature basis, of

---

20.   Louis Marin, *La Critique du discours. Sur la Loguique de Port-Royal et les pensées de Pascal,* Paris, 1975.
21.   Serres, op. cit., pp. 657ff.

mimesis. In this way resemblance acquires some semblance of pertinence to perspective, or to what perspective could be. "Thus paintings, seen from too far away or from too close; and there is only one indivisible point that is the truthful spot: the others are too close, too distant, too high, too low. Perspective designates [this point] in the art of painting. But who designates it in truth and ethics?"[22]

In the art of painting the impact of perspective is not limited to the register of the imaginary; it not only facilitates the construction of images, it assumes a role, a function that we may properly designate as symbolic. Perspective, I repeat, is not a code, but it has this in common with language, that in and by itself it institutes and constitutes itself under the auspices of a point, a factor analogous to the "subject" or "person" in language, always posited in relation to a "here" or "there," accruing all the possibilities for movement from one position to another that this entails. Such an observation should be sufficient to render suspect any assimilation of *perspectiva artificialis* to an instrument that has been incrementally perfected over time until finally, no longer responding to changing needs emerging through the evolutionary process, it must be replaced by another one better adapted to those needs: if the role of perspective in the realm of representation were a thing of the past, which is far from a settled question, the model it proposes would still retain its pertinence, precisely as *model,* one that might serve thought in the project of discovering what, in painting, are the conditions prerequisite to the making of statements (or: that might help us think, in terms of painting, what such conditions would be).

*

Perspective designates it in the art of painting. But who *designates it in truth and ethics?* The question can be construed in two ways and might even be said to have tricky implications. For the interrogative pronoun cannot be said a priori to refer to any specific class. In this statement it is the very process (and not the painter) that designates the "indivisible point," it being clearly implied that this selection is effected in strict accordance with rational pro-

---

22. "Ainsi les tableaux, vûs de trop loin et de trop près; et il n'y a qu'un point indivisible qui soit le véritable lieu: les autres sont trop près, trop loin, trop haut, trop bas. La perspective l'assigne dans l'art de la peinture. Mais dans la vérité et dans la morale, qui l'assignera?" Blaise Pascal, *Pensées,* Brunschvicg ed., no. 381; English trans. by A. J. Krailsheimer, London, 1966, p. 381.

cedures, *more geometrico*. But in truth, as in ethics, there is no single formal apparatus that facilitates deductive operations (not, at least, prior to Kant), and reference to the paradigm does not entail an appeal to reason. "Original sin is madness in the eyes of men, but it is put forward as such. You should therefore not reproach me for the unreasonable nature of this doctrine because I put it forward as being unreasonable. But his madness is wiser than all the wisdom of man, *sapientius est hominibus*. For without it, what are we to say man is? His entire being is dependent upon this imperceptible point. And how could he have become aware of it through his reason, seeing that it is something contrary to reason and that his reason, far from inventing it with its own means, draws away when confronted with it."[23] Thus it falls to God, to *the madness that comes from God*,[24] To designate this *mad* point (mad in Freud's sense when he describes the "primal scene" or the murder of the father) which reason cannot "invent," from which it turns away when "one" discloses it, as if it were the antithesis of all knowledge:[25] *one,* specifically the Church, whose history "should properly be called that of the truth."[26]

If I've made a point of citing Pascal at the beginning of this book devoted to perspective and to what we think we can call its "history," this is because he was the first to explore the paradigm with philosophical and/or apologetic ends in view, with full consciousness of its theoretical implications. The idea that truth, insofar as it can be historical, is itself somehow perspectival, entails a redoubled cleavage. A cleavage between, on the one hand, a knowledge that chops away at this point which is indivisible—which is not a *point of gaze* (*point de regard*, as Lacan so beautifully put it[27])

---

23. "Le péché originel est folie devant les hommes, mais on le donne pour tel. Vous ne devez donc pas me reprocher le défaut de raison en cette doctrine puisque je la donne pour être sans raison. Mais cette folie est plus sage que toute la sagesse des hommes, *sapientiius est hominibus*. Car, sans cela, que dira-t-on qu'est l'homme? Tout son être dépend de ce point imperceptible. Et comment s'en fût-il aperçu par sa raison, pusique c'est une chose contra la raison, et que sa raison, bien loin de l'inventer par ses voies, s'en détourne quand on le lui présente?" Ibid., Brunschvicg no. 445; English trans., p. 246.

24. *First Corinthians*, I, 25: "For the madness of God is wiser than men . . . ."

25. See Pascal, op. cit., no. 230: "Incomprehensible . . . that original sin should exist, and that it should not" ("Incomprehensible . . . que le péché originel soit, et qu'il ne soit pas"); English trans., p. 271.

26. Ibid., no. 858: "L'Histoire de l'église doit être proprement appelée celle de la vérité"; English trans., p. 262.

27. Lacan, *Le Séminaire XI*, op. cit., p. 89; English trans., *Four Fundamental Concepts*, p. 96.

but a point of view—and a vision (in Leibniz's sense) that is strictly determined, as the apex of a cone can be, and, on the other, a truth to which no knowledge corresponds. But a cleavage, also under the auspices of "man," between an incarnated subject, one whose only being is the one assigned him by the historical perspective in which he is caught (a perspective outside of which nothing can be said about him), and the subject who verifies this assertion and this designation. An entire history testifies to the fact that an analogous cleavage is discernable, in the field we are examining, between the painter's knowledge and the truth to which painting pretends (or can pretend), as is one between the point perspective is supposed to designate and the place of the subject (the question of the subject) in painting. This history is partly polemical, as we shall see with regard to Leonardo da Vinci, whose critique of "painters' perspective" contains features that are singularly attractive and singularly modern—or seem to be. But the fact that perspective has stimulated and continues to stimulate such heated debate suffices to establish that it is not an object, a fact of culture like any other, one that can be studied and discussed without implicating the nature of the "subject," in the most problematic sense of this term.

One thing is certain: if the subject is there, at the knot of difference, all humanist references to it become superfluous, for it undercuts their foundations.

JACQUES LACAN, "La Science et la vérité," *Écrits*, p. 857

Part Two

THE PROTOTYPE

Brunelleschi the inventor of perspective?

Alberti's dedicatory preface.

Filarete's *Treatise*.

Manetti's *Vita*.

Vasari.

FOUR

The Tradition

Tradition holds that Brunelleschi was one of the founding fathers of the Renaissance, one of the heroes of its narrative of origins, and makes him out to be the inventor of a method, if not of a form of representation, by means of which this same Renaissance summed up its key principles, making itself visible, rendering its composite matrix accessible in the guise of *paintings* (Though one sees immediately that the terms "tradition," "invention," "representation," "principle," and even "painting" call for critical scrutiny, and that questions concerning them cannot be separated from those raised by the very notion of "Renaissance").

As is appropriate for a "modern" hero—in fact one of the first heros of modernity if it is true that modernity is necessarily linked with novelty—this tradition is supposed to have been initiated in Brunelleschi's own lifetime. According to the avatars of history, no sooner had Leone-Battista Alberti arrived in Florence in 1434 than he undertook to write *Della pittura,* this "art of painting" in three books, the first of which includes, under the heading *rudimenta,* an exposition of what we might call the *princeps* of rational perspective construction and rational *more geometrico.* Proof that this treatise was the fruit of an encounter between a humanist advisor, one conversant with all the classical disciplines, and the principal artisans of the Florentine Renaissance can be found in the preface—written in 1436, for the Italian edition—dedicating the work to Filipo di Ser Brunellesco and, through him, to their common friend Donatello, as well as to Ghiberti, Luca della Robbia, and Masaccio: all "artisans" (*artefici*) but each of whom Alberti, in his posture as theoretician, unhesitatingly affirms to have disproved, in his own way, the dictum holding that nature, mistress of all things, had become so old and tired that she could no longer produce giants and geniuses comparable to those she had brought forth in her youth.[1] And, he continues, since they did this without the abundance of models and mentors available to the ancients, since they, "without teachers or models of any kind, discovered arts and sciences of which we have never previously seen or heard," their fame should be all the greater.[2] Take Brunelleschi, whose mind, perpetually active, made discoveries every day that would assure him eternal renown, and who was better equipped than anyone to judge, criticize, and even correct the "little text," the little "work on painting," which Alberti had written in his name—*a tuo nome:* the phrase is ambiguous, but can it not be taken to mean that the author of *Della pittura* had been somehow authorized to write as Brunelleschi's spokesman?[3]

The question seems all the more compelling given that this treatise (like Ghiberti's *Commentari,* a book, according to Vasari, written in the first person but entirely "done by others"[4]) makes no allusion to Brunelleschi's supposed role in the discovery—or the invention—of *costruzione legittima* and that Alberti states there will be other occasions to discuss Filipo's many titles to glory, as well as those of Donatello (*il nostro Donato*) and their followers. In the dedicatory preface explicit reference is made only to the monument that in the Florence of that time, as well as the one we know today, made an immediate visual impression: The immense dome of the cathedral, "rising above the sky, ample enough to cover with its shadow the entire Tuscan people," built without the aid of beams and without scaffolding, by means of technical procedures so astonishing that it was difficult to envision how the ancients might have conceived of them.[5] Doubtless Bru-

---

1.　"Onde stimai fusse quanto da molti questo cosi essere udiva, che già la Natura, maestra delle cose, fatta anticha et stracca, più non producea chome ne giganti cosi ne ingegni quali in que suoi quasi giovinili et più gloriosi tempi produsse amplissimi et maravigliosi." Leone-Battista Alberti, *Della pittura,* op. cit., p. 53. English trans., p. 39.

2.　"Confetossi se a quelli antiqui, avendo quale aveano chopia da chi inparare e imitarli, meno era difficile salire in cognotione di quelle supreme arti quali oggi annoi sono fatichosissime ma quinci tanto più el nostro nome più debba essere maggiore se noi sanza preceptori, sanza exemplo alchuno, troviamo arti et scientie non udite et mai vedute." Ibid., p. 54. English trans., p. 40.

3.　"Tu tanto persevera in truovare, quanto fai di di in di, cose per quali il tuo ingegnio maraviglioso s'acquista perpetua fama et nome et se in tempo t'acchade otio, mi piacerà rivegha, questa mia operetta di pictura quale a tuo nome feci in lingua toscana. . . . Piacciati adunque leggermi con diligentia et se cosa vi ti par da emendarla correggimi." Ibid.

4.　"Ne tacero che egli mostra el libro essere fatto da altri." Giorgio Vasari, "Vita di Lorenzo Ghiberti," *Le vite de' piu eccelenti pittori scultori ed architettori,* Milanesi edition, Milan, 1878, vol. 2, p. 247; English trans. by Gaston Du C. de Vere, New York, 1979, vol. 1, p. 368.

5.　Alberti, loc. cit.

nelleschi commented on Alberti's treatise, especially its first book, which is concerned with mathematics, with "the natural roots which are the source of this delightful and most noble art."[6] If the author turned to him for assistance, this was because, of all their erudite friends, he was the one best equipped to help defend him against the teeth of his detractors;[7] but erudition aside, Alberti says not a word concerning any authorization he may have received.

*

It was only a generation later, in the *Treatise on Architecture* by Filarete (probably written between 1460 and 1464), that Brunelleschi's name was explicitly associated with the "discovery" of perspective, in terms describing him less as a learned man than as a practitioner: a fabricator and, as Filarete emphasizes, a "most subtle follower of Daedalus" (the mythological inventor of both sculpture and architecture), who managed to revitalize in Florence, where he had started out as a sculptor, the ancient way of building.[8] An architect, what is more, for whom the problem of architecture was inseparable from that of representation and the problem of the representation of architecture inseparable from that of the architecture of representation, insofar as this latter can be formulated in terms of *construction*. So much is implied, at any rate, by the reference to Brunelleschi at the end of Filarete's description, in his treatise, of a perspective construction with a single vanishing point. But we must examine this passage more closely in light of its context. First, its historical context: Filarete had surely read Alberti, which makes this designation of an origin a kind of return, via *Della pittura*, to the lesson of Brunelleschi. But also its textual context: to anyone troubled, after delineation of the checkerboard underlying the perspectival scene, by

---

6. "El primo [libro], tutto mathematico, dalle radici entro dalla natura fa sorgiere questa leggiadra et nobilissima arte." Ibid.

7. "Niuno scriptore mai fu si docto al quale non fussero utilissimi gli amici eruditi et io in prima datte desidero essere emendato per non essere morso da detractori." Ibid.

8. "Et benedico l'anima di Filippo di ser Brunellesco, cittadino fiorentino, famoso et degnissimo architetto e sotilissimo imitatore di Dedalo, il quale risuscitò nella città nostra di Firenze questo modo antico dello edificare . . . ." Antonio Averlino detto il Filareto, *Trattato di architettura,* book VIII, fol. 59 recto; L. Grassi ed., Milan, 1972, vol. 1, p. 227; English trans. by John R. Spencer, *Filarete's Treatise on Architecture,* New Haven and London, 1965, vol. 1, p. 102. On the necessity of the connection, in the realm of myth, between sculpture and architecture, see my "Danse de Thésée," *Ruptures/cultures,* Paris, 1974, pp. 163–75.

seeing that the component squares are not square, and are not mutually identical, but rather become progressively diminished and deformed; to anyone remaining unconvinced by the argument advanced to explain this, namely that the point toward which lines perpendicular to the picture plane converge is in the image (*a similitudine*) of the eye, and that these lines correspond to the rays making up the visual pyramid;[9] to anyone dissatisfied with all "rational" justifications, Filarete suggests performing an experiment that seems trivial in itself but that revives the question posed since antiquity under the rubric of *scenographia*. On this point his argument is identical to that of Vitruvius: for both the problem was that of determining how to delineate *on a plane* the lines of a building (or any other object) in its designated spot, *con ragione,*[10] in conformity with the rule stipulating that the lines of lateral facades converge toward a single point, or, as Vitruvius would put it, toward a single "center."[11] To convince his skeptic that this is how it works for the eye, Filarete, rather than ask him to look at the ground, instructs him to lift his gaze—not, like Alberti, toward an immense dome but toward a simple ceiling whose rafters seem to shrink as they recede into space:

> The closer [the beams] are to you the more equal they seem to be, and the further away from you the more they seem to be so close together that one is on top of the other and they all seem to be one (*in modo che ti paranno tutt'una*). And if you wish to consider this more closely, take a mirror and look at them in it. You will see clearly that this is so (*e si meglio le vuoi considerare, torrai uno specchio, e guarda dentro in esso. Vedrai chiaro essere cosi*). If they are exactly

---

9.   "Perché questo [punto] è a similitudine del tuo occhio, e queste linee sono i razzi del tuo occhio, cioè e'razzi visivi antedetti." Filarete, op. cit., book XXIII, fol. 177 verso; cited ed., vol. 2, p. 652; English trans., p. 303.

10.   "Ora in questo ti voglio dimostrare come queste linee si tirano a volere fare uno casamento, e anche un'altra cosa fare posta ne'luoghi suoi con ragione in sul piano." Ibid., fol. 177 recto op. cit., p. 650; English trans., p. 302.

11.   "Item scaenographia est frontis et laterum abscenentium adumbratio ad circinique centrum omnium linearum responsus." Vitruvius, *De architectura,* book I, chapter ii. On the interpretation of this passage, and the translation of *circini centrum* as "compass point," which apparently refers not to a vanishing point situated on the picture plane but rather to a "center of projection" standing for the eye of the spectator, cf. Panofsky, "Die Perspektive . . .," op. cit., p. 106; English trans. p. 38.

opposite your eye (*al dirimpetto dell'occhio*) they will only appear
equal. I think it was Pippo di Ser Brunellesco, a Florentine, who
discovered the method of making this plane (*il modo di fare questo
piano*), which was certainly a subtle and beautiful thing, and by
rational means (*per ragione*), from what the mirror shows you (*che
nello specchio ti si dimostra*). Even so, if you consider it carefully, you
can see by your eye (*coll'occhio*) these changes and diminutions (*quelle
mutazioni e diminuzioni*).[12]

But the mirror is not only useful as a demonstrative aid. It also
offers practical assistance, a useful "short cut," a means of transferring to a
plane the outlines of figures subject to diminution that bypasses the difficulties and awkwardnesses entailed by "rational" construction:

> If you should desire to represent something in another, easier way
> (*per un'altra più facile via*), take a mirror and hold it up in front of
> the thing you want to do (*e tiello inanzi a quello cotale cosa, che tu
> vuoi fare*). Look into it, and you will see the outlines (*i ditorni*) of
> the thing more easily, and whatever is closer or further will appear
> foreshortened to you (*e quelle più di lungha ti paranno più diminuire*).
> Truly, I think this is the way Pippo de Ser Brunellesco discovered
> this perspective, which was not used in other times.[13]

Questa prospectiva, la quale per altri tempi non s'era usata: the problem,
as Panofsky was aware, is not so much one of discerning whether the art of
other periods and regions evinces knowledge of perspective as one of determining *what* perspective is in question in each case.[14] The kind of perspective
with which tradition has associated Brunelleschi's name has a singular character, one that is explicitly *originary* or *inaugural*. The text of Vitruvius was
there to attest antiquity's familiarity with the problem of receding nonparal-
lel lines as projected onto a plane, as well as with that of diminishing size.
Yet Filarete did not hesitate to write that "even though their intellects were

---

12.   Filarete, op. cit., fol. 178 recto; cited ed., p. 653; English trans., pp. 303–304.
13.   Ibid., fol. 178 verso–179 recto; cited ed., p. 657; English trans., p. 305.
14.   Cf. *supra*, chapter 1, pp. 12–13.

very subtle and sharp, this particular kind of perspective (*questo modo di questa prospettiva*) was never used or even understood by the ancients; while, in matters concerning them, the latter were able to exercise good judgment, they did not locate things on the plane in this way and with these rules (*pur non con queste vie e ragioni ponevano le cose in sul piano*)."[15] In Filarete's *Treatise,* intended to celebrate ancient ways of building and to announce, by way of a critique of the practices of the "moderns" (here, advocates of the "gothic" style), their immanent resurrection, the final chapters on *disegno* take on a paradoxical character: what becomes of the pretended superiority of the ancients if they did not dispose of an instrument that ostensibly assured man an unequaled grasp of the world, even as it testified to his capacity for formulating rational procedures? But the contradiction is only apparent, if one allows that the formation of the "antique" ideal and the project of the return to the origins of western culture need not be cut short by the discovery, or the invention, of perspective: the submission as evidence of the rupture in historical continuity after the fall of the Roman empire, and the adoption of a point of view into the past intended to establish classical antiquity as an impassable horizon, these moves posit a kind of temporal perspective effectively predicated upon a structure of referential return analogous in every respect to that for which *costruzione legittima* proposed a spatial model.[16]

As I've already implied, nowhere is the *constructive* character of the discovery ascribed to Brunelleschi so strongly affirmed as in Filarete's text. There it is stated that anyone wishing to erect a building should begin by preparing the necessary materials and then turn his attention to its foundations: "As it is necessary to have a site in order to build and to dig the foundations, so we too will first make the site in which we wish to make our drawing. First of all our site must be a plane that is made by rule."[17]

---

15. "Gli antichi, benché sottilissimi e acutissimi fussino, niente di meno mai fu usata né intesa." Filarete, loc. cit.

16. Cf. Giulio-Carlo Argan, "The Architecture of Brunelleschi and the Origins of Perspective Theory in the XVth Century," *Journal of the Warburg and Courtauld Institutes,* vol. 9 (1946), pp. 98–101.

17. "E così come è mestiere prima avere il sito per volere edificare e in esso cavare il fondamento, così ancora noi in prima faremo il sito a voler fare questo nostro disegno. In prima bisogna che questo sito ch'è piano si faccia con ragione." Filarete, op. cit., fol. 177 recto; cited edition, vol. 2, p. 650; English trans., p. 302.

This notion of a "site" prompted further developments which will be discussed where appropriate. For the moment I simply note that it fell to an architect, and not a painter, to bring to a point—as we shall see, this expression should be taken literally—the method of projection (*il modo di fare questo piano*) that Filarete describes in detail in his treatise. Coming after Alberti's description, the later one raises questions that are concerned with more than origins, even if this word is understood in both its historical and genealogical senses. While the passage might be read as advocating a direct return to Brunelleschi's lesson, sound method dictates that, despite the prominence the latter subsequently assumed in the history of theory and perspective, we fix our sights firmly on what Filarete clearly states about this matter. The observation that ceiling beams appear to merge as they become more distant, just as orthogonals in a painting seem to converge at a single point presented as analogous or similar to the eye; the idea that if one looks carefully with the eye (*coll'occhio*), one can observe (*de visu*) the same deformations that are revealed in a mirror; the emphasis on the notion of *diminution,* and on the *ratio* governing it: all these factors are consistent with what can be determined about the configuration conceived by Brunelleschi, as we shall see. But the essential thing remains the place, the function that Filarete assigns to the mirror in the circuit of representation: the mirror, the painter's guide, as Alberti had already maintained, by means of which one can judge not only the diminution of figures but also the distribution of light and shadow,[18] but the mirror, more important, whose image of the reality it faces will be implicitly understood as analogous to the one the painter has constructed on a plane, *con ragione.* Save for the fact that a single mirror is insufficient, since its image of the things in front of it is

---

18. "A questo fare specchio è buono aiutorio; perchè molto bene si discerne per questa mezzanità dello specchio i lumi e l'ombra." Ibid., fol. 180 recto; cited ed., p. 662; English trans., p. 308. Cf. Alberti, *Della pittura,* cited ed., p. 100: "Et saratti ad conoscere buono giudice lo specchio ne so come le cose ben dipinte molto abbino nello specchio gratia; cosa maravigliosa come ogni vitio della pittura si manifesti diforme nello specchio. Adunque le cose prese dall natura si emendino collo specchio." (English trans., p. 83: "A good judge with which to familiarize yourself is the mirror. It is marvelous how every weakness in a painting is so clearly [perceivable as] misformed in a mirror. Therefore things taken from nature are corrected with a mirror.") What is in question here is amending the painted work in light of what the mirror reveals, not imitating nature initially by means of it.

reversed, or turned around, and can only be set right if one repeats the transformation—nullifies it—by means of a *di-mostratio,* a double showing. In the matter of representation, the reflection will always be one mirror behind, and vice versa: "If you dispose of two mirrors facing one another, it will be easier to draw whatever you want to do."[19]

*

All indicators support an attribution of the *Vita di Filippo Brunelleschi* to the mathematician Antonio di Tucci Manetti,[20] a friend of Uccello's, with whom, according to Vasari, he liked to discuss Euclid,[21] and who is believed to appear in this connection on a small panel in the Louvre, attributed by Vasari to Uccello, at the side of Giotto, Donatello, Brunelleschi, and its putative creator, in the role—we might conjecture—Alberti would have coveted for himself, that of "theoretician" to the artisans of the Florentine Renaissance. This "life," the first masterpiece of its kind, though it did not lack for precedents, apparently written shortly after 1475,[22] contains a relatively detailed description of the perspectival experiments conducted by Brunelleschi. For the moment I want to feign ignorance of the information put into circulation by this text, unavailable to Vasari when he wrote his "Life of Brunelleschi" but subsequently the subject of extensive commentary, and focus exclusively on the assertion that in his youth, when his knowledge of construction, especially masonry, was beginning to attract the attention of prominent Florentines, Brunelleschi

> produced and himself practiced (*e misse innanzi, ed in atto, lui proprio*) what painters today call perspective (*quello ch'e dipintori oggi dicono prospettiva*) since it forms part of that science (*perche ella è una parte di quella scienza*) which, in effect, consists of setting down

---

19. "Ancora nello specchio e buon a ritrare, come t'ò detto; e se n'ai due, che si presenti l'uno nell'altro, ti sara più facile a ritrarre quello che vuoi fare, cioè quello que vuoi ritrarre." Filarete, op. cit., fol. 184 verso; cited ed., p. 655; English trans., p. 315.

20. Cf. the exemplary critical edition, by Domenico Robertis and Giovanni Tanturli, of Manetti, *Vita di Filippo Brunelleschi,* Milan, 1976; in English, *The Life of Brunelleschi by Antonio di Tuccio Manetti,* intro., notes, and critical text by Howard Saalman, trans. by Catherine Enggass, University Park, PA, 1970.

21. Vasari, "Vita di Paolo Uccello," op. cit., vol. 1, pp. 215–16; English trans., vol. 1, p. 350.

22. Tanturli, introduction to the *Vita di F. B.,* p. xxxv.

properly and rationally (*che è in effetto porre bene e con ragione*) the reductions and enlargements of near and distant objects as perceived by the eye of man (*le diminuzioni ed acrescimenti che appaino agli occhi degli uomini delle cose di lungi e da presso*): buildings, plains, mountains, places of every sort (*casamenti, piani e montagne e paesi d'ogni ragione*) and location (*in ogni luogo*), with figures and objects in correct proportion to the distance in which they are shown (*di quella misura che s'appartiene a quella distanzia che le si mostrano di lungi*); and it is he who originated the rule (*e da lui è nato la regola*) that is so important for everything of the sort done between that time and this (*che è la importanza di tutto quello che di cio s'è fatto da quel tempo in qua*).[23]

Brunelleschi *produced* perspective—more precisely what painters then (in 1475) referred to as *prospettiva;* but again we should note that Manetti's text was written a good half-century after the events it recounts, and forty years after Alberti's *Della pittura*.[24] He advanced it—in the sense of a *Vor-Stellung,* a re-presentation, even a *model,* for such can be the meaning of the word *innanzi* in the "elevated" style. He originated the rule so important for everything of the sort done between that time and this—as concerns perspective, but not necessarily painting, which should suffice to discredit careless discussions of possible examples revealing the impact of the perspective discourse on the practice of painters, prompting us instead to inquire (with a sounder methodological basis) into the status of perspective in its relation to painting. Brunelleschi himself is supposed to have put this perspective into practice, to have put it into action (*e misso in atto*). A *prospettiva* that is not *all* perspective but only *perspectiva artificialis,* painters' perspective, as opposed to the *perspectiva naturalis* of medieval authors, which was a theory of direct, reflected, or refracted vision that was easily confused

---

23. Manetti, op. cit., pp. 55–56; English trans., p. 42.

24. Manetti's remarks assume particular significance in light of the fact that Alberti was unfamiliar with the term *prospettiva,* which, as we have seen, was first used by Filarete (cf. M. Boscovics, "Quello ch'e dipintori oggi dicono prospettiva," *Acta historiae artium Academiae Scientiarum Hungaricae,* vols. 8 [1962] and 9 [1963]; as noted by Klein, *Form and Meaning,* op. cit., p. 140. This could be seen as the index of a conceptual development prompting replacement of the image of the "window" (and of *per-spective* as "seeing through") by the very different notion of the perspectival paradigm advanced by Piero in his treatise.

with optics. And yet, if something in the word *prospettiva* resounds, *rings out*—to use Piero della Francesca's language—with the force of the lines and angles produced by perspective, given prominence by it, put into play for the eye by it,[25] the pro-jection by means of which the painter appeals to the eye only has meaning to the extent that it is based on reason, *more geometrico*: as Manetti stresses, *prospettiva* is not all perspective, but it is linked to this science, in contrast with the recipes and studio tricks that Alberti was the first to denounce for their arbitrary, irrational character. Whereas *perspectiva naturalis* demonstrates the how and why of the apparent diminution of objects in proportion to distance, *perspectiva artificialis* would seem to have been a development of it—an unforeseeable one?—intended to subject representation to the laws of optics, or again, in the ancient sense of the word, to those of vision, the clear, distinct kind of vision that is understood in ancient discourse on geometry. The problem facing us is that of determining whether, in so passing from one register to another, one renounces traditional optics, appealing instead to a new idea of science, and of representation.

*

Vasari echoes this tradition in his own "Life of Brunelleschi," confirming its central tenet: the innovative, if not inaugural, character of Brunelleschi's contribution to the history of perspective, a perspective that was poorly practiced at the time, marked by countless errors, which Brunelleschi is said to have corrected as was necessary.[26] A century after Manetti, Vasari's text bears witness, here as elsewhere (notably in the "Life of Paolo Uccello,"[27] as well as in the second chapter of Vasari's "Della pittura," in the *Proemio* of his *Lives*), to the demotion of perspective to the status of a simple technique in the service of *disegno*. A technique, according to Vasari, that nonetheless

---

25. "Molti dipintori biasimano la prospectiva, perchè non intendano la forza delle linee e degli angoli, che da essa si producano. . . . Dico che la perspectiva sona nel nome suo commo dire cose vedute da lungi, rapresentate socto certi dati termini con proportione, etc." Piero della Francesca, *De prospectiva pingendi,* edition by Nicco Fasola, Florence, 1942, p. 128. Cf., *infra,* chapter 15.
26. "Attese molto alla prospettiva, allora molto in male uso per molte falsita che vi si facevano." Vasari, "Vita di Filippo Brunelleschi," cited ed., vol. 2, p. 332; English trans., vol. 1, p. 394.
27. Cf. my introduction to the volume in the series *Classiques de l'art* devoted to Paolo Uccello, new ed., Paris, 1985.

was difficult to understand and explain, an assertion that suggests that by then the word had lost many of the overtones to which Piero alluded. A technique allowing for the creation of effects of depth, diminution, and distancing, and of organization and composition, but one achieving results that seemed easy and unforced after the confusing lines of the geometric perspective construction had been painted over.[28] Thus the discipline's ambiguous status for Vasari, signaled by his statement that Brunelleschi wasted—this translation is not exaggerated[29]—much time before discovering, on his own, a way to make perspective accurate and perfect: which he found, Vasari asserts, in the method known as *intersegatione,* or sectioning, which amounted to "raising" the perspective of an object (a building, in the first instance) on the basis of its ground plan and a rendering in elevation, the plane of projection being itself assimilated to a planar section (*intersegatione*) of the visual pyramid. "A thing," as Vasari admits, "truly most ingenious and useful to the art of *disegno,*"[30] by which he means that of the sketch, of the "project," insofar as this is based, in painting as well as other arts, in procedures that are fundamentally graphic.

The discussion of this invention in the "Life of Brunelleschi" includes two descriptions whose relative precision testifies, if not to direct knowledge of the two panels in question, then at least to the prominent role they continued to play in the memory of the period, half a century, in all probability, after they had disappeared from view. Brunelleschi is reported to have been so pleased by his invention (*et di questa prese tanta vaghezza:* how can this fail to evoke the astonishing account, in the "Life of Uccello," of the latter painter's being so enamored of perspective that night after night he avoided the conjugal bed, despite the repeated pleas of his

---

28. "Bisogna poi che'l pittor abbia risguardo a farle con proporzione sminuire con la dolcezza de'colori, la qual'è nell'artefice una reta discrezione ed un guidicio buono: la causa del quale si mostra nella difficultà delle tante linee confuse, colta dalla pianta, dal profilo ed intersecazione; che ricoperte dal colore, restano una facilissima cosa, la qual fa tenere l'artefice dotto, intendente ed ingegnoso nelle'arte." Vasari, "Della pittura," *Proemio, Vite,* cited ed., vol. 1, p. 176; English trans. in *Vasari on Technique,* trans. by Louisa S. Maclehose, ed. by G. Baldwin Brown, New York, 1907, p. 214.

29. ". . . nelle quale perse molto tempo." Idem., "Vita di F. B.," loc. cit.

30. ". . . per fino che egli trovò da sè un modo che ella potessa venir giusta e perfetta, che fu il levarla con la pianta e profilo e per via della intersegatione; cosa veramente ingegnosissima, ed utile all'arte del disegno." Ibid.

wife, in order to study it?), that he himself painted "the square [of the baptistry] of San Giovanni, with all its mural revetments in black and white marbles, so that they diminished with a singular grace (*con tutti quegli sparmenti della incrostatura murati di marmi neri e bianchi, che diminuavano con une grazia singolare*); and likewise the casa de la Misericordia with its waffle shops and the corner of the sheep market, and on the other side the Saint Zenobius column." A work, as we also read in Vasari, which met with such great success, which was so highly praised by Brunelleschi's colleagues, that it wasn't long before he set about painting another panel representing "the pallazo, the piazza, and the loggia of the Signoria, together with the roof of the Pisani and all the buildings that are seen around that piazza."[31] According to Vasari, these two works excited the curiosity of artists, who studied them attentively, but it was his young friend Masaccio who is said to have profited the most from Brunelleschi's teachings, as can be seen from the architecture abounding in his paintings. To say nothing of masters of marquetry, whose art was predicated upon the feasibility of making images of perfectly interlocking parts on a plane: Brunelleschi had provided them with a compelling model in his perspectival rendering of the geometric ornament of the baptistry.[32]

Comparison of the texts by Filarete, Manetti, and Vasari allows us to assess the strength of the tradition assigning Brunelleschi a key role in the early Renaissance, although in Vasari this view is reached in a roundabout way whose twists and turns (for example, the placement in the *Lives* of the "Life of Paolo Uccello" before that of Brunelleschi, even though the latter was twenty years his senior) will be discussed where appropriate. But over the years the tone with which this position was advanced changed considerably. Whereas both his predecessors acknowledged the radical novelty of Brunelleschi's perspective and its rational character, if not its "truth" value, Vasari regarded it as no more than a useful and ingenious procedure facilitating the achievement of correct perspectival effects. In his view, Brunelleschi had not invented (or reinvented) perspective; he had simply discovered, after having wasted much time on the problem, a way to correct the

31. Ibid.
32. Ibid., pp. 332–33; English trans., pp. 394–95.

errors to which it was prone. He had done this to address the needs of painters, insofar as they included inanimate objects in their compositions, notably buildings of various kinds, for his method of planar projection, of perspective representation "by plan and profile" (*con pianta e profilo*), was particularly well suited to the depiction of buildings (it is still widely used by architects today). And not only painters, but also the makers of intarsia (*tarsie*), the art, as Vasari says with a hint of condescension, of inlaying colored woods.[33]

As if he wanted to exaggerate the strictly technical, empirical, even material character of the "thing," and in that way undercut speculation concerning its theoretical implications, Vasari sets out to persuade his readers that Brunelleschi had received no more than a basic education, and that he had only benefited from the lessons of Paolo Toscanelli late in his life, after returning from Padua, where he could have learned something from the teaching of Biagio Pelicani, author of the famous *Quaestiones perspectivae*. Toscanelli was undoubtedly the author of the short treatise *Della prospettiva* long attributed to Alberti, which is cast as a summary, in "vulgar" Italian, of the key concepts of medieval optics,[34] and of the remarks Brunelleschi is said to have found so interesting that he asked to receive instruction in geometry. That Brunelleschi would seem to have learned geometry *after* having executed—working, I again stress, on his own—his perspective experiments (which Manetti situated in his youth), and that his encounter with Toscanelli might have enabled him to give his invention its definitive form,[35] these two hypotheses, which are not mutually exclusive, do not seem to have interested Vasari. It seemed more important to him that "if Filippo was not well versed in letters, yet he knew so well how to reason in all things, with that natural facility born of practical experience, that he

---

33. "Le tarsie, che è un arte di commetterre legni di colori." Ibid.
34. Cf. Alessandro Parronchi, "*Della prospettiva* di Paolo dal Pozzo Toscanelli," *Studi . . .*, op. cit., pp. 583–641. There is only one surviving copy of this text (*Cod. Riccardiano* 2110), which was first published in 1849 by A. Bonnucci, in vol. 4 of the *Opere volgari* by Alberti. Robert Klein stated it was "without any doubt" derived from Biaggio Pelicani (*Form and Meaning*, op. cit., p. 103).
35. Parronchi, "Le due tavolette prospettiche del Brunelleschi," op. cit., pp. 242–43, and note 1, p. 243.

often confounded [his master]."[36] One could not better describe—despite the fact that Vasari's intentions were quite other, and opposed—or formulate in more striking terms the problem with which we will be dealing here: that of the status, in history, of the kind of "experiments" carried out by Brunelleschi, and of the experience accrued by means of them. A history, it must be emphasized from the start, that is not precisely that of art, nor that of science, and which has not yet become the focus of a constituted discipline—it is, rather, a field whose boundaries we must ourselves establish before setting out to explore it.

---

36. "Tornando poi da studio messer Paolo dal Pozzo Toscanelli, e una sera trovandosi in un orto a cena con certi suoi amici, invitò Filippo, il quale, uditolo ragionare dell'arti mathematiche, prese tal familiarità con seco, che egli imparò la geometria da lui; et sebbene Filippo non aveva lettere, gli rendeva si ragione di tutte le cose con il naturale della practica esperienza, che molte folte lo confondeva." Vasari, op. cit., p. 333; English trans., p. 395.

Milanesi identifies the two panels described by Vasari with two paintings on wood, one representing the Baptestry of San Giovanni and the other the Piazza della Signoria in perspective, which are mentioned in the inventory of the effects of Lorenzo the Magnificent (Milanesi, op. cit., p. 332, note 2). In his *Secret Notebooks* (1495–97), the doctor Francesco di Agostino Cegia refers to "un quadretto dipintovi San Giovanni di prospettiva, il quale aveva tolto el Grasso legnaiuolo" as being among the objects recovered by him after the flight of Piero di Medici (Cf. J. Schlosser Magnino, *La letteratura artistica,* 3d Italian ed., brought up to date by Otto Kurz, Florence, 1964, p. 711). I will discuss elsewhere the rather surprising reference here to the hero of the *Novella del Grasso,* a text contemporary with Manetti's *Vita,* and which Giovanni Tanturli has demonstrated, in my view decisively, cannot be considered apart from it (Manetti, op. cit., introduction, pp. xviiff.): its story is set in the baptistry piazza and its characters, aside from the victim of the farce, the carpenter el Grasso, are the people who wrote it, namely Brunelleschi, Donatello, and their friends from the San Giovanni quarter (cf. my *Théorie de l'échiquier,* in preparation). [There is now an English edition of the *Novella del Grasso:* Antonio Manetti, *The Fat Woodworker,* ed. and trans. by Robert L. Martone and Valerie Martone, New York, 1991.]

The invention of the rule.

The origins of perspective and geometry.

The meaning of history.

Perspective in practice and theory.

Knowledge and truth.

The Brunelleschi demonstration.

The textual tradition.

The Question of the Origin

Da lui e nato la regola. In constituting itself, the tradition had to assign *costruzione legittima* a concrete historical origin and—a subtler requirement— attach a name to it, that of its "inventor." Painters' perspective was discovered in a given time and place, by a man designated by name: a man who was not a painter, and who without doubt could not be one, seeing as the primary intent of this narrative of origin required that he belong to the race of constructors; a time whose *moment* is a matter of some importance because it presents itself as that of a rebirth, of a repetition of origin; and finally, a place—although we should allow for a likely intent to reinforce the image of Florence as "mother of the arts" and of the new culture by stressing local color—in which the tradition was deeply rooted, a region whose value as country *of origin* was not to be underestimated: this was self-evident for Alberti, who had recently returned to his native city after an extended exile imposed on his family; but Filarete too made a point of stressing Brunelleschi's Florentine affiliation each time he mentioned his hero's name. As if the legislative force of this cultural object, to whose legislative power as a binding rule the tradition attested (despite the fact that rules are not invented, nor are they discovered, being of institutional origin), was fully recognizable, fully justifiable, only if its sources were traced, its pedigree properly verified (a procedure requiring the testimony of witnesses, as we shall see). As if a single demonstration had not sufficed to guarantee its legitimacy, it being necessary to consider in addition the question of its origin, as well as the affiliated tradition and its preoccupation with historical specificity.

Insofar as it is framed in terms of tradition, the question of the origin of perspective blends into another that has consistently interested philosophers: that of the origin of geometry, and of the route it cleared for itself, after a prolonged period of tentative efforts, in the wake of a revolu-tion—to cite Kant—"due to a single man, whether known as Thales or by some other name," he who first gave the form and force of a theorem to geometric properties he had deduced himself, by common sense.[1] This con-nection is all the more justifiable given that the perspective rule is founded, geometrically speaking, on the so-called Thales theorem and the concept of *similitude* that follows from this. Every allowance being made (and my argu-ment makes no sense otherwise), the tradition transmitted and reworked successively by Filarete, Manetti, and Vasari holds that the revolution intro-duced by Brunelleschi in the matter of perspective (*la quale per altri tempi non s'era usata*) made such an impression that the event was saved from oblivion, just like that other inaugural event known to us thanks to the account of Diogenes Laertius. With the difference that, whereas we know nothing of Thales save his name (which could be mistaken), the history (*die Geschichte,* to use Kant's word) of the man who is supposed to have accom-plished this other "revolution" is relatively well known to us.

The very fact that despite a total absence, as we shall see, of spe-cific data concerning the precise nature of the procedure applied by Brunel-leschi, we nonetheless dispose of a great deal of information about the man and his life, about the circles in which he moved, and about his various activities, as well as about the circumstances of his discovery, this fact obliges us to fine-tune the parallel we might be tempted to draw between these two revolutions: the one, as a result of which science was somehow torn from its prehistory—out of a ground of pregeometric experience consti-tuting its "first attainments," to use Husserl's phrase—to take an ideal object, one liberated from all reference to an empirical subjectivity;[2] and the other, which was to result in an art as material—as profoundly implicated in the sensible world as was painting, in that art's appealing, by means of geometry, to "its roots in nature"—so as to impose, under the title of per-spective, a mode of representation linked, on principle, to the position assigned to the perceiving subject at the very departure point of *costruzione*

---

1.   Emmanuel Kant, *Critique of Pure Reason,* op. cit., English trans., p. xxxi.
2.   Cf. Edmund Husserl, *L'Origine de la gómetrie,* French trans. and introduction by Jacques Der-rida, Paris, 1962; English trans. (of the Husserl text only), "The Origin of Geometry," in *The Crisis of European Sciences and Transcendental Philosophy,* op. cit., appendix 6, pp. 353–78.

legittima, to its "origin," in the geometric sense of the word. In the eyes of tradition the question of the origin of perspective resembles that of the origin of geometry in two precise respects: in both instances the "revolution" is reputed to have been instigated by an individual mentioned by name, but in neither case can the meaning of the origin be isolated from that of history, whose task it is to produce such revolutions, ones that can figure (but figure only) as points of departure (here, for science or art), as absolute beginnings.

What can there be to the object of a deductive science or an "exact" practice, one supposed to have demonstrative value, if it cannot constitute itself as the object of this science or practice except at a given historical moment and in specific circumstances, and if it allows itself to operate, to unfold all its implications, only if in turn it clears the way for another history: a history that, while not subject to the same constraints as empirical history, nonetheless participates in its movement and is even capable of impeding this? And, conversely, what can there be to history in general, supposed to constitute the last horizon of all "meaning," as of all "truth," in comparison with the original mode of historicity characteristic of science, from the moment this latter conforms to a tradition—that precisely of "truth"—that appears to be the pure, ideal form, even the model of an authentic history, a history in the full sense of the word: a history irreduceable to a set of facts or a simple sequence of events but that would order itself in relation to a horizon of ideality from which, on the contrary, it would derive its meaning—in other words, something like perspective? To say that Brunelleschi discovered or invented perspective—or at least that he did not simply rediscover or reinvent it—is this to ascribe to that discovery an originary significance, to posit that it initiated both an object and a history, comparable to the one attached to the name Thales—whose endeavor "pointed unmistakably to the path that had to be followed, and opened and traced out for the most distant times the safe way of a science"?[3]

The question of the origin of perspective, which the tradition cannot ignore from the moment it has sufficiently constituted itself to pose it, this question, like its counterpart in geometry, thus takes on the value of an

---

3. Kant, op. cit., p. xxx.

example, from a phenomenological point of view (and in all senses of the word "example"), at the same time that it becomes the index of a task. As Jacques Derrida writes in his introduction to Husserl's *The Origin of Geometry,* "the possibility of something like a history of science imposes a rereading and a reawakening of the "sense" of history in general; ultimately, its phenomenological *sense/direction* will merge with its teleological *sense.*"[4] Or to put it differently, in words better suited to my argument here: the possibility of a history of science necessarily entails a reconsideration of the meaning of the word "history" and something like a "reawakening" of its meaning. This holds for the history of science. But what about that of art—which at a given moment in its history seemed to make a new beginning by linking its destiny to that of a discipline with scientific pretentions, one that could only impress as revolutionary? Especially given that the terms "rereading" and "reawakening" assume a singular resonance in light of the moment in which this narrative of origin was inscribed in history, took root in it—a moment that ever-present tradition dubs a "renaissance" or "rebirth," if not *the* Renaissance.

*

It will be asserted, correctly, that there is nothing of "pure ideality" about *costruzione legittima* and that it bears no resemblance to a geometric theorem, despite the fact that its theoretical justification, as well as the means that enable its demonstrative capacities and determine its normativity—in a word, its legitimacy—depend from geometry. It proposed only to apply this discipline to representational ends. Which did not prevent it from assuming, on the register of the imaginary, forms that were increasingly rigorous and pure, even abstract, to such an extent that finally it solicited geometric aid in the form of descriptive and projective geometry. But while it is true that much can be learned about the emergence of a theory from its develop-

---

4.   Derrida, in Husserl, op. cit., p. 5. Derrida's text is available in a separate English language edition as Jacques Derrida, *Edmund Husserl's "Origin of Geometry": An Introduction,* trans. by John P. Leavey, Jr., Lincoln and London, 1978; this reference on p. 27. ["Sense" is Leavey's rendering of the French term *sens,* but it can also signify "meaning" or "direction," a fact that Derrida exploits in the cited passage—TRANS.]

ment, its application,[5] and in general, to use Husserl's term, the field of work (*Arbeitsfeld*) opened up by it, this does not necessarily hold for painters' perspective. For it could be that originally this was but the result, the product of the progressive perfecting and normalization of a process, or of a set of empirical procedures, current in Florentine studios long before Brunelleschi: such as, if we are to believe the more convincing exponent of this hypothesis, the so-called bifocal method, probably in use since the fourteenth century, of which the procedure used by Brunelleschi would be only an a posteriori rationalization.[6] In the absence of all reliable information about the said method (having excluded Vasari's text, an attempt to remedy this lacuna a century and a half after the fact), it must be said that this hypothesis has nothing to support it save the reputations of those who espouse it. Unless one ascribes to Brunelleschi a perspective system confirming such a thesis, which is to fall prey, like Robert Klein, to circular reasoning.

But what is meant by "technique"? Either one can hold that this skill originated in a strictly material, mechanical way, which doesn't help us to understand how it came to be regarded as a *model*,[7] or one can espouse the idea—advanced with great subtlety by André Chastel—of a "knowledge contained within the figurative structures that administer it,"[8] effectively collapsing the question of origin into that of the modalities of this containment, of this "administration," and of the ways this implicit knowledge is rendered explicit. I recall here that Panofsky convincingly demonstrated how the most advanced Trecento artists, the most "progressive" ones (*die Fort-schrittlichen*), gradually perfected and came to systematically apply, with the aid of a checkered ground plane, a procedure that Duccio had used only for the central portions of coffered ceilings. But even if orthogonals visible

---

5.   Cf. Michel Serres, "Ce que Thalès a vu au pied des pyramides," *Hermès II. L'Interférence,* Paris, 1972, pp. 163–80.

6.   Klein, "Pomponius Gauricus on Perspective," *Form and Meaning,* op. cit., pp. 119–22.

7.   This argument was already made by the great Viennese art historian Aloïs Riegl at the end of the last century, in his criticism of theories positing a technical origin for ornamental forms (specifically, from textile production). Cf. Aloïs Riegl, *Stilfragen,* Berlin, 1893, chapter 1.

8.   André Chastel, "Présentation," in Klein, *La Forme et l'intelligible* (the original, French-language edition of *Form and Meaning,* op. cit., with additional articles), Paris, 1970, p. 14.

in the ground plane tend to converge at a single vanishing point, it doesn't
necessarily follow that this decisive step, attributable to the Ambrogio Lorenzetti, was made *"undoubtedly* with full mathematical consciousness."[9] In the
Annunciation in the Pinacoteca in Siena, commissioned from Ambrogio in
1344, the patterned floor is indeed systematically constructed in accordance
with the rules of perspective, in strict symmetry. But the point toward
which its orthogonals converge doesn't appear as such; it is dissimulated, or,
to be more precise, obliterated, obstructed by a column in low relief that

9.   "Es sind vor allen Dingen die Brüder Lorenzetti, die diesen wichtigen Schritt getan haben.
. . . Hier die sichtbaren Orthogonalen der Grundebene zum ersten Male sämtlich, und ohne zweifel
mit vollem mathematischen Bewusstsein, nach einem Punkte orientiert sind." Panofsky, "Die Perspektive . . .," op. cit., p. 117; English trans., p. 57.

corresponds exactly with the panel's axis of symmetry and that, although an extension of the gilded frame, is nonetheless firmly planted within the painting, in the foreground, on its lower edge. In its spatial ambiguity, functioning as it does as a kind of mask or screen, this architectonic element is the lynchpin of an eminently contradictory structure in which the paving's recession is in open conflict with the flattening effect created by the gold ground—within which the vanishing point is geometrically situated.

Numerous other examples of such contradiction could be cited; it is almost as though the point designated by the construction was somehow so powerful, yet so suspect, that it cannot be openly acknowledged, that it had to be dissimulated behind a mask or veil. Nonetheless, the discovery of the vanishing point, insofar as this was understood to affect the orientation of orthogonals well beyond those in the paving, to either side of it,[10] corresponded with the institution of a kind of "concrete symbol," in Cassirer's sense, eventually leading to the geometric definition of the "point of infinity." This idea is perfectly consistent with the central argument of *The Philosophy of Symbolic Forms:* henceforth this point will effectively function, not so much as a symbol of infinity, but as a *sign* whose inscription on the canvas or wall marked the initiation of a project of progressive theoretical articulation that was to achieve its logical conclusion only after a lapse of several centuries. But before arriving at a conception of a point as the image, at infinity, of the infinitely distant convergence point of all the orthogonals, defined as the reciprocal equivalent of a vertical (and inversely), it was necessary for mathematical thought to work through a sequence of stages corresponding, in part, to what is called the "history" of geometry—a history, to all appearances, in which art (that of the perspectivists) had its role to play at a given moment but which offers no support for the claim made by Panofsky that, like many other branches of modern "science" (the quotation marks are his, and significant), the projective geometry of the

---

10. "Die Entdeckung des Fluchtpunkts, als des 'bildes der unendlich fernen Punkte sämtlicher Tiefenlinien,' ist gleichsam das konkrete Symbol für die Entdeckung des Unendlichen selbst." Ibid., English trans., p. 58. The image of *all* orthogonals, whereas in Duccio only a few were oriented in relation to the same point: which doesn't imply that thenceforth the entire surface of the ground plane (*die ganze Bodebene*) was conceived as being organized in relation to a single vanishing point—only the squared surface in question.

seventeenth century was, in the final analysis, a product of the artist's workshop.[11]

It would seem that Panofsky merely diverted the movement of science in a way intended to turn it to art's advantage. A science so accomplished at integrating the stages of its own development that in each of these moments it appears to invent itself entirely in the present, outside history. But such an intention fails to take account of the paradox at the root of Husserl's reflections concerning the origin of geometry:[12] although the ideal entities that are the object of this science delineate for it a horizon of permanence and intemporality, at the same time it is impossible to conceive geometry (and science in general) apart from its history. In none of these moments is science *the* truth, given its inevitable ties to a specific time, and given that it always opens onto a future in which it will necessarily challenge its own attainments preliminary to surpassing them, though somehow steering clear of relativism and historicism. Husserl thought this double bind could be loosed with the notion of *horizon,* a horizon of ideality, a phrase I've used above; but a horizon, as well, that is temporal, a fact on which the future of science hinges, at every moment—on the extent to which truth exceeds knowledge, on the intention behind any founding act issuing in concepts that bring it to realization.

Such, in the field of art, was the discovery (prior to that of Brunelleschi) of the Lorenzetti; or, to use Panofsky's term, their disclosure (*Entdeckung*), as a result of which the vanishing point was brought to light, though this invention, in the archeological sense of the term, did not imply full consciousness of its theoretical implications. Panofsky comes very close to grasping the truth that concerns us here, and its sometimes tortuous developmental trajectory, when he states that painting made accessible to vision (*veranschaulischen:* to apprehend intuitively, to give to the senses, "to

---

11. "Auch sie [die projective Geometrie des XVIII. Jahrhunderts], wie so viele Teildiszipline der moderne 'Wissenschaft,' in letzem Grunde ein Produkt der Künstlerateliers." Ibid.

12. In addition to the introduction to *The Origin of Geometry* by Jacques Derrida, I here make use of an unpublished lecture course given by Maurice Merleau-Ponty at the Collège de France in 1959–60, under the title "Husserl au-delà de la phénoménologie," the last of his courses I was able to attend; my notes from it testify to my considerable debt to him. It was Merleau-Ponty who, while advising me during the period of my candidacy for the "diplôme d'Études supérieures," first had me read Cassirer, as well as Panofsky's text on perspective, and this at a time when no one else in Paris was interested in either of them.

illustrate") the *Systemraum,* the modern, systematic conception of space, in a concrete artistic sphere (*in einer künstlerisch konkreten Sphäre*), even before abstract mathematical science had given form and force to it as a postulate (*noch ehe das abstraktmathematische Denken ihn postuliert hatte*[13]). In this sense, and in this sense only, it might be maintained that, in the last resort, modern geometry emerged from "perspectival endeavors."[14] *In letzen Grunde*—the phrase can be taken literally, for the work carried out in the studios indeed furnished the indispensable grounding for future developments in geometry, as is illustrated by the example of Desargues. A grounding of pre-geometric experience, like that which was the basis, the condition, of the inversion described by Husserl of pure practice into pure theory, whereby the empirical skill of measurement was transformed in Thales's period into a method of geometric thought.[15] Brunelleschi's discovery cleared the way for a similar inversion, and perhaps even implied it.

*

In its constitutive, "revolutionary" moment, *costruzione legittima,* known as "correct" or "exact" perspective, is in direct conflict with the very idea of tradition: in effect no tradition could prevail against the force of its demonstrations. The paradoxical nature of history—a constant factor—would seem to dictate that this revolution be mastered in turn by a tradition that could only constitute itself as such by obscuring its more ambiguous aspects, by ignoring the implications of the event it acknowledged to be that of its origin. Thus the seeming tendency to confine the import of Brunelleschi's discovery within strict boundaries, evident as early as the first pages of Alberti's *Della pittura* (but *seeming* only, as the actual effect within the symbolic order will be precisely inverse), in the choice made by that author to treat in the terms of a specific discourse (*Parlo come pittore,* "I speak as a painter") an invention that, I repeat, could be ascribed to neither a painter nor a writer of treatises. That would not have been invented, that *could not* have been invented, if it were true that the historical importance of perspectival construction could be determined solely through examination of its

---

13. Panofsky, loc. cit.
14. "Und in der Tat sollte ja die projective Geometrie des XVII. Jahrhunderts aus perspektivischen Bemühungen hervorgehen." Ibid.
15. Husserl, Die Krisis . . ., p. 125; English trans., p. 28.

optical and/or geometric sources (in the scholarly sense of the word—primary sources), or its effects limited to the domain of painting, or its nature understood in terms of ideological fallout. What I refer to as Brunelleschi's demonstration—a demonstration that has nothing *ideal,* nothing "purely" geometric, about it—implicates another form of empirical or positivist history, even as it opens up a field of endeavor (and interrogation) that cannot be contained within the limits of any discipline, whether "art," "science," "technics," "geometry," "painting," "scenography," or other.

If such is the case, a new reading of the tradition through which this demonstration is known to us becomes obligatory: a reading that, if possible, is more naive (in the phenomenological sense), less *anticipatory,* but also more literal, more respectful of the texts, than those previously proposed. Not that I intend to minimize the interest of earlier research into the possible sources of the demonstration (notably that of Alessandro Parronchi) and its context (here I am thinking of the exacting work carried out by Robert Klein with the intention of recovering something of actual studio practice, though he was not fully conscious of the implications of the problem), or the many attempts (of Parronchi again, as well as Richard Krautheimer, Decio Gioseffi, John White, and, more recently, Edgerton, to name just a few) to reconstitute Brunelleschi's method of construction, to reconstruct his experiments.[16] If, as has been claimed, perspective is really a crossroads, if not of inceptions then at least of histories, this project is more than justified. But it nonetheless provokes the following question: After having been ignored or neglected for so long (Panofsky himself only alluded to it in passing, being less interested in the origin of perspective than in its properties as a "symbolic form," one purportedly linked to the *Weltanschauung* or world-view of the period), what can we learn today about the Brunelleschi episode, given that it is no longer accessible to us save through

---

16. Cf. Parronchi, "Le due tavole prospettiche del Brunelleschi," op. cit., pp. 226–312; Richard Krautheimer, *Lorenzo Ghiberti,* 1956, vol. 1, pp. 229ff.; Decio Gioseffi, *Perspectiva artificialis,* op. cit., pp. 73ff.; John White, *The Birth and Rebirth of Pictorial Space,* London, 1976, pp. 113–21; Edgerton, *The Renaissance Rediscovery of Linear Perspective,* op. cit., pp. 124–52. But the essential work, aside from the titles by Parronchi and Klein cited previously, remains that of Piero Sanpaolesi, "Ipostesi sulle conoscenze matematiche, statiche e mecaniche del Brunelleschi," *Belle arti,* 5 (1951).

a literature that is often paradoxical, even nonsensical?[17] If the tradition was able to constitute itself only by resorting to this designation of an origin, can we possibly hope, by analyzing the texts, notably their lacunae, to cast any new light on the original intent of this constitutive, if not constitutional, project?

I take this to be the index of a task that, while ultimately of phenomenological inspiration (which should not trouble those who've convinced themselves that much current theoretical work, far from having rendered the phenomenological project obsolete, sets out to address problems framed in crude, pre-phenomenological terms), must nonetheless be pursued in a way diametrically opposed to that adopted by Husserl in *The Origin of Geometry*. The fundamental difference between the two founding operations—that of Thales, which was rigorously idealist, and that of Brunelleschi, which was partly experimental—cannot be denied. Where Husserl aimed, by means of his "reduction," at recovering the original meaning of geometry by means of the eidetic of the spatiality of natural things and the index of scientificity in general, which entailed deciphering the meaning of the constituting act as this implicates the constituted object, in this instance developed geometry (thus the above-noted equivalence between meaning [*sens*] of the origin and teleological direction [*sens*]), we will be obliged, by contrast, to undertake a close reading of the single narrative that affected the introduction of Brunelleschi's perspective demonstration *into history*,[18] that of Manetti. A word-for-word reading, as regards both its content and the information it conveys. And this with the intention, not of uncovering its hidden meaning, or of interpreting it in light of its antecedents or of subsequent theoretical developments, but rather—in open defiance of philology if not of all pretense to objectivity, fortified, we might say, by a question utterly free of positivist certitude, a question that is essentially

---

17. Cf. Martin Kemp, "Science, Non-science and Nonsense: The Interpretation of Brunelleschi's Perspective," *Art History*, vol. 1, no. 2 (June 1978), pp. 134–52. I certainly do not concur with all his conclusions, but I am nonetheless indebted to a number of pertinent observations made by Kemp in this article, which led me to revise several of the arguments advanced in an early, highly preliminary version of the present work (Cf. "L'Origine de la perspective," *Macula*, no. 5–6, 1979, pp. 113–37).

18. On tradition as the "ether of historical perception," cf. Derrida, in Husserl, op. cit., p. 34; English trans., *Edmund Husserl's 'Origin . . .,"* op. cit., p. 49.

critical—in hopes of apprehending this tradition in the constitutive moment of its turning back on itself, using the *painting* which provides access, and on the point of origin with which it was, as we shall see, *pierced*. A hole, which it would appear Vasari significantly chose to ignore—unless it was quickly patched over to give the panel a more respectable appearance, one more in keeping with expectations as to what paintings ought to be. The project before us, then, is essentially that of directing attention to several features, if not *piercings*, absences, that are so many reference points along the path of another history, one that is resolutely speculative. And in implementing it—in this respect it resembles Husserl's, which addressed geometry within the context of western science in general—we must not ignore the question of its ties to a purported "crisis" from which it issued, the implications of which extend, under the standard of perspective, well beyond the crisis of the representational system inherited from the Renaissance, evidence for which can supposedly be found in painting since the epoque of Cézanne and the beginnings of cubism. For it is readily apparent that in the cultural field at large—encompassing prevailing modes of graphic design as well as information conveyed by photography, film, and computers—this system has lost none of its pertinence: even today our culture is massively informed by the perspectival model, far more so than was the Renaissance, for which perspective did not so much constitute a privileged ideological form as give historical *point* to the work of the symbolic.

Was der Fall ist.

The lost prototype.

And as for the sky.

Perspective and the built object.

Perspective shows.

The mirror demonstrates.

The Monstration

This matter of perspective (literally: this case of perspective, *questo caso della prospettiva*), the first thing in which he showed it (*nella prima cosa in che e'lo mostro*) was a small panel about half a *braccio* square (*una tavoletta di circa mezzo braccio quadro*) on which he made a painting that resembled (*a similitudine*) the temple of San Giovanni, seen from the outside; and of this temple he represented as much of it as can be seen from the outside (*e da quel tempio ritratto quanto se ne vede a un sguardo dallato di fuori*); and it seems that to represent it he stationed himself some three *braccia* inside the central portal of Santa Maria dei Fiori (*e pare che sia stato a ritrarlo dentro alla porta del mezzo di Santa Maria del Fiore qualche braccia tre*), the thing being done with such care and delicacy (*con tanta diligenza e gentillezza*) and so precisely (*e tanto a punto*) in the colors of the black and white marbles that no miniaturist could have done it better. And everything figuring around (literally: facing, *dinanzi*) that part of the piazza encompassed by the eye (*quella parte della piazza che riceve l'occhio*), namely, from the side facing the Misericordia up to the arch and corner of the sheep market, and from the side with the column of the miracle of Saint Zenobius up to the corner of the straw market, and as much of this place as one sees from some distance away (*e quanto di que'luogo si vede de discoto*). And insofar as he had to show the sky (*e per quanto s'aveva a dimostrare de cielo*), that is, where the painted walls stamped themselves against the air (*cioè che le muraglie del dipinto stampassano nella aria*), he used silver burnished in which a way that natural air and sky (*l'aria*

89

e'cieli naturali) were reflected in it, and even clouds that one saw pass by in this silver pushed by the wind, when it was blowing.[1]

Such was the prototype of perspective to which is attached, like a brand name, like a certification of pedigree, the name of Brunelleschi—if, that is, one accepts that the *tavoletta* used in the demonstration was a small painted wooden panel half a *braccio* square, or about the length of one's hand, wrist included, and thus easily handled.[2] Or to adhere more closely to the text: which abetted him in showing (but not, at first, demonstrating?) what there was to such a "case" of perspective (that is, one case among other possible ones), if not to perspective in general, to perspective as *the* "case." Or again—making free play with associations deriving from the use of this word in contemporary philosophy—to perspective as paradigm, as the paradigm of something in the representational order with implications bearing upon "what is the case," on what is at stake, on what is in question, that itself poses a question—*Was der Fall ist.*

"Prototype" should be understood here in the sense of *model*, though not one tied to a divine revelation, like icons of the Virgin in the Byzantine tradition, which held, at least ideally, that all such representations depended from Saint Luke's portrait of an apparition of Mary, the first link, necessarily an absent one, in a long chain of images. To say nothing of that other image, primordial if ever there was, the *vera icona* par excellence: the imprint of Christ's face on Veronica's veil, the record of direct contact, of immediate transfer of the real to the imaginary that took the form of a mirror image, a reversed or pivoted image, as in a self-portrait. Which was thus an *index,* in Charles Peirce's sense, the result of a quasi-photographic process, but one in which the distance implied by *prise de vue* (literally, captured view: the French phrase for an individual photographic exposure) plays its part: a distance, as we shall see, that perspective puts to constructive as well as demonstrative use. The image of painting that Brunelleschi used for his demonstration would have had to be *constructed* by him, and—as

---

1. Manetti, op. cit., pp. 57–58; English trans., pp. 42–44.
2. On the problems posed by the translation and interpretation of this passage, cf. *infra,* chapter 7., pp. 101ff.

was stressed by Alberti—without having at his disposition any *example* to inspire him. But this model—whatever the presuppositions and epistemological implications of the operation may have been—this prototype must also, of necessity, be absent from its place: the very structure of the tradition dictates this, as it could not have constituted itself as such except through the attempt to reactivate its traces. Such is the case with dreams, whose images, like this painting, are accessible to us only retrospectively, through descriptions couched in language, in conformity with the rule of *ekphrasis*. The descriptions in question can "make paintings" (*faire tableau*), but will only succeed in this task insofar as they make implicit reference to the constructive principle obeyed by the image of the baptistry, indicating with precision their origin, in the geometric sense.

According to Manetti, the constructive rule applied by Brunelleschi was such that, on the basis of an image in perspective of a building, one that could not have been more familiar to Florentines, the baptistry of San Giovanni, one could determine the spot on which the painter placed himself, at least ideally, to represent it—*a ritrarlo,* or, to take this phrase literally, to take its portrait, feature by feature. A *quantitative* matter, as Manetti specifies (*quanto se ne vede*): from a given point of view the eye can only perceive part of any opaque body, in particular a building whose regular form makes it amenable to calculation, a part that's larger or smaller in correlation with the limits imposed by the point of view in question. *E Pare che sia stato a ritrarlo:* in fact it matters little whether Brunelleschi went about producing his construction *in situ,* standing on the spot indicated by Manetti—the same spot upon which the text, a bit further on, states that any observer wishing to represent for himself the baptistry as it appeared in the *tavoletta* should stand. What was essential was that the chosen point of view could be *deduced* from the painting itself. And more: that the place be locatable in real space with relative precision ("about three *braccia* inside the central portal of the cathedral"), such that anyone at all who came to the spot might verify the accuracy of this designation.

It might seem surprising that Manetti has nothing to say about the method of construction used by Brunelleschi in his perspectival rendering of the baptistry, that his goal is to reveal its demonstrative power and experimental character. But one cannot use this apparent lacuna to argue that the

Brunelleschi's first experiment: overhead view of Florence Cathedral and the Baptistry with indication of the position of the observer inside the central portal and his two possible angles of vision.

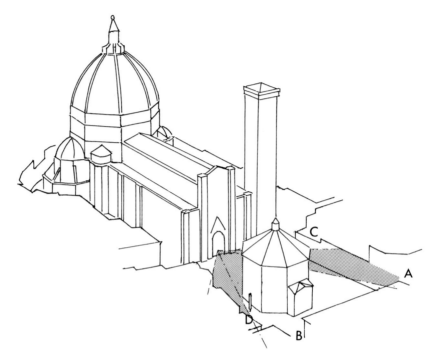

artist proceeded in a purely mechanical way, using a mirror, even painting on one, as has been proposed by Gioseffi.[3] In addition to objections to be discussed below, this hypothesis is difficult to reconcile with the function of the prototype in the tradition: in effect it is difficult to see how Brunelleschi could have derived a rule from a straightforward recording or graphic transfer. For even if, as Filarete would have it, he resorted to the use of a mirror the better to observe the way objects diminish in proportion with distance, it would still have been necessary for him to understand—like Kant's Thales—that he should not become fixated on what the mirror *demonstrates* (*che nello specchio ti si dimostra*), nor even on the concept derivable from it, but that he must engender this, "generate" it, using, as Vasari would say later, his own resources, and thus discover the rule *per ragione:* it being impossible in this instance for construction to operate a priori, its functioning being predicated on a foundation consisting of givens both the-

---

3.   Gioseffi, op. cit., p. 77.

oretical and practical, and of relatively developed measurement skills, in the context of which the mirror would have had a certain role to play.[4]

Vasari's indication that Brunelleschi, in constructing his perspective image of the baptistry and its surroundings, used a ground plan and an elevation of the buildings in question to correlate them with what he terms the *intersegatione,* that is, a plane of projection corresponding to the picture plane, the latter being assimilated to a slice of the visual pyramid, is a response to this epistemological requirement. This assertion, which would have been corroborated by standard architectural practice in Vasari's day, does not contradict Manetti's description. Thus it is easy to understand why numerous interpreters have accepted it; but Manetti's silence on this point merits our attention—it is, in fact, decisive. For the moment, however, I will merely note that if such had been the procedure used by Brunelleschi, he could have produced what appears to have been the first example of modern "scenography" without placing himself in the spot indicated by Manetti, and that a properly programmed computer provided with the necessary information would be capable of doing this without leaving the laboratory.

*

There remains the problem of the sky or, in Manetti's terms, of that portion of the little painting against which the walls of the buildings making up the background of the scene, as well as, it would seem, the pyramidal roof of the baptistry itself, should *stamp themselves.* It is worth pointing out here that, in Manetti's *Life,* the perspective episode follows immediately after an extended passage devoted to Brunelleschi's gifts as a *muratore,* which, it is claimed, in his youth first brought him to the attention of the authorities, who then summoned him *per architetto e per disegno.*[5] So much for the walls. But the sky? Doesn't representation of the aerial element, like that of clouds, those "bodies without surfaces," as Leonardo described them, fall outside the skills necessary for linear perspective, which can only function, as a rule of construction, on the condition that everything escaping its juris-

---

4. Cf., on this point, the invaluable observations of Martin Kemp, op. cit. 1978, pp. 158–59.
5. Manetti, op. cit., pp. 54–55; English trans., p. 40.

diction be excluded from its field? How is one to represent, feature by feature, a body that has no contours? How is one to trace its "portrait"?[6]

The new idea of the painting at the center of perspective's origin myth called for inclusion in the demonstration—on its margins, it would seem, and in the form of a reflection—of this unmastered, unmasterable background element, one that had to be *shown* but could not be except by use of a mirror—that is, paradoxically, by resorting to a *di-mostratio.* Thus the cloud mirror functioned as the index (narrowly construed) of a discontinuity between the order of that susceptible to representation by the means of *perspectiva artificialis,* and another element which, admitting of no term and no limit, seems to escape capture, demanding to be presented "in its natural form" (*l'aria e'cieli naturali*). The index of a discontinuity but also of a heterogeneity, if not of a heterotope (with the following reservation, which has its importance in an Aristotelian context: that the element reflected in the mirror, in its natural form, not be the entirely ideal one of light, but rather the atmosphere as the location of sublunar phenomena). *Casamenti, piani e montagne e paesi d'ogni ragione:* perspective is applicable to anything that will conform to its "reasons," however varied these might be. First of all, that product of art which, in its materials and its mechanics, borrows directly from nature: the thing built. Whereas according to Husserl geometry takes for its object the spatiality of natural things in general, perspective is indissolubly linked to built objects, and to architecture, as well as to the spatiality of the city as defined by the monuments punctuating it and the lines of the facades bounding and enclosing it. To such a degree that Rudolf Wittkower could argue, quite ingeniously, that Brunelleschi had been prompted to invent perspective by a requirement, a need, that was distinctly architectural: wanting to establish once and for all that the metrical coherence of a building remained constant regardless of the distance from which it was viewed, he had to demonstrate that the visible diminution of objects distributed in space conformed to a regular, invariable *ratio.* With the consequence that the proportions of a building can only be judged in perspective, in relation to an ideal plane of projection, which

---

6. On perspective as a structure of exclusion, and for a more fully developed analysis of this aspect of the Brunelleschian conception, cf. my *Théorie du nuage,* op. cit., pp. 166–71.

implies that the difference between architecture and painting is only one of medium, not of essence.[7]

But Manetti's attentiveness to the problem of the sky, and his failure to discuss the ground of the perspective construction, this textual given assumes symptomatic meaning if we note that Alberti holds the delineation of a checkerboard ground plane to be the first step in the construction of what must be called the perspective scene. In addition to conforming with the emphasis on the covering of buildings in the tradition—whether the dome of the cathedral of Florence or the row of beams that supposedly prompted Brunelleschi to formulate the notion of converging orthogonals, to say nothing of the coffered ceilings in San Lorenzo and Santo Spirito, or of the architect's probable participation in the graphic construction of the vault, also coffered, above Masaccio's *Trinity,* in which the ground plane on which the figures stand is reduced to a mere line corresponding with that of the horizon—it confirms a lesson to be learned from Manetti's account: in its moment of origin, perspective, like geometry, was less concerned with space, considered as the receptacle of bodies (and, a fortiori, with that homogeneous, continuous, and infinite space conceptualized by Descartes under the rubric of extended substance), than with objects themselves. Beginning with this octagonal baptistry, situated in the center of a square piazza, readily accessible to view, a perfectly regular figure presenting a similar aspect on each of its sides: the very type of those bodies of which Husserl spoke, having surfaces that are more or less smooth, angles that are more or less pure, and lines of intersection that are more or less clean; that instruct the mind and conduct it, in a sequence of incremental steps, toward the horizon of the pure "limit-shapes" that are the object of geometry.[8] But if one knows nothing about, cannot know anything about a volume except what its planes tell us, planes onto which, in a sense, it projects itself,[9] and if *projection* is as significant here as *plane,* then Brunelleschi's demonstration assumes, in this context, a singular *relief:* the first thing in which he showed and drew attention to *prospettiva* was a small painting

---

7.   Wittkower, "Brunelleschi and 'Proportion in Perspective,'" op. cit. 1953, p. 288.

8.   Husserl, *L'Origine de la géometrie,* op. cit., pp. 210–11; cf. *Die Krisis . . .,* op. cit., pp. 21ff.; English trans., pp. 25ff., 376ff.

9.   Serres, "Ce que Thalès a vu au pied des pyramides," op. cit., p. 173.

7   Masaccio, *The Trin-
ity*, 1426–27. Florence,
Santa Maria Novella,
upper portion of the
fresco. Photo: Alinari-
Giraudon.

The Prototype

made to resemble an object itself so manifestly rational that making a planar projection of it might easily appear to constitute a renewal with the inaugural act of geometry. In which task he could succeed only by reducing the visible bodies to an assemblage of surfaces—surfaces representing the limits of bodies, as lines represent the limits of surfaces.[10]

*

I have spoken of a "demonstration." But what, precisely, does Manetti say? That this matter, this "case" of perspective, Brunelleschi first *showed* it (*nella prima cosa in che e'lo mostro*) in a small panel on which he'd painted the baptistry of San Giovanni such that this appeared as if seen from a specific spot, namely from just inside the portal of the cathedral. The word *dimostrare* appears later in the text, in the phrase about the sky and the place reserved for it in the design (*e per quanto s'aveva a dimostrare di cielo*), which might seem to be a contradiction in terms, given that this "demonstration," purported or real, excluded all reference to geometry and was entirely dependent upon the operation of the mirror. But the difficulty—invoked in a number of texts dealing with perspective and the specular image—is only apparent. Perspective is, in effect, doubly a matter of *showing:* on the one hand, it provides rules for the diminution of objects in accordance with the distance at which they show themselves (*di quella misura che s'appartiene a quella distantia che le si mostrano de lunghi*); on the other, it lends itself to demonstration, by means of a mirror. If it is true, as Lacan would have it, that in a waking state our gaze is elided such that we imagine not only that we "see ourselves seeing ourselves" but that "we see it showing itself," by contrast, the perspective image, like the dream image, characteristically "shows itself" of its own accord—though even here there is some slippage of the subject, whereby it "demonstrates" its presence.[11]

That perspective, in and of itself, can be the object of a demonstration, if not of an explicit "monstration," is not necessarily self-evident. But that "it shows itself" of its own accord, often indiscreetly, is evinced by a substantial portion of quattrocento art. In the experiment to which Brunel-

10.   Alberti, *Della pittura,* book I, cited ed., p. 56; English trans., pp. 44–45. Cf. my *Théorie du nuage,* op. cit., p. 162.

11.   Lacan, *Le Séminaire XI,* op. cit., p. 72; English trans., *Four Fundamental Concepts,* p. 83.

leschi's name has become attached, this feature becomes not only figurative but also gestural and specular, all at once, by means of a mirror held at arm's length, which confers precise meaning on the distinction between *mostrare* and *dimostrare*. The word *di-mostratio* implies a process of duplication, of repetition, of doubling whose agent is the mirror. That Brunelleschi did not paint the baptistry with a mirror, or on a mirror, is confirmed by an attentive reading of the text: if such were the case, Manetti would have used the word *dimostrare,* as he did for the sky. The sky that Brunelleschi did not paint, leaving it to the mirror to reflect it, to "de-monstrate" it. As was already stated by Filarete, what is shown directly to the eye is demonstrated in the mirror (*che nello specchio ti si dimostra*). Painting shows; the mirror demonstrates.

The square of the *quadro*.

Windows and doors.

The schism between the eye and the gaze.

A matter of angle, distance, and point of view.

The Painting's Reasons

Before turning to the demonstration proper, it will be useful to pause and review the information presently at our disposal concerning the reasons shaping Brunelleschi's painting. First, its measurements.

Una tavoletta di circa mezzo braccio quadro: breaking with the generally accepted view, some have suggested that the word indicating approximation (*circa*) applies not to the dimensions of the *tavoletta* ("a small panel of about half a *braccio* on each side") but to its surface ("a small panel of about half a square *braccio*"), which would correspond to a square 41 centimeters to a side, and thus sensibly larger, though nothing in this reading necessarily entails the panel's being square in format.[1] But the argument that of the two interpretations this is the one more consistent with the usage of the period is contradicted by several contemporary sources.[2] Contrary to Martin Kemp, I opt for the prevailing interpretation, though I agree with his view that so small a difference in the dimensions is probably of little consequence. But the fact that in Italian the same word *quadro* can designate, when used as a noun, a "painting," and, as an adjective, a rectangle with four right angles and four sides of equal length, this fact points to a secret complicity between the two notions, and of them with the grid, as applied to the very ground of perspective, or a shortcut on which *costruzione legittima* is based: a complicity that, although its inscription in the language might seem to imply its having been a factor from the beginning, is not self-evident and has nothing "natural" about it—unless one refers it

---

1.   Cf. R. Beltrame, "Gli esperimenti prospettici del Brunelleschi," *Rendiconti della sedute dell'Accademia Nazionale dei Lincei. Classe di Scienze morale, storiche e filologiche,* ser. 28 (1973), pp. 417–68; cf. Kemp, "The Interpretation . . .," op. cit., 1978, pp. 137–38.
2.   "*Braccio quadro: si dice a quello spazio quadro che da ciascuno de'suoi lati sia di misura d'un braccio.*" Francesco Sacchetti (ca. 1335–1399), *Opere diverse,* Florence, 1857, p. 58. On the fundamental importance of the square for Brunelleschi, cf. Sanpaolesi, "Ipotesi . . .," op. cit., 1951, pp. 20–21.

to the model of a regular visual pyramid with a square base. If, to use Alberti's metaphor, a painting can be construed to resemble a window piercing a wall through which the spectator can look into an interior, it was not unreasonable for Filarete, pushing this figure to the point of redundancy, to specify for the plane of projection a square format that would subsequently assume the status of a principle, if not an archetype.[3]

And yet it must be admitted that, in the context of the myth of the origin, the prototype could have been other than square, could have correlated more with a door than a window. Whereas the image of the "window" implies a solution of continuity between the ground supporting the observer and that upon which the representation sits, this does not hold for a *door,* even when its threshold is preceded by a few steps or opens onto a sunken interior, as is the case in Florence today for, respectively, the cathedral and the baptistry. Given a door like that of Santa Maria dei Fiori, which is (currently) about six *braccia* wide and at least twice as high, and supposing that these dimensions were more or less the same in Brunelleschi's time,[4] and—a condition that has not been acknowledged in any previous reconstruction of the experiment—*that the doors were completely open,* the visual pyramid corresponding to this opening, whose apex would be situated three *braccia* inside the door, at a height of about three *braccia* (according to Alberti, the height of an average man[5]), this pyramid will have right rectilinear angles at its summit and a squared base or section corresponding to the plane of the door, as defined by its two framing verticals and its threshold, the upper limit of the *quadro* (assuming a square format) *stamping itself* against the sky, well below the lintel.

---

3.   "Perchè ogni cosa che l'uomo vuol fare si è mestiero di pigliare uno certo principio e forma, e con quello ordine che quella tal cosa merita sguire la cosa proposta, si che adunque noi prima fingeremo astare a una certa finestra, e per quella vedere tutte quelle cose le quali noi vorremo nel nostro . . . piano discrivere e disegnare." Filarete, *Treatise,* fol. 177 recto, op. cit., pp. 650–51; English trans., pp. 302–303. When describing how to construct a transparent net through which the painter can look, *as through a window,* the more easily to render the object which has thus been squared (*squadrato*), Filarete, significantly, specifies a square frame, made of four wooden strips on which should be stretched linen strings or copper wire half a *braccio,* two-thirds of a *braccio,* or a whole *braccio* in length (ibid., fol. 184 verso, op. cit., p. 677; English trans., p. 315).

4.   Cf. White, op. cit., pp. 114–15 and 130–31, note 4.

5.   Alberti, *Della pittura,* book I, cited ed., p. 70; English trans., p. 56.

*

The possibility, indicated by Manetti, of deducing from the perspective construction itself the point of view determining it was of course a function of the painting's representing not only part of the baptistry (*quanto ne se vede*) but a portion of the piazza in front of the cathedral, one that corresponded (allowing for a few subsequent changes in the street pattern) to what a spectator on the spot in question would see today. Or to what the eye takes in (*che riceve l'occhio*), in the curious phrase used by Manetti, as if to stress that where quantity was concerned the organ of vision should yield to the metric rule which is that of perspective. The painter (or the spectator) being free to direct his gaze wherever he likes, toward the baptistry, for example (*uno sguardo dallato di fuori*): if he arrests it there, the surroundings will organize themselves, *for the eye* (Lacan was not the first to explicitly indicate the schism between the eye and the gaze!), in conformity with a schema determined a priori whose limits, in the instance of a perspective as precisely framed as the one described by Manetti, can be deduced from its definition.

It is here that problems begin to arise. Working with a ground plan, we can determine that, assuming an angle of 90° between the sides of the visual pyramid, the "view" would have corresponded to the description given by Vasari, extending, on the left, as far as the casa della Misericordia, and on the right, beyond the Saint Zenobius column. Manetti's text, however, is nowhere near as clear as a first reading might suggest: assuming that the lateral limits of the painting would have corresponded, on the left, with the corner of the sheep market and, on the right, with the corner of the straw market, the perspective would imply a much smaller angle of vision, one of about 50°. But Martin Kemp, from whom I take the observation, has correctly noted that this passage can be construed very differently: if, on the ground plane, one draws lines from the point inside the cathedral indicated by Manetti to the two furthest extremities of the line delineated by the facades extending from the *volta* to the *canto*, behind the baptistry, the angle thus formed will be smaller still, and the mass of the baptistry will precisely screen out this line. Such that we cannot exclude the possibility that Manetti meant to say that the painting provided a view of that portion of the piazza extending, on the left, as far as the corner of the sheep

8   Florence, Baptistry
of San Giovanni viewed
from the cathedral.
Photo: Brunner.

The Prototype

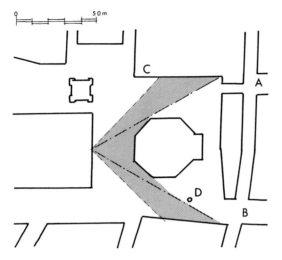

9   Plan of the environs of the cathedral and the
Baptistry of San Giovanni. The broken lines correspond to the two possible angles of vision. A. Volta
dei Pecori (corner of the sheep market); B. Canto
alla Paglia (corner of the straw market); C. Misericordia; D. Saint Zenobius column.

market (approaching from the Misericordia) and, on the right, beyond the
corner of the straw market, in the direction of the Saint Zenobius column.
As Kemp states, this reading is all the more credible given that one of the
aspects of perspective construction most frequently invoked in the literature
is precisely that opaque bodies screen out what is behind them in a way
consistent with basic geometric precepts.

    The choice then is clear: either the panel provided a view, in addi-
tion to the baptistry, of the two facades framing it on either side, whose
disposition was more or less perpendicular to the picture plane; or the view
concentrated squarely on the solid volume, the geometric body of the building itself, encompassing only two narrow strips representing the far reaches
of the piazza. In the first case—which corresponds with a schema that recurs
throughout trecento and quattrocento art[6]—the angle of vision would be
consistent with the one deducible from Manetti's indications about the spectator's position within the cathedral, namely a right angle. In the other

---

6.   Cf. *infra*, chapter 13, pp. 246–47.

case the angle would be one of about 50°, and the image, insofar as we can envision it, would bear a curious resemblance to Duccio's *Temptation of Christ* from the back predella of the *Maestà*. Which is a small square panel, or very nearly square, though of dimensions notably larger (43 × 45.5 cm) than those probably used by Brunelleschi, on which is depicted a building whose octagonal structure is very like that of the baptistry of San Giovanni, even if its style is different—Gothic, but with paneled ornament that retains something of the first Florentine Renaissance, that of the thirteenth century. The image of this monument, which corresponds to an extremely proximate view, occupies very nearly the entire surface of the panel, the building being cut off at the top, reduced to its prismatic mass and the merest fragment of its roof. While the volume is presented in a frontal view, the interior of the building is on a diagonal: through the door we see a floor whose checkered pattern delineates, not the prism surface parallel to the picture's ground plane, and on the same axis, as must have been the case, by definition, in the image of the Florentine baptistry, but rather an oblique view to the right. The whole being inscribed against a gold ground completely surrounding the structure, except for the ground, like a *veduta,* but one opening onto a pure element of light and ideality.

As Martin Kemp has said, the information provided by Manetti pertaining to the angle of vision and the relative breadth of the panorama presented to view is not sufficient to enable us to choose between the two hypotheses. Yet the text clearly suggests, once more, that from this perspective, from what it allowed to appear of the mass of the baptistry, from the angles assigned to elements other than parallel to the picture plane, one could deduce the point at which it seemed (*e pareva*) the painter had placed himself, at least ideally, in producing his construction. That implies that another given must be taken into account, that—whatever one might understand this to mean—of distance.

*

The problem of distance—distance between the point of view and the object perceived, and the distance between the eye and the picture plane, which are two different things—is to all appearances the heart of the question.[7] But it is not easy to formulate if one sticks to the letter of Manetti's text, refusing to extrapolate from it. Did Brunelleschi posit, in some form or other, the notion of the *distance point,* namely a point outside the field of the painting but on the same plane and on its horizon line, that would serve as a reference marker in determining the rhythm of diminution of transverse lines, the rapidity of foreshortening as a function of distance, in conformity with the principle of perspective construction? The assertion that he gave birth to the rule on which all subsequent work of the kind was based would seem to indicate this—if, that is, a debate that has agitated historians for a century can be considered closed: to maintain, with Panofsky, that Alberti was unacquainted with the distance point is to imply that it was not a necessary prerequisite of *costruzione legittima,* and that the institution of a

---

7.   Kemp, "The Interpretation . . .," op. cit. 1978, p. 138.

11 The principle of
costruzione legittima as
described by Alberti
(after Panofsky).

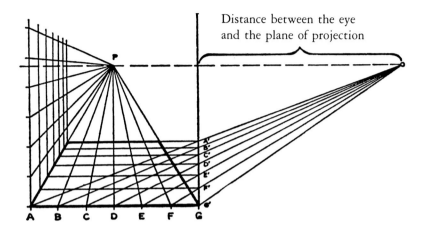

Distance between the eye
and the plane of projection

unique vanishing point and the assimilation of the painting to a plane of projection were sufficient to define it.[8]

So far, Manetti's text has scarcely helped us to clarify the problem. If one assumes that the plane of intersection corresponded to that of the cathedral door, the observer being situated three *braccia* inside it, then the distance separating the apex of the pyramid from this plane would have been equal to half the field of the work (6:3), and the distance point would be inscribed on the vertical edge of the painting. A hypothesis on the sole basis of which Robert Klein concluded that the method of construction used by Brunelleschi was a straightforward rationalization of the traditional bifocal system, and which John White found particularly attractive because he thought it implied that all the elements of the construction were contained within the limits of the painting, no exterior point, such as that posited by Desargues, being needed. That supposes, let it be said in passing, that a point inscribed on the edge of the painting, on its *border,* is to be regarded as within its field, which mathematically is far from self-evident: in the context of *costruzione legittima,* the inscription of a construction point on the edge of the painting might be taken to constitute a kind of *passage to the limit* which one would be obliged to interpret as such, a radically new development, as is signaled by Masaccio's *Trinity,* in which, as we have

---

8.   Panofsky, "Das perspektivische Verfahren Leone-Battista Albertis," *Kunstchronik,* new series, 26 (1915), pp. 504–16.

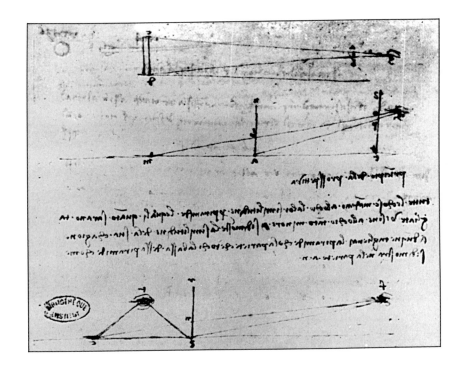

12   Leonardo da Vinci, schema of the perspective
construction of the distance point. Institut de
France, Ms. A, fol. 36 verso. Photo: Bulloz.

seen, the vanishing point is established on the baseline of the upper portion
of the composition, the ground being reduced to a mere line of no thickness
whatever.

Any argument based on the position assigned to the spectator
inside the door of the cathedral collapses as soon as it is conceded that the
angle of vision in question cannot be determined with any precision. The
information available to us at this stage only allows us to postulate a conclusion that might be termed elastic: one must either allow that the distance between the eye and the picture plane was equal to half the panel's
width, which would entail an angle of vision of 90°, as implied in Vasari's
description, and perhaps Manetti's, or one must opt for the hypothesis of a
smaller angle, about 50°, in which case the distance would have been very
nearly equal to the width of the panel, but without the distance between
the eye and the object being altered in any way. I raise the question of these
alternatives here, reserving the right to revisit it further along as it relates

13   Principle of ground-
plane construction using
the so-called bifocal
method (after R. Klein,
Form and Meaning,
p. 116).

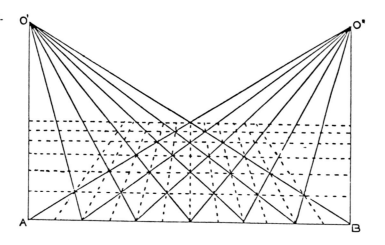

14   The *Tavoletta San
Giovanni,* construction
schema using both a plan
and an elevation of the
baptistry. A. Parronchi,
*Studi su la dolce prospet-
tiva,* fig. 90. Photo: Bibliothèque Nationale,
Paris.

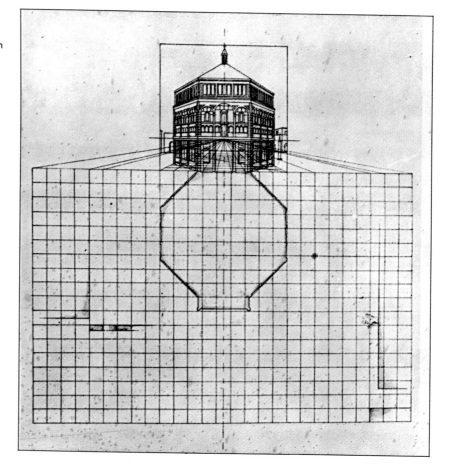

The Prototype

15   *Procession of the Banners of San Giovanni,* cassone panel, Florence, first half of the fifteenth century. Florence, Museo Nazionale del Bargello. Photo: Alinari-Giraudon.

to another example, one not without relevance to Brunelleschi's demonstration.[9] What if we didn't have to choose between these two hypotheses, since in the end the demonstration had meaning only if the possibility of a *variation* were left open, only if anyone participating in the experiment were accorded a carefully calculated margin of manoeuvre?

*

One last point remains to be resolved, one that has received scant attention in the literature. And *point* is the proper word to employ here, because the issue is that of determining where to situate the vanishing point on Brunelleschi's little perspective panel. Here again we are obliged to work with indications provided by Manetti: the position he assigns to the painter, inside the central portal of the cathedral and in all probability on its central axis, might be taken to imply that this point would have been at the geometric center of the *tavoletta,* at a height—allowances being made for changes in the floor levels of, respectively, the cathedral and the baptistry—corresponding to the door lintel of the latter monument. As plausible as it might seem, this hypothesis has its arbitrary elements, as Alessandro Par-

---

9.   Cf. *infra,* chapter 15, pp. 323ff.

ronchi has noted.[10] I will seize upon his observation to justify my own posture (here I stress the word *posture*) that this point was inscribed, incurring a bit of distortion, within the rectangle of this door, at the height of a man standing there, facing the spectator inside the portal of the cathedral. As we shall see, history justifies and, in a manner of speaking, verifies this adjustment, introduced into a demonstration that it does not alter but that it renders singularly more striking, even as it intensifies its symbolic impact: the image—and with it the demonstration of which it is the emblem—will work its way into the imaginary of the time, even accruing the force of an *imago*.[11] But the possibility of setting up, in Brunelleschi's own time, a direct opposition of the baptistry door and that of the cathedral along a single line is evinced by a precious *cassone* panel from the first half of the quattrocento, now in the Bargello in Florence: the procession of the festival of Saint John fills the interval between the two doors, symmetrically disposed at either end of the painting, which thus represents, or describes, in a longitudinal profile view, the very scene of Brunelleschi's experiment.

---

10. Parronchi, *Studi* . . ., op. cit., 1964, p. 249.
11. Cf. *infra*, chapter 15, pp. 319ff.

The mirror stage of painting.

Imago: the phase effect.

The double designation of the point.

The fissure.

Infinity, an idea of "what's behind one's head."

What is vision?

It's me, as if I were there.

A hole that's a stain.

A lentil for a ducat.

The two witnesses.

The value of the autopsy.

The "small" *braccia*.

E pareva che si vedessi 'l proprio vero.

The View

Since in such a painting the painter had to postulate beforehand a single point (*perchè 'l dipintore bisogna che presuponga uno luogo solo*) from which his painting must be viewed (*donde s'ha a vedere la sua dipintura*) taking into account the length and width of the sides as well as the distance (*si per altezza e bassezza e da'lati come per discoto*), such that no errors resulted from looking at it, as any divergence from this spot would alter what the eye perceived (*acciò che non si potessi pigliare errore nel guardarlo, che in ogni luogo che s'esce di quello ha mutare l'apparizioni dello occhio*), he had made a hole in the painted panel (*egli aveva fatto un bucco nella tavoletta dov'era questa dipintura*), located in that part of the painting [showing] the temple of San Giovanni (*che veniva a esserre nel dipinto dalla parte dello tempio di S. G.*), at that point where the eye struck (*in quello luogo dove percotava l'occhio*) directly from anyone looking out from that point (*al diritto de chi guardava da quello luogo*) from inside the central portal of Santa Maria del Fiore, where he would have placed himself if he'd had to depict it (*dove se sarebbe posto se l'avessa ritratto*). Which hole was as tiny as a lentil bean (*era piccolo quanto una lenta*) on the painted side and on the other one widened like a pyramid (*e da rovescio si rallargava piramidalmente*), like a woman's straw cap (*come fa uno cappello di paglia di donna*), to the circumference of a ducat or a bit larger (*quanto sarebbe el tondo d'uno ducata o poco più*). And he required that whoever wanted to look at it place his eye on the reverse side (*e voleva che l'occhio si ponessi da rovescio*) where the hole was large, and that the person looking (*per chi l'avesse a vedere*) hold it against his eye with one hand (*e con l'una mano s'accostassi allo occhio*) and with the other hold a flat mirror directly opposite

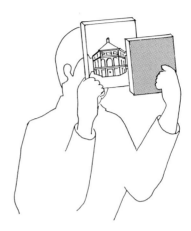

16 Brunelleschi's first experiment: how the *tavoletta* was used.

(*e nell'altra tenessi uno specchio piano al dirimpetto*) in such a way that the painting was reflected in it (*che vi si veniva a specchiare dentro la dipintura*); this distance (*quella dilazione*) from the mirror in the other hand corresponding roughly, in small *braccia* (*di braccia picoline*), to the distance in regular *braccia* from the place he appears to have been when he planted it up to the temple of San Giovanni (*la distanza velcirca, di braccia piccoline, quanto a braccia vere dal luogo dove mostrava essere stato a ritrarlo per insino al tempio di S. G.*), such that to look at it, under the various specified circumstances (*che al guardarlo, con l'altre circumstanze dette*) of the burnished silver and the piazza, etc., and of the point (*e del punto*), it seemed that one was seeing truth itself (*pareva che si vedessi 'l propio vero*); and I held it in my hands and saw it several times in my own day, and so can testify to it (*e io l'ho avuto in mano e veduto piu volte a mia dì, e possono rendere testimonanza*).[1]

Painting—or should I say representation?—in its "mirror stage," replete with its own mythic dimension deriving from a narrative of origin? In Lacanian terms Manetti's description of the experiment seems to justify the phase effect predestined for the perspectival painted image of the baptis-

---

1. Manetti, op. cit., pp. 58–59; English trans., p. 44.

try of San Giovanni and its surroundings: for it indeed inaugurates a new phase of history, at least of the history of painting. To such an extent that the antique term *imago* will be used throughout the remainder of this text each time explicit reference is made to the primordial figure under whose auspices perspective was first precipitated into the symbolic matrix established by Brunelleschi. What we are witnessing, retrospectively, an *invention* recounted to us by Manetti according the force of history to subsequent developments, a "drama" (to cite Lacan) "whose internal thrust is precipitated from insufficiency to anticipation,"[2] is clearly a matter of *identification:* if one considers a strictly perspectival painting in accordance with the conditions stipulated for the experiment—in other words, such that the painting gives way before its specular double—the representation will be substituted for the reality and will become confused with the "truth" (*e pareva che si vedessi 'l proprio vero*).

But why the mirror? As opposed to the unweaned child who acknowledges the mirror image as his own, and who anticipates, through this form, the *Gestalt* or bodily integration and coordination it still lacks, the painter's image is not transformed by the specular reflection. With regard to unity, the kind of perspectival coherence characteristic of Brunelleschi's panel, which made it novel, had nothing imaginary about it, being the fruit of precise calculations and a carefully considered decision: given a construction organized around a single point of view, the flat mirror did nothing but reverse its lateral orientation.[3] But this reversal is not without its problems. For it would seem to provide support for the hypothesis that Brunelleschi executed his painting with the aid of a mirror, directly on a reflective surface, in which case he would have needed to use a second mirror to reestablish conformity with the order of things, as this image, having been constructed directly on a mirror reflection, would have effected an exchange of left for right and right for left.

---

2.   Lacan, "Le Stade du miroir comme formateur de la fonction du Je," *Ecrits,* op. cit., p. 97; English trans. by Alan Sheridan, "The Mirror Stage as Formative of the Function of the I," *Écrits: A Selection,* New York, 1977, p. 4.

3.   To avoid confusion, I will conform to the usage now current among specialists and designate the lateral shift effected by the mirror as a "reversal," using the term "inversion" only when a shift of orientation in relation to the original is implied, for example, as in prints.

If the mirror's only role in the experiment were that of a simple corrective mechanism, as a number of commentators would have it,[4] there would have been nothing particularly revolutionary about it—nothing at least to justify comparing it with Galileo's discovery, as does Parronchi,[5] despite his endorsement of this view. The salient question then becomes that of determining whether the mirror was required during the actual execution, or was only used after the fact, not so much to confirm the accuracy of the perspective construction as to increase its demonstrative impact. This is a problem—that of the method of construction used by Brunelleschi—which Manetti chose to ignore in a way that must be deemed significant, and that left historians plenty of room to exercise their ingenuity. I will simply note that if one adheres to the procedure described by Vasari, a construction "by plane and profile," this need not imply any kind of reversal or pivoting, unless this be to assign to the notion of *intersegatione* a meaning other than that of a planar, transparent section of the visual pyramid, assimilating it to an opaque mirror. But if the image was indeed painted for the experiment, and if it was intended from the beginning to be viewed in a mirror, then surely the painter would have constructed it so as to make it symmetrically inverse. Such a task would not have posed any serious difficulties, given a monument whose frontal view resembles that of a regular prism and a surrounding piazza providing a roughly symmetrical setting: allowance being made for the Saint Zenobius column, the smaller the angle of vision the less apparent would have been the reversal, regardless of whether one were taking a direct view or one mediated by a mirror.

*

The difference, bordering on incompatibility, between the texts by Vasari and Manetti is clear. The one formulates the generative rule in accordance with which Brunelleschi's panel is supposed to have been executed but provides absolutely no information concerning the experimental circuit into which it was integrated, while the other provides the reader with directions

---

4.   Beginning with Giulio-Carlo Argan, whose work initiated the interest in the "inventor" of perspective that has now become so prevalent. Cf. Argan, cited article, as well as the invaluable small volume by the same author, *Brunelleschi*, Milan, 1955. In a similar vein, cf. Krautheimer, *Ghiberti*, op. cit., pp. 234ff.; Klein, *Form and Meaning*, op cit., pp. 120, 132, etc.
5.   Parronchi, "Le due tavole," in *Studi* . . ., op. cit., 1964, p. 231.

for its use without providing any information about the constructive principle employed; it is as though the biographer had decided that Brunelleschi's invention (or discovery) derived its initiatory significance less from the perspective construction itself than from the protocol of the experiment in which it figured. Such that those attempting today to learn more about the first while neglecting the second risk overlooking something essential, something articulated in Manetti's text as clearly as was permitted by the language of his time.

If the *princeps* experiment to which Brunelleschi's name has become attached was more than a simple "pictorial manifesto" (to use John White's phrase, which remains a happy one[6]), this is because its intention was not solely to reveal to the spectator the spot on which he would have had to place himself, at least hypothetically, to execute a painting analogous to Brunelleschi's; the painting alone would have sufficed to do this, without resort to a mirror. The experiment was also intended to reveal, by reflectively turning the structural disposition back on itself, nothing less than the premise of its own efficacity: namely that a painting constructed in perspective (*constructed,* not merely approximated) must be seen from one specific spot (*uno luogo solo*), governed by a system of rectangular cartesian coordinates distributed across three axes, two of them on the picture plane and the third perpendicular to it. The measure of height relative to the painting's baseline, that of the divergence from the two vertical sides, and that, finally, of the distance there ought to be between the eye of the spectator and the picture plane: these determine a point that Alberti held should correspond to the apex of the visual pyramid of which the painting should be a perpendicular planar section—and from which the eye cannot diverge without the image appearing to be deformed.[7] But the word *point* is not initially employed by Manetti; he first uses it a bit later, when enumerating the "circumstances" of the demonstration, which is to say its conditions and apparatus.

Self-referentiality is a trait characteristic of regulatory systems. This only confirms the importance for us of the description of the experimental protocol, and of what must be termed, as I've already suggested, the direc-

---

6. White, op. cit., p. 113.
7. Alberti, op. cit., p. 65; English trans., pp. 53–54.

tions for the use of Brunelleschi's little painting. Manetti implicitly says as much: if the panel was pierced by a hole, this was not with the idea that, if one placed one's eye against the other side of it to look at the mirror image, this latter would be corrected, but rather to satisfy a theoretical premise which he explicitly invokes (*perchè 'l dipintore bisogna che presuponga* etc.). What is astonishing here is that the spot on which the spectator should place himself, this unique location from which the painting must be seen if it is to produce its effect, has a respondant in the painting, and that it is within the field of the latter that it first manages to get its bearings, *by reflection*. What Brunelleschi's experiment demonstrates, in effect, is that the point we today call the "point of view" coincides, in terms of projection, with the one we call the "vanishing point": both are situated at the intersection of the perpendicular sight line and the picture plane—this perpendicular itself corresponding to the height of the visual pyramid, or, as it was dubbed by the perspectors, the centric ray; the same ray that Alberti qualifies as the "prince of rays," "the most active and the strongest of all the rays,"[8] and that pierces (*in quello luogo dove percotava l'occhio*) the picture plane, as would the point of an arrow the center of a target, coming straight from the eye (*al dirimpetto*) to that spot in the image homologous to the point from which a spectator established at the designated place would perpendicularly "pierce" the real object.

For the experiment to have any demonstrative impact, for it to access "truth" in a hitherto unprecedented way, the hole mentioned by Manetti had to pierce the entire thickness of the panel precisely at the vanishing point, which in the treatises is designated, significantly, as *il punto dell'occhio, das Augenpunkt*. I repeat: under the conditions specified by Manetti, this point would be inscribed on the central axis of the painting, at a height proportional to that of a man of average stature, or three *braccia*—if, that is, we admit that the painting corresponded to the plane of projection defined by the embrasure of the cathedral door, in its center where the diagonals of the *quadro* converged. It is there, in the precise geometric center of the panel, that this hole must have been pierced, at the

8.   Ibid., p. 62; English trans., p. 48.

point Filarete would say was made in the image of the eye (*a similitudine dell'tuo occhio*), just as the lines converging toward it resembled visual rays.[9]

*

There is a related point that must be stressed because it has been widely and grossly misunderstood: if we are correct in saying that the point of view and the vanishing point coincide on the plane of projection, it does not follow that there is symmetry between them. The vanishing point is not an image—narrowly constructed, a geometric image—of the point of view; if they coincide on the plane, this is due exclusively to an effect produced by the projection onto the mirror. Strictly speaking, these two points are situated, in three-dimensional space, on a line perpendicular to the picture plane. But whereas the *image* of the point of view should be inscribed on the painting—at a virtual distance corresponding to that separating the spectator from the plane of projection, like the symmetrical correspondent of an observer standing three *braccia* inside the cathedral, on its floor, at a like distance, the vanishing point being inscribed precisely opposite the eye within the frame of the baptistry door (or on its lintel)—it will on the contrary be thrown far behind the image of the observer, who will have it, so to speak, *at his back*—or, to use Pascal's language, "behind his head."[10] This fact makes it clear that even if the theme wasn't explicitly present in Brunelleschi's discovery, central perspective, like Greek geometry before it, however finite or finite-ist it might be, would have been preoccupied from the beginning by the question of infinity, and at the very spot, the very point that Viator, for reasons that surely remained unconscious, designated as the *subject:*[11] the force of perspective, the force—as Piero would put it—of its lines and angles, is such that the only way for the subject to obtain self-confirmation is for him to place himself behind the painting, to move behind it to look at it in the mirror, through the screen, pierced by a hole, of that same painting.

---

9. Cf. *supra* chapter 4, note 9.
10. On infinity as "an idea of what's behind one's head," cf. Louis Marin, *La Critique du discours . . .*, op. cit., pp. 394–96.
11. "Le point principal en perspective doit être constitué et assis au nyveau de l'ueil; lequel point est appelé fix, ou subject." Cf. Brion-Guerry, op. cit., p. 175.

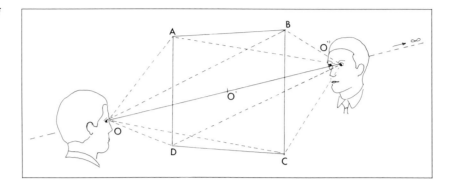

17 Infinity, "an idea of what's behind our heads."

*

The "subject" to which the perspective construction is attached, though we might say it is snatched away by infinity, is restricted by the hole Brunelleschi pierced through the panel to facilitate his demonstrative exercise. That the experiment had to proceed through this hole, and that its only meaning, its only goal, was to throw perspective back onto its presuppositions, to direct it back to its "origin," was confirmed by Leonardo: "But this said invention obliges the spectator to look through a small hole, and by means of this hole it shows itself well. But, if many eyes are brought together at the same time to see a single work produced by this art, only one will see the function of the said perspective clearly, while it will remain confused for all the others."[12] Such a constraint might seem unbearable, even unsustainable: Leonardo himself later allowed himself to express doubts about the cogency of a system that reduced the perceiving subject to an eye and the eye to a point. It nonetheless found justification to the extent that *perspectiva artificialis* seemed to reiterate the operation of vision by miming it. To employ terms very similar to those used by Leonardo, perspective is not alone in being subjected to the rule of a "small hole": the exercise of vision itself is predicated upon the condition that the images filling the atmosphere become concentrated in a given spot, that they be constrained to pass through a "small fissure" (*uno spiracolo*) that is like a point—but a

---

12. "Ma questa tale invencione costrignie il veditore a stare coll'ochio a uno spiracolo e allora da tale spiracolo si dimostrerà bene; Ma perché molti occhi s'abbattono a vedere a un medisimo tempo una medesima opera fatta con tale arte e solo un di quelli vede bene l'ufitio ti tal prospective e li altri tutti restano confusi." Leonardo da Vinci, Inst. de Fr., ms. E, fol. 16 recto; Richter, op. cit., vol. 1, pp. 63–64.

natural point, one that, unlike a mathematical point, has extension—where they intersect and interpenetrate yet remain distinct from one another.[13]

The task assigned the eye, or more precisely the "fissure" through which bundled lines constituting the visual pyramid pass as if to their origin (geometric or physical), renders it inevitable that, at this point in our analysis, we refer to the synthesizing function we currently ascribe to the "I" ("Ich," "moi," "ego"). As we have seen, Cassirer was convinced that this function was neither passive nor specular, but rather constitutive, within the register of representation, of the order and even the meaning of things and of the world.[14] In the same vein Freud said that "the relations of the I with the system of perception constitute its essence." But the definition of the "I" posited by Freud presents us with a new, unanticipated set of problems insofar as it appeals to the notion of *projection,* and in a way that supersedes all simple oppositions of the active/passive, specular/nonspecular sort: "The I is above all else a bodily I, it is not only a surfaced being but is itself the projection of a surface."[15]

I can already hear the cries of those lodging charges of anachronism: as if attentiveness to current effects deriving from the perspectival model—which have captured the attention of many fine minds who, following Lacan's lead, became interested in these questions—necessarily entailed betrayal of the most elementary principles of historical method. If there is any such thing as history, it must be conceded that it too takes the same route: one that leads through this echo chamber, this singular field of interference in which Freud's text resonates with those of Alberti, Manetti, and Leonardo. The "I" as "surfaced being," one corresponding to "the projection

---

13. "Prova come nessuna cosa po essere veduta, se non per ispiraculo, donde passa l'aria piena delle spezie delli obbietti, le quali s'intersegano nelli lati densi e oppachi de' predetti spiraculi. . . . Chi crederebbe che si brevissimo spazio fussi capace delle spezie di tutto l'universo? O magna azione, quale ingegno potra penetrare tale natura? Qual lingua fia quella che explicare possa tal maraviglia? Certo nessuna. Questo dirizza l'umano discorso alla contemplazione divina, ecc. . . . Qui le figure, qui li colori, qui tutte le spezie de la parte dell'universo son ridutte in un punto. O qual punto è di tanta maraviglia?" Idem., Cod. Atl., fol. 345, recto–verso (949 recto–verso in the Marioni ed., vol. II, Florence, 1980, pp. 50–53).

14. Cf. *supra,* chapter 1, p. 9.

15. "Das Ich ist vor allem ein körperliches, es ist nicht nur ein Oberflächenwesen, sondern selbst die Projektion einer Oberfläche." Sigmund Freud, *Das Ich und das Es,* Gesammelte Werke, vol. 13, p. 253; as cited by J. Laplanche and J. -B. Pontalis, *Vocabulaire de la psychanalyse,* Paris, 1967, p. 253. In the English trans. by Joan Rivière and revised by J. Strachey (Norton paperback ed., New York, 1962), this passage is on p. 16.

of a surface"? The meaning of this phrase in Freud's usage is not so difficult to grasp: the "I" corresponds to a real psychic operation, one by means of which organic sensual impressions are projected onto the psyche. But the very notion of *projection* implies that there is not, that there cannot be, a body to which it is linked save for a surface representation, just as Alberti maintained that painting could know bodies only through the surfaces delimiting them which can be projected onto a plane.[16] The "I" is the mental projection of the surface of the body, even as it represents the surface area of the mental apparatus. This definition provides us with sufficient justification to invoke the "mirror stage" in connection with Brunelleschi's experiment, insofar as the "subject" is implicated in the eye, and an eye definitively reduced to a point, but a natural point that occupies a certain *surface:* the hole pierced through the panel was shaped like a cone, such that, when the eye was held up to it, the eyeball was accommodated inside it, the pupil being flush with the surface of the painting through which opened this hole the size of a lentil—which was itself reflected in the mirror, *projected* onto it.

I repeat: when he eventually expressed doubts about the constraints linear perspective imposed upon painting, Leonardo argued that the eye cannot be assimilated to a point, nor vision to a process that is describable exclusively in terms of geometry. Paradoxically this criticism would lead him to question the strictly psychological notion of the "subject" dictated by perspective, which from the vantage point of the science of his day represented a step backward, as I shall show subsequently. In this context the reference to Freud's text has the additional merit of reminding us that the organizing function defining the "I" presupposes a certain energy—one that is desexualized, but one whose libidinal origin nonetheless reveals itself in its characteristic aspiration to linkage and unification: this compulsion to synthesis increases in proportion as the "I" develops and differentiates itself from the "that" ("*ça,*" "id"), which should not surprise us if it is true that perception performs the same function in the one instance as does the drive

---

16. "Delle chose quali non possiamo vedere, niuno nega nulla apartenersene al pictore. Solo studia il pictore fingiere quello si vede. . . . Più linee, quasi come nella tela più fili accostati, fanno superficie et è superficie certa parte estrema del corpo quale si conosce non per sua alcuna profondità ma solo per sua longitudine et lattitudine et per sue ancora qualità." Alberti, op. cit., pp. 55–56; English trans., pp. 43–44.

in the other.[17] With respect to the position assigned the subject at the beginning (or to put it better: at the pivot, *à la charnière*) of the perspective configuration, this remark implies a question: If this configuration is itself the product of a compulsion to synthesis, what is the source or origin of the energy upon which it in turn is predicated?

*

If those participating in the experiment believed they were seeing "truth" itself in the mirror, truth *proper* (*'l proprio vero*), that is because both the perspective construction and the experimental apparatus, of which the painting was an integral part, established conditions that are those, as Merleau-Ponty would say, of the "adult" vision (and, as such, desexualized?) of the world, the same one from which our reflexive tradition derives its standards of truth. As for the phase effect attached to the demonstration, it was the result, simultaneously (as if suggested by the reference to the "mirror stage"), of the discovery of a form that imposed itself on the gaze with an unprecedented pregnancy and of the properly reflexive character of an operation that invoked, through projection, an instance analogous to that of the "I"—insofar as it is true that the latter can only find satisfaction in a liaison, in a unification of surfaces, because it is from this synthesis, and from it alone, that it originates and derives the ground of its being.

This play of reciprocal implications meant in effect that the painting was not the only thing reflected in Brunelleschi's mirror: the "fissure" itself, the "light," the "gaze," each of these elements being required for the demonstration, and each of them opened in the center of the panel, at the knot of the perspective synthesis, in its antechamber, if you will, were also reflected there. As Leonardo observed,[18] images in mirrors exist only for those looking at them, whether they see their own reflection there or not. Lichtenberg's paradox (How can one see oneself in a mirror with one's eyes closed?) was countered not long after it was formulated: photography soon

---

17. Sigmund Freud, *Hemmung, Sympton und Angst, G. W.,* vol. 14; English trans., "Inhibitions, Symptoms, Anxiety," *Standard Edition,* vol. 20, London and Toronto, 1959.

18. "Describe how no object is in itself defined in a mirror; but how it is defined by the eye that sees it there." L. da Vinci, Windsor, ms. R 209; cf. E. McCurdy, *Les Carnets de Léonard de Vinci,* French trans., Paris, 1942, vol. 1, p. 240.

made it possible for anyone to take his own portrait, just as in a mirror, even when one's eyes are closed or covered by one's hands, as in Duane Michael's portrait of Andy Warhol. Brunelleschi's experiment was organized around an inverse aporia: How, facing a mirror, being caught in its field, can one look at it without seeing oneself there, if not, precisely, by means of a sight-hole, a per-spective, or (as Dürer would say) *Durch-sehung,* a seeing *through* (like Warhol, who tells us he's not looking at us, but looks through his fingers all the same?). Question: The eye being placed behind the panel and considering the reflection through an opening the size of a lentil, could this eye see itself, or its pupil, in the mirror? Or did it per-ceive only the *gaze* by which the panel was pierced and which pre-existed the design, a metaphor for this *seeing* to which the subject submits in its originary, constitutive moment (Lacan: "I see only from one point, but in my existence I am looked at from all sides"[19])? And what is *seeing,* if what I see *sees me?* Can a painting be *seen,* in this sense of the word *seeing,* in any way other than as positing itself to itself as the truth, through an elision of the gaze and the painting?

The "subject" as an effect of perspective, as it is of language? But of a perspective declaring itself to be *artificial*—whereas language is nor-mally presented as "natural"—one appearing at a specific historical moment so as to allow painting to reflect on itself, to use it to regulate itself, to derive demonstrative force from it. If Brunelleschi's sole intention was to localize, by means of the mirror, the point that perspective is supposed to designate, the experiment would have had consequences only for the imagi-nary. Its demonstration that the point of view can be posited, grasped as such, in its value and function as *origin,* only retroactively and by means of a relay mechanism, a subsequent scansion, this *di-mostratio,* in the strict sense of the word, provided a rule governing apportionment between the imaginary and the symbolic. Historically speaking, we would retain Panof-sky's argument that the discovery of the vanishing point, its being brought to light, chronologically preceded the invention of the point of view, which was linked to the assumption, precisely at the point of the eye, of a "sub-ject" to be defined as that of perspective, as distinct from that of science as

19.   Lacan, *Le Séminaire XI,* op. cit., p. 69; English trans., *Four Fundamental Concepts,* p. 72.

well as from the Freudian "I," but which, like them, is "all surface": an effect that is specular, and thus imaginary, but toward which the minimum requirements of naming, in the form of this indivisible point marked as that of the subject, the obligatory tribute to S (the symbolic, as noted by Jean-Claude Milner[20]), already *pointed,* just as in discourse. Whoever tried the experiment had to place himself behind the panel (though with his pupil just short of the surface of the painting), positioned as *here* in relation to a *there* looking at him from the depths of the mirror—in the absence, in Manetti's text, of any reference to a "distance point" or a "third point," by means of which the symbolic dimension would have been explicitly introduced into the disposition. To be more concise, the symbolic cannot be reduced to language, just as statements cannot be fully encompassed by a single system of pronouns or other linguistic elements indexing spatial and temporal position. The form of perspective Brunelleschi is traditionally held to have invented provides proof of this: with the corollary that it can only have come into the world, as Claude Lévi-Strauss maintains about language, at a single blow—what we call its "history" thus being reduced to the development or deployment, in the order of discourse and in view of the aims of discourse, of a configuration already constituted at the start, though in principle it was then still mute.

But the demonstration has implications aside from the double assignation of the point at which the subject believes it gets its bearings as such, within the painting, *as if it were inside it.* I repeat that up to this moment of his description Manetti has yet to introduce the term "point." The essential thing, for the present, the constitutive given of the experiment, the act organizing it as such, the invention—in the archeological sense of the word—was the piercing of a hole in the panel's center that defined something like a "view" (Leonardo: "Show how nothing can be seen except through a small fissure, etc."). But this is a "view" only in Raymond Roussel's sense, that of the *view* of a tiny photograph obtained by looking through a peephole fitted out with a magnifying glass enclosed in the bases of souvenir penholders from our childhood, or that in relief (dependent upon the use of binocular vision) procured by the stereoscope. For the hole

---

20. Jean-Claude Milner, *Les Noms indistincts,* Paris, 1983, p. 19.

Brunelleschi drilled in his *tavoletta* had nothing to do with "light" (*lumière*), in the sense of an opening onto the sky to access the light (one meaning of the Italian word *lume*), nor with a *veduta* directing the gaze over the surrounding landscape (which as a result accrues the value of an *over there*). Nor was the apparatus comparable to a darkened chamber or a telescope, for it was not directed toward the exterior but rather closed in on itself, all its elements being in that close proximity which was essential if the image were to be properly reflected and the eye to properly perceive the reflection. This proximity was indeed essential, as with the stereoscope, as is indicated by the fact that an observer placed on the spot indicated by Manetti, inside the cathedral portal, his eye fixed before a peephole, perfectly immobile, would perceive only a small portion of the mass of the baptistry (anyone can repeat this experiment today): if it is to take the full extent of the "view" that would be captured by a photographic apparatus situated on the same spot, the eye must move, must turn within its socket, performing a kind of sweeping motion inconsistent with the premises of the experiment.

In its strictly optical sense, perspective confers no dominating privilege on the gaze, but on the contrary imposes a condition of immediate proximity to the centric ray (the only one leading from the eye directly to the object, without any refraction) if vision is to be perfectly distinct. It is in this common place (*lieu commun*) of geometric optics—a place that plays an active role in Leonardo's writings, and in Lacan's, as we shall see—that *perspectiva artificialis* establishes limits, proposing an image so focused that all its component parts are of equal clarity, however distant they might be, on the plane, from the centric point (as for disappearance into depth, that's another matter, one that would only be regulated after the introduction of atmospheric perspective, of which Alberti already had a vague idea[21]). At the same time the apportionment one is tempted to effect between the eye and the gaze becomes jumbled: obliged to peer through a small hole at the image thrown back at it by the mirror, the subject in the experiment is reduced to the position of a voyeur. But a singular kind of voyeur, one who discovers that he is himself being looked at, and from the very spot from

---

21. H. D., *Théorie du nuage,* op. cit., p. 190, note 3.

which he himself looks, subjected as he is from the start to a form of seeing that elides his body, reducing it to an eye, and soon enough to a point. For the image cast back at him by the mirror is not his own but that of the painting that screens out his body, only to substitute its own, which the eye captures solely as a reflection. Under the conditions governing the experiment, the eye, in the mirror, does not see itself seeing, nor seeing that which it sees: there is someone there who looks at it, and whom it does not see. What it does see, directly in front of it (*al diritto*), on the spot supposed to correspond to the point of maximum clarity and distinction, is a hole blotting out the center of the image. At the very point (I use the word advisedly) most clearly illustrating the difference between *perspectiva naturalis* and *perspectiva artificialis*. I once again summon Lacan to my aid, and he comes through for me, if somewhat reluctantly (although he noted, apparently without having any knowledge of Brunelleschi's experiments, that the geometral dimension already allows us to observe how the subject is caught, captured by paintings): "There is something whose absence can always be observed in a picture—which is not the case in perception. This is the central field, where the separating power of the eye is exercised to the maximum in vision. In every picture this central field cannot but be absent, and replaced by a hole—a reflection, in short, of the pupil behind which is situated the gaze. Consequently, and in as much as the picture enters into a relation to desire, the place of a central screen is always marked, which is precisely that by which, in front of the picture, I am elided as subject of the geometral plane."[22]

*

Manetti specifies that the hole pierced, nonmetaphorically, in the center of the panel—conical in form, shaped like a woman's cap—had, at the back, the dimensions of a ducat (corresponding, *o poco più,* to the diameter of the eyeball), and that it was no larger than a lentil at its other end: as if the hole's precise cut had been calculated to ensure placement of the point of the eye at the apex of a pyramid symmetrical to the visual pyramid that

---

22. Lacan, *Le Séminaire XI,* op. cit., pp. 99–100; English trans., *Four Fundamental Concepts,* p. 108.

would have had the same apex—the cap image being repeated from Filarete, who applied it to this same pyramid.[23] If the critical operation should consist, here as elsewhere, of retrieving from underneath a purportedly "natural" state of affairs the implicit contract that regulates the functioning of a configuration, then it cannot but find justification in a metyonymic displacement imposing the idea of an exchange, one serving to distinguish *perspectiva artificialis* from *perspectiva naturalis:* the surplus value denoted by the passage from lentil to ducat, but also that from ducat to lentil (if we can see in it not only a modest vegetable but also an instrument of which Descartes speaks in his *Optics,* one capable of increasing the power of vision—the *forza del vedere,* a phrase already employed by Alberti—such that it carried "much further than our fathers could have imagined"[24]), this surplus value is an expression, in terms that are quite literally speculative, of the "truth" effect generated by the experiment.

The demonstrative force of the latter derived entirely from its verifiability, from the fact that one could look into the apparatus twice (*e veduto più volte*), as opposed to two looking into it at the same time: this would have required an optical configuration analogous to that imagined by Gottlob Frege, a kind of telescope equipped with several eyepieces directed at the same "view."[25] The experiment could be performed by anyone in turn, on his own, by taking the apparatus in his hands (*e io l'ho avuto in mano*) as Brunelleschi had intended and repeating it at will, such that he could subsequently bear witness about it (*e possono rendere testimonio*): like the painter of the *Arnolfini Wedding,* an image of which, returned by the mirror situated in the very spot on the picture plane toward which the orthogonals converge, bears the famous inscription *Jahannes Van Eyck fuit hic* and the date 1434, which is ten or twenty years later than Brunelleschi's experiments. *Hic* means *here,* in the spot from which I see it, as reflected, and not *there,*

---

23. "You can consider that these rays make a pyramid from the surface seen, full of rays and enclosing within it the aforementioned thing seen as in a bird cage made of very fine reeds, or like one of those caps young girls make out of rushes." Filarete, *Treatise,* fol. 176 verso; op. cit., p. 593; English trans., p. 301.
24. René Descartes, *La Dioptrique,* first discourse, *Oeuvres,* ed. by Adam-Tannery, vol. 6, Paris, 1965, p. 81; English trans., *Optics,* in *Discourse on Method, Optics, Geometry and Meteorology,* trans. by Paul J. Olscamp, Indianapolis, 1965.
25. Gottlob Frege, "Sens et denotation," *Écrits logiques et philosophiques,* trans. and intro. by Claude Imbert, Paris, 1971, p. 106.

where I see it to be by means of the mirror, in the position of the witness facing this man and woman whose portrait was executed by Van Eyck, if we are to accept Panofsky's classic reading, as a kind of marriage certificate.[26] But Deuteronomy had already laid down the law: in matters of proof, the testimony of a single witness is insufficient.[27] So there are *two* witnesses reflected in the mirror of the *Arnolfini Wedding*, placed in the frame of the door facing the mirror, slightly the other side of it, as in Brunelleschi's experiment, with which the Flemish painter seems to establish some objective relation, despite the strong probability that he had no knowledge of it. Two witnesses, and thus two vanishing points, quite close to one another, both falling within the circle of the mirror (if this is correct, we must seriously consider the possibility that the multiplicity of vanishing points, all situated in the same area of the painting, held to be characteristic of early Flemish painting might indicate not a problematic lack of systematic coherence but a deliberate choice, an acknowledgment or affirmation of the different perspectives of different subjects, first of all of different spectators simultaneously looking at the same painting).

But as "subject," how can the spectator in the *Arnolfini* configuration establish himself as a witness and repeat the operation recorded in the painting, except by identifying himself with the painter? The *Arnolfini Wedding* could almost have been modeled on Brunelleschi's demonstration. But with the intention of denying the spectator the place assigned him in the latter experiment. Behind the hole with which Brunelleschi had pierced his panel, one witness, and one only, could place himself. "Move so I can put myself there": this rule held for the experiment, just as it was fundamental to the *Novella del Grasso*, that inaugural text of Italian literature, authored by the same Manetti to whom we owe the "Life of Brunelleschi," whose complex intrigues unfold in the very locale to which the demonstration refers, the piazza of the Baptistry of San Giovanni.[28] Facing the *Arnolfini* mirror, which reflects not a voyeur's peephole but a door on whose threshold stand the painter and an associate, the spectator is incapable of finding his position, of which he would have been dispossessed from the origin.

---

26. Panofsky, *Early Netherlandish Painting*, op. cit., vol. 1, pp. 201–203.
27. "On the evidence of two witnesses or of three witnesses he that is to die shall be put to death; a person shall not be put to death on the evidence of one witness." Deuteronomy 17.6.
28. Cf. *supra*, chapter 4, note 36, and my *Théorie de l'échiquier*, in preparation.

The protocol described by Manetti provides confirmation that we are justified in speaking of an experiment in relation to the configuration conceived by Brunelleschi, for it explicitly states (a) that the experiment was repeatable and (b) that it lent itself to verification, of a kind we might designate by the word *autopsy:* to wit, I saw it with my own eyes (or rather, with my own eye, for it is to that that I was reduced).

The possibility of several observers succeeding one another behind the panel leads us to suppose that the "perspective subject" is somewhat different from that of the *cogito,* though not in contradiction with it. Like the reciprocity of perspectives which is its corollary, it authorizes us to posit a network of intersubjectivity, a kind of ideal community equivalent to Husserl's transcendental *nous* with pretentions to truth, in the very process of its historical production.[29] But as to this unique (though in one sense double) position that perspective construction assigns to the "subject"— indistinguishably both producer and consumer—in the way language can function only on condition that there is constituted, at the urging of discourse and in terms of the relation *I/you,* and relations of person generally, a center of internal reference[30]: Manetti goes so far as to assimilate it, when listing the "circumstances" of the demonstration, to a point (*e del punto*), thereby announcing, from the originary moment of "exact" perspective, the fixing, the focusing (*mise au point*) of a "geometry of visibility" that would be a necessary condition for the constitution of that "gazeless domain" about which Michel Foucault has written, that of modern science, a science preferring to experience bodies only in displays tending to suppress them.[31]

But the reduction of the subject to a point, for which Brunelleschi's experiment prepared the way, if it did not render it mandatory,

29. Derrida, in Husserl, op. cit., p. 49; English trans., *Edmund Husserl's "Origin . . .," an Introduction,* op. cit., pp. 64–65.

30. Benveniste, "L'Appareil formel de l'énonciation," *Problèmes de linguistique général,* op. cit., vol. 2, p. 82 [vol. 2 is not translated].

31. "Doubtless there has been, from Descartes to Monge, and earlier among painters and architects, a reflection on visible space; but it was a question of fixing a *geometry of visibility,* in other words of situating phenomena depending from perception within a *gazeless domain:* intelligible forms laid the foundations for forms perceived in displays that suppressed them." Michel Foucault, *Naissance de la clinique,* Paris, 2d ed., 1972, p. 88; English trans. by A. M. Sheridan Smith, *The Birth of the Clinic,* New York, 1973.

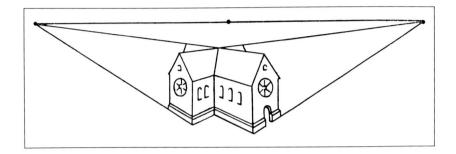

18 "Horned" perspective. Jean Pélerin, *De artificialis perspectiva,* 1505, fol. 8 verso.

entailed still more implications, all of them tending in the same direction.
Most commentators have noted that in frontal projections of the baptistry of
San Giovanni—a regular, quasi-platonic body, each adjoining pair of whose
eight sides forms an angle of 135°—the receding lines of each lateral facade
converge toward different points situated on a single horizontal line. In the
absence of lines perpendicular to the picture plane, such as paving lines (not
mentioned by Manetti) or lines delineated by the facades encompassing the
piazza, the perspective painted by Brunelleschi would have borne all the
earmarks of what Jean Pélerin dubbed "horned perspective."[32] Brunelleschi's
invention, which consisted of piercing a hole in the center of the panel, at
the vanishing point, in view of demonstrating that the latter corresponded,
by projection, to the point of view, this invention simultaneously conferred
upon the line including these two points the value of a *horizon.* That same
horizon, traded at eye height, with which Alberti counseled artists to align
the heads of all their figures, wherever they might be located in the perspective scene, on the sole condition that they be standing on the same
plane as the observer himself:[33] this being the simplest formulation of the
rule of declension from which the perspective disposition derives its value as
paradigm. Four centuries later, Poncelet provided a mathematical demonstration of the theorem maintaining, independent of all considerations of

32. Brion-Guerry, op. cit., p. 96.
33. "Veggiamo ne 'tempi i capi degli huomini quasi tutti ad una quantita ma i piedi de più
lontani quasi corrispondere ad i ginoche de più presso." Alberti, op. cit., p. 74; English trans.,
p. 58. Cf. Leonardo da Vinci: "Inperochè le cose poste sopra la pianura dove posi piedi, se sarà
piana, se detta pianura fusse infinita, mai passano più su, che l'ochio." Institut de France, Ms. A,
fol. 36 verso; Richter, vol. 1, p. 35.

"autopsy," that the place of all points at the infinity of a plane is a straight line. Here again, precise formulation (*mise au point*) of a geometry of visibility preceded the constitution of this gazeless domain in which, paradoxically, projective geometry itself participates.

*

But the experiment aimed at more than demonstrating the projective coincidence of point of view and vanishing point. This demonstration having been achieved, which required only that the panel on which Brunelleschi had painted his "perspective," having been pierced by a hole, be placed opposite a mirror, there remained the question of the distance at which the latter should be placed. Parronchi is right to note in this connection that in perspective drawing after nature, the fundamental operation consists of measuring objects with a ruler held at arm's length—as if the section of the pyramid fell there, at the distance of one *braccio*.[34] The analogy is misleading insofar as it suggests that such could have been the case with the mirror in Brunelleschi's experiment. But Manetti's description is no less so, for it leads us to think that if it were deployed with some freedom, changes in the distance of the mirror from the panel would be equivalent to displacements of the observer in relation to the object along the relevant line of sight: this at the cost, quite obviously, of more or less pronounced distortions in the diminution of transverse quantities. If one realizes, however, that the description makes no mention of a squared paving (in contrast to Alberti, who states its construction was the first step in *costruzione legittima*), and if one accepts that the eye could only take in, like a backdrop, a single line of facades parallel to the picture plane, then the only transverse quantities in question would be the foreshortened facades of the baptistry itself. Which is to say that however meticulously Brunelleschi had painted the ornamental marble insets (Manetti stresses that a miniaturist could not have executed them any better), however accurately he may have observed their diminution (as Vassari asserts), in every respect comparable to that of the squares on a two-colored checkerboard, the resulting effect would not have permitted a precise deduction of the distance of the construction.

---

34. Parronchi, op. cit. 1964, p. 306.

What does Manetti say? That the separation, the distance (*quella dilazione*) between the mirror and the panel, each being held in the hand, should correspond, more or less, in "small *braccia*," to the distance in regular *braccia* from the spot on which the painter was supposed to stand to the baptistry. In "small *bracchia*," which is to say in reduced *braccia*, in accordance with a graduated scale or a proportionate reduction: though these are not the same, in either case we are referred back to Thales's theorem concerning similar figures (the foundation of perspective construction, as it is the "origin" of geometry), and likewise to the notion of *similitude* central to geometry. That we are dealing here with circular logic is shown by the fact that the exact localization of the vanishing point, as it was supposed to be deducible from the perspective construction itself, was predicated upon an accurate determination of this distance. But there is, as we shall see, another difficulty, one of a properly theoretical order that is more serious.

If we follow Vasari and adhere to the given of the *intersegatione*, and if we admit (as his description stipulates) an angle of vision of 90°, the construction distance corresponding to a panel half a *braccia* square would be (by application of the properties of the right-angled isosceles triangle) a quarter *braccia*. The field of a mirror being defined as a pyramid with a summit corresponding to the eye, such that the image of the point-object corresponding to that from the eye was at the correct distance, the mirror must have been placed at a distance of about a quarter *braccia*, or about seven to eight centimeters. Which would not have been impractical, contrary to what Robert Klein maintained,[35] if the mirror itself had been of small dimensions (14 × 14 cm); all these givens must be revised if we hypothesize an angle of view of less than 90°, in which case the distance could have been as great as the width of the painting and the difficulty raised by Klein would be resolved without creating any new ones. The frame defined by the architecture of the door and the corresponding angle of vision could easily be modified, as I've already suggested, by adjusting the extent to which the doors were open or closed. In either case the reduced distance between the panel and the mirror was consistent, in principle, with a closer view, like the one of the baptistry obtainable today from the same spot.

---

35. Klein, *Form and Meaning*, op. cit., p. 120.

So Robert Klein is wrong to speak of Brunelleschi's first experiment as a failure, even in relative terms. On the contrary, having definitively demonstrated the projective coincidence of the point of view and the vanishing point, the arrangement had the additional advantage of allowing its inventor to pose the question of the construction distance in terms that certainly were experimental but that nonetheless led him to formulate the idea of what Alberti called *l'intersegatione* with perfect clarity. This makes it all the more surprising that the only distance taken into account by Manetti is that between the eye (or the "subject") and the object (if not the other seeing entity looking at him from the mirror as if he were there), while he says nothing about that between the eye and the plane of intersection. How is it that this renowned mathematician, whom we can be sure had read *Della pittura,* ignored this fundamental element, which Alberti, through use of the "window" metaphor, had made the theoretical centerpiece of the system? The answer is perhaps implicit in the question, or rather in its displacement, which entails our placing the accent on what remained unsaid in Alberti's account: it was only at the end of the century that Piero della Francesca and Leonardo da Vinci recommended that spectators position themselves at a distance from paintings proportionate with their dimensions, an extrapolation from construction distance.[36]

Brunelleschi cannot have been unaware of the problem: this is amply confirmed by Manetti's description of the experiment, beginning with the given of an observer positioned three *braccia* inside the cathedral portal, whose plane can then function as the imaginary equivalent of the plane of projection. In these circumstances and with all necessary allowances being made, the distance between the eye and the mirror should equal three *braccia:* "small" ones, because scaled down, reduced in the same proportion as was the cut of the panel in relation to that of the door. If, on the contrary, the distance between the eye and the object is taken into account, then these same "small *braccia*" must be differently understood: in the painting, as in its mirror image, the baptistry must have been itself set down at a virtual distance corresponding, in *braccia* not only reduced but having been subjected to the rule of proportionate diminution imposed by perspective, to the distance separating the cathedral portal from that of the baptis-

---

36. Cf. *infra*, chapter 15, pp. 374–75.

try. Thus the approximative character (*la distanza velcirca*) imposed on the experiment, an experiment that, *from this point of view,* called for a complement, one provided by the second experiment, this time in nonreflective terms: which brings us back, by way of concluding our discussion of the San Giovanni demonstration, to the role played by the mirror.

*

The truth effect attached to Brunelleschi's experiment was produced in the mirror. Thus it was an effect of the imaginary, even though it was produced by an apparatus which, as I've said, had the outward appearance of a symbolic disposition. As for painting, that's something else again, and we might well ask ourselves why it was necessary to use a mirror to pose the question of the "truth" of perspective. That this truth was an affair of the imagination, Diderot saw proof of this in the fact that a person blind from birth can form an idea of specular reflection, and even of perspective. When he asked the blind man of Puisaux what he understood by a mirror, he answered: "A machine that puts things into relief far from themselves if they are properly placed in relation to it." But as for "these kinds of perspective which give relief to objects, and which are simultaneously analogous to and different from our mirrors . . ., we perceived that they hindered as much as reinforced the idea he'd formed of the mirror, and that he was tempted to think that, seeing as the mirror painted objects, the painter, to represent them, perhaps painted a mirror."[37]

"A machine that puts us into relief far from ourselves": for a blind person, that wasn't so poorly observed, and Diderot was not wrong to note that many philosophers had employed less subtlety in reaching conclusions just as false. While Brunelleschi's machine also put the subject outside himself, this was not to give him relief but rather to treat him as a hollow, and as a negative. But the importance of manipulation in the experiment should not be underestimated. For it was this that made of the painting an object to be handled as well as seen, to be turned round and round, just as "savages," it is said, turned the first mirrors presented to them round and round

---

37.   Diderot, *Lettre sur les aveugles à l'usage de ceux qui voient, Oeuvres,* Bibliothèque de la pléiade, pp. 843–46; English trans., *Letter on the Blind for the Use of Those Who See,* in *Diderot's Early Philosophical Works,* ed. by Margaret Jourdain, Chicago, 1916.

to see what was hidden behind them. Brunelleschi did exactly the same thing: wanting to discover what was hidden behind perspective, he went to see for himself, going so far as to place his eye behind it to capture its operation in the mirror.

If Brunelleschi had painted the baptistry of San Giovanni with the aid of a mirror, perhaps even on its surface, why wouldn't Manetti have said so? The question is important, because it has a bearing on what I would call the system's point of reflexivity: to paint with the aid of a mirror (as in executing a self-portrait), or to bring in a mirror a posteriori, the better to judge a painting or, in the present instance, to submit it to a kind of *autopsy*—quite literally—; these are two very different things. The idea that Brunelleschi might have executed his painting directly on a mirror is absurd, and not solely from a theoretical point of view. If he had positioned himself in front of a mirror one-half *braccia* square, at a distance of between fifteen and thirty centimeters, with his back turned to the baptistry, the painter would have seen nothing but his own face, for his head would have screened out the baptistry. If he had placed the mirror at an oblique angle, as Gioseffi had suggested,[38] deformations would have resulted, and it was precisely these that Brunelleschi was trying to avoid. The only acceptable hypothesis then would be that he disposed of an apparatus like that used by Canaletto three centuries later, namely *una camera lucida,* which is historically impossible.[39] But the essential consideration lies elsewhere: If Brunelleschi had painted his perspective directly on a mirror, or with the aid of a mirror, or even (as suggested by Gombrich in a misguided attempt at simplification[40]) by using the *velum* procedure as described by Alberti, we would still be at a loss as to how, in the absence of paving lines whose converging vectors could have guided him, he would have been able to determine the location of the vanishing point to pierce the hole necessary for the experiment.

Thus Brunelleschi's first experiment did indeed correspond to a kind of mirror stage of painting, but one that implied no magic. Contrary

---

38. Gioseffi, *Perspectiva artificialis,* op. cit., pp. 78ff.
39. Gioseffi, *Canaletto. Il quaderno delle galerie veneziane e l'impiego della camera ottica,* Trieste, 1959.
40. Ernst Gombrich, "Standards of Truth: The Arrested Image and the Moving Eye," *The Image and the Eye,* Ithaca, 1982, pp. 256–57.

to what some have said,[41] the configuration was nothing like a machine, nor an optical box, and still less a *camera oscura,* seeing as it was designed to function in the full light of day. *A mia di:* the phrase is rich in meaning. For if Manetti was indeed able to hold the panel in his own hands, having been born in 1423, which is to say at the very moment, more or less, in which Brunelleschi was carrying out his experiments, then the hole against which he pressed his eye was in the image of his own "fissure," and of the "light" (pupil) that enabled him to see (*mia di,* as one would say of the "light" given off by a firearm). And it is because the configuration obeyed a principle radically different from that of the *camera oscura* that it could not produce the reversal that has been held, since Marx, to be characteristic of ideology, and with which magical connotations have sometimes been associated.[42] If there is any relationship to "truth" here, it is fundamentally the result of *construction.* In a word, and even though the photographic process would conform in every respect to the rule to which "he gave birth," the panel painted by Brunelleschi was totally different from a *snapshot.* The image that appeared in the mirror, at the rear of the configuration, was neither the imprint nor the reflection of an external reality (thus the importance, in this context, of the expedient of the plaque of burnished silver on which sky and clouds blown by the wind were reflected: the wind which, as Alberti notes, introduces movement, in drapery, hair, or clouds, into an otherwise static construction[43]). Far from capturing the real directly, as cameras and telescopes can, this "view" corresponded to a bracketing, to a veritable phenomenological reduction: within the brackets established by the panel and the mirror, the real was excluded, was outside the circuit (except, I repeat, for the problem of the sky). As was the subject itself, which gained access only by abstracting itself out of the specular relation. Thus

41. Cf., for example, Pierre Francastel, *Peinture et société,* Lyon, 1951, p. 19; Jean-François Lyotard, "La Peinture comme dispositif libidinal," *Des Dispositifs pulsionnels,* Paris, 1973, pp. 266ff.
42. "It is claimed that a magician can be recognized by certain physical peculiarities, with which he is branded and by which his calling may be discovered should he attempt to conceal it. It is thought, for example, that the pupils of a magician's eyes have swallowed up the iris, that his visual images are produced in reverse." Marcel Mauss and Henri Hubert, "Esquisse d'une theorie generale de la magie," in Mauss, *Sociologie et Anthropologie,* Paris, 1950, p. 19; English trans. by Robert Brain, *A General Theory of Magic,* New York, 1975, p. 27.
43. Alberti, *Della pittura,* op. cit., pp. 97–98; English trans., p. 81.

a system that, however empirically open it may have been, was theoretically isolated, closed in on itself, save for the cloud mirror and this hole, this "gaze" which the eye, held up against it, obstructed, or sutured. This "light" from which it derived its meaning and function, which was to render visible not reality but "truth," or its semblance.

The second experiment.

The indiscretion of he who looks.

The return of the denoted.

A positivist notion of truth.

The destruction of the painting.

The question of infinity.

An unprecedented idea.

Geometry Made Real

He made in perspective (*Fece di prospettiva*) the piazza of the Palazzo
della Signoria in Florence, together with all that is in front of it
and around it, insofar as it was accessible to view (*quante la vista
serve*), standing outside the piazza or better even (*o veramente al
pari*), with the front of the church of San Romolo, past the canto
di Calimala Francesca which opens into this piazza, a few *braccia*
toward Or San Michele; from which position one perceives the
Palazzo della Signoria in such a way that two sides of it are fully
visible (*in modo che due faccie si veggono intere*), the one facing west
and the one facing north. And it is a marvelous thing to see everything that appears, all together, with all the things apprehended
by [one's] view in this place. Fucci, and after him Paolo Uccello,
and still other painters wanted to copy it and imitate it; I've seen
more than one of these efforts, and none were done as well as his
(*e non stato bene come quello*). It might be said here: Why didn't he
make this painting, it being in perspective (*essendo di prospettiva*),
with the same hole for looking (*con quel 'busco per la vista*) as in the
small panel of the temple of San Giovanni? This is because the
panel (*la tavola*) had to be so large to accommodate so many different things (*che fussi si grande a mettervi tante cose distinte*), that it was
impossible to hold it up with one hand in front of one's face, with
the other one holding the mirror, a man's arm not being long
enough so that with the mirror in one hand he can be positioned in
front of the point at the appropriate distance (*e'le potessi porre dirimpetto al punto con la sua distanza*), nor [is it] strong enough to carry
it. He left it to the discretion of he who looks, as is the case for all
other paintings by other painters, even though he who looks is

never discrete (*Lasciollo nelle discrezione di chi guarda come interviene a tutte l'altre dipinture negli altri dipintori, benche chi guarda, ogni volta non sia discreto*). And in the place where he had put the burnished silver in that of San Giovanni, here he cut above the buildings (*da casamenti in su*) the wood on which he had painted. And he took it with him to a spot where he could observe it with the natural atmosphere above the buildings (*e recavasi con esso a guardarlo in luogo che l'aria naturale si mostrava da'casamenti in su*).[1]

What did Brunelleschi want to show by means of this second painting, a painting which Manetti warns the reader, without giving any specifics (contrast the detail contained in the description of the first experiment), was of much larger dimensions but not so large as to preclude his carrying his painting around with him—just as Braque, according to Jean Paulhan, was momentarily possessed by the idea of dragging his canvases around, of juxtaposing them with things, of taking them into a field, "to see how they held up."[2] And what was the relation between this second experiment and the preceding one? If the San Giovanni *tavoletta* was the first in which Brunelleschi showed the "case of perspective," in the words of his biographer, was the *tavola* of the Signoria a mere extrapolation from this demonstration, in the manner of a counterproof or simple corollary? Or did it embody a different project, even though it still was an exploration of the same "case"?

*

We have seen that nothing in Manetti's text allows us to conclude that the first experiment was a failure unless we ignore the function performed by the mirror. But as for this other experiment, whose chosen scene was the Piazza della Signoria, which was much larger than that of the baptistry, and which encompassed a larger and more motley set of component elements (express mention being made not only of the buildings circling the piazza but also of everything found within it—fountains, statues, various small structures—to the exclusion, should it be assumed, of any human figure

---

1. Manetti, op. cit., pp. 59–60; English trans., pp. 44, 46.
2. Jean Paulhan, *Braque le patron,* Paris, 1942, p. 60.

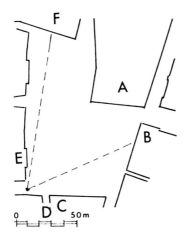

19 Brunelleschi's second experiment: plan of the Piazza della Signoria, with indication of the angle of vision adopted by Brunelleschi. A. Palazzo della Signoria; B. Loggia dei Lanzi; C. Tetto dei Pisani; D. Canto Calimata Francesca; E. San Romolo; F. Tribunale della Mercatanzia.

passing by, pushed by the wind?), it could not satisfy the same conditions nor aim for the same results.

Though it was constructed in perspective (*di prospettiva*) like the first one, Brunelleschi's second painting was not pierced by a hole. To preclude possible objections and justify what might appear to be a step backward from the demonstrative rigor of the first experiment, Manetti advances an argument that seems to be a material one. The clear and distinct representation of a scene of such amplitude supposed the adoption of a graphic scale considerably larger than that used for the San Giovanni panel; the dimensions of what was no longer called a *tavoletta* but rather a *tavola* necessitated that it be either held in both hands or—as seems more likely, and as Manetti's text discretely suggests—placed on the ground or some other support. This hypothesis, like the *tavola,* has, if I may say, all the more weight given that the criterion of distinction refers to an ancient meaning of the word *perspicere,* as well as to the Greek notion of optics.[3] But in reality Manetti's argument has a totally different import: he specifies that the distance at which the mirror ought to have been placed, for the experiment to conform to the same principle as the first one, exceeded the measure of one *braccio.* To be sure, the position ideally assigned the observer, at the entrance into the piazza and at its edge, *al pari,* recalls the situation of the eye in the first experiment, pupil flush with the surface of the panel. But this same observer, no longer obliged to hold the apparatus in his hands,

---

3.   *Cf.* Panofsky, "Die Perspektive . . .," op. cit., p. 127, note 3; English trans., pp. 75–76.

was now granted freedom of movement. While there's no point in toying with words, we should not allow Manetti's joke in the text at this point to go unremarked: we need only understand it literally, even at the cost of leaving ourselves open to additional charges of anachronism. If the one who looks is never "discreet" (*Benche qui guarda ogni volta non sia discreto*), this is because, in the conditions applying to vision under the perspective rule, he is always a *voyeur.* And this is true whether he dissimulates himself behind a panel pierced by hole so as to place his eye against it as if it were a keyhole, or whether he uses both eyes to take in the spectacle provided him by a painting, notably a scene presented to him under perspective's auspices. If perspective is a "scabrous" thing, as one reads in Filarete, this is not only because it is, with regard to the intellect, just as a surface can be, full of unevenness:[4] it is primarily because it appeals, in the subject, to the scopic drive, pretending to reduce it—Brunelleschi's experiments have no other meaning—to the function and status of a *witness,* if not—once again—of a *voyeur.*

The freedom now accorded the spectator did not imply that the second experiment represented a step backward from the first one. It could not even be said that it was less demonstrative, because it too was subject to verification, as we shall see. Undoubtedly it accorded a lesser role to reflection, as is signaled, quite literally, by the absence of a mirror. But this is because its purpose was different, Brunelleschi's intention this time being to show (and not to *demonstrate,* which was possible only with the aid of a mirror) that the constructive system founded on monocular vision, with the eye being confined to a fixed point, retained its pertinence and efficacy under conditions closer to that of normal vision. And the very object occupying the center of the scene, like the baptistry in the first experiment, constituted, in its geometric volume, and in light of the position assigned the spectator at the opposite corner of the piazza, a perspectival given subtly corresponding to binocular vision: whereas in the first instance the octagonal baptistry presented itself to frontal view (though two lateral facades were apprehended by the same gaze), the assymmetrical mass of the Palazzo della Signoria offered itself in an oblique view, the centric ray issuing from the

---

4.   "Siché attendi, et appri gli occhi dell'intelletto: che questo, che s'a dire, sono cose scabrose e sottili a intendere." Filarete, *Treatise,* fol. 177 recto; op. cit.,p. 600; English trans., p. 301.

eye in all likelihood bisecting the angle of vision: this perspective—uneven, angular *(scabrosa)* if ever one was—far from exploiting linear recession, introduced into the center of the arrangement a projecting *corner* and obliged the gaze to diverge and slide simultaneously over the two facades meeting at the angle of the palazzo, one facing north, as Manetti insists, and the other west. The resulting "horned" perspective effect was all the more pronounced because the angle at whose apex the centric point was established (in plan) was considerably exaggerated, in projection, by the diagonal perspective.

We have seen, with regard to the first experiment, in what terms the question of truth value assignable to perspective construction was posed. The image painted on the recto of the *tavoletta* had but one use value: if it lent itself to demonstration, this was to the extent that, to use Frege's terms, it could be recognized as a denotation. An image—as considered in the mirror—that was *virtual,* as Frege says of that formed in a telescope, and, as such, *partial (partielle),* if not biased *(partiale),* linked as it is to the observer's point of view (and meaningful, for Frege, only relative to this[5]). Yet this image, this view, was not a phantasm, and presented itself as objective upon being verified by several observers, on condition that the latter agree to place themselves, one after the other, at the obligatory point of view, just as anyone could position himself in the spot corresponding to the perspective view adopted by the painter and so verify the accuracy of the construction. While the arrangement devised for the first experiment situated the denoted element outside the circuit, so to speak, everything suggests that the panel in the second experiment screened it out, raising, in strictly experimental terms, the difficulty touching on the distance which is so frustrating in the first experiment, if one adheres closely to Manetti's description of it. We have seen that nothing in this description indicates that, in performing the first experiment, one ought to place oneself in the spot that corresponded, in reality, to the point of origin deducible from the perspective construction itself. But neither is there anything in the subsequent portion of the text to preclude our imagining that Brunelleschi could have set up his "painting" in the Piazza della Signoria itself, in the position

---

5. Frege, "Sens et dénotation," loc. cit.

appropriate for the contour of his panel as he'd cut it along the tops of the buildings, the arrangement thus confirming the hypothesis that assimilated the painting to one planar section of the visual pyramid, while at the same time turning this to account. So successfully that, the painting having been established as a kind of screen at the entrance to the piazza, and the spectator evincing the necessary "discretion" (in other words, placing himself at the distance appropriate for realization of the effect, such that the painting, to employ Braque's phrase, "held up" in comparison with its surroundings), the sky could be seen, *da casamenti in su,* without any need to resort to a mirror.

*

If Brunelleschi's discovery had inaugural import, this was to the extent it created the impression that, by its means, representation gained access to a new kind of "truth." A subject placing his eye behind the hole, this *lumière* or light hole pierced through the center of the San Giovanni *tavoletta,* could only confirm a precise correspondence between the perspective fiction and its object; just as a "discreet" observer would, of necessity, see the upper contour of the second *tavola* coincide almost perfectly with the silhouette of the

20 Brunelleschi's second experiment: the panel *in situ*.

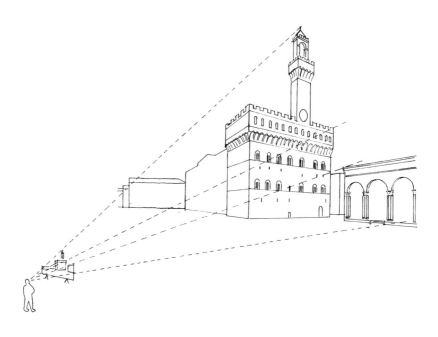

buildings in the Piazza della Signoria, without being required to use only one eye. Here again, anyone could repeat the experiment in turn, until becoming persuaded that neither magic nor tricks played any part in the result.

Doubtless a painting conforming to the rules of *costruzione legittima* responds, at least theoretically, to the given of the specular image, such representations ordering themselves in accordance with the traditional figures of resemblance, whose semantic web Michel Foucault has reconstituted for us.[6] But whereas Brunelleschi's arrangement appealed to *convenientia* and *aemulatio,* to resemblance based upon conjunction, coincidence, and adjustment, just like that in specular repetition, it did so in order to turn against itself that which appeared to be the fundamental experience, the primary form of knowledge, to unpack its implications, to resolve its paradoxes (and it is indeed a paradox, at least an apparent one, to which Filarete draws our attention, that a square seen in a mirror, or in planar projection, which amounts to the same thing, is no longer square, nor always comparable to another one), to put it to the test of a reasoned construction—of what in current parlance we would call a theoretical model. Far from "imitating" space, perspective was only able to feign it, and this from its origin—an origin with which it renews its relation at each moment. To feign it or (re)construct it, as is demonstrated by Brunelleschi's two experiments, each of which is centered around an architectonic object that was at the same time a basic, almost "ideal" body, a kind of *limit-shape,* to use Husserl's terminology, defined entirely by a set of surfaces. But what do we mean by "space" when we are dealing with a place that is itself a construct, namely a piazza surrounded by a series of facades? Rather than "imitate" space (insofar as the notion of imitation has any meaning in this context), it would be necessary to *produce* it, to constitute this space as an object, an operation that tends, as we see in Descartes, to deny it any quality other than that of pure extension and to exempt it from the reign of resemblance, compelling it to submit to that of "similitude," in a new, geometric sense of the word. It is to this moment—which escapes all periodization, though surely not all

---

6.   Michel Foucault, *Les Mots et les choses,* op. cit., chapter 2, "La Prose du monde"; English trans., *The Order of Things,* chapter 2, "The Prose of the World."

chronology—that Brunelleschi's discovery corresponds: an ambiguous moment, as is evinced by the fact that the discoverer, like the geometers of antiquity, was less interested in space itself than in the bodies it contained, and in their respective placement, beginning with built volumes and places, but one that retains its value as origin, and as radical origin, from the first steps forward, from the first synthesis, and that would serve as a ground for all subsequent developments, to the extent that, as a result of being taken to its limit, the relation of ressemblance between things and their image could only unravel, ceding its place to a comparison based upon order and measure. Its corollary being that henceforth the iconic operation would have less bearing on the elements of the representation than on the relations they maintained within a linked figurative proposition, one that derived its truth value from this linkage.

Some time later the French Academy would lash out against those who, like Abraham Bosse and his master Desargues, dared maintain that the proper task of painting was not to represent things "as the eye sees them or believes it sees them, but such as the laws of perspective impose them on our reason."[7] This debate must have preoccupied minds of the fifteenth century, as is indicated by Filarete's text when, against the objection he himself raises that perspective might be capable of deception through showing things that do not exist, the author responds that such is indeed the case, pointing out that *disegno* was not something true but rather the mere "demonstration" of the thing painted, of the thing one wanted to show.[8] Such that the only truth in painting, when it conforms with the rules of perspective, is demonstrative truth, and thus one that is founded on a constructive artifice. Which is to say that the truth value upon which such painting has a legitimate claim is not dependent upon resemblance, in any strict sense of the word, and that the relation of *aemulatio* between reality and its image is not of a kind allowing the two to be confused, to be mistaken for one another. In its moment of origin (an "origin" with which Desargues would renew ties, on another level), perspective construction

---

7. Abraham Bosse, *Le Peintre converti aux précises et universelles règles de son art,* Paris, 1637.

8. "Tu potresti dire: questa è falsa, che ti dimostra una cosa, che non è. Egli e vero; niente di meno in disegnio e vera: perche il disegnio ancora lui non è cosa vera; anzi, una dimostratione di quella cosa che tu ritrai o che tu voi dimostrare." Filarete, *Treatise,* fol. 179 recto, op. cit., pp. 618–19; English trans., p. 305.

did not aim at illusion, at least not the kind of illusion we designate with the term *trompe l'oeil.* But it ordered itself around a notion of truth that might be called realist, even positivist, if the import of Brunelleschi's discovery could be reconciled with any philosophy prepared to ignore the role of the subject in instituting a truth that it defines as the adequation of a proposition—figurative or other—to that which it denotes. An image constructed in perspective can be made perfectly coincident, optically speaking, with its object, such that it could be precisely superimposed over it or screen it out perfectly, but only if it is seen from the fixed point of view of an observer who could take in both of them in one glance. The sought-after adequation being possible only through resort to a rational method of construction, one governed by standards of order and measure, the *tavola,* having been so placed in front of one's eyes—*dinanzi agli occhi,* as Vasari put it[9]—would have initially functioned as a model whose coherence derived from the position to which it assigned the subject: a "subject," let it be repeated, whose body is elided from the beginning, and reduced—in the phenomenological sense—to a point—the one that would be inscribed, along with Descartes, at the beginning of modern science, even though the vision (*visée*) defining it is inseparable from what Husserl so aptly referred to as its "blinders."[10]

*

Brunelleschi's discovery did not, properly speaking, open the way for either an art or a science. If it has taken on the status of an "origin," this is in proportion, on the contrary, to its having transcended the boundaries separating art from science, to its having constituted a theoretical hammer blow that appears, in retrospect, to once more use a phrase of Husserl's, moving it from the register of "natural" optics to that of artificial representation, like an "effectuation accomplished." An effectuation accomplished (*e misse in atto*) in relation to the achievements of ancient and medieval optics, which Parronchi has shown to have contained, in a dispersed state, all the elements that would mobilize the demonstration; but an effectuation accom-

---

9. Vasari, "Della pittura," *Proemio, Vite . . . ,* cited ed., vol. 1, p. 169; English trans., in *Vasari on Technique,* op. cit., p. 209.
10. Husserl, *Die Krisis . . . ,* op. cit., p. 2; English trans., p. 4.

plished, as well, in relation to the entirety of the old perceptual ground serving as the basis for perspective construction, a discovery assuming originary value only to the extent that it awakens, outside the tradition initiated by it, an entire world of sedimented culture. That such an operation had to be the work of *one* man, identifiable as such, and that the invention of perspective (like that, in its time, of geometry) could only occur, in history, at an *individuated point* (*point nommé*), is confirmed by tradition: the act of election (*nomination*) supposed by the latter nonetheless provides a historical anchoring for the decision according to which the world would be constituted for the first time as a domain of pure visibility, "the unity," to cite Husserl once more, "of a ground and a horizon."

As already noted, Manetti's account makes no mention of the ground of the perspective construction, not of the horizon governing this. From which follow the difficulties we have catalogued, which Brunellechi's experiments, if they did not resolve them, would have at least exposed, simultaneously opening the way for new developments in the geometric order. The point of view being established at the edge of the line of facades enclosing the Piazza della Signoria, the second experiment was not subject to the "window" determination which, in the form a door framing the view, was one of the characteristic traits of the San Giovanni arrangement. It

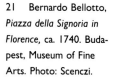

21   Bernardo Bellotto, *Piazza della Signoria in Florence,* ca. 1740. Budapest, Museum of Fine Arts. Photo: Scenczi.

would not have satisfied Brunelleschi's requirements to simply reject this given, which, in the last analysis, was illusionist. If we are to believe his biographer, he went further still, questioning the very notion of the "painting" such as it was then coming to be defined, and such as he himself perhaps had just invented it. By cutting out that portion of the panel corresponding to the sky, he doubtless produced the first *shaped canvas* in western art, though his intentions in doing so had nothing to do with *trompe l'oeil*.[11] From this assault on the integrity of the painting, as well as the hole piercing the first panel, Vasari set out to restrict the play of memory (unless overzealous restorers succeeded before him): the view Brunelleschi painted of the Piazza della Signoria thus belongs, as Manetti suggests, to a series that certainly does not come to an end with Uccello.[12] The second experiment nonetheless shared something with the first: in it, linear perspective appeared to apply itself only to solid bodies, notably buildings, which were solidly planted in the ground, to the exclusion of the sky and its phenomena. As if, faithful in this respect to the Aristotelian conception of the cosmos, the inventor of perspective had respected, in devising his experiment, the consecrated opposition between the celestial and terrestrial realms, even if in a strictly pictorial mode: Brunelleschi's sky is no longer that of medieval painters, nor is it the rarefied domain of the spheres so dear to philosophers and cosmographers; it is, rather, a meteorological site through which clouds move, pushed by the wind, and which thus escapes the measurements of geometry and perspective itself, here deliberately restricted to the *physical* components of the visible. And as for the places the artist chose to represent—two clearly delimited, enclosed piazzas—their very closure signals that he was not prepared to draw from his discovery the theoretical conclusions it implied: the world in which men evolve, in which they erect their constructions, beginning by tracing their foundations, this world is a world that is finite, closed, in which parallel lines, far from disappearing from view without meeting, converge upon a clearly visible point in the painting, and what's more, one that is governed, as specular

---

11. For an example of a panel whose shape was determined by trompe l'oeil intentions, cf. the *Lettres d'Italie* by the président de Brosses, Paris, 1928, vol. 1, pp. 11–12: "The painting is unframed and nonrectangular, being tailored according to the contours that would be the real ones of the pile of things represented in it, which contributes much to the illusion.
12. See the painting by Bernardo Bellotto now in Budapest.

coincidence has it, by the subject point as well as by the horizon line, to all appearances very close, onto which the latter is projected.

*

So one cannot maintain, as Panofsky does, that Brunelleschi's disposition *presupposed,* and even less that it *demonstrated,* the notion of an abstract, homogeneous, and isotropic geometric space, continuous and undefined, if not infinite, the *quantum continuum* central to postcartesian science,[13] nor that it bore witness to the destruction of the antique cosmos and its dissolution in the space of the new universe. And yet this world of—as Alexandre Koyré has written—*a geometry made real,*[14] in which the laws of physics will function, in a sense it was prepared by the disposition, in accordance with its own ways and means, even though no rigorous distinction is possible here between what belongs to practice and what to theory. The fact that Brunelleschi often carried his *tavola* with him to set it up where he thought best imposes upon us, in a very material way, the idea of displacement and transport, and also, through this, the fundamental operation of euclidean geometry, which is inconceivable save in and by the space of substitution which it establishes. But the first experiment already appealed to a properly geometric idea of similitude, itself based upon a work of idealization leading to the production of a very precisely articulated "limit-shape." In both cases the approximative character of the experiment, which Manetti did not attempt to hide, could be understood as contradicting the deep meaning of the scientific revolution of the seventeenth century, with its rejection of the world of "more or less" and its replacement by a universe of precision, of exact measurement, of rigorous determination.[15] The demand for measurement was nonetheless already present, here and there, as was that for precision, in the guise of the search for the proper viewing distance and for as close a correlation as possible between the image and its objective referent.

---

13. "The two qualities which characterize the space presupposed and presented in modern art up to the advent of Picasso: continuity (hence measurability), and infinity." Panofsky, *Renaissance and Renascences,* op. cit., p. 122. Cf. also the more nuanced statement in the same author's *Die Perspektive . . . ,* op. cit., pp. 121–22; English trans., pp. 70–71. On this point, see my *Théorie du nuage,* op. cit., pp. 225–26.

14. Alexandre Koyré, "Galilée at Platon," *Études d'histoire de la pensée scientifuque,* Paris, 1966, p. 151.

15. Koyré, *Études newtoniennes,* Paris, 1968, p. 28.

The demand for measurement and with it—to cite Husserl—for "the horizon of an open-ended infinity,"[16] the question of infinity being inscribed in the center of the San Giovanni *tavoletta,* on the spot marked by a point, if not by a hole.

The opposition between the two regions of earth and sky, or their ontological disparity, was not definitively put into question by the mirror reflecting both the silhouette of the buildings as the painter had captured them and the sky reflected in the surface of burnished silver: the mirror relay definitively manifesting that in principle they both belonged to a universe of "geometry made real." For all the consequences of Brunelleschi's experiments to be properly drawn, a prolonged effort would be required, one mobilizing painters and architects as well as philosophers and mathematicians; but the path had nonetheless been blazed, its direction had been clearly set, its horizon put in place, in what indeed appears, despite the contradictions inherent in it, as a definite advance—that "unprecedented" novelty of which Alberti spoke, that preliminary to the Galilean revolution, and to the idea, no less *unprecedented* if we are to believe Husserl, of "a rational infinite totality of being with a rational science systematically mastering it."[17]

16. Husserl, *L'Origine de la géometrie,* op. cit, p. 211; English trans. in *Crisis,* p. 374.
17. Husserl, *Die Krisis . . . .,* op. cit., pp. 19ff.; English trans., pp. 22ff.

The inversion.

The loss.

Truth of painting, truth in painting.

E iscritto non si truova.

Brunelleschi, "inventor of the Renaissance"?

TEN

The Renaissance and the Repetition of the Original

This is how I would sum up the epistemological question that concerns me here, and that raises certain difficulties as to how we ought to understand "history," whether of art, science, ideas, or thought itself: by what title, within what optic, if not within what perspective, can a demonstration conducted in accordance with the ways and means of art—in this instance those of *disegno,* borrowed from geometry—acquire the status of an origin, at least in its inaugural moment, in relation to theoretical, scientific, and even philosophical developments that manifestly transcend the boundaries of specific fields, of specific practices? A question of some urgency, if any meaning is to be ascribed to the project of an archaeology not only of knowledge, but of that thought qualifiable as "western," or—in Husserl's usage—as "European."

My hypothesis—to each his own; but this one has the merit of responding to the question one might well put to oneself concerning Manetti's text: Why does the latter breathe not a word about the construction process used by Brunelleschi, being interested only in the protocol of the experiment?—my hypothesis then will be that the position that tradition assigns to the discovery or invention associated with Brunelleschi's name corresponds to the moment of the inversion of practical interest into theoretical interest which was, for Husserl, the condition of science, in the western, European sense of the word: that is, it opened the way for it, or was predicated upon it. What Brunelleschi *discovered,* that to which he managed to give demonstrative force by building upon the experience of a millenium, was not that the vanishing point could be taken for the image at infinity of a painting's orthogonal lines (a notion that would only impose itself much later, and in a context utterly different from that of painting), but rather that it functioned, within the limits of the painting, and as

Filarete grasped perfectly, as the semblance of an eye (*a similitudine dell'occhio*)—the fan pattern of the receding lines representing the equivalent, on the plane, of that in space, of the rays included within the visual pyramid whose apex was the eye. In saying this, I do not mean to argue that with this *invention* Brunelleschi had opened up for art a field of ideality comparable to that of science, or that after this "first attempt" (as Kant would say) the route from which painting would never deviate was laid out. Manetti, when he ascribed to Brunelleschi the responsibility for everything that had been done after him in this matter, was doubtless thinking less of painting than of perspective itself. But that the latter was susceptible to reasoned development, and even abetted the ideal order of geometry, this is quite sufficient to demonstrate that it did more than correspond, in history, with a stylistic moment or with the constitution of a space of representation characteristic of an era: it suggests that a call for "truth" was present, was at work, and that art provided, for the first time, a place for it to manifest itself.

In this respect Brunelleschi's discovery was exposed to a wasting, a forgetting of its original meaning comparable in every respect to that, according to Husserl, undergone by the natural sciences after Galileo. The use of the word "Galilean" to characterize the revolution with which his name has come to be so conspicuously affiliated—because one was needed—only reinforces this connection. Like Galileo, Brunelleshi is inscribed, in relation to geometry, in the position of the heir: the geometry available to him knew nothing of its origins, or of the activities that had served as a foundation for the work of idealization.[1] Is this to say that it was empty of meaning, that the mutation transforming perspective into an "art," in Husserl's sense (that of obtaining predictable effects through application of a process conforming to precise rules), had already been effected? Or, to approach the question from the opposite tack: The operations serving as foundation for the kind of perspective that Brunelleschi *pro-duced,* which he foregrounded, if you will, were not these operations equivalent to a look backward, to a return to the sources of western science, insofar as they appealed, through the language of optical geometry and, beyond painting,

---

1.   Husserl, *Die Krisis . . .,* op. cit., p. 49; English trans., pp. 49–50.

to that primitive substratum of perceptual experience that constitutes, according to Husserl, the ground of all theoretical and practical life? Vasari's text provides evidence that once perspective construction became integrated into accepted custom (*moeurs*), as a fundamental disposition or *habitus* of the representation, it could no longer have any significance for painters other than a technical one, and not without providing a pretext for all sorts of games and effects, anamorphotic or other, which occasioned the ideological reduction of which it was very soon the object. But "exact" perspective, before appearing as a mere technique, a rival of the empirical recipes prevailing in the studios, before imposing itself as a code in the service of the *project*, a project impossible to disassociate from the notion of *projection* (Vasari's confused network of lines, *la difficultà delle tante linee confuse*, bringing to mind, in the verbal register, the future *Brouillon project* of Desargues), this kind of perspective would have necessarily implied a *theory*, in the mathematical sense of the word, which is to say "an open system of compatible propositions enunciating and linking the properties of an object domain in relation to certain explicitly formulated operations or relations."[2] And it is precisely as *theory* that *costruzione legittima* was to realize the paradox of opening the way to the most rigorous developments of descriptive and projective geometry, perhaps even anticipating them, while it furnished the ideology—by a trick that is itself properly ideological, unmindful of the origin and amalgam that photographic gadgetry would bring to term between the perspective configuration and the *camera oscura*—of the apparatus that seemed most suitable for its operation.

*

If Brunelleschi's experiment accrued any "truth" value, this was—yet again—in a specific, historically determined sense of the word. The preceding analyses effectively maintain that the question of the truth of painting, or of the truth *in painting*, was meaningful only on condition, for painting, of its participating in the history of truth, of its being linked to it at every moment. If we put the question of theoretical implications and, overall, of the historical significance of the requirement, emerging at the beginning of

---

2.   Jean T. Desanti, *Les Idéalités mathématiques*, Paris, 1968, p. 1.

the quattrocento, for a truth of painting (or a truth *in painting*) that was no longer theological or naturalist, but rather transcendental, in the philosophical sense of the word, a truth of understanding, and as such demonstrable, if not verifiable, what does this truth have in common with that to which Cézanne, five centuries later, would profess his debt:[3] a truth attributed not to the form of vision but to the very substance of the perceived, to its texture, though still remaining a matter of construction, of a construction by color, intended to be free of the rule of perspective, if not of all geometry?

We must still come to understand, in the one case as in the other, how a truth manifesting itself *in painting* can nonetheless simultaneously belong to the order of discourse, the discourse of theory as well as that of history. Just as we must still sort out the links between the assignation of origin and the idea of "Renaissance": presuming that a second birth is conceivable only in reference to a primordial time and place, whereas an origin (one has only to think of the lot of the question of the "beginning" in modern and/or contemporary cosmologies) is thinkable only on condition that the possibility of its being repeated remains open. Such is the very question of the "Renaissance," if one can accept its being formulated in terms other than philological ones, as is necessary in examining the perspective case brought to light by Brunelleschi. All evidence suggests that perspective theory belongs to that class of cultural products to which belong scientific formations, and the sciences themselves, as well as works of literary art: those objects that, according to Husserl, differ from tools (perspective can indeed be regarded as an instrument, at the cost of the above-mentioned reduction, but it certainly isn't a tool in the sense of a hammer or a pair of scissors), works of architecture, and all other products of this kind in that they cannot be duplicated or precisely repeated (but under what rubric are we to place paintings, and even photographs? Fifty years after the publication of Walter Benjamin's famous essay on *The Work of Art in the Age of Mechanical Reproduction,* the question should be considered anew). On the register of demonstration, this holds for perspective as soon as it is designated as being "scientific," as with Pythagoras's theorem and all

3.   "I owe you the truth in painting and I will tell it to you." Paul Cézanne to Émile Bernard, October 23, 1905, *Correspondance,* Paris, 1978, p. 315.

of geometry: it "exists once and once only, no matter how often or even in what language it may be expressed."[4] But the fact that Brunelleschi's "case," the kind of perspective he is imputed to have invented, was first put into circulation as a disposition that, whatever its demonstrative implications, borrowed nothing from the resources of writing or even language, this determination suffices to alter the givens of the problem. If all the elements of the demonstration were in effect present in the science called "perspective," a science of which *prospettiva,* as Manetti maintains, was but one part, it was still necessary, if the experiment were to take the form of an accomplished effectuation, for an empirical subject to repeat it with his own eye, each one placing himself in turn in the designated place, there where *costruzione legittima* finds its point of coherence, and at the same time proceeding to action: for there is never a "view" in a painting, nor an image in a mirror, save for the eye looking at it.

In theory, it cannot be excluded that the ancients knew and practiced a kind of perspective comparable, if not analogous, to that of Brunelleschi. In this respect too the subtlety of Manetti's text is astonishing. Whereas Filarete—to whom some attribute the first expression of this feeling of a "new birth" experienced by his contemporaries on seeing buildings constructed in an antique idiom[5]—did not hesitate to deny the usage and comprehension of this kind of perspective to the ancients,[6] Manetti held Brunelleschi's discovery to be all the more remarkable, all the "stronger" (*è più forte*), given that

> we do not know whether centuries ago the ancient painters—who
> in that period of fine sculptors are believed to have been good
> masters—knew about it or employed it rationally (*se lo sapevano e lo
> feciono con ragione*). But if they practiced it according to the rule (*se
> pure lo feciono con regola*) which I have not called a science without
> reason a bit earlier on (*che sanza cagione non dico io scienza poco di
> sopra*), as he [Brunelleschi] did later, those who could have taught

---

4. Husserl, *L'Origine de la géometrie,* op. cit., p. 179; English trans. in *Crisis,* p. 357.

5. Cf. J. R. Spencer, in *Filarete's Treatise on Architecture,* op. cit. 1965, vol. 1, p. 175, note 15, and Panofsky, *Renaissance and Renascences,* op. cit., p. 20.

6. Filarete, *Treatise,* for. 179 recto; op. cit., pp. 620–21; English trans., p. 305.

it to him had been dead for centuries and no written records about it have been discovered, or if they have been, have not been comprehended (*e iscritto non si truova, e se si trova, non è inteso*). Through industry and intelligence he either rediscovered or invented it (*ma la sua industria e sottigliezza, o ella la ritrovo, o ella ne fu l'inventrice*).[7]

Even supposing that antiquity knew perspective, or a kind of perspective, it would not have been able to give it the force of science. The rule discovered by Brunelleschi (if not invented by him), and which he may only have rediscovered, just as the young Pascal "rediscovered," without anyone's assistance, the first thirty-five propositions of Euclid, this rule could be taught him by no one. Because it was nowhere *written down* (or, if it were, was incomprehensible), and it lacked that "perdurable presence" (*das verharrende Dasein*) which Husserl regarded as characteristic of ideal objects, even when their inventors or those associated with their discovery had been dead for centuries. And *writing* should be understood literally here: for "the important function of written, documenting linguistic expression is that it makes communication possible without immediate or mediate personal address; it is, so to speak, communication become virtual . . . Accordingly, then, the writing-down effects a transformation of the original mode of being of the meaning-structure, for example, within the geometrical sphere of self-evidence, of the geometrical structure that is put into words. It becomes sedimented, so to speak. But the reader can make it self-evident again, can reactivate the self-evidence."[8]

Such a *tranformation* presupposes, in the first place, that Brunelleschi shift his gaze from a sky irremediably mute to direct it toward the earth. This earth—as he must have realized in the course of his trip to Rome—on which the past has everywhere left its mark, often undeciphera-

---

7. Manetti, op cit., p. 56; English trans., p. 42.
8. "Es ist die wichtige Funktion des schriftlichen, des dockumentierenden sprachlichen Ausdrucks, dass er Mitteilungen ohne unmittelbare oder mittelbare personliche Ansprache ermoglicht, sozusagen virtuell gewordene Mitteilung ist. . . . Danach vollzieht sich also durch das Niederschreiben eine Verwandlung des ursprunglichen Seinsmodus des Sinngebildes, in der geometrischen Sphäre der Evidenz des zur Aussprache Kommenden geometrischen Gebildes. Es sedimentiert sich sozusagen. Aber der Lesende kann es wieder evident werden lassen, die Evidenz reaktivieren." Husserl, *Die Krisis* . . ., appendix 3 (*Die Ursprung der Geometrie*), op. cit., pp. 371–72; English trans., pp. 360–61.

ble; archaeological traces intermingling so completely with new foundations that one cannot say, when excavations have been carried beyond a certain point, whether invention brings about the discovery of a buried treasure, or, by dint of turning over the constant ground of human experience, it takes root there. On this point, see La Fontaine ("Travaillez, prenez de la peine; c'est le fonds qui manque le moins"; "Work, take the trouble; it's the foundations that are least lacking"), and what Alberti says about the assertion to which the first book of *Della pittura* is a response: that his is an entirely mathematical book which, from roots put down in nature, sends forth this charming, very noble art.[9] Discovery, or invention? The question is meaningless to the geometric mind: "What 'exists' ideally in geometric space is univocally decided, in all its determinations, in advance. Our apodictic thinking, proceeding step-wise to infinity through concepts, propositions, inferences, proofs, only 'discovers' what is already there, what in itself already exists in truth."[10] According to Manetti, Brunelleschi did not regard his "inventions" as a source of pride but made do, when the occasion presented itself, with giving concrete, factual demonstrations (*ma nelle occorenze che venivano, lo dimostrava co'fatti*[11]). At the beginning of the quattrocento the time had not yet come, without doubt, for a perspective demonstration conducted in accordance with the ideal ways of geometry. But what the painters would call *prospettiva* nonetheless originated with this invention in the form of a *di-mostratio*: so true is this that the question of the origin allows of no response other than an invention, whether the latter assumes the status of the origin or there never was any but an *invented* origin.

Brunelleschi, "inventor of the Renaissance"? In the end this formula is acceptable only if we admit that in its inaugural moment—the one assigned it by a tradition which in Manetti, as opposed to Alberti, is anything but rhetorical—the Renaissance had no models at its disposition other than those it had itself produced, made available for its own use, subsequently being reflected, in conformity with the deep-seated movement of reactivation that characterizes it, in the mirror of its own origin. *E pareva che si vedessi 'l proprio vero.*

---

9.   Cf. *supra* chapter 4, note 6.
10.   Husserl, *Die Krisis . . .*, op. cit., p. 19; English trans., p. 22.
11.   Manetti, loc. cit.

*

Even if the Brunelleschi configuration served only to demonstrate the specular coincidence of the point of view and the vanishing point, this demonstration would suffice to confer upon such an "invention" its value and meaning as an *origin,* without there being any need to attribute to its author a premonitory view of subsequent theoretical developments. The essential thing is that this discovery opened a new way, like that of Thales, with which it is implicitly associated. According to Vasari, Brunelleschi understood this very well, soliciting the instruction of geometers in hopes of going beyond "natural" practice to attain the truth of science, whatever might be the possibilities perspective had to offer as means, as technical process. As if this craftsman, this artisan, this constructor, had become conscious of the inversion, implicit in his invention, of practical interest into purely theoretical interest: an inversion by which—to paraphrase Husserl once more—an art founded on measure transforms itself, by way of idealization, into a process of pure geometric thought: the art of perspective, like that, in its time, of measurement, prepared, in accordance with its own ways and means, and in a repetition of the inaugural act of geometry, the appearance of projective geometry, itself linked to a new world of "pure limit-shapes." But Brunelleschi's discovery remains nonetheless paradoxical, with regard to history, as soon as we have access to it only by detouring through tradition and the secondary elaborations occasioned by it, whether Alberti's text or Filarete's, which demand to be investigated as such. And such is, in the end, the original meaning of this discovery (or this invention), that it cannot be regarded as fully secure unless it is seized upon in the moment of its repetition, if not already of its decline: a lost prototype, necessarily so if it was to occupy the originary position in its own field, but one that cannot be confined within the boundaries of either painting or geometry.

When I've made a good painting, I have not written a thought. That's what they say. How simpleminded they are. They deprive painting of all its advantages.

Eugène Delacroix, *Journal,* October 8, 1822

Part Three

SUSPENDED REPRESENTATION

The *Città ideale* and the "Urbino perspectives."

Inventories.

Proof by context.

The Mandrake.

What is thinking?

"Et anticho in prospettiva"

And now, this painting. This painting that you know as well as anyone: which fact obliges me, at this point, to invoke your testimony and pass—in conformity with a usage often encountered in old treatises—from the *I* to the *you*,* and from one discursive regime to another, one that is explicitly "dialogical." The said "Ideal City," because it is under this title that it is currently exhibited in the National Gallery of the Marches, in Urbino. Though you might deem it more consistent with the experience of anyone who goes there to say that this is the title under which the painting *presents itself* in that place, *exhibits itself* there, in the sense of Serlio's *discoprirsi* of a theatrical scene "made by the art of perspective," which he numbers among those things according the greatest pleasure to the eye and satisfaction to the spirit:[1] the reflexive form signaling from the start that we cannot pretend, without considerable impertinence, that such a painting is to be treated however we like, as merely one object or document among others, given that its pictorial mechanics seem to have been conceived precisely to lure anyone stopping in front of it into its game.

(A city, or rather a place, an urban site frozen in a perspective, deploying before the eye the symmetrical fan of its receding lines. The image of a deserted square, roughly rectangular, paved in polychrome marble, bordered along three of its sides by the fronts of palaces and middle-class houses, with a circular building, having two superimposed columnar

---

*   *Tu,* the French familiar form, which Damisch uses from this point to the end of the book—TRANS.
1.   Sebastiano Serlio, *Il secondo libro di prospettiva,* Paris, 1545, fol. 64 verso; in English, cf. facsimile of 1611 edition of the *Treatise on Architecture,* New York, 1970; cf. also *infra,* chapter 12, p. 213.

22 The *Città ideale*, known as the Urbino panel. Urbino, National Gallery of the Marches. Photo: Martino Oberto.

orders and crowned by a conical roof, occupying its center. A view of architecture that connotes "renaissance," and in which the gaze, despite the apparent simplicity of a construction organized around a unique vanishing point established on the central axis of the painting, does not really manage to anchor itself anywhere but rather proceeds, without one's being able to figure out why at first, by successive slippages and—as one would say of an equestrian mount—by ambling about: being continually sent back from the center to the periphery, its allure limited by the extremely wide angle of vision, which seems to have determined the panel's oblong format [239.5 × 67.4 cm] as well as the structure of what is presented as a scenic configuration in which the forward-most lateral structures, two buildings of cubic form, each with one facade parallel to the picture plane, challenge the importance of the central cylindrical volume, somewhat recessed and on a curved surface over which the eye tends to skid.

What is the value of such a "description"? Each of its terms invites discussion, as does the choice of characteristics held to be relevant, and the list of those that were excluded: the problem precisely will be to determine whether, and under what conditions, in accordance with what criteria of relevance and in what order of consequence, a painting such as this permits itself to be described, and demands to be.)

You knew it from your first inspection, which occurred some thirty years ago now: this painting (if such is the appropriate term) is clearly not a painting like others, like, also in this same museum, the *Flagellation* of Piero della Francesca and the *Pentecost* of Signorelli—to choose by design two works in strict perspective, at least one of which (the Signorelli) is not, properly speaking, at least originally, a "painting" at all because it was the banner of a confraternity intended to be carried in processions, subsequently transferred to canvas. In the circumstance the poetic effect (for that is what is in question) owes nothing to fable, or history, unless this be negatively and in a way yet to be defined. The image of this *ideal city* offers nothing to view that can be *narrated:* which provides sufficient justification, in the view of some, for its genre to be qualified as "abstract," for it to be assigned a value that is essentially "decorative." Unless one were to cast into narrative form, or at least that of a *program,* the ordered sequence of trials awaiting any analyst who lets down his guard the least bit, through which he must necessarily pass, for otherwise the title borne by the panel in the museum will be of no help to him.

For soon enough the spectator—or as we ought to say, *il riguardanto,* "the observer," a usage still employed by Poussin: this question is related to that of the "painting"—cannot help but discover that he is implicated in a perfectly calculated apparatus. And this, at least in the first analysis, by the sole effect of a construction that, while it keeps him in a position of exteriority in relation to the "scene" before his eyes, summons him, by the same operation, to its center, to the point henceforth marked, in the painted surface, by a small conical hole, but without furnishing him, as to all appearances would be necessary under the perspective rule, with a stable, secure point, in relation to which he could easily get his bearings in the game in which he must take a stand, however much he's inclined to resist. Hence the suspicion that takes hold of him, before attempting any interpretation, that this game might be governed by a scenario that's more complex than it seems, first, because of the over-ostentatious perspective construction, and then the luminosity, the chromatic brilliance which a recent restoration, directed (you are well placed to judge of this) by a master's hand, restored to a painting long believed lost in a mist accentuating its mysterious character. In its symmetry, also too marked not to be suspect, this painting is the image of the fascination it exerts, to which you yourself have succumbed utterly: to such an extent that you've come to doubt, after having studied it for so many years, whether you've done anything other than try to distance yourself from its power in order to begin to *see* it. The paradox being that this painting exercises its fascination over anyone approaching it, over anyone entering its field of attraction, only by presenting itself as stupefied, fraught in its very visibility (this latter already difficult to understand) with a kind of blindness: there being something in it, to quote Jean Cocteau in one of his great moments, of "that wary eye with which the public recognizes masterpieces."[2] But this paradox, how to account for it, and in what terms? And how are we to say, poetically speaking, what is "proper" to this painting, at least to its difference, without renouncing the exigencies that are those of history, nor the rigor of "scientific" analysis?

*

These questions occupied you while the cleaning was underway, step by step, sometimes separated by long intervals that testify to an infinite num-

---

2. "Cet air d'oeil crevé à quoi le public reconnaît les chefs-d'oeuvre": Jean Cocteau, *Essai de critique indirecte,* Paris, 1932, p. 8.

ber of scruples and precautions even as they facilitated multiple consulta-
tions and deliberations. A task that took almost ten years, at the end of
which, it stands to reason, we ought to know a good deal more about this
painting. More, in any case, if we keep to its visual appearance, than Fiske
Kimball could have known when he undertook to demonstrate, in a key
article, on the basis of evidence internal to the work (a work, I repeat, which
was then drowning in semidarkness, whose graphic aspect seemed to carry
over all others), that its author was Luciano Laurana, the architect of Federico da Montefeltro[3]—an attribution first proposed by Franz von Reber, in
1889, which had hitherto been supported by evidence that was essentially
literary, if not epigraphical (we'll return to this point). To summarize:
according to Kimball, an analysis of the "architectural content" of this *perspective* qualified as "from Urbino," as well as that of another panel, of similar inspiration, in the Walters Art Gallery in Baltimore, which he regarded
as its pendant, this analysis, without becoming caught up in its details,
confirmed the attribution and clarified the debt of Bramante and Raphael,
both from Urbino, to Laurana. Which was held to be so considerable that
the latter merited a place, immediately after Alberti,[4] among the founding
fathers of that moment in the history of art to which specialists refer—
without the epithet signifying anything other than "monumental," in
Nietzsche's sense of the word—as the "High Renaissance": that stature was
not established, still according to Kimball, by an examination of the substantial transformations effected by this architect on the old castle of the
Montefeltre, despite the fact that these make the palace of Urbino (the same
one now housing the National Gallery of the Marches, and thus the *Città
ideale*) one of the key monuments of the era.

Despite the subtlety of Kimball's analysis, you cannot help but
observe that in this trial the presumed author is accorded greater prominence than this work, which is dealt with only as a legal exhibit. The so-
called "internal evidence" operates on two different, though related, levels:
the taxonomic one of names, Laurana competing with other possible

---

3.   Fiske Kimball, "Luciano Laurana and the 'High Renaissance,'" *Art Bulletin,* vol. 10 (1927–
28), pp. 124–51.
4.   Alberti probably met Laurana at Mantua, where he was himself in the service of the Gonzaga
from May 1465 to November 1466; cf. Kimball, ibid., p. 129, note 13.

"authors," whether painters (including Piero della Francesca himself, to whom this painting was long attributed) or architects (such as Francesco di Giorgio Martini, who was placed in charge of construction at the Urbino palace some years after Laurana); and the genealogical one of influences and affiliations, if not that of the periods and epochs according to which the discourse of the history of art is organized. How you regret, given its remarkable pictorial quality, that the nature of the arguments advanced to support this thesis leads us to assess the importance of this painting, and to an even greater extent that of its author, more in terms of architecture than of painting. Its "architectural content" receives greater emphasis than its "pictorial form," about which Kimball admits he has little to say, though he does note the new dimension here bestowed upon architectural surroundings in the name of compositional support, stating that the perspective construction, which he regards as closely related to the diagrams of Piero

della Francesca, implies no theoretical advances upon Alberti, though it does evidence a hitherto unexampled ease in the projection of complex volumes onto a plane.[5]

Kimball's study is without doubt an essential contribution to the large file that has gradually accumulated around the pictures often called, rightly or wrongly, the "Urbino perspectives": mention should here be made of a third panel, at first glance quite different from the other two though it clearly belongs to the same "genre," now in the Bode Museum in Berlin. A file opened for the first time by Passavant when, setting out to reconstitute the milieu shaping of the young Raphael, he studied the Urbino panel, which was then in the sacristy of the convent of Santa Chiara (now

---

5.   Ibid., pp. 148–50.

24 *Architectural Per-
spective*, known as the
Berlin panel. Berlin, Staat-
liche Museen. Photo:
Museum.

"Et anticho in prospettiva"

25   Master of the Barberini Panels, *Birth of the Virgin*. New York, Metropolitan Museum (Rogers and Gwynne M. Andres Fund, 1935). Photo: Museum.

26   Master of the Barberini Panels, *Presentation in the Temple*. Boston, Museum of Fine Arts (Charles Potter Kling Fund). Photo: Museum.

destroyed), and challenged the traditional attribution to Bramante.[6] And that, half a century before this panel entered the collections of the ducal palace, where it joined a small group of important works regularly associated with the reign of Federico di Montefeltro, including the *Flagellation* and the *Madonna of Senigallia* by Piero, the *Desecration of the Host* by Uccello, the portrait of the duke painted by Pedro Berruguete, and the marquetry interior of the *studiolo.*

The fact that the *Città ideale* is now exhibited in a room known as the "dressing room," adjacent to this same *studiolo,* rather begs the question, though this decision is apparently justified by documents that attest the presence, in a neighboring room, in the form of an oblong panel (*un quadro longo*), of an "old but beautiful perspective" which an inventory of 1599 attributed to Fra Carnevale.[7] Fra Carnevale is only a name to us today, but Vasari maintained that Bramante, when still a child, made a study of his works,[8] and some have been tempted to attribute to him the famous "Barberini panels" now in the United States, which feature highly developed, quite sophisticated architectural elements framing their narratives, whether representing the *Birth of the Virgin* (Metropolitan Museum) or the *Presentation in the Temple* (Boston Museum of Fine Arts).[9] (The same observation

6.   Johann David Passavant, *Rafael von Urbino und seine Vater Giovanni Santi,* Leipzig, 1839, vol. 1, p. 422; French translation, Paris, 1860, vol. 1, pp. 380–81. The only reliable information concerning the provenance of this painting is found in a notice dating from 1775, where it is said to be in this same convent, and where it is attributed to Bramante (cf. M. Dolci, *Notizie delle pitture che si trovano nelle chiese e nei palazzi di Urbino, Rassegna Marchigiana,* 1933, pp. 281ff.). This reference, which I take from the excellent catalog prepared by Dante and Grazia Bernini at the conclusion of the restoration performed by Martino and Anna Oberto (*Il restauro della Città ideale di Urbino,* documentary exhibition, Urbino, 1978, p. 12), is not mentioned in the useful survey by Alessandro Conti, "Le prospettive urbinate: tentativo di un bilancio ed abozzo di una bibliografia," *Annali della scuola normale superiore di Pisa, Classe di lettera e filosopfia,* series 3, Pisa, 1976, pp. 1193–1234.

7.   Cf. F. Sangiorgi, *Documenti urbinati. Inventari del palazzo ducale,* Urbino, 1976, p. 76. Inventory of 1599, no. 97: "Un quadro longo di una prospettiva anticha ma bella di mano di Fra Carnevale." Inventory of 1609: "Quadro uno longo de una prospettiva anticha ma bella."

8.   "Ma il padre . . . vedendo che egli si dilettava molto del disegno, lo indirizzo ancore fanciulletto all'arte della pittura, nella quale studio egli molte le cose di fra bartolommeo, altrimenti fra Carnevale da Urbino." Vasari, "Vita di Bramante da Urbino," *Vite,* vol. 4, p. 147.

9.   Cf. Adolfo Venturi, "Nelle pinacoteche minore d'Italia," *Archivo storico dell'arte,* 1893; George Martin Richter, "Rehabilitation of Fra Carnevale," *Art Quarterly,* vol. 3, no. 4 (fall 1940), pp. 311–24; and, most recently, L. de Angelis and A. Conti, "Un libro antico della sagrestia di Sant'Ambrogio: entreta e uscita del podere della Piacentina," *Annali della scuola normale superiore di Pisa,* cited series, pp. 97–105. The attribution to Fra Carnevale is contested by Federico Zeri (*Due dipinti, la filologia e un nome. Il maestro delle Tavole Barberini,* Turin, 1961). Alessandro Parronchi

holds, a fortiori, for several of the *Miracles of Saint Bernardino* panels in Perugia, which have even been attributed to Bramante himself and are often mentioned in studies of the pictures referred to, rightly or wrongly, as the "Urbino perspectives."[10])

---

thinks the two panels are the work of Alberti and that they belonged to an altar frontal, a *sgabello* of much larger dimensions than a traditional predella ("Leon-Battista Alberti pittore," *Studi . . .,* op. cit., pp. 437–67). On the notion of the *sgabello,* see *infra,* chapter 16, p. 402.

10. George Martin Richter, "Architectural Phantasies by Bramante," *Gazette des Beaux-Arts,* vol. 23 (January 1943), pp. 5–20.

notes that the name of the Palazzo Accoramboni in which it was housed suggests a direct link with the Urbino milieu: Ottavio Accoramboni da Gubbio was bishop of Fossombrone from 1579 to 1610 and archbishop of Urbino from 1621 to 1623, and seems to have been much esteemed by the duke Francesco Maria II della Rovere.[17] As for the Berlin painting, acquired in 1896 on the Florentine market, a natural outlet for Urbino collections, under Piero's name, its proportions (140 × 253 cm) are closer to the measurements listed in an inventory of 1582:[18] if, that is, we overlook that it is painted on a panel much too high for an overdoor and that its appearance seems ill-suited to such a function. A document of 1651, preserved in the Archivo di Stato in Florence, lists among the goods of the deceased Agostino Velluti, the former steward of the Della Rovere, *una prospecttiva in tavola lunga palmi 13 et alta palmi 3; di mano di f{ra} Carnevale, pittore celebre et anticho in prospettiva.*[19] While these measurements (approximately 300 × 75 cm) do not correspond with those of the Urbino panel, which we know, since its recent cleaning, has not been cut down, contrary to a hypothesis that has occasionally been advanced, it should be noted that the Baltimore panel is not only the right height (being 220 × 77.4 cm), it also seems to have been altered at both ends; but given the composition, you think it unlikely that it could have been shortened by forty centimeters on each side.

*

Why pretend otherwise? You take great interest in such considerations, even a certain pleasure. It's not only a matter of hearing you pronounce phrases from the inventories: *quadro uno lungo, una prospettiva anticha ma bella,* as well as the enigmatic *et anticha in prospettiva,* which seems to apply less to the painting than to its author and which you find as enchanting as others have found the more noble and poetic *Et in arcadia ego.* . . . Judging from

---

17. Bernini, cited cat., p. 11. Cf. A. Vernarecci, *Fossombrone dai tempi antichi ai nostri,* Fossombrone, 1903, vol. 2, p. 602. The inventory made in 1631, on the occasion of the duke's death, lists under no. 171: "Quadro uno lungo dove vi è dipinta una prospettiva."

18. The 1582 inventory lists, among the "quadri e ritratti diversi," under no. 233, "un quadro lungo tre braccia o poco più e alta una braccia e mezzo in circa con una prospettiva sopra una porta delle camere ducale" (Sangiorgi, op. cit., p. 43).

19. Cf. G. Gronau, "Zu Luciano Laurana," *Repertorium für Kunstwissenschaft,* 1905, p. 95.

the Urbino inventories, it's possible that at the end of the sixteenth century and at the beginning of the seventeenth the style of architecture, if not the image of the city, proposed in the panels they mention might have seemed old-fashioned, out of date.[20] But these inventories explicitly indicate that their archaic effect derived not only from their "architectural content" (to use Kimball's phrase) but was seen, as well, to be a function of the very form of their representation, perspective *as such* having ceased by then to be a subject for painting, at least in quattrocento terms: though its beauty could still be appreciated, the *genre* had become unfashionable. The Florentine inventory, aside from the curious fact that it repeats the attribution to Fra Carnevale (which suggests we might be dealing with one and the same painting), plays upon calculated slippages of meaning: in the Urbino inventories it is "perspective" which is qualified as "ancient," if not "antique" (so true is it that the myth of the origin of perspective imposes an ambiguous reference to the heritage of antiquity, whether the Renaissance properly speaking invented it or only rediscovered it), whereas in the present inventory this descriptive is applied to its author. So the epithet could mean that, however famous he was, this painter gave himself away as a "master of times past" by his interest in perspective as much as his way of using it; unless we are to understand that his celebrity derived from his talent as a perspectivist (evidenced by the fact that the *Brera Altarpiece,* now known to be a work by Piero, was long attributed to him), in which field he had shown himself to be the ancients' equal.

This interest, this pleasure, is justified if, without pursuing the matter any further, we accept that, in studies of art, history always has the first, if not the last, word. The first, which implies that the analysis should be organized, from the beginning, around the questions *When?* and *Where?* But the last as well, seeing as the only interpretations acceptable to it must be verified and validated—when it does not proceed to this task directly— by careful examination of the social and cultural context within which the work first saw light.[21] This argument, which sounds like a summons to

---

20. Bernini, cited cat., p. 7.
21. Cf. Carlo Ginzburg, *Indagini su Piero,* Turin, 1981; English trans. by Martin Ryle and Kate Soper, *The Enigma of Piero,* London, 1985, p. 12.

"scientific" rigor and cannot easily be refuted, nonetheless belongs to a positivist conception of history whose current resurgence is symptomatic. It isn't only that assimilation of the historian to a detective whose task it is to discover the truth about "what really happened" concerning works of art, and the conditions of their production, is naive and dogmatic. In addition to renewing with a shallow historicism,[22] it evidences—which is disturbing in another way—a reversion to a pre-critical approach to cultural history. It is as though historians were willfully ignoring the *fact*—rendered conspicuous by Walter Benjamin and the "reception" theorists—that works cannot be seen (or read) except as filtered through a history that has left the intentions of their creators and the reactions of contemporaries far behind; their pretensions to objectivity go hand in hand with a refusal to acknowledge the implications of the historical moment in which they themselves live, and with a failure to discern the strands that continue to connect the past to the present: "For it is not a question of presenting works in correlation with their time, but rather, in the time in which they are born, of presenting the time that knows them."[23]

That is to say, there's something perverse about your interest in investigating sources in hopes of clarifying the relations between the so-called Urbino perspectives and their original context, not to mention the nature of the "commissions" prompting their production. Let's suppose that these panels were indeed painted in Urbino, during the lifetime of Federico da Montefeltro or shortly after his death, by one of the artists the duke managed to associate with his enterprise, which was both political and constructive; or, alternatively, that they were intended to function as part of the refined exercises indulged in by the court in the environment created for it, where, as Castiglione attests, the memory of his *virtù* had remained remarkably present: the palace, as we read in *The Courtesan,* which he had

---

22. "'The truth will not escape us.' This formula, by Gottfried Keller, designates the precise place in the vision of history proper to historicism in which this last is broken open by historical materialism. For it is an irreplaceable image of the past that threatens to disappear along with everything in the present which is not acknowledged to be implicit in it." Walter Benjamin, "Edward Fuchs, Collector and Historian," *Zeitschrift fur Sozialforschung,* 1937; French trans., *Macula,* no. 3/4, p. 42.
23. Walter Benjamin, "The History of Literature and the Science of Literature"; French trans., *Poésie et révolution,* Paris, 1971, p. 14.

built on the awkward site of Urbino and which, by consensus, was the most beautiful to be seen in all Italy, and so well fitted out in every respect that it seemed "more like a city than a mere palace."[24] These perspectives could then be the typical products of an essentially creative culture which Arnaldo Bruschi has gone so far as to qualify as a *civiltà prospettiva,*[25] dominated from the beginning by the personality of Piero della Francesca, who was soon joined by Laurana, Francesco di Giorgio, Baccio Pontelli, and others, and which shaped men like Bramante and Raphael. Or, alternatively, they could be the fruit of a later moment of the Urbino milieu during which reflection prevailed, without eliminating it completely, over experimentation: the word *esperimentare* appears in the first lines of *The Courtesan.*[26] Although theory was not absent from the era dominated by the figure of Duke Federico: it was for him that Piero wrote his *De prospectiva pingendi,* though the work was not placed in circulation until after the duke's death.

But there is more, demonstrating the degree to which a contextual approach can orient interpretation and influence it, nourish it, without offering any reliable control mechanisms. Confronted with the urban ensembles of which these *perspectives* propose the image, we might well ask ourselves how the idea for them could have developed in a fortified mountain stronghold like Urbino established on the summit of a steep hill in the heart of the Appenines. Some, extrapolating from this fact, have suggested another track, and also a geneology that suits them better. Assuming the question makes any sense at all, the beautiful essay by Fabio Cusin on the Montefeltro dynasty[27] provides us with some of the elements needed for a response. In the Middle Ages the country of the Montefeltre was but one of several *terre castellate* that had sprung up along the indeterminate and mountainous frontier between the domain of the Church and the plains controlled by the emperor. If the land there was not as fertile nor the air as placid as

24. "Questo, tra l'altre cose sue lodevoli, nell'aspero sito d'Urbino edificiò un palazzo, secondo la opinione di molti, il più bello che in tutta l'Italia si ritrovi; e d'ogni opportuna cosa si ben lo fornì, che non un palazzo, ma una città in forma di pallazo esser pareva." Baldasar Castigilione, *Il cortegiano,* book I, section 2; English trans. by George Bull, *The Book of the Courtesan,* Baltimore, 1967, p. 41.
25. Arnaldo Bruschi, *Bramante,* Rome, Bari, 1977, p. 23.
26. "In ultimo, dopo molto pensieri, ho deliberato esperimentare in questo." Castiglione, op. cit., book I, section 1; English trans., p. 39.
27. Fabio Cusin, *La personalità storica dei Ducchi di Urbino,* Urbino, 1970.

Castiglione would have us believe, the profession of arms must have permitted the first Montefeltre to obtain from the emperor titles of nobility guaranteeing control of the lands bearing their name, and at the same time strengthened their power over vassals for whom war represented the only possible source of revenue. Under Federico the dynasty would transfer its allegiance to the Church and break with the Ghibelline model of tyranny to rally, motivated by power politics as much as by reason, behind the idea of a state authority founded on *virtù,* and above all on prudence. Such, in effect, is the first virtue attributed to Federico in *The Courtesan,* whereas his military talents appear well down the list, after humanity, justice, generosity, and unconquerable spirit: and this despite the fact, acknowledged by Castiglione, that mastery of arms had made the fortune of the Montefeltre and provided the duke of Urbino with occasions for him to demonstrate his parity with a number of the more celebrated figures of antiquity.[28] (To cite Walter Benjamin again, this is another indication of the extent to which all cultural productions are always, indissolubly, documents of barbarism.[29])

Et anticho in prospettiva: within the renewed perspective of a history in which reference to antiquity should function as both a principle of intelligibility and as the index of a political task, Federico's enterprise assumes the character of a singularly innovative and original project. Whereas his ancestors had managed to remain in power regionally, and occasionally play roles effecting all of Italy, only by playing the card of war as best they could, notably in view of financial gain,[30] the duke, the first to bear that title by the Pope's grace, opted for peace. But it was an armed peace, and thus a relative one that, what's more, would net this *condottiere* political as well as financial advantages. That indicates that, like his ancestors, he knew how to profit from the strategic position that was his own, somewhat remote from the great urban centers, but setting himself apart from them

---

28. Castiglione, op. cit., book I, section 2; English trans., p. 41.

29. Benjamin, "Edward Fuchs . . .," op. cit., p. 45.

30. If Machiavelli saw in Federico only a formidable man of war, and what's more one who had shifted his allegiances from Florence to the Church, it should be noted that the Montefeltre do not figure in the list he provides "of small princes and men without estate" (*o de' minori principi o di uomini senza stato*) in whose hands were concentrated, in the Middle Ages, all the arms of Italy and who, living from warfare, had formed amongst themselves a kind of tacit understanding that it was a profession, if not an art (*il quale stando in sù la guerra, avevano fatto come una lega e intelligenzia insieme, e riduttala in arte*). Machiavelli, *Istorie fiorentine,* book I, chapter 39; English trans. (unattributed), *The History of Florence,* New York, 1960, p. 45.

he ceased to conduct himself as the leader of a band of mercenaries, fixing his gaze on the plains, turning his attention to acquisition of the means, in the seat of his power, which would permit him to comport himself like a prince, in the modern sense of the word—beginning with a palace, the first of its kind.[31]

In this context we can well imagine that the image of a city on a plain surrounded by steep hills like the one provided by the Urbino panel, that of a city also on a plain and surrounded by walls but rich in antique monuments like the one provided by the Baltimore panel, and that of a city on the coast, at the water's edge such as we see in the Berlin panel—that all these images would have appealed to the minds of an age in which, to cite Machiavelli, the appeal of an easy life encouraged men to emerge from isolation.[32] The well-known portraits of Federico and his wife Battista Sforza now in the Uffizi, which Piero painted as a diptych, meet the same criterion, as the subjects' profiles are inscribed against landscape backgrounds with horizons blocked by a line of hills or mountains, and which, while a bit rough behind the duchess, opens behind the duke onto a large, navigable body of water. The same opposition—which thus accrues a programmatic meaning—is to be found on the backs of the two panels, which bear representations of the triumph of Federico and Battista: almost as if these were the two complementary wings of a single political agenda, one of them affirming the dynasty's geographic roots, the other signaling the opening to the exterior reflected in the duke's enterprises. But if there is a *città ideale,* its image takes on a particular valence when exhibited in the palace at Urbino, in the immediate proximity of the duke's private rooms, and of the *studiolo* which was their inner sanctum. Here again Cusin's text comes to our aid, showing how the construction of this palace (like that of Versailles much later) was both the instrument and the symbol of that of the state, in accordance with Federico's cherished pretentions of seeing the court of Urbino prevail over all others through the order and method—what the French would term *étiquette*—reflected in the arrangement of its spaces. The consummate science presiding over the erection of the gigantic founda-

---

31. Cusin, op. cit., pp. 51ff.
32. Machiavelli, op. cit., book II, section 2; English trans., p. 48.

28   Piero della Francesca, *Battista Sforza* and *Federico da Montefeltro,* dyptich, ca. 1472. Florence,
Uffizi. Photo: Anderson-Giraudon.

tions—which only military engineers of the stature of Laurana and Francesco
di Giorgio could have conceived—makes the structure seem liberated from
topographical constraints, less like a palace poised on the edge of a cliff
than like a city in the form of a palace, to use the phrase coined by Castiglione that would be taken up by Perrault in his evocation of Versailles:[33] a
city, at least in terms of image, and one that, as such, might be reflected in
the idealized representation of an imaginary city with a circular temple at
its center, like the dynastic monument Federico had foreseen erecting in his

---

33. "This is not a palace, but a city entire, / Superb in its grandeur, superb in its materials":
Charles Perrault, *Le Siècle de Louis le Grand,* Paris, 1687.

palace.[34] To such an extent is it true that in Urbino, reality—insofar as this encompassed what was dreamed—preceded utopia.[35]

At a moment when in Rome itself the popes had renounced national ambitions and embraced the necessity for regeneration of the cultural model of the so-called "eternal" city, the project or dream of a "New Rome" could not help but find echo wherever the humanist spirit, far from seeking refuge in contemplation of an inviolate nature, had set itself constructive, urban projects.[36] Some credence is accorded to this project, to this pretention (which extends to the comparison, in Machiavelli's phrase, of small things to large ones, Florence to Rome, for example[37]), to this dream, finally, by the Baltimore panel, with its two typically Roman monuments, its amphitheater and its triumphal arch figuring prominently among other buildings with antique ornament. Save for the fact that the statues supported by the four columns framing the fountain in the foreground correspond to only three of the cardinal virtues, Strength, Justice, and Temperance, with Abundance having taken the place of Prudence. As Federico Zeri has noted, there is nothing accidental about such a substitution, which suggests a mode of government in which the quest for profit carries over all other considerations[38]: which is hardly consistent with what I've just said about the idea of state authority founded on *virtù* and prudence, the primary virtue for Duke Federico, or with the ideal of a "New Rome"

This would present no obstacle, and would rather act as a stimulus to interpretation, if we had proof that these panels were indeed painted in Urbino. But while the inventories of the ducal collections attest the presence in Urbino, from the end of the sixteenth century, of one or more old "perspectives" painted on wooden panels of oblong format, nothing allows us to conclude that these were of Urbinan provenance, or that these were the panels now under discussion. And as for the date of the execution of these latter works, we are reduced to conjecture based primarily on stylistic considerations which, given the highly idiosyncratic genre to which these

---

34. Bruschi, op. cit., p. 29.
35. Cusin, op. cit., pp. 84–88.
36. Ibid.
37. "Questo tenne disunita Roma; questo, si gli è lecito le cose piccole alle grandi aggagliare, ha tenuto diviso Firenze." Machiavelli, op. cit., book III, section 1; English trans., p. 108.
38. Zeri, cited cat., p. 144.

29   Baltimore panel, detail of its central portion.

paintings belong, is rendered even more fragile and subject to doubt than that concerning panels clearly ascribable to a painter designated by name. Like the *Flagellation* by Piero, which has been assigned dates varying as much as twenty and thirty years[39]: discrepencies comparable to those encountered not so long ago in studies of the "Urbino perspectives," dated by some, like Kimball, to the years 1470–1480, while others, including Robert Klein, tended to place them later, in the years around 1500.[40]

A date close to the end of the fifteenth century, or at the beginning of the sixteenth, is supported by those who, like Piero Sanpaolesi and Howard Saalman, remove these panels from the context of Urbino and declare them to be products of Florentine studios somehow linked to the activity of architects such as Giuliano da Sangallo or Baccio d'Agnolo, maintaining that they contain numerous archeological references to contemporary Florence.[41] That does not exclude the possibility that one or another of these paintings, beginning with the *Città ideale,* might have quickly found its

---

39.   Ginzburg, *The Enigma of Piero,* op. cit., chapter 3.
40.   Robert Klein and Henri Zerner, "Vitruve et le théâtre de la renaissance italienne," in *La Forme et l'intelligible,* Paris, 1970, p. 299 (not published in *Form and Meaning,* op. cit.). As for André Chastel, he adopted the theory of their being of Florentine origin: cf. *Art et humanisme . . . ,* op. cit., p. 305, note 2, and p. 364, note 1.
41.   Piero Sanpaolesi, "Le prospettive architettoniche di Urbino, di Baltimora e di Berlino," *Bolletino d'arte,* vol. 34, no. 4 (1949), pp. 322–37; Howard Saalman, "The Baltimore and Urbino Panels: Cosimo Roselli," *Burlington Magazine,* vol. 110, no. 748 (July 1968), pp. 376–83. As the title indicates, Saalman attributes these two panels to Cosimo Rosselli, while allowing that the latter could have based them on drawings by Sangallo.

way to Urbino, where it would have been very well received for all the above-cited reasons.

But the subtlest and most systematic advocate of the hypothesized Florentine origin has been Alessandro Parronchi.[42] Basing his argument on a passage in the "Life of Franciabigio" in which Vasari recounts that this painter conceived, in collaboration with Ridolfo Ghirlandaio, a scenic apparatus including two "perspectives" for the comedies mounted in Florence during the festivities occasioned by the marriage of Lorenzo di Medici and Madeleine de la Tour d'Auvergne, in September 1518,[43] he has assembled an astonishing set of proofs, with Machiavelli's *The Mandrake* serving as the touchstone. Parronchi interprets this comedy, written at the beginning of 1518,[44] as a somewhat satyric allegory of the return of the Medici to Florence, incarnated in the character of Lucrezia who, from the arms of her old husband, passes into those of the handsome and martial Callimachus. Which suggests that the play may have been specially commissioned of Machiavelli and performed for the first time during the first of the three days of celebration, namely on September 7, 1518. And what do we read in the prologue to *The Mandrake?* An invitation for the spectator to consider the scenic apparatus in front of his eyes: "Florence we'll show you now, your home; Tomorrow, maybe, Pisa, Rome."[45] From which derives the idea of identifying the Urbino panel as one of the scenic "perspectives" mentioned by Vasari, and of seeing in it an idealized image of Florence, an argument that is reinforced by the similarity Parronchi perceives between the arrangement of this piazza, with a circular temple at its center and part of the facade of a basilica visible in the background, and the project to transform the surroundings of the Palazzo Medici drawn up by Leonardo da Vinci:

---

42. Parronchi, "La prima rappresentazione della Mandragola. Il modello per l'apparato. L'allegoria," *La Bibliofilia,* vol. 64 (1962), pp. 37–86, and "Due note, 2. Urbino-Baltimora-Berlino," *Rinascimento,* vol. 29 (December 1968), pp. 355–61.

43. "Fece con Ridolfo Ghirlandai un apparato bellissimo per le nozze del duca Lorenzo, con due prospettive per le commedie che si fecero, lavorate molto con ordien e mestrevole giudizio e grazia, per le quali acquisto nome e favore appresso a quel principe." Vasari, "Vita del Franciabigio, *Vita,* vol. 5, p. 195.

44. Cf. Roberto Ridolfi, *Vita di Niccolo Machiavelli,* 7th ed., Florence, 1978, pp. 532ff., note 19, and (concerning the interpretation proposed by Parronchi), p. 538, note 29.

45. "Vedete l'apparato / Qual or vi dimostra: / Quest'è Firenze vostra, Un' altra volta sarà Roma o Pisa." Machiavelli, *La mandragola,* prologue; English trans. by Frederick May and Eric Bentley, *The Mandrake,* in *The Classic Theatre,* vol. 1, Garden City, 1958, p. 3.

Didn't the latter envision tearing down the church of San Giovannino, thereby facilitating the creation of a large piazza in front of San Lorenzo in which he proposed to construct a circular temple with a cupola, an emblem traditionally associated with the glory of the Medici?[46]

Quest'è Firenze vostra. Un' altra volta sarà Roma o Pisa: several texts brought together by Parronchi indicate that on an undetermined date Lorenzo Strozzi had had one of his comedies performed at the Medici palace, in Lorenzo's presence, using a "perspective" by Ridolfo Ghirlandaio, and that a comedy entitled *La Falargo* was given on the night of September 8, 1518, as part of the Medici festivities. Parronchi identifies the Baltimore panel with the *Commedia in versi* by the same Lorenzo Strozzi, which is set in Rome and was thus consistent with the announcement made in the *Mandrake* prologue on the first day. The Baltimore panel having been situated in this way, it remained only for the Berlin panel to be identified as an evocation of Pisa, where another of Strozzi's comedies, *La Pisana,* takes place, and which would have been performed on September 9, within the above-mentioned apparatus: Pisa, which had been revivified under the Medici and which provided Florence with a natural outlet to the sea, even if, as Machiavelli observes, its lagoon was less extensive than the sea at Livorno.[47]

The fact that at least one of the so-called "Urbino" perspectives soon found its way to that city is easily explained: Lorenzo di Medici, having been named Duke of Urbino by Leo X, who had just deposed Francesco Maria della Rovere, would have brought it with him when he made his entry into the city early in 1519. Does not Vasari mention this prince's interest in the scenic apparatus devised by Franciabigio, which led to the latter's being summoned to work on the decor of the villa at Poggio e Caiano, where he could give free reign to his architectural fantasies while continuing to display his gifts for perspective?[48] And the *Città ideale* may not have made the trip alone: Parronchi has uncovered, in a manuscript account of a trip to Urbino made by two envoys of Clement IX, evidence

---

46. Cf. Carlo Pedretti, *A Chronology of Leonardo da Vinci's Architectural Studies after 1500,* Geneva, 1962, pp. 124ff; Parronchi, "Due note . . .," cited art., pp. 357–58.

47. Machiavelli, *The Mandrake,* act I, scene ii.

48. "Laonde il Francia fece nella parte sua, oltre la bellezza della storia, alcuni casamenti misurati molto bene in prospettiva." Vasari, "Vita del Franciabigio," op. cit., p. 196.

for the presence, in one of the patrician residences they visited, of a painting of oblong format by Ridolfo Ghirlandaio, "among the oldest we have," representing a temple with several delicately colored figures, a panel which he believes is to be identified with the one in Baltimore.[49]

If I've described this theory in some detail, this is because it has been very poorly received, in some instances by individuals who are far less demanding than Parronchi where proofs are concerned. At a moment in which young historians tend to dismiss any interpretation not based upon "an analytical reconstruction of the intricate web of minute relations that underlies the production of any work of art, however simple,"[50] Parronchi's work on *The Mandrake* should be saluted as a precursor of "micro-history." But the resistance he has encountered is of an entirely different epistological order: in the current climate of opinion, any suggestion of a date as late as 1518 for the panels in Urbino, Baltimore, and Berlin seems a deliberate provocation. It's all very well for Parronchi to say he is convinced (as you are not) that the spatial construction of the *Città ideale* would have been impossible before Leonardo's work on atmospheric perspective had made an impact on painterly practice: the fact remains that the theatrical "perspectives" developed by Franciabigio and Ridolfo Ghirlandaio could only have been perceived, at this date and within the context of contemporary Florentine painting, as archaicizing. In this instance, as in others, we must come to terms with a well-established prejudice holding that any work of importance must be a beginning, if not an origin, which would seem to preclude us from regarding a painting of the manifest quality of the *Città ideale* as (to use contemporary French slang) a *rétro* exercise or, to use Parronchi's term, as an example of "neo-quattrocentism" at the beginning of the sixteenth century.[51] But don't the inventories from this same sixteenth

49. "E d'più antichi, che abbiamo." Parronchi, "Due note . . .," cited art., p. 358.

50. Ginzburg, op. cit., English trans., p. 12.

51. Parronchi, "Due note . . .," op. cit. 1968, p. 359. Elsewhere Parronchi observes that according to Vasari Franciabigio owned a painting by Masaccio, which some are tempted to identify with a perspective exercise by Masolino, of which the well-known small panel which Berenson attributed to Andrea di Giusto, *The Healing of the Lame Man* in the Johnson Collection in Philadelphia, would be a copy (cf. Curtis Shell, "Francesco d'Antonio and Masaccio," *Art Bulletin*, vol. 47 [1965], pp. 465–69). The resemblance between the interior of the church in which the scene unfolds and that of the cathedral of Florence brings us back to Brunelleschi.

30   Andrea di Giusto (?), *Healing of the Lame Man*. Philadelphia, Museum of Art (John G. Johnson Collection). Photo: Museum.

century insist, precisely, on the archaic connotations of the *perspectives* listed in them?

Parronchi's argument has a certain coherence, though its logic is circular.[52] But in your view the essential considerations lay elsewhere. You accept the idea that these three panels conventionally designated as the "Urbino perspectives" make up a coherent, systematic group, though in ways not spelled out in previous studies, however interesting these may be. Riding the demon of attribution so far as to attribute to Franciabigio the Urbino panel (whose "shadowy" appearance before the recent cleaning struck him as consistent with this painter's style), and giving those of Baltimore and Berlin to Ridolfo Ghirlandaio, Parronchi takes from Vasari the idea of a possible collaboration between the two artists, and does not exclude the possibility that they may have used drawings by Sangallo and Domenico Ghirlandaio, Ridolfo's father, just as the comedies by Lorenzo Strozzi may well have been the fruit of a collaboration between their avowed author and Machiavelli.[53] What strikes you as important here is that this would allow one to entertain the possibility that, in strictly historical terms, not only might these three panels be related, not only might they belong to the same family, more or less extended, they might have resulted from a single commission and thus echo a single project—in short, *respond to one another.*

Is the historian obliged to seek out a hypothetical document that would permit him to settle the debate between partisans of relatively early or relatively late dates, and between supporters of an Urbinan as opposed to a Florentine origin? You point out that the spread of possible dates implied by the various hypotheses has widened, now spanning half a century (surely some kind of record), and that the focus of attention has moved from Urbino to Florence, without there having been any change in the way the *theoretical* problem of these panels is posed. And more serious still: without the results of the recent cleaning, which completely transformed the appearance of the *Città ideale,* having been taken into account in any serious way. It's not that there's nothing to be said about these panels, considered in and

---

52. It is not altogether legitimate to maintain that, once the comedies corresponding to them have been identified, these latter enable us to date the panels; for these comedies would not have been identifiable or datable (except for *The Mandrake,* and in relation to it) save on the basis of the panels themselves and of the trio Florence/Pisa/Rome with which they are consistent.

53. Parronchi, "La prima rappresentazione della mandragola . . .," op. cit. 1962, pp. 72–76.

of themselves, that might interest historians and from which they might eventually profit, if only they knew how to hear and understand questions put to them in terms of structural analysis. On the contrary, the failure of positivist, factual history seems to you to justify, *in this particular case,* an approach to these works conducted differently, by other means and according to methods different from those of detective work, with greater attention being paid, in terms of style and iconography, to what determines their originality, their specificity in the context implied by their having been posited as a series, today, "in the time in which they are known." An approach, in a word, that is less casual and more respectful of the play of thought which is manifestly a factor here. But what then is thinking, if painting can present it with options and offer it means, be constitutive of it—the only question, in the end, that matters to you, or to me?

Evasive tactics.

The tragic scene and the comic scene.

The view (continued).

Architectural references.

The theater and "flat" painting.

Illusion and trompe l'oeil

Scenography.

The case of set design.

A long-established procedure.

T W E L V E

Distancing Maneuvers

I term here "distancing" (*désinvolture*, from the Italian *dis-* and *involta*, "enveloped," "packaged") the liberating resolution, taken in the presence of a painting such as the Urbino *Città ideale*, to resist giving in to it and to persist in putting questions to it, in considering it from different angles and submitting it to sustained interrogation: Who can have been the author of this painting? When was it painted, and where, in what context, to what end, in response to what commission? And further: What exactly does it represent? To what genre does it belong? What could have been its *function*? All these questions are standard ones in the history of art, though they are usually formulated separately from one another. But the last one, that which deals with use value, is rarely framed so directly, so plainly: and the fact that I so frame it can be taken as an indication of just how urgently many feel a need to keep their distance from a work that is so unseemly, even *indiscreet,* and, if not rid themselves of it altogether, then—an appropriate phrase here—keep it in its place. Such distancing gestures then appear to be just what they are: tactics of evasion or flight—flight from thought as much as from the painting.

Let's be frank: the question of attribution does not particularly interest you, although you're intrigued by it. But what intrigues you even more is the strange discomfort you feel on reading Richard Krautheimer's well-known study of the Baltimore and Urbino panels[1]: you're not convinced by it; its argument, though seductive, strikes you as untenable, at least as presented; and yet you prefer its virulence, always active, to the

---

1.   Richard Krautheimer, "The Tragic and Comic Scenes of the Renaissance. The Baltimore and Urbino Panels." *Gazette des Beaux-Arts,* vol. 33 (1948), pp. 327–48; republished in R. K., *Studies in Early Christian, Medieval and Renaissance Art,* 1969, pp. 345–59.

31   Sebastiano Serlio,
*Comic Scene. Il secondo
libro dell' architettura,*
Paris, 1545, fol. 67 bis.
Photo: Bibliothèque
Nationale, Paris.

32   Sebastiano Serlio,
*Tragic Scene. Il secondo
libro dell' architettura,* fol.
69. Photo: Bibliothèque
Nationale, Paris.

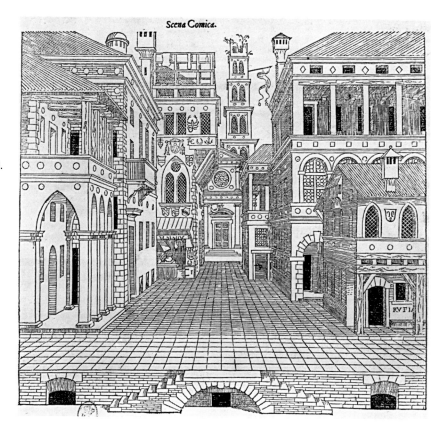

Scena Comica.

swarm of objections it prompted, and you agree with Parronchi that without doûbt it was dismissed with undue haste.[2]

At first this publication, which appeared twenty years after Kimball's, seems to address a very different problem. Krautheimer makes no
pretense of proposing new information bearing on the attribution to
Laurana. Nor does he deny that these panels have a niche in the history of
architecture. His goal is quite different: he intends to explicate the thematic
material of these paintings, their "subject matter"—in a word, to determine
what they "represent." Which amounts to situating them within another
context, inscribing them within another history. Krautheimer notes that
these panels are often designated, described, cited, invoked in the specialized literature as either "architectural perspectives" or as "stage designs."

2.   Parronchi, "Due note . . .," op. cit., p. 355.

Now these two appellations are not incompatible, given that so-called "Italian" theatrical decors were largely the province of architects (to become convinced of this one has only to read the *Trattato sopra le scene* which Serlio inserted into book II of his *Architecture, Libro de prospettiva*); but Krautheimer aims to prove that these are examples of theater architecture: the panels in question would be the first figural representation of the "tragic scene" and the "comic scene" as Serlio was to describe them, borrowing from drawings by his master Peruzzi and from the text by Vitruvius maintaining that different kinds of scenery are distinguished by ornamental elements that observe, in their distinctions from one another, precise rules and reasoning (*inter se dissimili disparaique ratione*[3]). In conformity with this text, which in

---

3.   "Genera autem sunt scaenarum tria: unum quod dicitur tragicus, alterum comicum, tertium satyricum. Horum autem arnatus sunt inter se dissimili disparique ratione, quod tragicae deformantur columnis et fastigiis et signis reliquisque regalibus rebus; comicae autem aedificiorum privato-

Perrault's translation specifies that "the tragic scene must have columns, elevated pediments, statues, and other such ornamental elements appropriate for a royal palace," the Baltimore panel features noble, severe pedimented buildings resembling ancient palaces framing a small piazza adorned with columns surmounted by statues, as well as, in the background, a veritable museum of ancient architecture, replete with amphitheater, triumphal arch, and even an octagonal temple with marble revetments suggestive of the first Florentine "Renaissance." As for the Urbino *Città ideale,* it is characterized by facades largely devoid of ornament, by the opening of a broad loggia on the upper floor of the palace in the left foreground, and by the presence, in the center of the composition, of a circular building which Krautheimer doesn't hesitate to identify as a *macellum,* a Roman open market, all of which is consistent with the Vitruvian definition stipulating that "the decoration of a comic scene should represent private houses, with balconies and windows treated like those of common, ordinary buildings."

You maintain that, despite appearances, Krautheimer's argument is not so very different from Kimball's, that in its way it "distances" just as much, because both authors avoid the question posed by these paintings as they are presented (or as they present *themselves*) in museums. And because they avoid it by pretending that the only thing that interests them about these works is what they "represent," that to which they refer, the key to which is to be found by searching in books: but not without the accent thus placed on "content" referring them back to a notion of "form" predicated upon a strict adequation of container and content, of representation and represented. Between form and content, and between "architectural" and "theatrical" content, no contradiction, and no solution of continuity (save in the case of the supposed *macellum*). If we are to believe Kimball (and Krautheimer certainly doesn't contradict him on this point), the panel in Urbino, like that in Baltimore, instantiates an architectural ideal inherited from Alberti, one that reveals itself, on a formal register as well as in the buildings' arrangement and their regular alignment surrounding one or more isolated monuments, designated as poles of these urban compositions, in the *all'antico* treatment of the facades, the continuity of rooflines, cor-

---

rum et maeniarorum habent speciem profesctusque fenestris dispositos imitatione communium aedificiorum rationibus. . . ." Vitruvius, *De architectura,* book V, chapter 6.

33   Baldassare Peruzzi, *Architectural Perspective.*
Florence, Uffizi, Department of Drawings. Photo:
Museum.

nices, etc.[4] Now this ideal accords nicely with the system that would
become the norm in sixteenth-century theatrical decor and of which Serlio
was the principal advocate. But in your view this is not the essential point:
you hold this to be rather that in this context perspective appears to be no
more than a simple means in the service of architecture or scenography. Of
architecture *and* scenography, if it's true that these "became nearly synony-
mous,"[5] as in the drawing by Peruzzi preserved in the Uffizi and which,
while it may represent a theater set (as is suggested by Serlio's having used
it for his engraving of the tragic scene in his treatise), nonetheless seems to
belong to the genre of architectural *vedute.*[6]

4.   Kimball, op. cit., pp. 145–46.
5.   Krautheimer, "The Tragic and Comic Scenes . . .," op. cit., p. 328; *Studies . . .*, p. 346.
6.   Uffizi, Department of Drawings, no. 291 A; cf. Serlio, *Il secondo libro dell'architettura*, fol. 69
recto; English facs. ed., op. cit., 1611/1970, fol. 25 verso; and Klein and Zerner, "Vitruve et le
théâtre . . .," in *La Forme et l'intelligible*, op. cit., 1970, p. 298.

34 The *Città ideale* or Urbino panel, left portion.
Photo: Martino Oberto.

You want also to be very clear about what this means, which is far
from obvious. You question the meaning of the word *veduta* as employed in
the expression *veduta architectonica,* as well as that accruing to the term *archi-*
tectonica when coupled with the word *prospettiva,* a phrase used to designate
the Urbino panel until very recently (it was still employed in the catalog of
the exhibition at the National Gallery of the Marches in 1973, where the
painting was displayed half-cleaned, with two strips emerging from the gray
murk laid over it by time[7]): "View," "perspective" *of architecture? Architec-*
tural "view" or "perspective"? The choices available to the translator only

7. *Restauri nelle Marche,* Urbino, 1973, cat. no. 54, pp. 228–32. The accompanying entry by
G. Marchini refers to the appellation *Città ideale* only to dismiss it.

35   The *Città ideale,* or Urbino panel, right portion. Photo: Martino Oberto.

serve to emphasize the reciprocal implications linking perspective to architecture, and the idea of the "view"—in the sense of the word we acquired
through analysis of Brunelleschi's experiments—to that of construction.

*

The questions raised by the phrases "view of architecture" and "architectural
perspective" cannot be contained within the limits of a problematics of
"genre," any more than within those of a regional history like that of architecture and/or scenography. But you do not maintain that the Urbino perspectives have nothing to do with the form of architecture admired at the
time, which architects endeavored to realize, or of which they dreamed, or
in which—as the term "renaissance" implies—the future was conjugated
with the past in a kind of dream work in which contradiction, displace-

36 Leone-Battista Alberti, Palazzo Rucellai in Florence, built by B. Rossellino after designs by Alberti, 1447–51. Photo: H.D.

37 Baccio d'Agnolo (?), Palazzo Cocchi in Florence, early sixteenth century. Photo: H.D.

ment, and condensation eventually played a role, even in architecture that was actually built. You wouldn't dream of denying this. How could you, given the exceptional grasp of architectural renderings, at least in the form of graphic representations, apparent in these works?

For the moment you want to remain focused on a few exemplary characteristics of the Urbino panel that manifest the complexity of the problems that lead historians to contradictory conclusions. In the facades of the palaces in the foreground, you single out the rhythmic bays *all'antico,* a motif introduced by Alberti in the Palazzo Rucellai, constructed in Florence, and according to his plans, by Bernardo Rossellino between 1447 and 1451, and taken up by Laurana in the court of honor of the palace in Urbino. But which is given a new inflection in the palace on the right, where the bays are separated, at each story, not by a pilaster but by a half-

column, fixed to what seems to be a pier that's shallow but rather wide and that supports the springs of the arches above the windows: a motif rarely encountered in built architecture, in this form, prior to the late fifteenth century or the beginning of the sixteenth, as in the facade of the small Palazzo Cocchi on the Piazza Santa Croce, attributed to Baccio d'Agnolo.[8]

You also single out the wide exterior loggia on the top floor of the palace to the left: again, a motif that appears in urban architecture only at the beginning of the sixteenth century, in Florence, and in the context of a facade design that's much more archaizing than this one: as in the Palazzo Guadagni on the Piazza Santo Spirito, erected 1503–1506, probably by Cronaca, or the Palazzo Nicollino on the via della Spada, built in 1550

---

8. Sanpaolesi, "Le prospettive architettoniche . . .," op. cit., p. 329.

according to designs by Baccio d'Agnolo—the same Baccio d'Agnolo to
whom some have been tempted to attribute the Palazzo Guadagni, and
whose name has been linked, as we shall see, with the Baltimore panel.
According to Serlio, the loggia or, as it was then called, the *pergola* is
extremely effective in the theater, for its openings facilitate the evocation of
tall buildings behind it and its deep cornices, whether in relief or painted
on backdrops, emphasize corners and allow for striking effects of foreshortening and depth.[9]

 Again, you draw attention to the highly original solution to the
problem of the perpendicular articulation of two facades *all'antica*. Alberti's
Palazzo Rucellai has only a fragment of a lateral facade, its single corner
pilaster being joined to that of the street facade. And as for the Palazzo
Piccolomini, erected by Rossellino along the same lines in Pienza (that

9. "Come saria portico traforato, dietro del quale si vegga un altro casamento, come questo
primo. . . . Li poggivoli, altri le dicono pergola; altri renghiere: hanno gran forza nelle facie che
scurzano, e cose qualche cornice che li suoi finimenti vengono fuori del suo cantonale tagliati
intorno ed accompagnati non l'altre cornice dipinte: fanno grande effetto." Sebastiano Serlio, *Il
secondo libro di perspettiva. Trattato sopra le scene,* Paris, 1545, fol. 67 recto; English facs. ed., 1611/
1970, fol. 24 verso.

39   Bernardo Rossellino, Palazzo Piccolomini in
Pienza, 1459–63: loggia overlooking the valley.
Photo: H.D.

40   Luciano Laurana, Court of Honor in the Palazzo Ducale in Urbino, 1468–72: corner detail.
Photo: H.D.

other "ideal city," though one that was actually *realized*), the *all'antica*
facade abutting the three-floor loggia opening toward the valley is simply
stuck onto it, its cornice brutally interrupted to make way for a projecting
roof. Whereas in Florence the archaizing formula of corner embossments
would prevail (as in the Palazzo Guadagni), this problem here finds its
clearest resolution in the guise of two antithetical solutions presented on
opposite sides: the corner is either marked by an apparent pier constituted
by two pilasters joined at a right angle, as in the Palazzo Rucellai, a solution retained by the painter for the two palaces on the left; or the exterior
bays are slightly recessed in relation to the corner wall, which is exposed in
the interval between two columns of pilasters. Having admired the elegance
of the palace in Urbino on each of your visits there, you know very well
that this last solution, employed in the palace on the right, was used by
Laurana in his court of honor, its novelty there consisting of its being

41 The *Città ideale,* the "basilica."

applied to a real building's exterior, and to enclosing corners rather than projecting ones.

And finally, at least for now, you point to the facade of the basilica glimpsed at the back of the piazza, half obscured by the mass of the circular building in its center, its polychrome marble ornament so reminiscent of the church of the Madonna delle Carceri in Prato, noting its resemblance to a drawing by the latter's architect, Giuliano da Sangallo. Which has prompted some to connect the Urbino panel to the circle of Sangallo,[10]

10. This hypothesis was first advanced by C. Huelsen, in connection with a drawing in the Sangallo notebook (C. H., *Il libro di Giuliano da Sangallo Codice Vaticano Barberino Latino 4424,* Leipzig, 1910, pp. 15–16.

suggesting that he either painted it himself[11] or had someone else execute it after one of his drawings.[12]

You're conversant with all these suggestions, which have the merit of obliging us to consider the painting very carefully, focusing our attention on numerous details that might be thought to be of interest only to specialists in architectural history but all of which you sense to be important, to be potentially relevant, despite the fact that structural analysis has not been able to make much of them. And you're perfectly aware of what's at stake in these discussions: whether one inclines toward Laurana (who died in 1479), toward Francesco di Giorgio (who died around 1502), or toward an architect of the generation of Sangallo (who died in 1515), the probable date of the panel's execution must be calculated in relation to these death dates: situated in the 1470s, in the case of Laurana; around 1500, or even later, if one accepts the Sangallo hypothesis. Which decision is not without consequences by the standards of art history: in one case the painting would be remarkably precocious, to the point of seeming to be an "avant-garde" work, in any case one by a personality of the first order, which as such would pose certain problems; in the other, we would be dealing with a production that required less impressive skills and that might eventually be attributed to a lesser artist, one who as a result would gain in stature, even if he'd collaborated with an architect in producing it.

*

For Kimball the matter admits of no doubt: the Urbino panel is in every respect an innovative work demonstrating the degree to which Laurana set the tone for the generation of architects succeeding him, several of whom, including some of the greatest, must have undergone apprenticeships of one kind or another at Urbino. As for Krautheimer, he has no problem with the date (the 1470s) seemingly implied by a set of arguments which I'll address

---

11. Cf. Bernard Degenhardt, "Dante Illustrationen Giuliano da Sangallos in ihren Verhältnis zu Leonardo da Vinci und zu den Figurenzeichnungen den Sangallo," *Römische Jahrbuch fur Kunstgeschichte,* vol. 7 (1955), pp. 233–35.

12. Sanpaolesi (op. cit., p. 335) maintains that the Urbino and Baltimore panels are the work of a Florentine painter, executed after drawings by either Sangallo alone (for the Urbino panel) or by Sangallo and Baccio d'Agnolo (for the one in Baltimore).

briefly below (perhaps not so briefly). But for him, as for Kimball, the goal was to demonstrate that we are dealing with an inaugural work, with a kind of origin (in other words with a question, that of the "origin" and its repetition, from which one can never escape in Renaissance studies): as the first representation of the "comic scene" which Serlio would derive from Vitrivius seventy or seventy-five years later, this panel would initiate a series, one not without connection, by way of the theater, to architecture.

No one would deny that this "ideal city" (in this context, after all, the title should have a certain appeal for you), that this survey, better yet, or that this *view* of an urban complex then without example in reality, simultaneously gives every appearance of being a theater set, one in the Italian style with an illusionist character borrowed from perspective. This is due of course to the very nature of the perspective configuration and to the task Alberti assigned to the painter: that of constructing a scene in which, by a kind of *repetitio rerum,* the *istoria,* the main focus of painting, could be represented.[13] The impression of "theatricality" is reinforced by the disposition of the various elements, which creates two lateral flanks, in imitation— as Alberti says of buildings intended for theatrical presentations—of an army in battle formation.[14] And also, as has often been noted,[15] by the absence in this theater of any and all human presence. This absence or imminence being signaled by two pigeons on the cornice of the palace in the right foreground, reminiscent of the two doves in the story of Noah's ark.[16] A desert, then, but of architecture, and of architecture seemingly untouched by time, there being no traces of rising waters or accumulating sand, and only the slightest hints of invading vegetation, though the plant on a windowsill near the two birds spreads its foliage incongruously. A desert, but one in which everything speaks of man, beginning with the obstinate repetition of doors and windows, open, closed, or somewhere in between, one of the features that most interests you. It's as though the operations of art had been halted midway and the painting thrown back-

---

13. Cf. my *Théorie du nuage,* op. cit., pp. 152–58.
14. "Spectacula ferme omnia structam cornibus ad bellum aciem imitantur." Leon-Battista Alberti, *De re aedificatoria,* book VIII, chapter vii; cited from the edition by G. Orlandi and P. Portoghesi, Milan, 1966, vol. 2, p. 729.
15. Conti, op. cit., p. 1195.
16. Bernini, cited cat., p. 6.

ward into an indeterminate time, a purified interval in which before and
after are blended and merged, a moment of representation indefinitely
suspended.

Contemplating this scene—if "scene" there is—one cannot say
whether man has just withdrawn or whether he's about to make his appearance. As in the theater when, between acts or scenes, the lights are about to
go out or have just been turned on again. But Krautheimer—like Kimball,
and most of those who've written about it—was only able to study the
painting prior to its recent cleaning, in the course of which it emerged from
the shadows not with a slow consistency but fragment by fragment, like a
work of marquetry accumulating over a period of years, until the entire
surface was uncovered, a process that began with the preliminary removal of
patches of thick varnish, revealing the astonishing pictorial quality of what
lay beneath. A quality that, in itself, poses a problem. If we persist in
seeing this painting, like those linked with it, as a singularly precocious
representation of Italian scenography, then we are confronted with a paradox: How can that which constitutes the ground, the basis, the frame if not
the form of the representation be figured, as such, using means belonging
to painting, and with what consequences for our idea, our very conception
of *representation*? Then again, these works might simply be scenic designs
similar in type to those Serlio was to describe admiringly in his treatise
(here I cite from Serlio's text via a translation by Jean Martin which contains several errors, noting that this description is especially relevant to the
Baltimore panel):

> Among the things made by the hand of man capable of inducing
> wonder, and of providing pleasure to the eye as well as satisfaction
> to the mind (*fra l'altre cose fatte per mano degli huomini che si possono
> mirare con gran contezza d'occhio e satisfationi d'animo*), in my judge-
> ment [one should place] scenic apparatuses which have just been
> revealed (*il discoprirsi lo apparato di una scena:* literally, the way a
> scenic apparatus *reveals itself* when the curtain hiding it *falls*). The
> reason for this is, that one sees such and such a palace made by the
> art of perspective (*dove si vede in piccol'spazio fatto da l'Arte della
> perspettiva, supervi palazzi . . . .:* perspective allows for the construc-
> tion of scenic places such that in these "small spaces", these

reduced areas, buildings which appear to be superb palaces can be invoked), with large temples and diverse houses both near and far off, beautiful and spacious piazzas ornamented with various buildings (*amplissimi tempii, diversi casamenti, e da presso, e di lontano, spacioso piazze ornate di varii edificii:* it is the piazzas as much as the buildings that are said to impress the eye as being at different distances, which implies that within the frame of a given scene other perspectives could be introduced, thereby multiplying or redoubling the configuration), long straight streets crossed by transverse ones, triumphal arches, columns of great height, pyramids, obelisks, and a thousand other beautiful things (*dritissisme et longhe strade incrociate da altre vie, archi trimphali, altissisme colonne, obelischi, et mille altre cose belle*[17]).

A scenic model, in the generic sense of the word, or a design for a specific production: this latter interpretation, however seductive (and which, as Parronchi observes, doesn't exclude the possibility that the painter set out to demonstrate his talents, perhaps aiming to give the force of painting to simple theater "perspectives" in hopes of attracting attention), is deficient in your view because it fails to take account of the considerable difficulties raised by any realization of such a model or design. You caution that when we speak of scenic perspective, we must be careful not to take it for granted that the perspective in question is that of painting, even though Italian scenic design acquired its unity in reference to an ideal plane and the point of view of a privileged spectator seated in the center of the auditorium at

---

17. Serlio, *Il secondo libro,* op. cit., fol. 64 verso; English facs. ed., fol. 24 recto. This text should be considered along with Vasari's description of the scenography and "perspectives" conceived by B. Peruzzi for a production of *Calandria,* a comedy by Cardinal Bibiena, one of the first in "vulgar" Italian, mounted by Pope Leo X in 1513, in which year the play was also performed in Urbino (Cf. below, p. 216). "Basta che Baldassare fece al tempo dit Leone X due scene che furono maravigliose, ed apersono la via a coloro che hanno poi fatto a'tempi nostri. Ne si può immaginare, come egli in tanta strettezza di sito accommodasse tante strade, tanti palazzi, e tante bizzarie di templi, di loggie, e d'andari di cornici cosi ben fatte, che parevano non finte, ma verissime, e la piazza non una cosa dipinta e picciola, ma vera e grandissima. Ordino egli simultaneamente le lumiere, i lumi di dentro che servono alla prospettiva, e tutte l'altre cose che facevano di bisogno, con molto giudizio, essendossi, come ho detto, quasi perduto del tutto l'uso delle comedie. . . ." Vasari, "Vita di Baldassare Peruzzi," op. cit., vol. 4, pp. 600–601; English trans., vol. 2, p. 1000. This text confirms the importance of Peruzzi's role as scenographic architect, even as it reinforces arguments dear to his disciple.

the proper distance.[18] Under such a hypothesis no attempt is made to solve the problem of how to proceed from a wholly imaginary perspective, that—to cite the French translator of Serlio—of *la plate peinture,* of "flat painting," to this other mode of perspective which was that of the theater, which had its own distinct rules from the moment it dealt with real depth and volume, even though these were presented in foreshortening: the one being *imagined,* as indicated by Serlio's phrase, on a flat surface, the other being material, and in relief.[19]

The few descriptions of theatrical productions dating from the end of the quattrocento and the beginning of the cinquecento, including the evocation, in Castiglione's correspondence, of the performance of Bibiena's *Calandria* at Urbino in 1513, in a production overseen by Girolamo Genga, contain little that might help us to understand how a two-dimensional model would have aided, in the absence of an actual theater, in the construction of even a temporary set. It would be different if we were dealing with simple backdrops, as may have been the case in the first performance in Ferrara, in 1508, of Ariosto's *Cassaria,* with scenery painted by Pellegrino di San Daniele consisting of a "perspective" with various buildings, houses, churches, and towers surrounded by gardens, which was so well conceived and so agreeable to the eye, we are told, that it would have been worthy to preserve for use on other occasions:[20] and this is the earliest known mention of an illusionistic decor painted and/or constructed in per-

18. Georges R. Kernodle, *From Art to Theater: Form and Convention in the Renaissance,* Chicago and London, 1944, pp. 178ff.

19. "Pure quantunque questo modo di Perspettiva di ch'io parlaro sia diverso dalle regole passate: per essere quelle imaginate sopra li pariete piani: e questa per essere materiale e di rilievo e ben ragione a tener altre strade." Serlio, loc. cit.. The problem of the relation between architecture that is built or sculpted, in three dimensions, and painted or feigned architecture, in two dimensions, is not limited to scenography: it is also important in altar painting, notably in Siena. In the work of the Lorenzetti brothers, as in that of their Flemish imitators, the architectural frame of the representation is extended onto, or echoed by, the sculpted or constructed frame of the altarpiece. Cf. Lotte Brand Philip, *The Ghent Altarpiece and the Art of Jan van Eyck,* Princeton, 1971, pp. 8–9.

20. Cf. the letter from Bernardino Prosperi to Isabella d'Este, cited by G. Campori, *Notizie per la vita di Ludovico Ariosto,* Modena, 1871, p. 68 (Conti, "Le prospettive urbinate," op. cit., p. 1206, note 14): "Di quello che è stato il meglio in tutte queste feste e rappresentazioni è stato tutte le scene dove si sono rappresentate, quale ha facte uno maestro Peregrino depintore che sta con il Signore, che una è contracta e prospettiva di una terra cum case, chiese, companile e zardini, che la persona non si può satiare a guardarle per le diverse cose che ge sono; tutto de inzegno e bene intese quale non credo se guasti, ma che la salarono per usarla da le altre fiate." On Pallegrino di San Daniele, a painter from Friulia, cf. Conti, loc. cit.

spective. But questions remain in connection with the text by Vasari describing the scenic apparatus and the "perspectives" conceived by Franciabigio and Ridolfo Ghirlandaio for the comedies mounted in Florence on the occasion of the marriage of Lorenzo di Medici, as with Castiglione's description of the sets devised by Genga for the performance of Bibiena's comedy: this description, though relatively detailed, does not allow us, given the conventions of dissimulation at work in the scene, to determine precisely which elements were painted, which were in relief, and which were "really" constructed.

What in fact does Castiglione say in this oft-cited letter? That the scenery represented, first of all, a space, a street separating the last houses of the city from the surrounding wall, which was "simulated" as convincingly as possible, with its two towers, by a kind of screen stretching from floor to ceiling (*dal palco in terra era finto naturalissima il muro della città, con due torrioni*), and that it was then transformed (though nothing is said of the mechanism effecting this change) into a magnificent city with streets, palaces, churches, and towers (*la scena poi era finta una città bellisima con le strade, palazzi, chiese, torri*). Castiglione notes that there were "real" streets (*strade vere*) and many things treated in relief (*ogni cosa di rilievo*), but with the aid of fine painting, which conformed to a well-conceived perspective (*ma aiutata da bonissima pittura con prospettiva bene intesa*). One saw there, among other things, an octagonal temple in "semirelief" (*un tempio a otto facce di mezzo rilievo*), entirely of stucco (*tutto di stuco*), with beautiful figurated "histories," feigned alabaster columns, architraves and cornices of azure and fine gold, meticulously worked small columns, faux-marble sculptures, etc., and which was more or less in the center (*questo era quasi in mezzo*), while to one side of it was a triumphal arch, clearly detached from the wall (*Da un de'lati era un arco trionfale, lontano dal muro ben una canna*), decorated with trompe l'oeil marbles (*era finto di marmo, ma era pittura*). All of which was so well executed that one could only marvel that, despite the many obligations facing the state of Urbino (*che con tutte l'opere dello stato d'Urbino*), only four months were needed to realize it.[21]

---

21. Castiglione, letter to Lodovico Canossa, February 6, 1513; cited by Mario Apollonio, *Storio del teatro italiano*, Florence, 1940, vol. 2, pp. 19–21.

With respect to iconography alone, there is a striking analogy between this description and the Baltimore panel (to say nothing of the text by Serlio, and of the way the circular temple in the middle of the *Città ideale* "turns"). But it doesn't help us clarify the nature and function of the "Urbino perspectives," insofar as these may relate to the theater. Though Genga may well have had some perspective tools at his disposal, nothing in Castiglione's letter authorizes us to think that painting was reduced to operating its effects on a backdrop. On the contrary, the terms of the letter suggest the coexistence and interaction of planar perspective, which is the painter's province, and that in full or partial relief, in a way similar to that used by Bramante in 1480–81 in his famous trompe l'oeil choir of Santa Maria presso San Satiro, in Milan. The same Bramante with whom Genga, also from Urbino, had worked in Rome before returning to Urbino to serve Duke Francesco Maria, there to construct the "beautiful scenes" (*le belle scene da lui fatte*) mentioned by Serlio, which demonstrated his mastery of the two arts of architecture and perspective.[22]

(You note in passing that, strictly speaking, trompe l'oeil must be distinguished, phenomenologically, from illusion because it is impossible to exempt oneself from its dissimulation, even if informed of it in advance, if one stands in the right place: trompe l'oeil, like its reciprocal analogue anamorphosis, assigns an indivisible point that corresponds—to use Pascal's phrase—to the *véritable lieu* or right place, by which is meant the place where it takes on the appearance of reality, of "truth," or, in the case of anamorphosis, from which its mechanics become visible. The technical distinction consists in the fact that illusion has only flat planes at its disposal, while trompe l'oeil exploits every available resource, including the judicious use of nominal depth to suggest one that's much greater, as in Santa Maria presso San Satiro,[23] and the grafting of painted architectural elements onto real ones, as in the decor of the *studiolo* in Urbino, as well as both at once,

---

22. Serlio, op. cit., fol. 25; English facs. ed., "The Second Book," opening statement.

23. Eugenio Battisti has drawn my attention to Cesare Cesariano's emphasis, in the commentaries to his translation of Vesuvius (Como, 1521), on the pronounced inward curve of the wall on which Bramante (whose student he was) painted this trompe l'oeil. Research conducted by Gabriella Ferri Piccaluga under Battisti's direction seems to indicate that this trompe l'oeil corresponds not to an apse but rather to the arm of centrally planned building, which Santa Maria presso San Satiro originally was.

as in Pozzo's trompe l'oeil ceiling in Saint Ignazio in Rome: thus trompe l'oeil intensifies the problems associated with so-called illusionist set design, of an apparatus combining elements treated in "flat painting" and three-dimensional volumes, some of which are depicted as foreshortened.)

*

So it was not without good reason that André Chastel rejected Krautheimer's "brilliant demonstration," and that Francastel drew proofs from it supporting a direct relation between the "montage" procedures which he took to be characteristic of Italian quattrocento painting and the contemporary theater.[24] If one sets out to stick to the "facts," it doesn't make any sense to speak of theater in connection with the panels in Urbino, Baltimore, and Berlin, especially if one opts (as did Francastel) for a relatively early date, given that the long delay between Alberti's call for a rebirth of the ancient theater and the first attempts to realize this goal on the stage is a matter of record. Any more than to see in them the first Renaissance representations of the tragic and comic scenes on the basis of descriptions of these by Serlio half a century later: For what would it mean, in the realm of interpretation, if textual proofs, the only ones considered legitimate in the history of art, led us to reverse the conventional order of precedence and accord priority to images rather than to the writings purportedly providing us with the key to them?

And raising the stakes even further, at the risk of burning our bridges behind us: Don't we move a bit too fast and allow ourselves to be taken in by appearances if we see in these panels a "prefiguration of the cubical, unitary framework of the classic scenography to come,"[25] given that there would be nothing cubic about the scenery constructed by Serlio except, precisely, its appearance? In doing this, don't we fail to take into account something justifiably emphasized by Chastel, namely the problematic usage of a term borrowed from Vitruvius which the latter derived from a context very different from that of the theater, for *scenographia* consists, as

24. André Chastel, "'Vues urbaines' peintes et théâtre," in *Fables, Formes, Figures,* Paris, 1978, vol. 1, pp. 497–503. Cf. Pierre Francastel, "Imagination plastique, vision théâtrale et signification humaine," *La Réalité figurative. Éléments structurels de sociologie de l'art,* Paris, 1965, pp. 211–38.
25. Francastel, op. cit.

we've seen, of the representation on a plane (*adumbratio*) of the facade and receding side walls of a building all of whose lines were meant to converge—if one accepts the argument of Panofsky's lecture—toward a single point?[26] Which is one of the ways to graphically represent architecture, like the *ichnographia* (ground plan) and the *orthographia* (elevation), and which was surely used in the theater, but without the word being pronounced, and without this kind of "perspective" having necessarily have acquired a scenic connotation?

Anyone determined to see in the three panels in Urbino, Baltimore, and Berlin scenic models in a generic sense, namely designs for scenery for specific productions, must ask himself, as you point out, just what sort of concrete uses they would lend themselves to. And pay heed to the specific objection raised by Chastel, who maintains that their oblong format is incompatible with the proportions of scenic curtain or backdrop.[27] You suggest that the unusual format of these panels could itself be a kind of ruse or trompe l'oeil, though one in no way implying that the perspective to which they conform is as completely open as it seems at first glance. Since you're anxious to husband your arguments, you choose, for the moment, to focus only on a perspectival given corresponding to an angle of vision greater than 90°. Even in this case could it not be imagined, as a working hypothesis, that compositions of this kind might have been meant to be enlarged to serve as illusionist backdrops within a relatively archaic theatrical framework; and this, in the place of the *frons scaenae,* of the screen of arcades or *portico della scena* (such as would be imagined by Serlio in his reconstruction of the theatre of Marcellus[28]), so favored by those who saw themselves as the interpreters of Vitruvius after Giovanni Sulpizio da Veroli produced the first edition, doubtless in 1486?[29]

What we know about the proportions of the wooden theater erected in the plaza of the Capitol in 1513, in honor of Lorenzo and Giuliano di Medici (an acting area about 32.4 meters wide and 7.8 meters deep, in

---

26. Francastel, op. cit.
27. Chastel, "'Vues urbaines' peintes et théâtre," op. cit., 1978, p. 498.
28. Serlio, *Il terzo libro . . . nel quale si figurano e descrivano le antichita di Roma,* etc., Venice, 1540; English facs. ed., op. cit., 1611/1970.
29. Joannes Sulpitius, *L. Vitruvius Pollionis ad Caesarem Augustum de architectura liber primus (-decimus),* Rome, ca. 1486.

front of a screen of five bays), indicates that stages of this kind were generally four or five times wider than they were deep. Which is to say that, if
we suppose a painted drop to be hung behind it (but you insist this is no
more than a working hypothesis, and a rather absurd one), this would have
proportions comparable to those of the Urbino perspectives. To be sure, the
image of the tragic scene which Serlio based on Peruzzi is roughly square in
format, but this is because, far from describing the full width of the stage,
it corresponds only to that part of the scenery constructed in perspective on
an inclined plane (marked *B* on Serlio's plan) receding toward the backdrop
and linked to the stage proper by means of a double sequence of flats, in
conformity with a kind of scenographic treatment that's later and more
complex than that of the "Vitruvian" stage. As for the area on which the
action unfolded, namely the horizontal platform (marked *C*) across which
the actors moved, its grid of 34 × 5 squares also corresponds to a stage
much wider than it is deep, as is confirmed by the image of the comic

42   Serlio's stage,
ground plan. Serlio, *Il
secondo libro . . .*, fol. 66
verso. Photo: Biblio-
thèque Nationale, Paris.

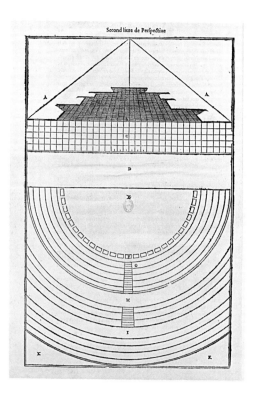

scene, where the forward location of this platform is clearly indicated in the foreground, even though the entire stage is not represented.

The Capitoline theater bears further discussion here. First of all because the man in charge of its construction seems to have been the Florentine Pietro Roselli, a close collaborator of Giuliano da Sangallo. Sangallo who was then in Rome as part of the Medici retinue, taking measurements of ancient monuments, the Coliseum among them. It is possible that Roselli, who helped him with this project, was inspired by a design by his master. Or that we worked from an idea by Peruzzi, as is suggested by the striking similarity between the theater's internal organization and that of the northern facade of the Farnesina, with its central element of five bays placed between two advancing wings, where open-air performances were

43   Pietro Rosselli (?), Capitoline Theater, Rome,
1513. Reconstruction by A. Bruschi (F. Cruciani,
Il teatro del Campidoglio, plate 3).

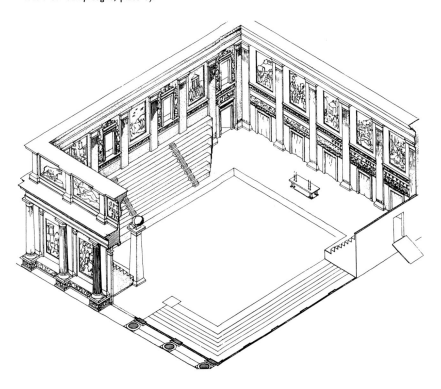

given on several occasions.[30] The surviving descriptions of the Capitoline theater indicate that its stage was backed by a blind portico of five bays, each of them pierced by a door surmounted by a cornice and a painted panel, and that this same arrangement recurred around the periphery of the room as well as on its facade. Certainly there's nothing about such a scheme suggestive of a continuous backdrop; but Vasari's mention, in this connection, of a "perspective" devised by Peruzzi as a scenic apparatus for a comedy in which the beautiful arrangement of buildings, the multiple loggias, *the bizarre quality* (your underlining) *of the doors and windows,* in short everything one saw in it of feigned architecture was nothing less than *astonishing,*[31] supports your suggestion, even though Vasari confused a reading on the Campidoglio of Plautus's *Poenulus* with a much later production by Peruzzi, but one that echoes descriptions of performances given earlier in Ferrara and Urbino.[32]

Nonetheless, the motif of a portico that, replacing the *frons scaenae,* supports the facade behind the stage is incompatible with the idea of an illusionist perspective deployed across its full breadth. This motif, which successive editions of Terence's theater would disseminate throughout Europe, republishing with variations the illustrations of the Trechsel edition (Lyons, 1493), has been qualified by Robert Klein as "proto-Vitruvian," by which he means that it was based on a reading of Vitruvius that was still inflected in accordance with medieval theatrical tradition.[33] But the performances organized by the Roman Academy of Pomponius Laetus for Cardinal Riario, at the very moment in which Sulpizio's *princeps* edition of Vitruvius appeared, seem to have featured a scenic arrangement that was much less lucid. In the dedication to his work, in which he praises Alfonso Riario as a protector of humanists, Sulpizio congratulates him for having been the first to organize the performance of an ancient tragedy on a permanent stage set,

30. Cf. C. L. Frommel, *Die Farnesina und Peruzzis architektonisches Frühwerk,* Berlin, 1961.
31. "Ma quello che fece stupire ognuno, fu la prospettiva ovvero scena d'una comedia, tanto bella, che non è possibile immaginarsi più: perciocche la varieta e bella maniera de'casamenti, le diverse logge, la bizzaria delle porte e finestre, e l'altre cose che vi si videro d'architettura, furono tanto bene intese e di cosi straordinaria invenzione, che non si puo dirne la millesima parte." Vasar, "Vita di Baldassare Peruzzi," *Vite,* Milanesi ed., vol. 4, pp. 595–96.
32. Fabrizio Cruciani, *Il teatro del Campidoglio e le feste romane del 1513, con la ricostruzione architettonica del teatro di A. Bruschi,* Milan, 1968, pp. lxxix–lxxx.
33. Klein and Zerner, "Vitruve et le théâtre . . .," in *La Forme et l'intelligible,* op. cit., 1970, pp. 302ff. Cf. Kernodle, op. cit., pp. 160–64.

beneath a tent stretched over the courtyard of his palace, which was the Cancelleria, a building with some bearing on the Baltimore panel, as we shall see. And also the first, *nostro saeculo* (I remind you that we're still in the quattrocento), to have shown a painted scenic facade, *picturatae scenae faciem*.[34] But how are we to understand this? According to Krautheimer, Sulpizio was thinking of a stage consisting of a platform (the *pulpitus* of Vitruvius, which is not to be confused with a *proscenium*) and a *facies*, which was either a "stage prospect" erected downstage or a canvas backdrop. The fact that Sulpizio boasts a bit further along of having managed to devise *facies* that pivoted like the *periaktoi* of the ancient theatre, or could slide into the wings like moving elements in modern stagecraft (*versatilem et ductilem quando libuerit facies non difficulter*), seems to indicate that they were toward the back of the stage. It follows from this that they may have been modeled after the *frons scaenae* of Vitruvius, even though the columns of this were only painted. But this correct understanding of Vitruvius only became current in Italy with the translation by Daniele Barbaro, published in Venice in 1568, with some help from Palladio.[35]

It is nonetheless true that Alberti had long since called for a revival of the ancient theater, claiming the church was determined to eradicate all memory of it,[36] and that he was perfectly cognizant of the distinction between the three genres of dramatic poetry: the tragic, which recounts the adventures of tyrants; the comic, which describes the difficulties and lives of family fathers; and the satyric, which sings of the pleasures of the country-

---

34. Joannes Sulpitius, *L. Vitruvius . . . de architectura . . .*, as cited by Krautheimer, op. cit., 1958, p. 340.

35. Perrault understood perfectly the difference between *versatilis* and *ductilis*: "Our French word for theatrical decorations is a happy rendering of that of Vitruvius, which is *ornatus*. These decorations were of two kinds, according to Servius in Vergil's *Georgics*. In addition to the machines in triangular form which the Greeks called 'Periaktous,' which means 'turning,' and which allowed for three distinct changes, each of their faces bearing a different painting, the ancients also had others that are still used in our theaters, and whose artifice consisted of making different things appear when they were made to move to the side, such that when one of them was pulled away, it revealed another hidden behind it. The latter was called a *ductilis* and the former a *versatilis*. It is nonetheless difficult to believe that these changes were effected as quickly as those in our theaters, which occur almost instantaneously and without our perceiving them: for we read that when the ancients wanted to change their scenic decorations, they drew a curtain that was called the *Sigarium*, behind which they made whatever changes were necessary at their leisure." Perrault, op. cit., book V, chapter vii, note 22.

36. "Et nostros non audea improbare pontifices morumque magistros, si consulto spectaculorum usum prohibere." Alberti, *De re aedificatoria*, op. cit., p. 724.

side and of the loves of shepherds—a turning device (*versatilis machina*) facilitating changes of decor at will.[37] Eugenio Battisti has attempted, in a very original way, to reconstruct the "implicit" scenography of *Filodosso*, a comedy written by Alberti in Bologna after 1425, and revised by its author in 1436–37 (which is to say before writing *De re aedificatoria*), in hommage to Lionello d'Este, who had declared his approval of a revival of public performances in the antique mode. Battisti does not claim that this comedy was ever actually produced, but he notes that it had been conceived with such a production in mind and that everything about this text suggests the idea of a unitary spatial "cage" within which the characters operate, prisoners of the law and of social circumstances, just as Fortuna herself must submit to the inexorable march of time.[38] Can we go further and identify the *angiportus* mentioned in the dialogue as a forward portico opening onto the back of the stage, along lines similar to those of the Berlin panel? This hypothesis is seductive insofar as it's based solely on textual considerations, which indicates that a problem of *visualization* was at issue, one that could be resolved, at least initially, outside the theater.

But the first attempts at scenography, at the end of the fifteenth century and the beginning of the sixteenth, were something else again. However awkward they may have been, these efforts must have basically conformed to one of two approaches. To be sure, from a material point of view there is no great difference between a stage background conceived after the "Vitruvian" model, with its screen of arcades, and a painted perspective, except that working doors set into a frontal arcade pose fewer problems than those incorporated into an illusionistic backdrop. But this relative difficulty did not prevent the public from quickly manifesting its preference for scenery in perspective. You take pleasure in Robert Klein's demonstration of this: All evidence suggests that the theater, like other sectors of Renaissance culture, was a site of conflict between simple theater lovers, on the one hand, and humanists, archeologists, and scholars, on the other, with the former applauding striking scenic effects (though at the beginning of the sixteenth century we are still quite far from the possibilities of so-called

---

37. "Non deerat ubi versatili machina evestigio frons porrigetur expictus et appareret seu atrium seu casa seu etiam silva, prout iis condiceret fabulisque ageretur." Ibid., p. 728.
38. Eugenio Battisti, "La visualizzazione della scena classica nella comedia umanistica," *Rinascimento e barocco*, Turin, 1968, pp. 102–105.

"Italian" scenography) and the latter, at the risk of seeming to be pedants, supporting a revival of ancient stagecraft. But this last goal would be realized only by Palladio, in his *teatro olimpico*.[39]

It is a certainty that the genre, to use André Chastel's name for it, of "urban views in perspective," which encompasses the "Urbino perspectives" as well as many marquetry panels and cassone frontals, was not directly intended for the theater. And if we invoke in its connection the category of the "spectacular" (specifying what we mean by the term), the historical context obliges us to take this as referring to the street rather than the theater. According to Chastel, paintings of this kind were intended to valorize, in representational terms, the space of the city: "In the end it's a matter of using perspective to define *solemn places,* ennobled by forceful architectural references, Colissea, triumphal arches, temples . . ., so as to suggest singular, crystalline spaces set apart in the interior of the city, ideal for processions. . . . One should think of them in the context of ritual entries, of ceremonial decorations."[40] The idea that such *fragments of the city,* insofar as, in their being set apart within the urban tissue, they constitute the perfect framework for representations, suits you very well, save perhaps for the solemnity and ceremony. For the city, as much and even more than a place of celebration, is one of festival, of diversion, of masquarade, and, above all, of the comedy—and tragedy—of everyday life; you think this is demonstrated by the *Novella del Grasso,* which I've already mentioned several times, whose action unfolds in the very place where Brunelleschi's first experiment was set, the piazza of the Baptistry of San Giovanni, the organization of which is not unrelated to that of the *Città ideale.*

In fact the question strikes you as being badly formulated to the extent that it isn't posed in the most general terms: those of the production, in painting and in accordance with those means proper to it, of a space of representation, or, as Walter Benjamin would phrase it, of *an acting/gaming space for the figures.*[41] But let us be clear on this point: talk of a

---

39. Klein and Zerner, "Vitruve et le théâtre . . .," in *La Forme et l'intelligible,* op. cit., p. 294.

40. Chastel, "'Vues urbaines' peintes et théâtre," op. cit., p. 501.

41. Benjamin, "Edward Fuchs . . .," French trans. in *Macula,* no. 3/4, p. 57, note 18. [The French rendering of Benjamin reads *"du'un espace de jeu pour les figures." "Jeu"* can mean "acting" (as in the theater), "game" (as in card games), and "play" (as in the play of a join in carpentry). In the next sentence Damisch glosses the second of these meanings—TRANS.]

game has no meaning unless its rules are clearly established from the outset, and its area precisely defined, within the field and in accordance with the terms that are those of painting, as opposed to those of its referent or its destination, its supposed function. Now the power of the perspective config- uration, and its primary characteristic, is such as to confer a *scenic* value on every action, including processional ones, unfolding in its theater (one has only to think of the great Venetian cycles of Gentile Bellini and Carpaccio, to which I shall return). Here as elsewhere, invocation of the referent or of "function" tends first of all to obscure the operation of that which is proper to painting. Though the latter declares itself openly to be a representation, or *the representation of a representation,* it doesn't necessarily follow that its model, its occasion, or its pretext must be sought in a reality that is itself a kind of spectacle. In painting, the strength of classic representation is dis- closed in its very configuration, and in the disjunction this implies between the two moments to which the painter's brief can be reduced—the painter, whose task it is to open up, in an initial moment, a field to serve as that of the *istoria,* to construct, to establish, a scene within it using the tools of *costruzione legittima* and to subsequently introduce into it the figures of fable or narrative.[42] We could almost say that the "Urbino perspectives" propose emblematic images of this fundamental disjunction; and you find it extremely facile to assign them a primary function or destination relating to spectacle, which is to disregard the—seemingly intentional—effects result- ing from the blockage of representational mechanics in midcourse.

We must indeed speak of theater here, even though the externals of the scene take the form of a fragment of a city. But the theater in question is that *of painting* and must be analyzed as such, whatever its eventual rela- tions to the universe of spectacle. The fact that the properly scenic implica- tions of *costruzione legittima* were rapidly acknowledged changes nothing. Walter Benjamin said of works of art that "the complete circle of their life and their action has as many rights, let's say even more rights, as the history of their birth";[43] and it is always detrimental to abstract the phe- nomenon of refraction and maintain that they are accessible to us only

---

42. On the constitutive doubling of representation, cf. my *Théorie du nuage,* op. cit., pp. 92ff.
43. Benjamin, "Histoire de la littérature et science de la littérature," *Poésie et révolution,* op. cit., p. 14.

through the traces they've left in history. This determination obliges the historian to be particularly attentive to the empirical conditions shaping such a trajectory. Regarding the so-called "Urbino perspectives," rejection of the "Vitruvian" interpretation, and your entire argument, which urges us to stick within the register proper to painting, certainly doesn't preclude us from examining the lessons and suggestions that men of the theater and overseers of spectacle in general have been able to derive from the workings of perspective—workings that they can clarify retrospectively, even though these may not originally have had anything to do with the theater proper. And this without taking into account that if one dates these panels to around 1500 (as does André Chastel) or to the beginning of the sixteenth century, the gap separating them from the first productions of Peruzzi and Genga isn't so great. Much less, in any case, than the two or three centuries elapsing between the first perspective efforts, graphic and pictorial as well as theoretical, in the period of Brunelleschi and Alberti, and the renewal of these in the realm of geometry with Guidobaldo dal Monte and Desargues.

*

In both cases the problem is the same: we cannot see in the quattrocento *veduta architectonica* a prefiguration of classic scenography, any more than we can pretend that Brunelleschi's experiments and the rule that painters derived from them presupposed a notion of "crystalline" space (as Chastel would call it, playing on two meanings of the word) which would only be conceptualized much later, and in another context, on another level. But we can no longer ignore the fact that Renaissance painters and architects posed themselves, in terms and under auspices yet to be specified, a certain number of problems and proposed solutions to them that would subsequently lead to decisive developments in areas as unrelated to one another, to all appearances, as mathematics and scenography. This play across the centuries of practice and theory, as well as across their various sectors, surely constitutes one of the most recalcitrant enigmas in all of cultural history and is also one of the most powerful mainsprings of the evolution of the arts and sciences themselves, and of what we call their "history." If there's no question of seeking to establish relations of cause and effect, or of derivation, between this manifestation and that, between this production and that, from heterogeneous domains, and if the links that can be established between diverse fields of knowledge are usually of an analogous, if not an imaginary or even fantasmatic, character (when they're not simply anecdotal), such juxtapositions nonetheless oblige us to jettison the compartmentalization of discourses imposed by the academic categorization of knowledge and to pose questions about the irreducible, necessary multiplicity of the forms that thought can assume.

We are still very far from doing this today, at least with regard to art and more particularly to our concern here, namely perspective, despite the considerable amount of work devoted to the subject by several generations of historians. And it's in this connection that the distancing tactics we've examined strike you as most vulnerable to criticism. Tactics that are certainly not the sole province of art historians. Alexandre Koyré has taught us that the surest way—if not the subtlest—to be rid of the epistemological problems implied by the idea of a "scientific revolution" is to derive all scientific advances from purely technical and conjunctural developments.[44] The same tendency, positivist in inspiration (when its goals are not obscurantist), has become prevalent in the domain of the arts. And you deplore the fact that its advocates seek justification in Robert Klein's superb work on the *De sculptura* by Gauricus: for the documented existence, at the side of so-called "scientific" forms of perspective, of workshop traditions established at some earlier point in the past (as with the system Klein terms "bifocal") does not suffice to demonstrate that *costruzione legittima* can be reduced to a matter of perfecting a procedure that evolved in Tuscany, from the fourteenth century, through a process of empirical normalization.[45]

One might be tempted to see the "urban views" and other "architectural perspectives," so prevalent in art of the quattrocento, as no more than exercises in the deployment and control of perspective effects. But would it necessarily follow from this that they conformed, without exception, to a simple schema, easy to establish and almost mechanically applied,[46] as in the art of marquetry? Certainly perspective construction was

---

44. On this subject, see Alexandre Koyré's critique of positions defended by A. C. Crombie in his classic book *Robert Grosseteste and the Origins of Experimental Science, 1100–1400,* Oxford, 1953, and in his *Augustine to Galileo: The History of Science, A.D. 400–1650,* London, 1952. Cf. A. Koyré, "Les Origines de la science moderne. Une interprétation nouvelle," *Études d'histoire de la pensée scientifique,* Paris, 1966, pp. 61–86.
45. Chastel, "'Vues urbaines' . . .," op. cit., pp. 500–501, note 8.
46. Chastel, ibid., p. 501.

particularly well suited to the practice of *intarsia,* "this art," Vasari writes, "of combining stained woods of various colors to create perspectives, scrolls, and other objects of fantasy which was introduced in the time of Filippo Brunelleschi and Paolo Uccello":[47] Aren't the effects of depth and relief at which marquetry aims the result of assembling on one plane component surfaces that are precisely crafted and of different chromatic values? André Chastel long ago noted the relation between these two series: "The simple armature of orthogonals and converging receding lines determined through the play of its 'intersections' a geometric network; this network resolved itself into a play of elementary figures easy to carve, with the little blocks placed on the surface becoming, as the result of perspective effects, trapezoids, squares rotated to assume the form of lozenges, etc.; what was collected as a result of spatial decomposition was brought together on the image plane like a puzzle, which is just the way marquetry works."[48] It is easy to imagine that the celebrated panels used by Brunelleschi in his demonstrations—beginning with the one on which he'd painted the Florence baptistry "with such delicacy precision (*e tanto a punto*) in the colors of the black and white marbles that a miniaturist could not have done it better"[49]—would have been of interest not only to painters but to marquetry craftsmen as well. Which is why Masaccio would not have neglected to tell them about them. "And it stimulated them so much, that it resulted in fine practices and many useful things done under its auspices (*che si fece di quel magistero*), as well as a number of excellent things that brought Florence profit and renown."[50]

For all that, *intarsia* was anything but a school of facility. If many marquetry panels feature conventional, repetitive schemes, others bear witness to a sophisticated exploration of the geometric elements of illusion, if not of trompe l'oeil, as we defined it above. But more to the point—and this applies above all to the decor of the Urbino *studiolo,* because of its date (1476) a decisive contextual factor for us—they feature a number of traits

---

47. Vasari, "Vita di Benedetto da Maiano, op. cit., vol. 3, p. 333. Cf. Chastel, "Marqueterie et perspective au XVe siècle," in *Fables, formes, figures,* op. cit., vol. 1, pp. 317–32, and my *Théorie du nuage,* op. cit., pp. 159–66.
48. Chastel, "Marqueterie et perspective au XVe siècle," op. cit., p. 321.
49. Cf. chapter 6, pp. 89–90.
50. Vasari, "Vita di Filippo Brunelleschi," op. cit., vol. 2, p. 332.

44 Domenico Rosselli, marquetry door, Urbino, Palazzo Ducale, room VIII. Photo: Anderson-Giraudon.

45　Domenico Rosselli, *Studiolo,* Urbino, Palazzo
Ducale, 1476. Photo: Alinari-Giraudon.

and motifs intended to reinforce these effects: objects—scientific and musical instruments, pieces of armor, books, boxes and containers of all sorts—
that lend themselves to purely "descriptive" reconstitution, by projection
onto a plane of the surfaces into which they can be broken down (a skill of
which Paolo Uccello was a past master); and, above all, solid or grilled
doors, open, closed, or somewhere in between, creating a strong impression
of protruding from the plane of the wall, and behind which the interiors of
feigned cabinets are visible—an idea brought to its maximum degree of
sophistication when incorporated into a real door, as in Urbino; and, finally,
vedute of architecture or landscape, opening like so many windows in the
paneling. Such as, in the Urbino *studiolo,* the view of the river or a lake
surrounded by hills similar to the landscape in the background of Piero's
portrait of Duke Federigo, here seen from above through three arches of a
portico situated on the edge of a terrace with a checkerboard paving, and

which is itself framed by two pilasters joined by a balustrade on which is placed a basket full of fruit, near which a squirrel—the symbol, as is only proper, of the eminently political virtue of Prudence—busies itself gnawing a nut.[51]

The nature of marquetry precludes approximation and improvisation; all the pieces of its puzzle must fit together with great precision, totally covering the surface to which they are applied. That makes it an exercise ideal for demonstrating the coherence of the system. But all the same you are not disposed to accept, even though the unifying function of perspective expresses a coherent mathematical thought, that the process of analysis and construction deriving from it can be reduced to marquetry technique.[52] To maintain this is to ignore both the singular importance of reference to geometry in the constitution of the system and the specific status assigned to *costruzione legittima* in the context of painting (that painting of which it is the daughter, as Leonardo would say) and, in general, of classic representation. Painter's perspective did not evolve from empirical technique, but neither was it born of purely abstract, theoretical speculation: the invention, the discovery to which tradition attaches Brunelleschi's name appealed to geometry more than it proceeded from it; but it is precisely there, in the invitation to a work of idealization that became manifest through the hole Brunelleschi placed in the center of his *tavoletta,* that its meaning and its value as an origin resides.

It is a certainty, as both Francastel and Chastel have emphasized, that paintings constructed in strict conformity with perspective rules were the exception in the quattrocento. But you don't see this as proof of any reticence on the part of painters with regard to a system that, it has been argued, restricted their freedom of movement.[53] Let it be said in passing: If any restriction was in question, wouldn't this consist of the discipline's having been less "inoffensive" than Robert Klein maintained? I agree with you that the idea, widely accepted, that some sort of violence inheres in the perspective configuration is a complete absurdity, and bears the mark of a

---

51. Luciano Cheles, "The Inlaid Decorations of Federico da Montefeltro's Urbino Studiolo: An Iconographic Study," *Mitteilungen des Kunsthistorischen Institutes im Florenz,* vol. 26, no. 1 (1982), pp. 1–46.
52. Chastel, "Marqueterie et perspective," op. cit.
53. Ibid.

specific ideology. This commonplace dates back, as we've seen, to Vasari, to the opposition he posited in his "Life of Paolo Uccello" between two types of artists: the first, of which Donatello was an example, being preoccupied above all else with the expressive powers inherent in painting as such; and the other consisting of men, like Uccello, who approach things systematically, through methodical study. But this view is accompanied by a theoretical error of far greater consequence, which consists in thinking, or wanting to think, particularly in relation to those applications to which it lends itself in the field of architecture, that perspective construction constitutes a kind of code, even a language, when in fact it only gave painters a model, in the epistemological sense of the word, providing at the same time a regulating configuration intended not so much to inform the representation as to orient and control its regime (this being said without denying the possibility of a form of representation that would not be subjected, in Leonardo's words, to a "brake" as well as a "guide").

You grant that this is not easy to understand: it depends upon other developments, such as the fact that, among the first demonstrations of the power of such a model, the one proposed in 1425 by Masaccio's *Trinity*, for which it seems Brunelleschi provided the schema, is characterized by a remarkable variation: if one considers only the upper portion of the fresco, the question of the *ground* of the perspective construction is somehow elided, as if the rule had to proceed from the beginning by exception, or by a regime that was somewhat forced, in order to prevail.[54] Conversely, how can we fail to see that the so-called Urbino perspectives, in their exaggerated symmetry, correspond to a similar intention, and at an historical moment in which, according to André Chastel (taking him at his word), such an approach had become unfashionable?[55]

As soon as we decide to view this as no more than an accessory trait, a mere episode, acknowledgment of the system's mathematical implications brings us back to questions of style and ultimately cuts short all critical reflection on the theoretical difficulties—and, to utter the word, the philosophical ones—raised by so-called scientific perspective. If on this point you had an annoying tendency to become irritated in your disputes

---

54. Cf. above, chapter 6, p. 95.
55. Chastel, "'Vues urbaines' peintes et théâtre," op. cit., p. 498.

with Robert Klein, this was because you perceived in them the echo of a very old procedure, as well as the resurgence of a reductive ideology whose ravages in the field of the study of art are spreading. As long as the latter limits itself to agreeable games, to speculation that is wholly formal and gratuitous, no one will object, save to express regret for a lack of "poetry" and the "picturesque." But when one maintains that thought is at work in painting, that here and there it can awaken echoes of things that escape all departmental and disciplinary control, this is held to be intolerable. If works appear that risk lending themselves to such discussion, the best way to deal with them is to preemptively deny them all genuine originality, and to try to force them back into formation by assimilating them to a class of objects considered (perhaps mistakenly) to be insignificant. Those singular works known as the "Urbino perspectives" are a case in point: there was a rush to affirm, not implausibly, that all the panels of this kind were originally intended to serve as cassone frontals, or produced for decorative ensembles in which they vied for attention with works of marquetry.[56] This operation is not an isolated one; it is part of a concerted strategy intended to reduce to a matter of mere fashion the work carried out through painting, under the auspices of perspective, during the quattrocento and well beyond, to say nothing of subsequent developments within a scientific context. The same distancing maneuvers would be used with Uccello, leading to his being regarded as a minor master with archaizing tendencies, and with the "mathematical curiosities" used in marquetry before they were employed in theatrical architecture, scenography, and trompe l'oeil: as if it had been deemed important to avoid being taken in by them, to strip them from the beginning of all resonance, all reverberation they might have within the orders of art and thought.[57]

---

56. Chastel, ibid.

57. The operation is taken to caricatural extremes in a chapter of the recent *Storia dell'arte italiana* devoted to perspective, which focuses, in a calculated, polemical way, on the practice of marquetry, in reaction to the theoretical incoherence for which, it is stated, Panofsky would have to bear the blame, if it were not for the fact that it derived from excessive attention devoted to a work (a folly?) of his youth; cf. Massimo Ferretti, "I maestri della prospettiva," *Storia dell'arte italiana*, part III, vol. 4, *Forme e modelli*, Turin, 1982, pp. 457–585. The refusal of "philosophy," and even thought, cannot be taken any further. I will only note here that Panofsky was in his thirties when he gave the lecture that is the basis for *Perspective as Symbolic Form*.

The descriptive illusion.

Meaning and reference.

What is describing?

Reckoning with painting without being taken in by it.

Poetry as precision.

The representation's absence from its place.

Perspective transfixed.

Perspective and architecture.

Sites of writing.

The Reading at an Impasse

Thus you count three varieties of what I've termed distancing maneuvers: the first consists of insisting that the Urbino panel (and all those related to it, however large this *corpus* might be) is an extension of architecture; the second that it's an extension of the theater; and the third, that it's an extension of "decoration." Three maneuvers that are clearly linked, as decoration is linked to the theater, the theater to architecture, and architecture to decoration and even to painting, from which Alberti maintained it had borrowed most of its ornamental elements: columns, pilasters, cornices, pediments, etc.[1]

You are far from thinking that these maneuvers could have been dispensed with altogether: some kind of distancing was doubtless inevitable at the beginning of the inquiry. You are the first to concede that reference to the universe of architecture and the theater, if not that of decoration, provides us with a language enabling us to describe these panels in great detail. Without Fiske Kimball, who had the idea of taking an inventory of the architectural features which, by their quality and complexity (we'll see some further examples of this), would suffice to set the so-called Urbino perspectives apart from the rest of the family to which they're held to belong and from which, according to André Chastel, there's no reason to isolate them.[2] And you say without the slightest hesitation that you prefer this reading, though it's a bit myopic, to excessively casual views of the unitary character of the perspective scene and the purported decorative intentions of such compositions. The difficulty in this instance consists of

---

1. Alberti, *Della pittura*, book II, cited ed., p. 77; English trans., p. 64. For a more extended discussion of this question, see my article "Ornamento," *Enciclopaedia* Einaudi, vol. 10, Turin (1980), pp. 227–28.
2. Chastel, "'Vues urbaines' peintes et théâtre," op cit., p. 498.

accommodating features it's tempting to regard as accessory, while at the same time leaving oneself open to the calculated play of the perspective construction: having spent long hours in front of the *Città ideale,* and having often bent over to study it through a magnifying glass while it lay on the conservator's table in Urbino, you have come to believe that nothing in this painting was left to chance, and that any interpretation must take into account its every detail, but without losing from view the enigma that it initially proposes to the eye.

You do not deny, then, the importance of the work in this area already accomplished by the history of art. You retain from it, above all, the injunction to proceed as closely as possible to the painting, without being afraid of the analysis becoming overly technical or erudite. But without hesitating to address more abstract considerations. Your hypothesis is that these are veritable demonstrations, and that as such they oblige us, once we've grasped their premises, to thoroughly follow through with them. In the end, a demonstration is not a matter of observation or proof, much less verification, but rather one of reasoning, in the Kantian sense of analytic reconstruction or, as Poincaré would have it, in the inductive mode of a recurrent reasoning founded upon a synthetic judgment a priori that authorizes passage "from the finite to the infinite."[3] Not that you pretend to assimilate the procedures of art to those of science. Especially given that *perspectiva artificialis* did not proceed initially from a basis of geometry, save indirectly, by means of a detour through optics. But insofar as it did invoke geometry, this movement without prior example in art manifested the demonstrative rigor characteristic of it. Which prompts the question: How could perspective, born as it was of painting, in turn provide a demonstration of it? And how would such a "demonstration" compare with one in geometry?

These questions take us far afield from architecture and the theater, and decoration too, though they may bring us back to them at the end of our travels. But they have the merit of preventing us from lapsing into what I will call, borrowing a phrase from philosophers of language, the *descriptive illusion,* which consists in the view that representation is the primary function of both language and art, a pictorial proposition, like a lin-

---

3.   Henri Poincaré, *La Science et l'hypothèse,* Paris, 1906, p. 22.

guistic statement, having meaning only to the extent it describes the "state of things" and refers to facts presented as real, or at least as thinkable.[4] Under the so-called "representationalist" hypothesis, a proposition or statement has no meanings other than those it designates, it being supposed that the sign effaces itself before that which it denotes, just as does painting—or *pourtraicture,* as it was called in sixteenth-century French—before that of which it is the "portrait," feature by feature (*trait pour trait*). The city given to view in the Urbino panel can well be taken to be an *ideal* one. Utopia, while accessible to description, nonetheless participates in the circuit of representation, if only as a kind of prefiguration: the non-place which it designates is one only because the city here represented has no other place, precisely, but *here,* a here that doesn't consist of a painted surface and a network of lines and animating patches of color but rather is the ideal site constituted by painting by means of perspective construction. In other words the site of a fiction, there being no better illustration of the transparence of the sign implied by the representationalist hypothesis than the celebrated formula in which Alberti assimilates the rectangle of the painting to an open window through which the gaze travels toward what's painted there;[5] and Leonardo maintains that perspective was nothing other than "the vision of an object behind smooth, transparent glass, on the surface of which everything beyond it has been marked."[6]

*

But if these paintings must be described, how can this be managed without first dealing with what they *represent,* namely buildings of various kinds? "Ideal" city or not, the descriptive illusion consists in maintaining that these buildings, or at least some of them, have referents in reality, whether archaeological or contemporary. Thus Kimball felt obliged to point out that the amphitheater in the second row of the Baltimore panel, to the left, doesn't correspond to any Roman model (it lacks the entablature surmounted by a parapet featured in the Colisseum and the theater of Marcel-

---

4.   Cf. François Recanati, *La Transparence et l'énonciation. Pour Introduire la pragmatique,* Paris, 1979, p. 96.

5.   "Un quadrangolo di retti angoli . . . el quale reputo essere una fiestra aperta per donde io miri quello che quivi sara dipinta." Alberti, op. cit., p. 70; English trans., p. 51.

6.   Leonardo da Vinci, Inst. de Fr., Ms. A., fol. I verso; cf. MacCurdy, op. cit., vol. 2, p. 306.

46   Berlin panel, left
portion.

47   Leon-Battista
Alberti, Palazzo Rucellai
in Florence: detail of the
facade. Photo: H.D.

48　Baltimore panel, left portion.

49　Baccio d'Agnolo (?), Palazzo Cocchi in Florence: detail of the facade.

50   Baltimore panel,
right portion.

51   Andrea Bregno (?),
Palazzo della Cancelleria,
after 1489: detail of the
main facade. Photo: H.D.

lus) but rather to the amphitheater in Pola, which he takes as further support for his attribution to Luciano Laurana, who was from Istria. Likewise the triumphal arch, whose motif of independent bays separated by pairs of columns, unknown in Rome, also occurred in Pola.[7] As for the octagonal temple in the same row as these other two ancient monuments, in the literature it is regularly compared with the baptistry in Florence, which features the same decorative scheme of inlaid marble and has the same lantern topped by a sphere supporting a cross.

If we should want to be attentive to contemporary references, the corner palace on the left of the Berlin panel appears to be a double of Alberti's Palazzo Rucellai, or rather (given that it has more than one full-dress facade) of the Palazzo Piccolomini by B. Rosellino: which in this context qualifies as a gesture of pronounced archaism. Conversely, we will recognize in the facade of the partially obscured basilica to the rear of the piazza, on the right, in the Urbino panel a model close to buildings by Antonio da Sangallo, while the palace in the left foreground of the Baltimore panel has an elevation rather similar to that of the Palazzo Riario in Rome, or the Belvedere courtyard in the Vatican (after 1503), with the "triumphal arch" motif appearing again, somewhat later, in the Palazzo Cocchi in Florence, perhaps by Baccio d'Agnolo, and on the interior facade of the Villa Imperiale in Pesaro, by Girolamo Genga (1521–1540). The motif of independent bays separated by doubled pilasters, but without arches, visible in the palace on the right, also occurs in the Bramante-like facade of the Palazzo della Cancelleria and in Raphael's palazzo.

So the mode of reference can vary, depending on which depicted work of architecture is being considered, each one referring back to the denoted, describing it, representing it, in its own way. In the interests of time, you distinguish three such modes. Sometimes the representation will refer, as if it were a kind of citation, to an old or an ancient model: such is the case, in the Baltimore panel, with the amphitheater, the triumphal arch, and—forcing the point just a bit—the octagonal temple (the reference here could be textual rather than archaeological, as is suggested by the

---

7. Kimball, op. cit. 1927–28, p. 145. F. Zeri maintained, *contra* Kimball, that the amphitheater was indeed modeled after that in Rome, as is indicated by the superposition of Tuscan, Ionic, and Corinthian orders, whereas the amphitheater in Pola is entirely in the Tuscan order.

columns surmounted by statues, which refer directly to the *signa* of Vitruvius). Sometimes it will be inspired by "modern" models, whether a notable building such as the Palazzo Rucellai or examples of the "anonymous" architecture that makes up the greater part of the urban tissue, useful in creating a background that is neutral, sedimentary, serving to throw more monumental elements into relief. And sometimes, finally, it will present itself as a proposition whose sole reference is a virtual one, as the annunciatory sign of a renewal, *all'antico,* of architecture, whereas ordinary buildings present themselves as the traces, the depositories of another history, one that's inscribed within a quasi-geological continuity and gives no indication of the possibility of a "renaissance," of a concerted attempt to bring the past into the present, to deliberately enhance the new through recourse to the old.

Let it be stated in passing that this kind of mix, with some elements being borrowed from reality of different periods and some being models that had not yet proceeded beyond the project stage, is characteristic of utopias, which can assume their proper figurative function only by bowing to the regimen of representation.[8] In a parallel way Federico Zeri speaks of "imaginary cities" (but what does "imaginary" mean here?). As Pierre Francastel has demonstrated, architectural depictions can precede the realization of comparable designs by several decades: "The architecture of the Renaissance was painted before it was built."[9] So we cannot accept Eugenio Battisti's suggestion that these panels represent not so much an "ideal" city as an ancient one reconstructed according to diverse sources.[10] Any more than we can accept, without further data, that the simultaneous presence in the Baltimore panel of archaeological monuments and buildings reflective of an advanced taste for an *all'antica* idiom, typically Roman, is an illustration of the marriage of ancient Rome and modern Florence that was the goal of humanist circles at the end of the fifteenth century.[11] But we can say that this panel offers up a veritable display of ancient and modern architecture, something resembling a repository of monuments, the equivalent of a care-

8.   Cf. Louis Marin, *Utopiques: Jeux d'espaces,* Paris, 1973; English trans. by Robert Vollrat, *Utopics: Spatial Play,* Atlantic Highlands and London, 1984.
9.   Pierre Francastel, "Imagination et réalité dans l'architecture civile du quattrocento," *La Réalité figurative,* op. cit., pp. 290–302; *Peinture et société,* op. cit., p. 70.
10.   Battisti, op. cit., p. 109.
11.   Howard Saalman, "The Baltimore and Urbino Panels: Cosimo Roselli," *Burlington Magazine,* vol. 110, no. 784 (July 1968), pp. 376–83.

fully preserved "historic district," though one into which buildings have been introduced that must be qualified as "avant-garde," even if the panel was painted in the years around 1500: the fact that the new architecture was in an *all'antica* idiom guaranteed the possibility of an integration consistent with trends in scenography—in the Vitruvian sense—facilitating the incorporation within a single perspective of the two foreground palaces and the background of ancient monuments.

In the most recent literature the descriptive illusion is embraced without qualification: Sanpaolesi, Parronchi, and Howard Saalman take it to be out of the question that this genre of "perspective views" might have

52   Baldassare Peruzzi, Hall of Columns, Villa
Farnese, before 1516. Photo: Scala.

54 *Miracle of the Man Wounded by a Shovel,* from the "Miracles of Saint Bernardino." Perugia, National Gallery of Umbria. Photo: Alinari-Giraudon.

At the end of the fifteenth century, the motif of the centrally planned temple could only be considered in light of the contemporary projects for Saint Peter's in Rome: Perugino's *The Consignment of the Keys to Saint Peter* in the Sistene Chapel, painted in 1482, is set before an octagonal temple framed by two Roman triumphal arches which evokes (rather distantly) traditional depictions of the Temple of the Rock in Jerusalem, which was consistently confused in medieval descriptions with the Temple of Solomon. An analogous building, though of smaller proportions, is visible in an anonymous Florentine woodcut from the end of the fifteenth century, illus-

55   Episode from the *Gesta Romanum,* woodcut,
ca. 1460–80. Florence, Uffizi, Department of
Drawings. Photo: Museum.

56   Buckle of Saint
Césaire, *Guardians at the
Tomb,* Provence, before
543. Arles, Church of
Nôtre-Dame-la-Major.
Photo: Giraudon.

57   Bonanno Pisano,
*Presentation in the Tem-
ple,* panel from the
bronze doors of Pisa
Cathedral, 1180. Photo:
Fotocelere.

58 Pietro Cavallini, *Presentation in the Temple,*
mosaic in the choir of Santa Maria in Trastevere,
Rome, late thirteenth century. Photo: Richter.

trating an episode from the *Gesta romanorum:*[15] flanked by two small buildings placed further forward, the temple is not without similarity to those in
Perugino's *Consignment* and Raphael's *Marriage of the Virgin.* Two features
strike you as worth noting: first, the recurrence of the motif of a centrally
planned temple or building in the context of certain episodes from sacred
history—the marriage of the Virgin, the presentation in the temple, the
guarding of the tomb, etc.; and second, the pronounced symmetry that
characterizes compositions of this kind, in their architecture or their figure
distribution, when the building doesn't occupy the center of a piazza whose
bordering facades recede on either side of the scene, as in the famous predella panel of *The Presentation in the Temple* by Gentile da Fabriano,[16]

15. Florence, Uffizi, Department of Drawings, Inv. 125 st sc. Cf. A. Hind, *Early Italian Engrav-
ings,* London, 1938, vol. 1, p. 46, where this print is dated 1460–80.
16. Paris, Musée du Louvre. The rotunda of the sepulcher appears on a Roman ivory from the
early fifth century (Munich, Bayerische National Museum) and, in a less sophisticated form, but one
in which two flanking arcades create an emphatically symmetrical effect, on the buckle of the belt
of Saint Césaire preserved in Arles (Provence, before 543). It recurs in several Carolingian ivories.
The building in the presentation in the temple is visible (among many examples) in the bronze

59　Gentile da Fabriano, *Presentation in the Temple*, predella panel from the *Adoration of the Magi* altarpiece, Florence, 1423. Paris, Louvre. Photo: Lauros-Giraudon.

which is precisely contemporary with Brunelleschi's experiments. But it is in the frescos of late antiquity, as in proposed reconstructions of ancient scenography, that the motif takes the form of a "view" framed by two rows of columns. And as to circular temples with conical roofs featuring colossal orders of columns, the Temple of Vesta in Rome offered a model closer to that in the *Città ideale* than Bramante's *Tempietto;* a second-century relief in the Uffizi bears a particularly interesting image of it in which the walls between the columns are reticulated in a way not dissimilar from what we see in the Urbino temple.

*

A model does not ascertain a fact but rather aims at an effect, in the sense in which André Chastel could say that the so-called Urbino perspectives were intended to valorize the space of the city. If, like Krautheimer, one

doors of the cathedral in Pisa [1180]: here again it occurs in a symmetrical composition of a kind of which the Sagolacheni plaque (Southern Georgia, 10th–11th centuries) in the Tbilisi Museum offers a particularly interesting example from a semiological point of view; the building is metonymically reduced to a simple baldachino placed above the central group, which is flanked on either side by attendants (cf. *Au Pays de la Toison d'or. Art ancien de Géorgie soviétique,* Paris, 1982, cat. no. 60, ill. p. 136).

views the Urbino and Baltimore panels as the first representations of the "comic" and "tragic" scenes of the Renaissance, the problem in question is only displaced slightly.[17] Here again, you point out that the interpretation is predicated on a confusion of meaning with reference. And you find it amusing (as did Krautheimer) that, basing his argument on ancient and modern tragedies, Serlio maintained that uncommon loves and adventures, and cruel, violent deaths, could only take place in the houses of the great, of dukes, princes, or especially the king:[18] thus the apparatus of the tragic scene should feature exclusively buildings connoted as "noble" (*in cotali apparati non si sarà edificio che non habbia del nobile*), even when there were only canvas facades, with the action taking place not within the buildings but in the space between them. An injunction that the Baltimore panel effectively seems to anticipate, even as it conforms to Vitruvius's stipulation that the tragic scene should be decorated—as we've seen—with columns, pediments, statues, and other "royal" accessories (you note, however, that Vitruvius's text describes the scene only by citing these signs, and in no way implies that it must be cast as a piazza or a street). In its overall organization, this panel also conforms to Serlio's recommendation that the scenographer choose objects that appear to "turn well" under the spectator's gaze, or that of the *regardants* ("lookers" or "observers") in Jean Martin's literal translation;[19] in particular he should take care to place small buildings in front of larger ones, and carefully place all those elements—chimneys and bell towers, but also the buildings farthest from the eye—to be simply cut from wooden panels or painted on hanging canvas in such a way that their edges do not show.[20]

---

17.   In a postscript to his study, appended when it was published in a collection, Krautheimer was careful to emphasize that he considered the panels in question to be *reflections* rather than *representations* of the comic and tragic scenes as conceived in the Renaissance, which clarification only results in the question of their referent being posed with even greater clarity. (*Studies . . . ,* op. cit., p. 359.)

18.   "Li casamenti d'essa vogliono essere di grandi personnagi: per cio che gli accidenti amorosi: e casi inopinati, morte vilenti e crudeli (perquanto si lege nelle tragedie antiche et anco nelle moderne) sono sempre intervenute dentro le case de signori, ducchi o gran principi, imo di Ré." Serlio, op. cit., fol. 68 recto; English facs. ed., fol. 25 verso.

19.   "Et sempre si di fare elettione di quelle cose che tornano meglio a riguardanti, non havendo rispetto a mettere un edificio piccolo davanti ad uno grande." Ibid.

20.   "Tutte le superficie sopra li tetti come saria camini, campanili, et cose simili, se faranno sopra una tavola sottile, tagliati intorno, ben lineati e coloriti . . . , poi si metterano alli svoi luochi, ma siano talmente disposti, et lontani che i spettatori non li possino vedere per fianco." Ibid.

There is nothing in this panel that doesn't find an echo in Serlio's text, including the human figures—which may or may not have been added later. He observes of the tragic scene—and you are surprised that Krautheimer took no note of this—that some had proposed painting living figures in it, such as a woman on a balcony or in a doorway; but he counsels against this, because figures deprived of movement cannot "represent the living."[21] On the other hand, one would do well to fit out such a scene with feigned statues and reliefs made of wood or paper, and with fables and stories painted on canvas partitions, which could later be placed wherever appropriate (*e poi si metterano alle suoi luochi*). This could be said to apply, in the Baltimore panel, to the gilt bronze statues mounted on the fountain and surmounting the columns framing it, and to the reliefs decorating the triumphal arch: sculpture, through the painting which pictures it, being thus alloted the task of representing movement and "the living," by strictly static means, in contrast with the theater, where machines moving across the stage (Serlio notes this in relation to the satyric scene, citing performances mounted by Genga for the Duke of Urbino) can create the illusion of life.[22]

Krautheimer admitted it before anyone else: the "Vitruvian" interpretation of the Baltimore panel cannot be regarded as established. Though it may be well founded, it has yet to be verified. And the similar argument advanced concerning the Urbino panel has not found many takers. You note that there's consensus about the brio of the analysis, that it sticks in the memory, but also that it has no ardent enthusiasts and has not been subjected to serious scrutiny. In your view the only person to have attempted this, André Chastel, failed to address the main point, focusing less on the details of Krautheimer's text than on the consequences that others—beginning with Francastel—have derived from a hypothesis that, according to him, can be summed up in two lines. The work remains ahead of us: if it hasn't yet been done, this is because it necessarily entails challenging the privileged status of the representational function in painting. And another difficulty as well, which gives every appearance of being a paradox.

---

21. "In queste scene benche alcuni hanno dipinto qualche personagi che rappresentano il vivo, come saria una femina ad un balcone, o dentro una porta, etiamdo qualche animale: queste cose non consiglio che si faccino, perche non hanno il moto, e pure rappresentano il vivo." Ibid.
22. Ibid., fol. 70 recto; English facs. ed., fol. 26 recto.

If Krautheimer had essentially restricted his argument to the Baltimore panel, the scenographic interpretation would have been difficult to refute. You have proceeded, like many others, to the manifest parallels between this panel's iconography and Castiglione's description of the performance of Bibiena's *Calandria*. To be sure, this play was a comedy; nonetheless, the scenery featured an octagonal temple and a triumphal arch decorated with reliefs not unlike those on the arch in Baltimore (in one case mounted engagements, and in the other, according to Castiglione, a man on horseback spearing a nude man with his lance[23]). If we then compare, with no ulterior motive, the Urbino panel with the one in Baltimore, the same impression persists, by metonymy, of a theater set devoid, this time, of all human presence, but one that doesn't give the impression, at least initially, of having any specific character. Now this is precisely the way the hypothesis has functioned in practice, being either rejected, placed between parentheses (Klein: "Whatever one makes of this hypothesis, it cannot be used to date the appearance of theater scenery differentiated by genre"[24]), or taken to such an extreme as to see in the panels models for scenery intended for specific performances (in French, *représentations*): which, within the representationalist framework, is the reference to be preferred above all others, as there is never a representation, according to a remark made by Peirce that I like to cite out of context, that is not of another representation.

But Krautheimer's argument presupposes that a term-for-term opposition can be set up between the Urbino and Baltimore panels. And it is on this opposition, this systematic positing of series, that its prestige rests—a prestige whose basis is epistemological. Krautheimer holds that the character of the "scene" represented on the Urbino panel is much less solemn and "antique" than that in Baltimore. This is not only a matter of its not featuring comparable archaeological material, lacking an amphitheater, a triumphal arch, columns surmounted by statues, and a monumental fountain. The two wells symmetrically disposed in the foreground, in front of the two corner palaces, are broken down into simple, regular volumes on octagonal bases, as in the example Serlio took from Piero to explain the method for constructing bodies in elevation on the basis of ground plans

---

23. Castiglione, cited letter.
24. Klein, *La Forme et l'intelligible,* op. cit., p. 299.

60   Method for con-
structing wells in eleva-
tion. Piero della
Francesca, *De prospectiva
pingendi,* fig. XXXVIII.

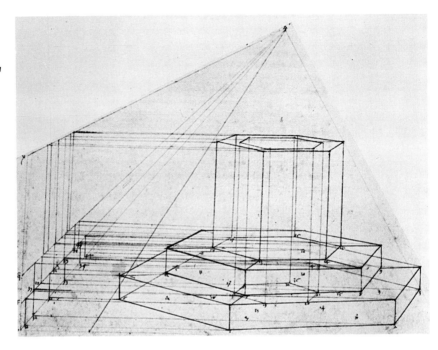

(*i corpi levati dal piano*[25]). As for the polychrome pavement, if it too seems simpler in design than that in Baltimore, it is far from clear that, as Krautheimer maintains, it presupposes any less skill in rendering figures of plane geometry in perspective. Here again the repertory of forms corresponds to those in Serlio's *Trattato di perspettiva, quanto alle superficie,* but were already used by Piero: losenges or octagons inscribed within squares, eventually divided into quarters, with borders in the form of bands or strips, etc. You point out that in the Urbino panel the marble pavement stops at the level of the second space which opens up in the background, in front of the basilica, and whose ground is of indeterminate color (brick? terra cotta?)—the important point being that the perspective checkerboard is interrupted to reveal what is *beneath* it. The same opposition occurs in Piero's *Flagellation,* with the difference that in the *Città ideale* the marble mosaic—or as some would say, the marquetry—occupies most of the surface of the painting corresponding to the ground of the scene. This is not quite

---

25. "Ma vorra l'Architetto esempio gratia dimostrare in perspettiva una forma ottogona come saria un pozzo." Serlio, op. cit., fol. 35 verso; English facs. ed., fol. 6 verso; cf. Piero della Francesca, *De prospectiva pingendi,* book I, xiv.

the case in the Baltimore panel, where only the low foreground area is decorated in this way, with the upper level over which are distributed the monuments and palaces, extending beyond the triumphal arch to the wall of the city, apparently lacking any such pavement.

But the crucial element of Krautheimer's argument concerns the depicted architecture. And it cannot be refuted by alleging that the presence of similar buildings in both panels destroys the opposition he sets up between them.[26] To consider only the corner palaces, Kimball's lesson has lost none of its pertinence: the elevations of the Baltimore palaces, which seem to answer, in the doubling of their columns and pilasters, that of the triumphal arch in the center of the composition, derive from a much more "advanced" model than those of the Urbino palaces. Without taking into account that in the supposed "comic scene" the two palaces on the left feature, in one case, a broad loggia running the entire circuit of the top floor and, in the other, a balcony on axis with the central door: Is the presence of these features sufficient justification for invoking Vitruvius's text recommending that the comic scene include imitations of private homes with conventional balconies, overhangs, and windows?[27] Rather than to these palaces, Serlio's call for handling the small houses in the comic scene like those of private persons such as citizens, lawyers, merchants, hangers-on, and so forth[28] seems more applicable to the ordinary buildings distributed around the periphery of the piazza, though these lack the projecting elements envisioned by Serlio, save for the setback of the line of facades on the edge of a second space, in the right background, as well as the shifts in scale and height he held to be characteristic of the comic scene in which, by contrast with the tragic norm, buildings in the foreground should be lower than those behind them, creating a calculated impression of disorder.[29] As for those other buildings which Serlio regarded as integral to the comic

---

26. Chastel, "'Vues urbaines' peintes et théâtre," op. cit., p. 498.
27. Vitruvius, loc. cit.
28. "I casamenti delle quale vogliono essere di personnagi privati, come saria di citadini, avocati, mercanti, parasiti, ed altre personne." Serlio, op. cit., fol. 67 recto; English facs. ed., fol. 25 recto.
29. "E sopra tutte le altre cose si de fare elettione delle case piu piccole e metterle davanti: accio che sopra esse si scuoprano altri edifici . . . onde per tal'superiorita della casa piu adietro, viene a rappresentar grandezza, e riempisse meglio la parte della scena, che non farebbe diminuendo se le summita delle case diminuissero l'una dopo l'altra." Ibid., fol. 67 verso; English facs. ed., fol. 25 recto.

scene, namely the tavern and the house of the *Rufiana* the procuress or, in Jean Martin's translation, the *maquerelle,* they are nowhere to be seen.

(It's true that in the Baltimore panel the examples of more modest, rustic architecture, while numerous, can barely be deciphered between the "noble" structures and archaeological monuments. But the proximity of the city wall, visible beyond the triumphal arch, cannot but confer on this entire portion of the scene—as Krautheimer said of the set for *Calandria*—connotions much less exalted than those called for by a definition of the "tragic" in terms of the social hierarchy, and Krautheimer's designation of the entry tower as a *regia* or castle cannot alter this.[30])

*

There remains the circular structure occupying the center of the Urbino composition, in the place taken by the triumphal arch in Baltimore, and which has already attracted our attention. If the comic scene is to include, in addition to the house of the *rufiana* and a tavern, a *tempio,* it's difficult to see how this one might satisfy the stipulation that it be in a "modern" style, which is to say a Gothic one, rather than an antique idiom. Which occasions, here again, an astonishing sleight of hand on the part of Krautheimer, who maintains that this centrally planned monument is not a sacred building but the product of a fusion of the enclosed circular hall and the *tholos* with conical roof which occupied its center in the empirial period, and which reappeared, as we've seen, in ancient stage scenery: in other words, a *macellum,* which scholars of the time thought to have been the essential element of the ancient market.[31] You see this designation, which is at the very least audacious, and that of the *regia* already mentioned as remarkable art historical examples of the linguistic abuse to which, according to the philosopher of language J. L. Austin, the illusion that a statement's function is essentially descriptive lends itself.[32] An abuse that also reflects back on the description itself. If it's true that describing an image requires one to list its elements, to name them, then the representationalist hypothesis can lead to absurdities: in order for his description to agree with the *macellum*

---

30. Krautheimer, "The Tragic and the Comic Scene . . .," op. cit., p. 333; *Studies . . .,* p. 349.
31. Ibid., pp. 334–38.
32. Cf. Recanati, *La Transparence et l'énonciation,* loc. cit.

identification, Krautheimer went so far as to maintain, contrary to the evidence, that the entire perimeter of the building in question was open, that the columns of its first floor were separated by low lattice-work stalls in *opus reticulatum*.[33]

What can we retain of Krautheimer's thesis if this building cannot be a *macellum*, as has become clear with the recent cleaning? Is the fact that the differences between the Baltimore and Urbino panels don't readily lend themselves to the establishment of simple, unequivocal oppositions, of the kind called for by the Vitruvian characterization of two kinds of scenes, the tragic and the comic, the noble and the "ignoble," sufficient to completely discredit the idea of a relation, in this case a specific one, with the theater, and to simultaneously undermine the attempt to compare the paintings term by term? This question only makes sense to you insofar as it leads to a questioning of the privileged status granted the iconographic and referential level in the analysis of paintings. This is not the place to discuss the problems posed by the distinction between the two levels of signification of the work of art introduced by Panofsky, namely a primary level posited as "natural" and "pre-iconographic," one that lends itself to spontaneous apprehension, being founded, as Roland Barthes said, upon "anthropological awareness," and a secondary or "conventional" level calling upon acquired knowledge that is explicitly erudite. But this distinction is exemplified in the case before us, which shouldn't surprise us in light of Krautheimer's tendency as an historian to pay close attention to the iconographic aspect of architecture, and given that he set out, with regard to the "Urbino perspectives," only to clarify their meaning, what they "represent." If it's true that the depictions in a painting exist only declaratively, then it is one thing, operated on one level, to note the presence in the center of the composition of a circular building with a double order of columns and conical roof, and quite another to designate this as a temple or—better yet—a *macellum*.

For Krautheimer, the difference between the two scenic types, the tragic and the comic, is first of all a matter of vocabulary: the question of the meaning of these panels is essentially reduced to that of the significance to be assigned the objects represented in them, their context having been

---

33. Krautheimer, op. cit., pp. 334–35; *Studies . . . ,* p. 350.

taken into consideration. Where perspective is concerned, all he feels he must do is note that the characterization of the tragic scene implies that the buildings included in it be symmetrically disposed and regularly aligned, and that those in the comic scene be distributed irregularly and asymmetrically. A single "form" can thus serve to express different "contents." And the spectator, the "observer," must be capable of grasping the operation: the identification of any motif implies, in every instance, an act of recognition whose more or less automatic character is itself a function of the evidence relative to the representational means deployed. In the case of paintings whose most "natural" features, to our eyes at least, however they may in fact embody restrictions placed on vision, derive from perspective construction, the problem of how the painting might allow itself to be described and given discursive form remains to be addressed.

And what, exactly, is describing, if the element of illusion upon which every description is predicated can lead to blindness, in Krautheimer's case quite patent and, far from limited to the *regia* and the *macellum,* extending over the entirety of the composition: for there can be no doubt but that the arrangement of the *Città ideale* does not feature, in its perspective regimen, any of the ruptures and level shifts that Serlio held to be characteristic of the comic scene, save for the effects of transparency created by the porticos and the loggia visible in the palaces in the foreground. But there is equal blindness among those who dismiss his interpretation on the basis of strictly iconographic considerations, as in the argument that the *macellum* identification could not be retained because the building in question was surmounted by a cross: this emblem could very well indicate a change of affectation, and there are many examples of pagan structures transformed into Christian ones, beginning with the baptistry in Florence, which tradition holds was once a temple of Mars. And in light of this argument, what are we to make of the "basilica" partly visible in the background, which bears not the smallest indication of its being a Christian edifice?

*

You also see as symptomatic the fact that some can maintain that the iconography of the Baltimore panel is more *legible* than that of the panels in

Urbino and Berlin.[34] This is partly because in our culture amphitheaters and triumphal arches are more readily identifiable than the circular structure in Urbino or the fortresslike structure visible against the watery horizon in Berlin. But above all it is because the Baltimore panel contains figures, whether decorative elements, such as statues and relief, or actual figures scattered throughout, that seem to have been included only *as figuration:* in other words, to imply by their very presence an historical or allegorical dimension. Iconography abhors a vacuum, just as it abhors any kind of painting that seems to exploit the resources of representation for the sole purpose, where the painting is concerned, of baffling the *reading* metaphor.

That paintings cannot be related verbally, this—as you pointed out by way of introduction—is considered scandalous in the context of a culture as massively informed by the philological model as ours. To such an extent that they're first subjected to being "read" in accordance with appropriate figures, the most privileged being that of narrative.[35] It's with good reason that semiology is today asking under what conditions a discourse *about* painting might be possible: for, taking up where iconography leaves off, the latter being incapable of dealing with anything in a painting that can't be named or articulated in accordance with the linear dimension of the syntagm, the only alternative option it sees is that of assimilating paintings to texts, and simultaneously to a system of reading. To describe, in this sense, is always already to narrate, insofar as all description—even the geometers admitted this—refers to an action: to describe a curve is to trace it, if only in the imagination, just as describing a painting amounts to clearing a path, laying out a route through it for discourse (when it's not a question, as in Diderot, of remaking it in the mind).

The reading metaphor presupposes that a painting allows itself to be defined, at least initially, as a "path for the gaze."[36] But it has meaning

---

34. Saalman, op. cit., p. 380.

35. Cf. Jean-Louis Schefer, *Scénographie d'un tableau,* Paris, 1969, and Louis Marin, "Élements pour une sémiologie picturale," *Études sémiologiques,* Paris, 1971, pp. 17–43; English trans., "Towards a Theory of Reading in the Visual Arts," in *Calligram: Essays in New Art History from France,* ed. by Norman Bryson, Cambridge, 1988, pp. 63–90. Cf. also the critique of the Marin article by J. -L. Schefer, *Semiotica,* vol. 4, no. 2 (1971), pp. 171–93.

36. Marin, article in *Études sémiologiques,* op. cit., p. 19; English trans. in *Calligram,* op. cit., p. 66.

only within the framework which is that of discourse pretending to take the measure of painting and "paint" it in turn, with the means proper to it. Which implies, again, that a painting can have meaning only insofar as it presents itself as a "bound and fettered" totality,[37] and to the extent that the paths in question can be translated into language. (Diderot: "The paintings I describe are not always good paintings; those I don't describe are sure to be bad."[38]) It is far from clear that we've escaped this circle today, or that there's any way to escape it other than by rejecting the notion, in the end a strictly empirical one, of the *path* (*parcours*) and with it the reading metaphor: a metaphor that has been productive, within certain limits but that is nonetheless misleading when the purported "text" of the painting is not construed a priori as a proxy for the person behind it, and when, if there must be a reading, this is understood to be something other than an *analogon*.[39]

That prompts the following question: Could there be a form of analysis whose aim was not to capture painting in the net of discourse but rather to allow oneself to be educated by it, even at the risk of undermining the linguistic model? A form of analysis that would be based not so much on the collation of iconic signs as of those features in paintings that resist being named and in which can be recognized the indexes of work which, leaving the iconic to one side, cannot be reduced to the order of the sign?[40] A form of analysis that would not be linked to any path, narrative or other, but on the contrary would reject on principle the notion of the inventory, and that would be capable in turn of *making pictures* [*faire tableau*])? Without taking into account that the very notion of the path of reading is highly ambiguous, given that—as Walter Benjamin observed after Gotthold Lessing, though in his case in relation to Chinese painting—it can be understood in two ways: either the description is held to advance along the lines of a promenade offering successive partial glimpses of the surrounding landscape, or it takes its place within a view from above, the pathway being

---

37. Ibid., p. 23; English trans., p. 70.

38. Diderot, *Salon de 1767*.

39. Marin, article in *Études sémiologiques*, op. cit., pp. 22–23; English trans. in *Calligram*, op. cit., p. 70; and the critique of this article by J. -L. Schefer.

40. Cf. Meyer Shapiro, "On Some Problems in the Semiotics of Visual Art: Field and Vehicle in Image-Signs," *Semiotica*, vol. 1, no. 3 (1969), pp. 223–42; reprinted in *Semiotics: An Introductory Anthology*, ed. by Robert Innis, Bloomington, 1985, pp. 206–25.

inscribed within the encompassing geography.[41] A form of analysis, finally, equipped to deal not so much with the question of representation as with that of painting's operation.

For in the end the problem comes down to this: Is it possible to escape the descriptive illusion in any way other than by denouncing the representationalist hypothesis from which it proceeds, while retaining the rights to an analysis that's not *about* painting but rather proceeds *with* it, but that doesn't necessitate our allowing ourselves to be spoken by it, like that "experiment with the past" which, according to Walter Benjamin, is history?[42] Or to put it another way: an analysis aimed less at helping us to understand than at helping us to see, and which would strive for a renewed intimacy with the work that is painting's own province? For *representing* is not the only function of painting: it aims at many different kinds of effects, in some of which theoretical aspects compete with poetic ones, so they're arguably closer to the realm of the ideal than to the field of affect. Such that for any discipline committing itself to a pictorial pragmatics, there would be no way to gain access to the conditions under which painting can be carried out other than to seize them in the very moment—as you said a moment ago—of their operation, of their effectuation: the English word *painting* indicating, as a progressive form of the verb, the essentially performative nature of a practice that has no existence, in contradiction to language, save in the act, the exercise.

Such an attempt would presuppose that language had uses other than purely descriptive ones. By way of broaching a response to the question implicitly posed by Benveniste about the specificity not so much of painting, considered as a semiotic system, as of the meaning it produces, and better yet of its characteristic mode of *signification*,[43] I here posit that there's a mode of meaning proper to *painting* that can only be brought to light by a linguistic operation that is not declarative but rather demonstrative in character. If perspective has any demonstrative value in relation to

41. Walter Benjamin, *Einbahnstrasse*, Frankfurt, 1955, pp. 16–17; French trans., *Sens unique*, preceded by *Enfance berlinoise*, Paris, 1970, pp. 156–157.

42. Idem., "Joseph Fuchs, collectionneur et historien," French trans. of 1937 article published in *Macula*, no. 3/4, p. 42.

43. Émile Benveniste, "Sémiologie de la langue," *Problèmes de linguistique générale*, op. cit., vol. 2, p. 57; English trans. of this article by Genette Ashby and Adelaide Russio, "The Semiology of Language," in *Semiotics*, op. cit., 1985, this ref. p. 238.

painting, this is to the extent that it furnishes the means and the occasion for such an operation: discourse's first brief being not to interpret painting, to deliver up its meaning, but to work along with it as it does, in geometry, with geometric figures. It being understood that it's one thing for a geometer to do geometry—as Poincaré would put it—with a piece of chalk, and quite another for discourse to measure itself against painting, thereby becoming vulnerable to being taken in by it: while geometry in its analytic mode has only, in the end, to dispense with figures, the pertinence of analysis where painting is concerned is determined in relation to its holding true that the discourse taking it for its object has no meaning, in each moment, save insofar as it derives its reason for being from the painting, and from it alone, and allows itself to be worked by it as much as it works it.

*

If there's any work of idealization in question here, that of which the "Urbino perspectives" strike you as typical examples doesn't necessarily have any connection with that of utopia, and they have even less to do with that of anticipation. To see these panels as models for a town or a stage setting is to effectively construe them as *representations,* even though the things to which they refer are presented as no more than possibilities. Unless one maintains that the utopia, or the model, belongs to the order of neither the concept nor the image, and these allow themselves to be comprehended, as Louis Marin has shown, in their capacity as figures or schemas of the imagination, in the Kantian sense of these terms: which is to say in the moment of the figure's reflecting on itself, of a "reference without referent," the sole aim of the fiction's operation being to clear a space in which the concept will be able to articulate itself in terms that are tangible, accessible to intuition, and to constitute and delineate, *in the form of an absence or lack* (note emphasis), the site of its emergence.[44]

Paradoxically Krautheimer's interpretation is apposite here, in that it maintains that the place the "Urbino perspectives" aim to constitute and delineate is not so much that of a utopia as that of a model of "representation," in the sense of a theatrical performance. For this interpretation outlines precisely the form of an absence, in this instance that of the

---

44. Marin, *Utopiques . . . ,* op. cit., pp. 40–41; English trans., p. 22.

performance to take place in this setting, but that remains as though suspended such that one can't decide, as you noted above, whether it has just concluded or has not yet begun, creating a feeling of anticipation blended with ambiguous imminence. You think of those photographs by Eugène Atget which Walter Benjamin compared to the "scene of a crime." As they display only a scene, with the emptiness of the setting paradoxically reinforcing the "theatrical" effect they produce. "In these images the city is emptied like a lodging that has yet to find new tenants. In such works surrealist photography prepares the way for the salutary movement leading to an estrangement between man and the surrounding world. To the politically informed gaze, it clears a space in which the clarification of details is given pride of place over all intimist considerations."[45]

Even in its comparable determination to clarify details, painting would have thus pursued, since the quattrocento, a project very similar to that of the photography of Atget, the surrealists, and a few others (I cannot resist mentioning, once again, the journalistic photographs, the first of their kind, taken by Roger Fenton during the Crimean War, in particular his image of a deserted valley filled with cannon balls, the real allegory of a history in which man no longer has a place, even in the form of cadavers, a history from which, as a result of that art alleged to be the most objective of all, he has become estranged). We shouldn't be surprised by the interest in our "perspectives" during the 1920s, which thanks to surrealism was not limited to specialists in art history. Surrealism and Giorgio De Chirico, whose "metaphysical paintings" Cocteau held to be similar to the *Città ideale,* that *grisaille.* De Chirico, who "had in common with dreams their impression of transporting us into indeterminacy, but nonetheless into constructed places whose every stylistic detail speaks of sleep,"[46] and some of whose perspectives, according to Cocteau, "are not only asleep: they are, between us, transfixed."[47] For the *Città ideale,* between us, has that same aura of, as Cocteau put it (you noted this at the beginning), a "wary eye": wary or transfixed, just like, in that photograph accompanying the story of

45. Benjamin, "A Short History of Photography," French trans., *Poésie et révolution,* op. cit., pp. 27–28.
46. Cocteau, *Essai de critique indirecte,* op. cit., pp. 167–68.
47. Ibid., p. 261.

a convict returned from Rio del'Oro, "the gaze that gazes at us and that sees the city."[48]

If there is no gaze save gazed at, how can we come to terms with what's striking about this painting: a painting that is not, at first, a path for the gaze but rather a trap for it? You note with delight that readers committed to the picturesque will have long since closed this book: this is because, like Cocteau, you wanted to consider only the facts here, and because, despite your predilection for myths, fables, and novels of all kinds, you chose to *systematically avoid telling stories*.[49] As for those smitten by poetry, they're another matter entirely: for them to be tempted to continue reading, they need only accept that "poetry is precision, as with numbers."[50] But what of photography? What of the subject, summoned to take its place in front of the lens (it's not only in moviemaking that he's forewarned not to squint at the camera: but the photographer can rest assured that once caught, fixed, immobilized on paper, the eye of the subject will not stray)? The lens *behind* which there need not be an eye, a computer would suffice: think of the photographs of distant planets sent back to us by NASA through space, opening up successive new vistas of the uninhabited universe. These waves are transfixed, and we along with them. As are you yourself before these windows, these doors that are open, closed, or something in between, wondering whether there is or isn't someone else on the lookout behind them, and if so, whose indiscretion is the greater: yours, looking at the city, or the city's, looking at you with all its eyes, wary though they may be, but arrayed like the keys of a keyboard you don't know how to play, nor from what score.

Remark 1: Whenever you enter the *studiolo* in Urbino, and that "space in which the clarification of details is given pride of place over all intimist considerations" opens up before you, you feel as though you're committing an indiscretion. And the discovery, each time, of the figure of the prince emerging from the wings is not sufficient to banish this malaise, which

---

48. Ibid., p. 229.
49. Ibid., p. 229.
50. Ibid., p. 16.

derives from a sense of suspension that's vague, yet strong enough to make you feel as though you have no business here.

Remark 2: In the Berlin panel there are boats which, given the absence of any sign of human presence, seem like so many ghost ships. Which leads you to suspect that there might be, in this theater, protagonists, actors, extras other than human ones: like the light throwing some details into prominence while casting others into shadow; or the architecture, the marine horizon, the clouds, to say nothing of the observer who finds no point within the painting in which he's reflected or at which he can anchor himself.

*

The representation's absence from its place delineates, in formal terms, the figure of a scene. But the construction of this "in perspective" entails certain consequences, is predicated on certain presuppositions. For perspective, as conceived by the men of the Renaissance, aimed at nothing less than the establishment, even before that of a "space" (supposing this notion had already acquired the meaning we ascribe to it today), of a site where everything would be, to use Serlio's phrase, inscribed in its place, *a suo luogo*. In this sense the opposition one might be tempted to posit between two kinds of perspectivists, those for whom *costruzione legittima* was indistinguishable, as Alberti professed, from the production of a scene within which an *istoria* could unfold, and those, like Piero, preoccupied with the possibility it offered of constructing, in planar projection, volumes such as they appear to the eye, this opposition—as can also be demonstrated using Uccello as an example—is in the end untenable: in both cases the same representational principle is at work that precludes us from thinking of bodies apart from the places they occupy, just as it precludes us from conceptualizing extension in any way other than as their receptacle or support—a receptacle or support that is itself inconceivable without resort to a *construction*.

And so it goes, a fortiori, for a "void" (the empty scene) the idea of which painting can only convey negatively, in the form of an absence: the scene being able to make itself seen, to make itself known, as such, and as the scene of the representation, only by means of an inversion of the positions traditionally assigned to the "container" and the "contained": the "container" (the scene) assuming the figure of the painting's "contained" (the subject). Which explains why we've been so preoccupied with determining what the "Urbino perspectives" *represent*, with discovering their content, when, as even André Chastel admits, "they seem not to have any":[51] as though it were necessary, whatever the cost, to assign them a referent to put an end to the kind of scandal provoked by placing parentheses around the representation, around the suspension of same, around its *épochè*. But here we are broaching what is without doubt the most difficult question raised by these panels, one having to do with the very form of representation, insofar as the perspective paradigm proposes the most consequent image of it. For what can it mean to designate the panels that concern us as "perspectives," and what's more as "old perspectives" or "perspectives in the antique style" (*et antico in prospettiva*), as do the sixteenth-century inventories? Can perspective in itself constitute the subject of a painting, to the point of defining a genre, or is it just a predicate, a property, in the sense in which we speak of a perspective drawing or a view in perspective? A question that appears to be eminently "modern," because it amounts to asking whether or not painting can be self-reflective in its operation, to the point of taking itself as an object, in its very form. That which our century has named *abstraction* would encourage us to respond affirmatively; but the problem persists with regard to paintings that cannot be called "abstract" (conforming to the usual tendency of art historians when dealing with the "Urbino perspectives") only on condition that we understand, from the start, the implications of such a predicate, of such a "property," in the context of representation.

In Wittgenstein's terms, an "image," a "portrait" (as was current usage in sixteenth-century French, and this is without doubt the best rendering of the word *Bild* as used in the *Tractatus*), can describe, picture, represent, in the mode of the *Abbildung,* any reality whose form it has, for example, spatial or colored form.[52] But as for the form of the representation, of the a-presentation (*die Form der Abbildung*), the image or

---

51. Chastel, "'Vues urbaines' peintes et théâtre," op. cit., 1978, p. 501.
52. "Das Bild kann jede Wirklichkeit abbilden, deren Form es hat. Das Raumliche Bild alles Räumliche, das farbige, etc." Wittgenstein, *Tractatus logico-philosophicus,* 2.171.

portrait cannot describe or represent this but only show or display it,[53] which is to say—as is the case here—*stage it,* in the way painting deploys and makes play with color, displaying it, exhibiting it, but not describing it, depicting it, or simply *imitating* it. To be sure, nothing in the *Tractatus* authorizes us to draw an analogy between perspective and the logical form of the *Abbildung*—nothing, that is, but the fact that Wittgenstein himself worked ceaselessly to break down this metaphor, ever active, ever recurrent.[54] If I make such free use of the term (deliberately misconstrued and out of context), this is because Wittgenstein's language is perfectly suited to the question I'm addressing here. *Painting in perspective* (*de prospectiva pingendi*) is certainly not the same as *painting perspective:* a drawing or painting can be *in perspective;* but *perspective itself,* how can this be produced, made prominent, if not in the form of *a* perspective—which immediately implies reference of some kind? The question becomes even more pressing if perspective is held to be the preeminent paradigm of representation, as well as the configuration through which the latter reflects on itself and reveals its operation. And this question is not as "modern" as it seems, if it's true that classic philosophy never stopped searching for a middle way between two extreme and antithetical conceptions of the sign: one maintaining that the sign can only turn back on itself at the cost of becoming opaque, thereby severing its connection with the thing it purports to represent; and the other, conversely, emphasizing its constitutive transparency and the impossibility of its reflecting on itself in the process of representation.[55] To become convinced that reference (necessarily "abstract") to painting has played a role in this debate, one has only to read Descartes or Berkeley, the *Logic* of Port-Royal or Condillac, and above all Pascal. But can we look to the fact that the question has lost none of its meaning and relevance today as authorizing us to construe it in terms that would have been those of painting, one or two centuries before the constitution of what Foucault designated as the classical *episteme?*

---

53. "Seine Form der Abbildung aber kann das Bild nicht abbilden: es weist sie auf." Ibid., 2.172.

54. Cf. Gilles-Gaston Granger, "Le Problème de l'espace logique dans le *Tractatus* de Wittgenstein," *L'Age de la science,* July–September 1968, pp. 181–95.

55. Recanati, *La Transparence et l'énonciation,* op. cit., pp. 20–21.

With regard to the art of perspective, *la sottil arte di perspectiva,*
Serlio states, from the start, that it is very difficult to convey in written
form and more susceptible to being taught directly than through doctrine or
drawings.[56] But he didn't dwell on this difficulty (which calls for closer
examination): far from spending time philosophizing about and discussing
what perspective might be, and from whence it came, with regard to these
points he was content to refer the reader to Euclid's *Optics,* if not his *Catop-
trics:*[57] which constituted an implicit response to the question concerning the
origin of perspective, though one that was not necessarily self-evident. In
fact Serlio's primary intention was to satisfy the needs of architects, for he
held perspective to be nothing other than what Vitruvius called *scenography:*
to wit, a means in the service of representation.[58] Perrault recalls, in this
connection, that Aristotle had used the word differently, as designating the
"scenic paintings" allegedly introduced into the theater by Sophocles:[59] a
reference that has a certain pertinence here, if we recall that at the dawn of
the sixteenth-century scenic designs seem to have been conceived in terms of
painting rather than architecture, with scenography subsequently coming to
exploit the resources of both, but not without Serlio's noting, as we've seen,
the difference between two kinds of perspective: one (that of painters) that
made its appeal to the imagination, and another (that of architects) that,
working with *real* depth and volume, of necessity conformed to rules different from those applying in the first kind.[60]

But the important thing, for the moment, lies elsewhere, in the
fact that perspective, whether the work of a painter or an architect, was
inseparable from architecture. You cite Serlio's remark that "the perspectivist will be able to do nothing without architecture, nor the architect with-

56. "Anchora che la sottil arte della perspettiva sia molto difficile a scrivere . . . e massimamente
de i'corpi levati del piano. Ansi e arte meglio se insegna conferando presentialment, che in scritto,
et in disegno." Serlio, *Il secondo libro,* fol. 25 recto; English facs. ed., "The Second Booke," opening
statement.
57. "Ne mi stendero in philosophare o disputar che cosa sia perspettiva ne donde sia derivata;
percio che il profondissimo Euclides ne tratta sottilmente con la speculatione." Ibid.
58. "Ma venando alla pratica et al bisogno de l'architetto, diro bene che perspettiva e quella cosa
che Vitruvio domanda Scenographia, cioe la fronte e li lati di uno edificio, et andro di qualunque
cosa o superficie o corpo." Ibid.
59. Perrault, *Vitruve,* book V, chapter viii, p. 178, note 1; cf. Aristotle, *Poetics,* 1449a.
60. Cf. *supra,* chapter 12, pp. 214–15.

out perspective."[61] But what does this mean, with regard to perspective, if not that in no case does the latter constitute an empty form, and that there can be no perspective—as Sartre said of color—save *of something*—this something being above all architecture, from the moment there's not, and cannot be, anything but a constructed perspective, and that perspective is, fundamentally, an architectonics? From that follows the seeming redundancy, if not pleonasm, attached, as I've intimated, to the notion of "architectural perspective." Which does not preclude the possibility of perspective's being conceptualized as a kind of scenography: quite the contrary, as is confirmed by the fact that the period's greatest architects—including Bramante and Raphael—started out as painters, whereas others, and not insignificant figures, got their start in the theater—such as Peruzzi and Genga, to whose scenery for Duke Francesco Maria in Urbino Serlio refers in passing. Not to mention Serlio himself, whatever his individual status with regard to the prevailing division of labor: Serlio, who says he began by practicing painting *and* perspective, which led him subsequently to the study of architecture.[62]

In fact the designation "perspective" in inventories from the Renaissance and the classic period denotes, in every case, a "view of architecture": the term carrying an important nuance, however, as it seems to imply an emphasis on the form of representation that these paintings exploit in such a way that this monstration takes the form of a demonstration. And yet, despite their manifestly ostentatious evidence, such "perspectives" always elicit a suspicion of deception: witness how, in built architecture, the term "perspective" is often used to designate elements in which trompe l'oeil plays a part. The fact that the term was used less as a title proper than as the indicator of a genre does not resolve the difficulty, which is simultaneously theoretical and epistemological, but rather exacerbates it, as can be seen each time a catalog proposes a description of a painting of this kind. For either the description is not accompanied by a reproduction and pretends to give us an idea of the painting, or even itself make a painting,

61. "Imo il perspectivo non fara cosa alcuna senza l'architettura, ne l'architetto senza perspettiva." Serlio, op. cit., fol. 25 verso; English facs. ed., "The Second Booke," opening statement.
62. "Et io, quale i mi sia, essercitai prima la pittura e la perspettiva, permesso delle quali a gli studi de l'architettura mi diedi." Ibid.

61   The *Città ideale*, inscription on the pediment of the palace to the left. Photo: Martino Oberto.

62   The *Città ideale*, inscription on the pediment of the palace on the right. Photo: Martino Oberto.

through an exercise in the genre of *ekphrasis;* or it uses the reproduction to suggest that paintings exist only to be described. In the one case as in the other, the hypothesis, with regard to paintings constructed "in perspective," that the latter has a privileged relation to description, perhaps constituting its most fundamental ground, is reinforced by the fact that the set of discrete elements included in the description are organized as a progression commencing on the ground, checkered or not, which is the foundation of the representation, thence proceeding from bottom to top and from foreground to background:[63] the synchronic configuration of which perspective

---

63.   Cf., for example, G. Bernini's description of the *Città ideale* in the catalog published on the occasion of the cleaning of the painting, cited cat., p. 6.

is an example functioning, simultaneously, as a model for the successive articulation of the components of the image in the three dimensions of projective space.

*

There remains a problem that you've already mentioned once or twice: that of the inscriptions on tablets within the two small pediments atop the foreground palaces in the Urbino panel (three lines in length on the right, and four lines on the left). These inscriptions, which include not only Latin letters but also characters that seem to be in Greek or Cyrillic, have long interested scholars. But the history of the attempts to decipher them is itself revealing of the interests prevailing in the history of art, and of the priority accorded questions of attribution and dating by it.

The first to describe these inscriptions, Passavant, was able to decipher only the four letter sequence M G–F G, which he thought might be the initials of a certain Maestro Giapo Cebdroli da Gubbio, of whom nothing is known save that he was a ceramist.[64] At the turn of the present century, when the idea of attributing this panel to Luciano Laurana was beginning to gain ground, scholars pointed to a passage in the *Descrizione del Palazzo Ducale in Urbino* by Bernardino Baldi, published in 1587, where it was stated that "Luciano Laurana had a perfect mastery of drawing and painted in a most accomplished way, as can be seen in certain small panels on which are delineated, in conformity with the rules of perspective, and colored some scenes which are without doubt from his hand, given that his name is inscribed on them, as are other things, in Slavic language and characters."[65] Budinich profited from a 1901 cleaning to make a close study of these inscriptions, particularly the one on the left, in which he thought he could make out two sets of characters, one indicating a date (147–), and another corresponding to the birthplace of Laurana, URANNA.[66] Dis-

---

64.   Passavant, *Rafael* . . ., op. cit., vol. 1, p. 442; French trans. vol. 3, pp. 380–82.

65.   "Che Luciano Laurana avesse buonissimo disegno e acconciamente dipingesse si vede in certe tavolette nelle quali son tirate con ragioni di prospettiva e colorite alcune scene, delle quali non si puo dubitarsi che siano sue essendovi scritto il suo nome, e alcune altre cose cl' caratteri e linguaggio schiavone." Bernardo Baldi, "Descrizione del palazzo ducale in Urbino," as cited in *Vita e fatti di Federico di Montefeltre,* Bologna, 1826, pp. 264ff.

66.   Kimball, "Luciano Laurana and the 'High Renaissance,'" op. cit., pp. 125–29.

patched to Urbino on behalf of Fiske Kimball, Richard Offner, while sympathetic to the attribution to Laurana, found no evidence to support these assertions.[67] That did not prevent Kimball from arguing that the "slavic" character of the letters was sufficient to prove the argument based on the text by Baldi (ignoring the fact that he used the term *tavolette,* which could scarcely apply to the cumbersome Urbino panel).

More recent attempts at deciphering have led some to identify in the inscription on the right, which is the more clearly visible one, sequences of letters in which Greek and Latin characters are mixed together with a series of numbers, 1 4 9 ., which suggests a date that Zeri points out, as if by chance, is more consistent with the style of the depicted buildings,[68] and with the now prevailing tendency to date the "Urbino perspectives" later than is consistent with an attribution to Laurana. But the recent cleaning of the Urbino panel, though rendering the inscriptions more clearly visible, has cut these speculations short, one hopes definitively. For the conclusion of those in charge of the cleaning, Anna and Martino Oberto, as well as of those writing in the catalog reporting its results, is that these inscriptions are examples of *simulated writing,* which excludes all possibility of specific names and dates being mentioned in them.[69] That has not prevented others from wanting to reopen the question, as if the idea of such a closure to reading was as unbearable for them as was, for Krautheimer and all those emulating him, contradictions and all, that of an indefinite suspension of representation.

You are tempted to take a hint from the very insistence with which these inscriptions solicit deciphering, only to repeatedly frustrate the hopes they've raised of putting an end to the debate dividing historians. To assert that, in effect, these epigraphs function like the *absence* characteristic of the representation. Like an allegory of the deadlocked reading: but its *real* allegory, from the moment this figure delivers up its meaning only on condition, for the "observer," of playing along with the signifier, of borrowing the accoutrements of reading only the better to reveal the impasse into which it has fallen. Inscribed as they are within the configuration of the

---

67.   Ibid.
68.   Zeri, cited cat., p. 145.
69.   D. and G. Bernini, cited cat., p. 12.

painting, the inscriptions also carry, with regard to the perspective construction and the entire apparatus of the scene, a symbolic significance: if the principle of *costruzione legittima* aims at painting's effacing itself before what it represents like the sign before the signifier, the fact that the reading is frustrated in this way, and that the process of decipherment has hit the wall of the signifier, takes on an emblematic value (*wall* being here understood quite literally, as both the partition serving to support the inscriptions and as the one into which the "window" opens which is equivalent to the painting).

This argument will become clearer if we observe that, whereas in the Urbino panel the sites of writing are disposed symmetrically, on either side of the scene, the triumphal arch in the center of the Baltimore panel features a similar image, in this case the site of an *absence:* the place traditionally set aside on such a monument for the epigraph here bears no inscription indicating its date or purpose. Between the two panels a play of opposition is set up which only accrues meaning in the context of a configuration, a perspective encompassing them both, which immediately comes to seem absolutely essential. Admittedly this opposition is somewhat mitigated by the presence on the left side of the painting of a pediment with a tablet that might or might not bear an inscription. And it might not seem to hold up at all, save for one thing: this unique site, established like the painting's vanishing point along its central axis, itself seems to solicit, in the context of comparisons with works that are more or less contemporary, a kind of decipherment and interpretation different from those used in attempts to settle questions of dating and attribution. We have only to think of the Arch of Constantine in Rome, and of its depiction in late fifteenth century paintings, and in compositions not without similarities to the "Urbino perspectives." Like the frescoes by Botticelli (*The Punishment of Corah*) and Perugino (*The Consignment of the Keys to Saint Peter*) facing one another—here too in accordance with a deliberate play of opposition—on the walls of the Sistine Chapel. In Botticelli's fresco the image of the Arch of Constantine, accurate in every ornamental detail, centrally disposed, occupies the background, while further forward and to either side of it are a palace and an open portico, with the "storia" being organized around an octagonal altar very reminiscent of the two wells in the foreground of the Urbino panel. As for Perugino's fresco, there the action unfolds in a large

63   Botticelli, *Punishment of Corah,* ca. 1482.
Vatican, Sistine Chapel. Photo: Anderson-Giraudon.

piazza with regular squared pavement, with three monuments disposed
along the same line visible in the background (as in the Baltimore panel): a
domed, centrally planned building, of a type analogous to the one in the
Marriage of the Virgin, but here flanked by *two* triumphal arches of a very
different type, with doubled columns, like the one in the Baltimore panel.
In both cases the inscriptions dominating the attics emphasize the intrinsic
meaning of the represented scenes or give us the key to it, in one instance
positing a parallel between the sacerdotal authority of Christ and that of
Moses, and in the other proposing a symbolic demonstration of the superiority of the Christian Church and the primacy of papal authority.[70]

---

70.   Leopold D. Ettlinger, *The Sistine Chapel before Michelangelo: Religious Imagery and Papal Primacy,*
Oxford, 1971, pp. 66–70 and 90–93. This portion of the decoration of the Sistine was realized
during the pontificate of Sixtus IV, between 1481 and 1483, which doesn't take us very far from
the "Urbino perspectives."

FOURTEEN

To See Them, You Say, and Describe Them

You insist on this point: the problem is not to determine what the "Urbino perspectives" *represent*, nor to decide, from the start, to what genre they belong. Initially it's one of trying to see them, of learning to see them, of managing to describe them. Without, all the same, feigning to ignore the considerable work accomplished by the history of art with regard to them. And this for two reasons, which strike you as mutually supportive of one another.

The first corresponds to the need for finesse in observation of which you have so often spoken, and which allows us to summarily dismiss any interpretation that isn't at least on a par in this respect with those proposed by Kimball and Krautheimer, to cite but two. Whatever the means employed, no analysis need be seriously entertained unless it's as attentive to detail as those two authors and subsequent ones, like Sanpaolesi and Parronchi, who pretend to have reoriented the question: in the case of Sanpaolesi, by suggesting that the "perspectives" originated in Florence rather than Urbino; and in Parronchi's, by maintaining that they're not generic models for the different scenic types described by Vitruvius but rather set designs conceived directly for the theater, for specific productions. This last hypothesis having the merit of obliging us to consider the three panels as a *group,* an ensemble, though one whose coherence and internal consistency has yet to be demonstrated by means other than historical or referential ones.

But you feel that the work focusing on questions of attribution and date must be kept in view, like that concerned with possible connections with theater design, given that all comparison entails, of necessity, the establishment of series. To maintain that the Urbino and Baltimore panels are by the same hand while that in Berlin is by another; to connect all three to the Urbino milieu, linking them to Piero or Laurana, or perhaps Francesco di Giorgio, or to see them as the productions of a Florentine artist or studio connected to the circle of Giuliano da Sangallo; to isolate, within these compositions, elements properly architectural in conception, ascribable to this or that specialist in the art, as opposed to other elements of which one or several painters may have been in charge (a hypothesis that, on a theoretical level, you find particularly seductive, as it leaves open the possibility that these panels were the results of encounters and exchanges—in other words, of collaboration): all these subtleties in which connoisseurs and scholars have taken pleasure not only oblige us to look more carefully, they also, and above all, make it easier to perceive that there's a link between these three panels that's not merely nominative, one that resists all attempts to disassociate them on the basis of formal or stylistic arguments, as well as all operations intended to integrate the group thus defined into a much larger corpus, without taking account of the exceptional workmanship characteristic of these panels. It cannot be repeated too often: Marquetry, however perfectly executed, could never aspire to a luxuriance of detail such as that seen here. Superficial analogies won't suffice to convince us of this, we'll have to take a closer look, yet again. But this is precisely the problem, and it may be that the paintings themselves, in their very mechanics, impede this.

*

You dream of an exhibition that would unite the three panels, today separated by thousands of kilometers, one of which, at least, is difficult to see: which makes you relish all the more the luck we had, after countless failed attempts, to be present, wandering hopelessly through the few publicly accessible rooms of the Bode Museum, in East Berlin, at a moment when the curator walked through them, and immediately brought us into its presence. How many have seen it, this panel, and studied it as we were able to do then, in semidarkness, among those who judge it to be of a quality inferior to those in Urbino and Baltimore? Or is this because its architectural content strikes them as less elaborate, less sophisticated, less "avant-garde," despite the interest, from a theatrical perspective, of this view of a deserted square opening onto the sea through the columns of a portico situated in the foreground: Doesn't this three-bayed portico, with coffered ceiling and pierced walls on either side suggestive of wings, closely resemble a *proscenium* as well as a Vitruvian arcade screen? It's not without reason that Eugenio Battisti has maintained that, considered from a scenographic point of view, this panel is the most interesting of the three. Krautheimer, on the other hand, was obliged to ignore this "scene," for it's difficult to see how he could have brought it into line with the Vitruvian trilogy: To what does this view of a maritime city correspond, if not to a harbor with several ships gliding through its waters? You're tempted to play the erudite scholar, citing the description Pollux gives in his *Lexicon* of the facade of the stage of a Hellenistic theater: to either side of the two doors flanking the central portal were two others functioning as *periaktoi,* the one on the right offering a view of the city's exterior while that on the left opened onto a port.[1] But such an exercise in innocent pedantry would only bring you back, against your will, to the theater.

It would seem that we just can't get away from it. And this is not only because scenic connotations inevitably attach themselves to representations of this kind. On a subtler level, the Vitruvian interpretation strikes you as owing much of its prestige to an epistemological effect that has not yet been identified as such. If Krautheimer used comparison of the Urbino and Baltimore panels to posit the existence of a set of systematically articulated binary differences and oppositions (*inter se dissimili disparique ratione,* to cite Vitruvius's phrase), then it must be conceded that one can do structuralism, just as others write prose, without knowing it. And I can't help but be amused when I see that some of the individuals most fiercely resistant to structural analysis, those blindest to its potential benefits to art history, and who are in the greatest hurry to relegate it to the ash heap (as if one could dismiss as obsolete, in our field, a method one hadn't even tried out)—I can't help but be amused, I say, when I see these people succumb to the brilliance of an interpretation which they seem to secretly regret isn't more convincing. The reason for this being, of course, that Krautheimer sacrificed to the law of genre, which stipulates that the only proofs to be credited in the history of art are textual ones. Had he managed to come up with even a vaguely convincing representation of the third of the scenes described in the treatises, the "satyric" one, his interpretation would have struck them as

---

1. Pollux, *Onomasticon,* IV, 126; edition by E. Bettie, Leipzig, 1900; as cited by A. M. G. Little, "Scaenographia," *Art Bulletin,* vol. 18 (1936), p. 408.

even more impressive, though without increasing their awareness of the structural imperative underlying their expectations.[2]

The strength of Krautheimer's argument then owes less to its content than to its form: if his demonstration is not really convincing, its project, on the other hand, if not its modus operandi, is somehow pleasing to the mind, at least in principle. But the implications of this are clear: first, a refusal, from the start, to assign the depicted elements hard and fast meanings refering to things outside the painting, on a level transcending its own. However preposterous it might seem, the idea that the structure in the center of the Urbino panel is a *macellum,* an ancient covered market, would nonetheless be acceptable, at least hypothetically, if it were justified by pointing to a network of polar oppositions shown to hold sway over it. There's nothing about the actual appearance of the monument that lends credibility to this hypothesis: it can only have been prompted by the game in which Krautheimer allowed himself to become caught up; it can only find justification in the rules of this game. As Claude Lévi-Strauss has written, symbols never have intrinsic, unchangeable meanings; their value is a function of their position, and is always relative.[3] But this observation applies not only to individual motifs; it also holds on the level of the paintings themselves, from the moment they're considered as figurative propositions whose coherence is a function of that of the system of which they're integral parts. Paintings don't derive their meanings from contemporary or archaic institutions whose reflections they are (in this case, the Vitruvian scene, in its three manifestations) any more than myths do: they're a function of the position these occupy in relation to others in a transformation group.[4]

The true weakness of Krautheimer's demonstration lies here: rather they sticking to the syntagmatic context, as methodological rigor would

---

2.   Some have researched the relatively late appearance of the satyric scene, for example, in the drawings of Battista da Sangallo (cf. A. Conti, "Le prospettive urbinate . . .," cited article, p. 1205). But it was in the strictly scenographic art of a Buontalenti as well as in landscape painting that the satyric genre would finally make itself felt (cf. Ernst Gombrich, "The Renaissance Theory of Art and the Rise of Landscape," *Norm and Form: Studies in the Art of the Renaissance,* London, 1966, pp. 119–21).

3.   Claude Lévi-Strauss, *Mythologiques I. Le Cru et le cuit,* Paris, 1964, p. 64; English trans. by John and Doreen Weightman, *The Raw and the Cooked,* New York and Evanston, 1969, p. 56.

4.   Ibid., p. 59, note 1; English trans., p. 52.

dictate, and proceeding first with a comparative analysis of the panels and subsequently querying whether the play of formal oppositions revealed by it were echoed in nonpictorial series, he preferred to invoke the Vitruvian paradigm (subsequently revised and completed by Serlio) at the start, and use it as a kind of preestablished, preconstituted interpretive framework. Now this paradigm could serve to construct a transformation group only to the degree that it was itself susceptible to development of a structural kind. As described by Vitruvius, it would appear that the satyric scene *transforms* nothing, that it retains none of the traits of either the comic scene or the tragic, being decorated only by trees, caves, mountains, and rustic accessories of all kinds, like a landscape[5]—which perspective could not teach one how to construct, save by reducing it to the measure of architecture. But if Vitruvius presents the satyric scene as the antithesis, the absolute negation of the two scenes connoted as architectural, with caves and mountains being opposed to structures built by the hand of man like nature to culture, this is no longer the case with Serlio. In addition to fountains and streams, snails and other "strange little beasts," he introduced small huts *alla rustica* similar to those—again—in settings designed by Girolamo Genga for the Duke of Urbino: in other words, a primitive, even archetypal mode of architecture, one in clear opposition to more cultivated varieties, be they noble or common, tragic, or comic.[6] But there's also something of the nature/culture opposition in the absence of rules typical of the satyric scene, at least on the level of its protagonists; for satyrs are preoccupied with those who unstintingly give themselves over to voluptuousness, indicating them by, so to speak, pointing them out (*quasi mostrati a ditto*); such licence being admisable only for characters who do not themselves command respect, which is to say for figures who are *rustic* (like the huts).[7]

As a prisoner of the referential prejudice, Krautheimer was unable to develop the acute intuition which initially prompted his study of the

---

5.   "Satyricae vero ornantur arboribus, spelucis, montibus reliquisque agrestibus rebus in topoedi speciem deformati." Vitruvius, *De architectura,* book V, vi, 8.

6.   Cf. Josef Rykwert, *On Adam's House in Paradise: The Idea of the Primitive Hut in Architectural History,* New York, 1972.

7.   "Perho tal'licentia si puo comprendere che fuse concessa a personnagi che senza rispetto parlassero, come sarra a dire gente rustica." Serlio, *Il secondo libro,* fol. 69 verso; English facs. ed., fol. 26 recto.

"Urbino perspectives." The only differential variants he was willing to recognize were hierarchical ones: "noble" architecture as opposed to "common,"
like great men as opposed to commoners. Which led to the iconographic
deformations we've examined, with context dictating whether a given motif
is to be ennobled or relegated to an inferior status (the case of the *macellum*).
But he could not have proceeded otherwise: the absence from Krautheimer's
paradigm of a straightforward representation of the satyric scene precluded
him from taking any account of the operations establishing systematic relations among these three panels. Note well: I said these *three* panels. For the
fact that there's a term-for-term or feature-for-feature opposition between
two figures, two scenes, two paintings is no guarantee that there will be
transformations, much less that these transformations will constitute a
group. And with regard to structure, as Lacan liked to point out (and Lévi-

Strauss said the same thing), one must learn to count higher than two, and at least to three: for works of art, like myths, like man himself, can "converse" among themselves only insofar as they conform to the regimen conditioning all discourse, that of a polar opposition and regulated exchange of positions of enunciation, in which reference to a third party is obligatory (*I, You, He*).

The idea that works of art can "converse" among themselves in some systematic way is not a new one. Panofsky provided an example, perhaps an overly literal one, when he showed how the first series of great Gothic cathedrals was organized in a way paralleling the scenario of the scholastic *disputa*, with its sequence of questions and answers, objections, etc.[8] From a strictly semiological perspective, the stakes are high from the moment the hypothesis permits us to get beyond the aporia in which the question of artistic "language" comes to grief, and painting can be considered as a semiotic system: in other words, as soon as the problem—as Benveniste would say—of its mode of *signification* can be engaged. Whether one argues that there is no system other than that of "language" or "code," a position that still doesn't help one to produce a repertory of traits, primary elements, in short of the *unities* (colors, etc.) of painting, or a grammar presiding over their deployment, their combination—unless one remains on the level of iconography, in other words, of *motifs*, which yield of necessity to an initial verbalization, as Benveniste pointed out. Or one maintains that ultimately the only system is that of the painting, as Jean-Louis Schefer has stated,[9] or—basically the same position, but formulated in a way consistent with contemporary aesthetic preoccupations—agrees with Benveniste that the significance of a work of art varies fundamentally from viewer to viewer and that, if any significant relations are in question, these are to be discovered within the work itself, considered in isolation from all else: "Here art is never anything other than a specific work of art into which the artist freely sets up contrasts and values over which he assumes supreme authority, answering to no one, unobliged to eliminate contradictions, having only a vision to express, in accordance with criteria that can be conscious or uncon-

8.   Erwin Panofsky, *Gothic Architecture and Scholasticism*, New York, 1957.
9.   Schefer, *Scénographie d'un tableau*, op. cit., pp. 167–94.

scious, of which the composition as a whole provides evidence and becomes a manifestation."[10]

Formulated in these terms, the paradox is subject to the same constraint as Saussurian linguistics, which maintains that analysis can only be carried out with regard to statements (*énoncés*), and is inapplicable to any level higher than that of the sentence. Whatever one makes of the thesis assimilating paintings to articulated propositions (which is not the same as saying they are cast in the forms and terms of verbal language), one might expect that the establishment in series of several paintings within a single transformation group would focus attention on certain modes of signifying that are less a matter of competence than of performance, and on a work of meaning that presupposes, if it makes any sense at all, that the artist has something other, something more to do than "express a vision." And, for example, as is posited by a stronger theory of symbolism in painting, that he can question himself about the conditions, with regard to pictures, of visibility and representation—in other words, of statement—reflect on them and, even at the risk of contradiction, interpret the system in question in accordance with its own ways and means, without resort to language as an intermediary. For this, it suffices to posit—replacing "mask" by "painting" in the analysis of Lévi-Strauss—that one painting *responds* to another by assuming its individuality, and that what matters "is not primarily what it represents but what it transforms, that is to say what it chooses not to represent. It denies as much as it affirms. It is not made solely of what it says or thinks it is saying, but of what it excludes."[11] With the caveat that while the reply, in the case of masks, forms an integral part of a given *repertory* (that of masks), the competence evidenced in a painting through its assumption of its individuality can only be demonstrated a posteriori, and by way of logical analysis. If there's such a thing as a system of painting, this is not to be sought in the convention authorizing the dialogue, nor in the *unicum* of the painting, but in the play of questions and answers, or

---

10. Benveniste, "Sémiologie de la langue," *Problèmes de linguistique général*, op. cit., vol. 2, p. 59; English trans. in *Semiotics*, op. cit., p. 239.
11. Claude Lévi-Strauss, *La Voie des masques*, Geneva, 1975, vol. 2, p. 117; English trans. by Sylvia Modelski, *The Way of the Masks*, Seattle, 1982, p. 144. On the decisive importance of this approach for the study of art, cf. H. D., "L'Éclat du cuivre et sa puanteur," *Critique*, no. 349–350 (June–July 1976), pp. 599–625.

responses (in every sense of the word*), of variations and transformations, that is central to art and is its mainspring.

*

But you grow impatient. Rather than spending more time on theoretical matters, you'd prefer that we try to verify the hypothesis we've just advanced as quickly as possible, that we get down to the paintings themselves. Because it seems to you that just as with myths, of which nothing can be understood until they're placed in series, the construction of the transformation group constituted by the three panels that interest us should finally allow us to see them, and describe them, while at the same time clearing a way for interpretation. For if thought is indeed at work here, of a kind that uses the means proper to painting, the only way to familiarize ourselves with it will be to track it as it operates, to put the paintings back to work, to deal with them as configurations that, in addition to demonstrative value, have a cognitive function. It cannot be said of painting, as Lacan said of language, that it *knows:* for painting never disposes of an instituted language and must work obstinately to provide itself with the means necessary to it. But the *will to language* that inheres in painting, that animates it, is eventually doubled by a will to knowledge, by an incitement to thought that must forge its own instruments, beginning with the perspective paradigm and the transformations to which it is susceptible. That is sufficient to displace the problem of reference—within this framework the referent is primarily an other, or other paintings—as well as that of context. If these panels inscribe themselves within history, it is not the history known to art historians: the effects of anticipation and release characteristic of it are not solely, nor even initially, of a stylistic or iconographic order. Any more than they are solely, or even initially, of an artistic order: it would be better to speak in this connection of aesthetics in the ancient sense of the term—which is not the Kantian one.

To see them, you say, and describe them. The establishment of the transformation group should encourage us to look more carefully at the panels, and to discover in them a number of features not previously ascer-

---

* Damisch's word is *réplique,* which can refer not only to a reply, a retort, or a rejoinder, as in English, but also to a musical repeat, a theatrical cue, or a cinematic retake.—TRANS.

tained, leading to the production of a kind of symbolic configuration that will itself constitute a sort of painting or tableau—one that, while it couldn't be substituted for the works themselves, will aid us in describing them better, more rigorously and systematically. The rule stipulates, in effect, that the configuration (the painting) encompass all traits, motifs, elements, and relations previously inventoried by art history, distributing them in an ordered way, the sole condition being that they derive their meaning, their "significance," not from what they purport to represent but rather from what they transform. Conversely, all traits, motifs, elements, and relations generated by the establishment of the series must be considered pertinent and subject to interpretation. And as for those that might become manifest through other means, they are to be taken into account only when they can be integrated into the group thus constituted.

Which is to say that this rule should permit us to escape from the other paradoxical stipulation that attention be paid, in the analyses of paintings, only to those elements organizing themselves, more or less spontaneously, along the thread of a discourse, of a continuous "reading," or that, on the contrary, the initial goal of the pursuit be maximal description, with the decision about which features to retain as pertinent being taken subsequently: a task impossible by definition, if it's true that pictorial transformations, like mythic ones, occur in multiple dimensions that cannot be explored simultaneously,[12] and that the very advance of the analysis will necessarily result in the appearance of new parameters and unsuspected traits. Just as a simple play of binary oppositions is not sufficient to determine that there will be transformations, so the operations to which a given trait is susceptible are insufficient to found a group. If there is a group, its logical consistency will be verifiable, in the last analysis, by its facilitating the description, by degrees, of the system holding sway over the "Urbino perspectives," and in such a way that—to the extent possible—there's nothing left over. I say its *logical* consistency; its possible historical consistency is another problem entirely.

*

---

12. Lévi-Strauss, *Le Cru et le cuit,* op. cit., p. 126; English trans., *The Raw and the Cooked,* p. 118.

The concept of transformation, like that of the group, is taken from mathematics. It seems only logical then that our analysis begin with geometrical transformations; specifically with that of a group encompassing the kind of symmetry common to the three panels: which is to say a feature whose character, insofar as this is *abstract,* makes it resemble a principle, even a foundation. But the difficulty we mentioned earlier in relation to perspective here comes into play once more: in the register of the visible, there is and can only be symmetry *of something,* through which it manifests and asserts itself as a property; and this something is, once again, architecture—that of the scene as well as that of the buildings occupying and circumscribing it.

It makes sense then for the description to commence with the foreshortened plane that is the scene's ground. In this respect the Urbino panel (subsequently designated as U), if we exempt two tiny glimpses of a mountainous landscape to either side of the central edifice, features a single continuous ground plane, on a single level, corresponding to the horizontal plane of projection. By contrast, the "scene" in the Baltimore panel (hereafter BA) is on two levels: in the foreground, a small depressed square disposed like a proscenium; in the background, its terraces projecting forward on either side of the "stage" and encroaching upon the proscenium, a second, higher level linked to the lower one by three stairways, in accordance with the disposition Serlio was to recommend for the tragic scene, which is sufficient to make the theatrical reference unavoidable, in some form or other, at least with regard to BA.[13] This second level continues, beyond the triumphal arch disposed as though it were a semitransparent screen, until the wall of the city marking the back of the scene, above which, as in U, a row of hills is visible. As for the Berlin panel (hereafter BE), its disposition is rigorously inverse: it has an elevated foreground level that's part of the portico framing the square, extending beyond it on a lower level, the drop being signaled by an interruption of the receding lines of the paving which, far from being an indicator of incoherence as some have maintained, bears witness, on the contrary, to careful planning which here becomes apparent: for this effect is explained if one postulates the existence of several steps, blocked by the raised proscenium floor, linking

---

13. Cf. *supra,* chapter 13, p. 253.

U Urbino panel.

BA Baltimore panel.

BE Berlin panel.

the two levels of the scene. In the background, finally, the sea, which is even lower than the square and the quay prolonging it, stretches to the horizon, though this latter is blocked by the silhouette of several islands— intended to recall the hills in U and BA?

On the ground level, or shift of same, thus defined, the architectural elements distribute themselves in roughly analogous ways in all three panels. But here too there are differences to be noted, some of them subtle. Beyond the open area in the foreground whose plan resembles an upside-down *tau* or *T,* and which evokes the proscenium of Serlio's theater, being occupied only by two symmetrically disposed wells, the unity of the ground plan in U determines that all the buildings are on the same level. But some of them are on plinths of various heights: relatively high in the case of the two wells, whose bases have four steps; still higher (five steps, to which the building's basement must be added) for the circular temple in the center of the composition as well as for the basilica visible to its right; but only three steps for the two lateral palaces, and only one for those beyond them.

BA conforms to a different schema. Except for the fountain in its center and the four columns framing it, the stage or proscenium, again in the form of an upside-down *tau* but clearly delimited in this case, is free of all construction. In conformity with the disposition of Serlio's stage, all the buildings are relegated to the second level, though the two lateral blocks are a bit further forward; but whereas Serlio, beyond the foreground slice of his stage, has its ground incline visibly toward the horizon, here there is continuity and consistency between the first and second levels, the break between them being bridged by the three sets of stairs, in the center and at the two sides (as would be the case, as we've seen, in the image of the "tragic scene"). And though this second level seems to serve as a kind of plinth for the buildings it supports, some of these nonetheless have bases of their own: four steps high in the case of the palace on the left, and only one for that on the right—an opposition that's reversed in the background: four steps for the octagonal temple (on the right) and only one for the amphitheater (on the left).

BE uses all these givens but deploys them in opposing ways. The first rectangular level is indeed demarcated by a difference in level, but in this case a positive difference that makes it into a kind of plinth itself. The four columns of the foreground in BA recur here, but integrated into a structure in which they lose all symbolic autonomy. Far from being empty of architecture, the BE proscenium is itself a piece of architecture. If there is an empty space here, a plan in the form of a *tau,* it extends beyond the proscenium and, once again, on a lower level. Finally, among the buildings symmetrically distributed in the background, only the palace on the right has any steps, but these can't really be said to constitute a plinth; and as for the one facing it on the left, if it appears to have a basement level with a single step, this is interrupted by the door, which amounts to an implicit negation of the very notion of a plinth.

U	BA	BE
Single level	Two levels	Three levels.
Background of towering hills.	Depressed foreground and background of towering hills.	Foreground elevated, with two successive incremental drops. Islands on the horizon.
Proscenium undelineated and empty of architecture, but marked by two symmetrical wells.	Proscenium delineated by level drop; empty of structures, except for fountain and four symbolic columns.	Proscenium delineated by level increase, itself architectural, with columns here assuming constructive value.
Buildings on plinths.	"Plinth" effect intensified by level shift.	Buildings lack plinths, with proscenium constituting its own plinth.

And then it scarcely makes sense to speak of the ground in any terms but those of level(s), if one sets aside the tracings with which every perspective construction must begin. This proceeds, in U, in accordance with a regular square grill, itself based on a division of the painting's baseline into three equal segments and two narrower ones to either side, the dimensions of the grid becoming smaller in the painting's extremities. This schema is rendered visible by gray bands whose intersections are marked by a change of color, in accordance with conventions then current in the arts of mosaic and marquetry. Inside the 3 × 4 set of squares extending over the center of the scene, rather like a carpet, from the baseline to the steps leading to the *tempio,* are shapes whose repertory corresponds to the exercises, included in all the treatises of the time, from Piero to Serlio and beyond, demonstrating how to render figures of planar geometry in perspective: diamonds and octagons, solid or in outline, inscribed within squares, and in the foreground, on the painting's central axis, an octagon in which is inscribed a Maltese cross.

In addition to the particularly careful, even luxuriant, handling lavished on this portion of the scene, whose ornament, I repeat, spreads like a carpet before the circular building occupying its center, U is also notable for another important feature: a break in the continuity of the paving, which is replaced by a ground of indeterminate color in the square in the background, to the right of the *tempio* and in front of the basilica. As we've seen, this is analogous to a gesture, more discrete, in Piero's *Flagellation,* where the interior/exterior opposition is doubled by one between the polychrome marble floor of the room in which Christ is punished and the brick paving of the street.

In a way consistent with his thesis, Krautheimer judges the design of the paving in U to be "simpler," "less precious" than that in BA. Let's just say it occupies a smaller portion of the painting's surface, and so is less conspicuous. For its ground plan is something else again. Whereas the baseline of U is divided into five segments—of unequal length but corresponding to a regular grid—with decorative motifs in only three rows, the paving design in BA is a bit more complex, having a large central square flanked on three sides by squares of like dimensions, with that occupying the proscenium recess and the two others, severed by the edges of the painting (as in U) and constituting the two sides of the "stage," being accompanied by bands of olive green filling the intervals between the proscenium and the squares. Within the squares are two diamonds, or, in the case of the central square, two concentric octagons. The apparent complexity of the design results from the fact that the lines of the grid pattern here define five bands of inconsistent width: three corresponding to the aforementioned squares, inlaid with polychrome marble—white, gray, and olive green—and two others that are white and narrow that cannot (in contrast with U) be assimi-

lated to the otherwise prevailing grid. The design thus derives its relative
subtlety from the fact that this schema appears only as a negative. And
from its color range being richer than that in U: whereas in U the chromatic contrast is limited to gray (corresponding to the outlining of lines
and figures) and the white ground, BA offers three colors: gray and olive
green on white, the latter serving as ground and coming into play as a
result of the spacing of the figures. It should also be noted that the continuity of the ornament seems to be interrupted before the baseline, as the
foreground of the "stage" is occupied by three discontinuous bands marking
the closure of the proscenium. But the essential point remains that in BA
the marble paving is restricted to this proscenium. The second level of the
scene being devoid of all outlines other than the bases of the buildings
situated on it, and a fortiori of all ornament.

In BE, by contrast, once beyond the proscenium decorated by
twelve squares containing diamonds, there's a schema in which red brick
alternates with black against a white ground, its elementary grill deriving
from the division into five equal segments of the base line corresponding to
the posterior limit of the proscenium, and which extends, red brick against
white, over the full depth of the recessed level of the scene. Over its depth

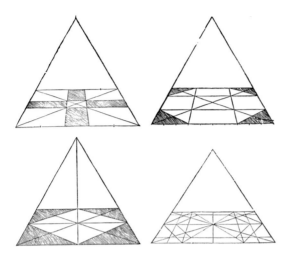

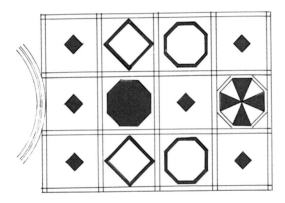

67   Perspective renderings of planar geometric
figures. Serlio, *Il secondo libro* . . .. Photo: Bibliothèque Nationale, Paris.

68   Schema of the paving design in the *Città
ideale.*

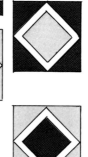

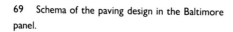

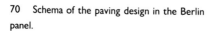

69 Schema of the paving design in the Baltimore panel.

70 Schema of the paving design in the Berlin panel.

but not its width, as the two lateral branches of the upside-down *tau* features only transverse lines, all perpendicular ones having been excluded. Here again we obtain a subgroup of transformations that is perfectly rational and, what's more, consistent.

U	BA	BE
Positive grid deriving from quintuple division of the baseline, except for the background square.	*Negative* grid driving from a division of the baseline into 3 + 2 segments, covering only the proscenium level.	*Negative* grid on the proscenium (3 × 4 squares). *Positive* grid deriving from a quintuple division of the rear line of the proscenium, covering only the central portion of the scene.
Bichromatic design scheme, gray on white, covering 3 × 4 squares and defining a differentiated area in front of the temple.	*Trichromatic* design scheme, gray and olive green on white.	*Bichromatic* design scheme for the "stage," red on white, and a *trichromatic* one for the proscenium, red and black on white.

*

While not all on the same level, semiotically speaking, the traits we've inventoried share a relative independence from iconography. They clearly function on different levels: it would be untenable to consider the makeup of the ground of the perspective scene, figure/ground relations, the use of color, the presence or absence of plinths, etc., under the same rubric. But, if one understands iconography to mean primarily the identification of figures and their labeling by means of language, then it's not so easy to distinguish between what, in the painting, makes an image (in the sense of "making a sign") and what can be assigned to a strictly formal level of articulation. For reasons that are easy to grasp, you haven't refrained from using terms ("triumphal arch," "colisseum," "palace," etc.) and metaphors (like that of the proscenium) that unavoidably engage the work of interpretation. Certainly you could have excluded these terms and metaphors without prejudicing the demonstration. On the other hand, the very fact of recognizing, within the image, something as a *ground,* with one or more levels, as depth, as geometric figures in planar projection, as the vanishing point, etc., presupposes an acceptance—in perceptual terms, independent of the question of its intrinsic value—of the convention that implies the perspective construction, or from which this proceeds: a construction whose arbitrariness, or—as we perhaps ought to say—whose relative necessity is confirmed by the fact that its parameters can be modified or transformed, within certain limits, without fundamentally disturbing its internal economy or the constants on which this is based.

You're prompted by this remark to advance more rapidly to another transformational subgroup which you hold to be of great importance, but to which for the moment you only want to draw our attention, as you intend to examine it in a more developed, systematic way further on. This subgroup consists of several traits related to iconography in only a mediated way, their primary linkage being to the perspective regime. A case in point is the *veduta,* an opening that offers a *view* onto the exterior (in contrast with *luce* which, as the word indicates, are intended to provide light); in other words, a kind of escape hatch giving onto the painting's background or a distant landscape, opening like a window or hole in the perspective configuration, [14] or penetrating through its mesh—in a way consistent, once again, with the given of "seeing through," of *perspicere,* of the *Durchsehung,* that shapes it.

Of these "openings" and the closure on which they're predicated, in conformity with the principle of the "Vitruvian" theater, U offers two more or less symmetrical examples: two fragments of landscape visible to the left and right of the central volume, through two openings in the architectural screen. A landscape that, as you've noted, is mountainous: the fragment on the left quite narrow, wedged between the cornice of one of the palaces and that of the *tempio* but that nonetheless provides a view of a slope covered by vegetation and dominated by a bare ridge; and that on the right, somewhat wider, framed by the upper facade of the basilica and that of the two houses

---

14. Cf. Pierre Francastel, *Peinture et société. Naissance et destruction d'un espace plastique,* op. cit., p. 65.

on the other side of the street, and in whose foreground we can make out a roadway ascending among a few trees, while in its background are juxtaposed, in the distance, the aforementioned ridge and a higher, more distant peak. But perhaps we must also, in U, take account of another *veduta,* in the sense we've specified: that consisting of the opening to the right of the *tempio* onto a second square further back, introducing into the composition an element of dissymetry accentuating the effect of depth, with the facade of the basilica being itself partially obscured from view by a carefully calculated framing effect.

BA also features two *vedute* onto the surrounding landscape. One is wedged between the palace to the left and the colisseum, above the roofs of the houses, opening onto a ridge topped by a crenellated wall interrupted by a door surmounted by a tower, the operation of the *veduta* being interrupted or cut short by the insertion of this screen, which is itself pierced by an opening. The other, broken into three parts by the three arches of the triumphal arch, features two successive ridges topped by a screen of trees blocking the escape into an infinite distance, as in U. But rather than these openings as quickly closed off, it is the entirety of the perspective visible through the arches, from one side to the other of the arch and including a second square that's itself closed at the back of the crenellated wall whose center is pierced by a door surmounted by a tower, which should be regarded as a *veduta,* as should the two narrow views opening onto the city's wings, just beyond the far corners of the palaces in the foreground. The situation being further complicated by the fact that the views into the interior of the amphitheater also create an effect of baffled depth and are blocked by another door, another opening.

As for BE, it features on the right, through one of the portico's lateral arcades (its "wings"), a narrow view of a crenellated wall above which a tree is profiled against the sky. In the center of the composition, the view of the sea is framed by a fortified tower (on the left) and a palace of Florentine type on the right, the horizon proper being intermittently blocked by mountainous islands (or are they promontories, the *veduta* thus giving onto a semi-enclosed bay?). But the transformation resulting in the opening, at the composition's center, of a seemingly limitless perspective is conjugated with the foreground placement of the portico framing the scene, as could be the case with a triumphal arch; there's no place in BE for other *vedute* save

of the sky and the horizon, and there can't be any others, if it's conceded
that the painting, the "perspective" itself, considered as a whole, is in the
end nothing other than a *veduta* in the sense we've specified.

　　The evidence suggests then that the play of *vedute* is linked to a
systematic variation that leads, in a calculated though easily reversible progression, from the wedged spaces of U to the open space of BE, by way of
the semiopen spaces, their openings baffled, in BA. You make no mystery
of the fact that, for you, this is the crucial point, the argument that sums
up all the work that can be done with these panels. And if you say *point,*
it's with the intent of invoking the vanishing point established on the central axis of the painting (in all three cases), and which is situated (another
constant) within the central door of a building: in the case of U, one that's

72   Berlin panel, central portion.

relatively close; in BE, within the central bay of a portico in the foreground; and in BA—a particularly subtle transformation that effects the
shift between U and BE—within the central opening of a triumphal arch in
the middle distance, one that opens onto another much more distant door
to which we might say the vanishing point has been referred. For, as
Alberti observes, a triumphal arch serving as the principal ornament of a
square or a crossroads is nothing other than a perpetually open door.[15]

15.   "Sed quod ferosque triviaque maiorem in modum exornent, sunt arcus ad fauces viarum sta-
tuti. Est enim arcus veluti perpetuo patens porta." Alberti, *De re aedificatoria*, book VIII, chapter
vi, op. cit., p. 716.

U	BA	BE
Perspective closed but adjusted down or up (the second open space in the background).	Perspective semi-open and adjusted down or up.	Perspective open.
Vanishing point established on the axis of the temple door, relatively close.	Vanishing point relegated to background beyond and through central opening of the triumphal arch.	Vanishing point relegated to the horizon, but framed within the central bay of the portico.
Two vedute, opening onto distant mountains.	Two vedute summarily interrupted by a wall or a screen of trees.	No vedute proper, the "perspective" itself taking its place.

*

We must still take stock of one last (?) non- or infra-iconographic structure (which doesn't preclude its generating meaning, its eventually accruing a conventional signification): that of light. In U it comes from the left, from a point situated slightly forward from the plane of the painting and quite high up: as is evidenced by the well-lit lateral facade of the palace on the right, the shadow cast by the palace on the left, those of the columns and pilasters of the porticos, as well as the play of light and shadow over the cylindrical volume of the *tempio* and, above all, over the four visible faces of the two octagonal wells in the foreground (we will return to these).

In BE the light also comes from the left, but from a point situated within the depth of the painting, beyond the portico. An apparent incoherence in the distribution of light and shadow (the frontally aligned facade of the palace on the left is in the light, while that of the palace on the right is in shadow) is explained by the fact that the palace on the right is somewhat further back than is that on the left, its facade sitting just beyond the fifth horizontal line of the checkerboard, while that on the left commences after the fourth. So what's in question here is a kind of false symmetry, a characteristic that calls for further explication and development. On the other hand, the light source seems to correspond to a point situated at only mod-

73 Baltimore panel, the triumphal arch.

erate height, since the ceiling of the proscenium, like that of the portico of the palace on the right, casts no shadow.

In a way consistent with the rule of transformation, the light in BA, by contrast, comes from the right, and from a point situated well in front of the painting and very high (note the shadows cast by the columns, the triumphal arch, and the palace on the right, as well as by the ceiling of the portico of the same palace). But here again the situation is complicated by the fact that, in addition to the light source outside the scene which determines the distribution of light and shadow, we observe in the sky, on the painting's left, above the amphitheater but not very high, a small golden sun surrounded by a few clouds (a propos: nothing has yet been said

74   Baltimore panel, the amphitheater and the
"sun."

of the admirable clouds in U, as they've been revealed by the recent cleaning). This manifest but apparently intentional inconsistency might be seen as providing a supplementary argument—and, in this case, a decisive one—for those maintaining this panel's direct relation to the theater. While, as we've seen, it shares a number of features with the sets used at Urbino in 1513 for a production of *Calandria* (though this doesn't permit us to draw any further conclusions), you point out that, according to Castiglione's description, on that occasion the auditorium was brightly lit (so providing a light source in front of the scene). As for this incongruous sun, you're tempted to find an a posteriori explanation of it in Serlio. In a passage in the *Trattato sopra le scene*, which follows immediately after the text you've just cited and in which he deals with questions of scenic apparatus and squares decorated with buildings rendered in perspective, as well as the columns, triumphal arches, etc., that can also be used in sets, Serlio specifies that in the course of the performance one saw the sun rise, traverse the heavens, and, at the end of the comedy, set, by means of an artifice which many found astonishing:[16] a sign of temporal unity, as the spatial disposition of the scene could be a sign of the unity of place. Unless (as some have maintained) what's in question is not a sun but a moon, in which case it should be classified as superfluous and ignored.

U	BA	BE
Light source to left. Placed high and in front of the painting.	Light source to right. Placed high and in front of the painting.	Light source to left. Placed rather low, within the painting's depth.
	Sun(?) at the end of its course, in left background.	

Your remarks about iconographic operations per se will be brief. But they nonetheless figure in your argument. Most of the features previ-

---

16. "Lo levare del sol; e il suo girara, e nel finire della comedia tramontar poi con tale artificio che molti spettatori di tal'cosa stupiscono." Serlio, op. cit., fol. 64 verso; English facs. ed., fol. 26 verso.

ously dealt with by art historians can be integrated into the transformation groups already constituted on the basis of essentially formal, or constructive, considerations, and this supplementary evidence will tend to attract their attention. And then the fact that a given motif can itself be subjected to ordered transformations, and that elements of "architectural content" (to use Kimball's phrase) can expand into a cluster that will conform to rules of operation analogous to those of the formal system in which it finds its place, has theoretical implications: it confirms Lévi-Strauss's assertion that, in structural analysis, content and form are not distinct entities but rather "complementary points of view each of which is essential for full understanding of a single object of study."[17]

Whether it's a matter of facade elevations or their coloring, of the opposition between sacred and profane monuments, of "noble" and common structures or ancient and modern ones, etc., pictured architectural elements constitute a register of oppositions that's sui generis, and that functions within each of the panels as well as among them. In U the bays beneath entablatures of the palace on the left, colored a bluish gray, are opposed to the relief arches above the windows in the palace to the right, which are colored ocher, this opposition of hot and cold being reversed in the two palaces beyond them, just as the circular *tempio* is opposed to the basilica, noble buildings (all of which are not in the foreground: there's a palace in the left background) to "ignoble" ones, etc. In BA there's the same play of color schemes, and the opposition between bays under entablatures and bays under relief arches recurs, in reverse, in the two foreground palaces, the reversal of the color schemes corresponding to that of the shift in lighting. And then the palace on the right has a portico, while that on the left does not. The opposition between noble and ignoble buildings also recurs here but is complicated by the presence of a fortified wall, which is inconsistent with the scene's purported "tragic" connotation, as we've seen.

If all the buildings pictured in U (unless the *tempio* is misidentified as a *macellum*) seem to be from the same period, in BA, by contrast, there's an unmistakable opposition between the foreground palaces, in a style we might crudely term very "advanced," and the three archaeological edifices

---

17. Lévi-Strauss, *Le Cru et le cuit*, op. cit., p. 106; English trans., p. 98.

arrayed in the background, of which at least two, the amphitheater and the triumphal arch, are strictly consistent with ancient practice, while the octagonal building evokes a medieval structure of the first Florentine "Renaissance." And you point out that the lines incised in the underpainting indicate that initially the second story of this building was not set back, making for an even closer resemblance to the San Giovanni baptistry. In Florence it was believed that this had been a temple of Mars, subsequently consecrated for Christian worship. If the establishment of a parallel between this structure and typically "pagan" monuments reinforces the attribution of this panel to a Florentine painter,[18] the crucial point remains the clearly established opposition between ancient architecture and contemporary avant-garde, *all'antico* architecture.

In this context Kimball's analyses assume a new pertinence. We've seen that the facade elevations in U are singularly innovative, even if one accepts the attribution to Laurana, and found no equivalents in Florentine architecture until the late fifteenth and early sixteenth centuries. What then are we to make of the doubled pilasters characteristic of the facades in BA, and of their independent bays, which would be characteristic of Roman architecture in the period of Bramante and Raphael? What are we to make of this doubling, which echoes that—as we've seen, without Roman equivalent—of the columns in the triumphal arch, if not that this trait maximizes the discrepency between the ancient and the new, between the antique and the "reborn" pretending to renew with it by means of a "middle" age, one which, in Italy at least, had never completely forgotten the lessons of the ancient world nor fully ruptured with its traditions?

Some, on the other hand, have taken the more archaic facade treatments in BE as indicating that the quality of this panel is inferior to that of the two others. The elevation of the palace to the left recalls that of Alberti's Palazzo Rucellai, while that of the one on the right is in a newer idiom, though one that's still ill defined.[19] The opposition recurs here between a white, porticoed building (on the right) and a gray building with a ground

---

18. Parronchi, "Due note . . .," op. cit., p. 360. Parronchi goes so far as to see in the disposition of the amphitheater and the triumphal arch at a certain distance from an enclosing wall an echo of the arrangement of the ancient Roman Capitol, etc.

19. One would be tempted to compare it with some of Antonio da Sangallo's work (Palazzo Tarugi in Montepulciano, etc.) if it didn't lack the essential component of a classical order.

floor that's almost blind (on the left). As for the other buildings, they have a pronounced Tuscan allure (the palace by the sea, to the right, is a replica of the Palazzo Borgherini in Borgo SS. Apostoli) and are frankly medieval (note the second palace on the right, with its crenellated culmination). To say nothing of the tower on a cubic base decorated with antique garlands, in which Parronchi recognizes—according to his own logic—the arsenal in Pisa, while Sanpaolesi sees in it a reminiscence of Castel Sant'Angelo as it was prior to the destructive renovation of Alexander VI, as pictured in Giuliano da Sangallo's Roman notebook.[20] If we exclude this last hypothesis, as well as the proposal that the portico framing the scene is an avant-garde motif taken from Peruzzi, which is far from evident,[21] the play of the pictured architecture, that in the "stage" proper, is based on a progressive exacerbation, from U to BA by way of BE, of the discrepancy between the present and the past, between new and ancient architecture. In fact there could be no better illustration of the difference between the mode of reasoning typical of traditional art history and the one you're attempting to apply here: for the same archaic character that led Kimball to conclude that the Berlin panel could not be from Laurana's hand[22] has served to further convince you that this panel participates in the same set of transformations as the two others. But just as it cannot be considered separately from them, the Baltimore panel cannot be arbitrarily set apart and, to cite Howard Saalman, viewed as "a graphic illustration of 'Modern (Florentine) Art Triumphantly Equal to Ancient (Roman) Art.'"[23] Aside from the fact that such "triumphalism" gives short shrift to Machiavelli's reservations about the possibility of comparing "small things" to "great" ones, specifically Florence to Rome, such similarities seem insignificant when compared with the subtlety of the configuration emerging from our comparison of the three paintings:

---

20. Cf. Parronchi, "La prima rappresentatione . . .," op. cit., p. 82, and Sanpaolesi, "Le prospettive architettoniche . . .," op. cit., p. 328.
21. Cf. *supra*, chapter 13, p. 246.
22. "The arguments for Luciano's authorship do not apply to the Berlin panel. Here the architectural forms show no innovation." Kimball, "Luciano Laurana and the High Renaissance," op. cit., p. 131.
23. Saalman, op. cit., p. 380.

U	BA	BE
Relatively homogeneous period indicators but connoted as "avant-garde."	Maximal discrepency between two periods, the contemporary one and antiquity, on which the first is modeled.	Relatively homogeneous period indicators but archaic in character, except for the portico framing the scene.

*

The human figures scattered over the scene of BA pose a delicate problem, whether they are subsequent additions or not. Neither U nor BE has any such figures; and as you've noted, it's this, at first glance, that constitutes the most striking feature of the "Urbino perspectives." To such an extent that it's easy to forget the presence of such figures in BA. In U, the only trace of animal life is provided by the two pigeons snuggling on the first floor cornice of the palace on the right. In BE, a human presence is intimated by the move of the ships, at least two of which are in full sail. But it isn't legitimate to argue that, because the small figures in BA seem to have been added on top of the paving and architectural background, their presence can be dismissed and the scene considered "empty":[24] in terms of technique this was standard practice in painting at the time, establishment of the perspective scene being regarded as a necessary condition for deployment of the *istoria*. Federico Zeri, who's inclined to ascribe these figures to a hand different from that responsible for the architecture, maintains that their meaning is as yet unexplained. But he rejects the notion that their inclusion was somehow accidental, holding that the introduction of unconnected figures into such a scene is inconsistent with early Renaissance imagery.[25] The detective who's a part of every licensed historian will be tempted to search for a fable or story that might explain this man who, using a cane, ambles by in the foreground, on a level with the fountain from which

---

24. A. Conti ("Le prospettive urbinate . . .," op. cit., p. 1195) excludes the possibility that these figures could have been added later. But the "proof" he evinces for this is surprising, to say the least: the shadows cast by the figures are consistent with those of the buildings, etc.
25. Zeri, cited cat., p. 144.

of the painting, above the vanishing point: on the attic of the triumphal arch, where convention would dictate the presence of an inscription specifying the monument's meaning, or providing the interpretive key to the figurated scene in which it is a motif,[28] is a plaque that has been left blank. This observation leads us to reconsider the notion of *motif,* to assign it a meaning that is not its conventional iconographic one. A motif is not defined on a single level, but rather specifies itself on a succession of different registers: the same triumphal arch that functions initially as a "door" within which the vanishing point is framed, subsequently accruing an "antique" connotation, and finally contributing, through its doubled columns, to a play of architectural oppositions, this same motif assumes yet another role on the level of a reading, this time construed nonmetaphorically. In the only one of the scenes in which man is admitted, if not as protagonist then at least as *figurant,* and the only one too that includes explicit "images" (the *signis* of Vitruvius), writing has its assigned place, but in the form of an absence, a lack; and an absence, a lack, situated on the very axis of the gaze, or close enough as no matter: evidence of another incremental gradation, again carefully calculated (and again one can start with any of the panels to grasp it), which in progressing from BE, straightforwardly presented to vision (here too absence generates meaning), to U, which pretends to solicit a reading only to baffle it with an illegible text, must of necessity pass by way of BA and its "blank" on a wall, which acquires the force of an enigma.

---

28. Which is the case, as we've seen above (cf. chapter 12), in the frescoes by Botticelli (*The Punishment of Corah*) and Perugino (*The Consignment of the Keys to Saint Peter*) in the Sistine Chapel.

Epistemology of the group.

The painting of reference.

The prototype, again.

Clouds in painting.

Symmetries and automorphisms.

Aberrations and curious perspectives.

The hole.

Transgressing the limits.

Piero's demonstration.

The genius of perspective.

Ensigns in painting.

The consistent angle.

De prospectiva pingendi

Here we must pause for a moment. Not to pardon ourselves, to justify this accumulation of seemingly heteroclite traits, but to prevent any misunderstanding about the meaning of an operation whose premises we have yet to pass beyond. The ensemble of features already discussed constitutes, in its particulars as well as its systematic articulation, a first set of proofs justifying—pending verification—the hypothesis that the three "Urbino perspectives" belong to a single transformation group which they suffice to define. At this stage of the inquiry this is the only thing that should concern us, and it will prove fundamental to all subsequent efforts at interpretation, if such is the appropriate word. But it's important to stress what differentiates our project from those of our predecessors. Whether it's a question of Kimball or Krautheimer, or of still others, they set out to gather stylistic and iconographic data that would allow them to situate the panels in relation to other, more or less well defined corpuses: the oeuvre of this or that specific artist; the series of monuments, real or pictured, that might be connected with those represented in them; the set of perspective exercises produced not only by painters but by decorators, above all specialists in marquetry; the set of visual and written documents relevant to the disposition of the theatrical scene, etc. By contrast, our project is oriented in a precisely inverse way: we intend to demonstrate that the three panels *constitute a system,* and that this system demands to be considered as such, prior to all other considerations, given both its internal coherence and its ramifications, which apply well beyond the frontiers of the group itself and affect a field that cannot be determined a priori—and which can only be defined in terms of the operations to which it lends itself.

We should also be very clear about the status and epistemological limits of the object we will be striving to construct, largely on a foundation of descriptive and logical givens, meticulously avoiding supposed arguments of a stylistic or empirical bent, which you regard as insignificant in the face of the structural apparatus produced by our analysis. The fact, for example, that the dimensions of these panels are not identical, and that the one in Berlin is situated above feigned wooden paneling that appears to suggest a decorative function, and the questions of possible different "hands," dates, and provenances: none of this strikes you as being decisive. For you are far from pretending that the "Urbino perspectives" were painted by a single artist (supposing each of them to be the work of a single "hand"), in a single place, and for a single occasion. Allowing that they were probably produced within a period not exceeding two or three decades, and in a relatively circumscribed geographic and cultural milieu within which information circulated freely, you affirm simply that they answer one another, that they make *objective* rejoinders to one another. Which certainly doesn't preclude their having been produced in succession (all dialogue unfolds over time), nor even their having been intended for different destinations, with their apparent changes of function constituting yet another, equally subtle kind of transformation.

Truth to tell, you don't expect our demonstration to convince many "connoisseurs," or those art historians who are content with a brand of reasoning innocent, even on their own terms, of the most elementary evidentiary requirements, and who have lost all contact with a half-century's worth (and more) of developments in anthropology, linguistics, and even history. Why pretend otherwise? You look forward with relish to the resistance (it's a given, you've already had a foretaste of it) with which this incursion into a long-restricted domain will inevitably be met: you see it as an indication that the analysis has attained its goal, that it has touched a sensitive point, that of repression. And you derive satisfaction from the thought that this would already have been the case in the period of Alberti and Piero, and in those of Leonardo, Vasari, Abraham Bosse, and Desargues: all had like tribes of "contradictors," of those who rejected, as do many today, the idea that art might be linked to theory and provoke thought, denying that obscure desire for "science" which inhabits it—a desire of which perspective is simultaneously the expression and the fruit. But we must also deal with another objection, one that's better founded: a group such as the one we're attempting to constitute is not only the product of a history; it is also the legacy of one, and is subject to all the contingencies this entails. Structural analysis makes no attempt to account for the material genesis of individual works or those of the ensembles to which they belong, beyond the hazards of time. Nonetheless, there's nothing arbitrary about the structures it uncovers; and if it necessarily borrows from history, this is in order to raise questions about it, in the hope that some individuals, among the most curious and best informed, will pay attention to them.

Thus we cannot be sure, a priori, that other paintings, other works, obscure or previously unknown, won't eventually become part of the group, though they can only do so on condition that they put into play all the requisite features and introduce a new transformational twist, correcting, modifying, or rearranging the model: if a painting were to appear, for example, that satisfied the laws of the group but included a clearly legible inscription, the analysis could encompass it. But you think the appearance of such a painting unlikely. And this as a matter of principle (as we've seen, the very idea of a "reading" runs counter to the group's identity) as much as fact: the few known panels or frescoes that might be compared to the "Urbino perspectives" (those already mentioned and some others to be discussed below) fail to satisfy the stipulated condition; and as for the *cassone* panel published by Paul Schubring and now in the Kunstgewerbe Museum in Berlin,[1] while it might seem to belong to the group, a summary examination suffices to convince that it lacks the same luxuriant detailing and adds nothing new to its definition. This is not to say that the group is necessarily a closed set, nor even that it couldn't encompass others: on a strictly epistemological level, its power would, on the contrary, be commensurate with its capacity to organize and structure the field that is its own, and to facilitate an analysis, beginning with a more developed description.[2] Should we wish to go further and assign the group some kind of historical existence, we would have to resort to arguments other than structural ones.

---

1. Cf. Paul Schubring, *Cassone, Truhen und Truhembilder in der Italienischer Frührenaissance. Ein Beitrag zur Profanemalerei in Quattrocentro,* 2d ed., Leipzig, 1923, and Heinze Lehmann, "Une Vue de la place Ognissanti à Florence," *Gazette des Beaux-Arts,* vol. 15 (April 1936), pp. 244–47.

2. With regard to the panel I've just mentioned, for example, to isolate an interesting *variation:* and in fact the vanishing point is not situated within a door but is obscured by the fountain in the center, while *two* doors, one one either side, open into the wall in the background.

Which is precisely what I propose we do next, even as we bring the transformational analysis to term and give it some real demonstrative force.

The group we've constructed has only a logical existence. But it's impossible to avoid ascribing one of the three panels, that in Urbino, a privileged position in the circuit of transformations, to such an extent that it functions consistently as the painting of reference at the beginning of these investigations. And this for reasons that are extrinsic as well as intrinsic. History records that this panel was the first to attract the attention of connoisseurs and scholars, and that in the late nineteenth century it entered a collection—that of the future National Gallery of the Marches—which was relatively accessible, and which provided it with a context giving it a particular allure. Not without marking a few reservations, you've reviewed the reasons suggesting the *Città ideale* was linked to the Urbino milieu, and even to Duke Federico himself: among others, the mention of an "old perspective" (*una prospettiva antica ma bella*), painted on wood panel of an oblong format, in several inventories of the ducal collections. Such that it seems only natural for this panel to be exhibited close to the marquetry of the *studiolo,* and even Piero's *Flagellation,* which is certainly much earlier, though its author lived a sufficiently long time to have dedicated *De prospectiva pingendi,* his treatise on painter's perspective, to Federico's son Guidobaldo, though he'd originally intended it for his father.

The "historical" arguments implied by the museum context might very well be misleading. But there can be no doubt about the intrinsic quality of the painting. Its quality as a construction, in the geometric sense, and as graphic representation of architecture; but also its more specifically pictorial quality, which can now be properly judged thanks to the recent cleaning, masterfully carried out by your friends Martino and Anna Oberto; that of a painting whose strictly symmetrical perspective—which might be considered relatively archaizing—is combined with a feigned negligence, a *sprezzatura* (as Baldassare Castiglione would say) that seems astonishingly modern in the handling of the sky, especially the clouds, reduced to simple tracings of white against a blue background: they could be by Poussin, or even, given their luminism and the close observation they reflect, some of the meteorological studies at which nineteenth-century painters so excelled. Considering these slender markings, which appear to be the product of brushstrokes so effortless "that it seems the hand is completing the line intended by the painter by itself, without any effort or guidance,"[3] one can't help but be tempted to see them as evidence setting the Urbino panel apart from the two others (pending the day when the exhibition of your dreams provides an occasion for direct comparison).

As for the perspective itself, it will appear to be archaizing (*et anticho in prospettiva:* unless, as you've suggested, the adjective refers to the painter and was intended as praise, or to hint at a certain reserve) if one situates the execution of the painting in the years around 1500 or later, and to an even greater extent if one holds to the date of the inventories, the oldest of which are from the late sixteenth century, in which case the above-mentioned quality of *sprezzatura* is no longer so remarkable. But the archaism stands—we've learned from the formalists not to make undo haste to view this is the indicator of a survival but rather to analyze it *as process*—even if one opts for an earlier date: in which case the pictured architecture takes on an "avant-garde" connotation, without this entailing any contradiction. To say nothing of the clouds, which are strikingly different from those—highly elaborated but utterly conventional—of Mantegna. "When the temporal dimension comes into play in a system of symbolic values . . ., it becomes itself a symbol and can be used for stylistic purposes."[4] But the process in question here goes well beyond effects of style. On the constructive level as well as the iconographic one, the *Città ideale* effectively renews with the prototype inscribed within the mythic departure, if not the ideal, of Renaissance perspective, which has taken on the force—as I've said—of an *imago:* the small panel painted by Brunelleschi and through the center of which the latter, according to his biographer, had pierced a hole so that, applying one's eye to its back and considering it in a mirror placed at the proper distance, one could look at this *tavoletta* on which he'd represented the baptistry of San Giovanni and its environs as seen by an observer situated inside Florence cathedral, on the axis of its central portal—the monument being framed on one or three sides, according to the angle of vision adopted, by facades of the buildings on the piazza, itself rectangular, whose center it occupies. Which is to say a strictly symmetrical composi-

---

3. Castiglione, op. cit., book I, section 28; English trans., p. 70.
4. Roman Jakobson, "Le Langage commun des linguistes et des anthropologues," *Essais de linguistique générale,* French trans., Paris, 1963, p. 37.

76   The *Città ideale*,
details of the sky. Photos:
Martino Oberto.

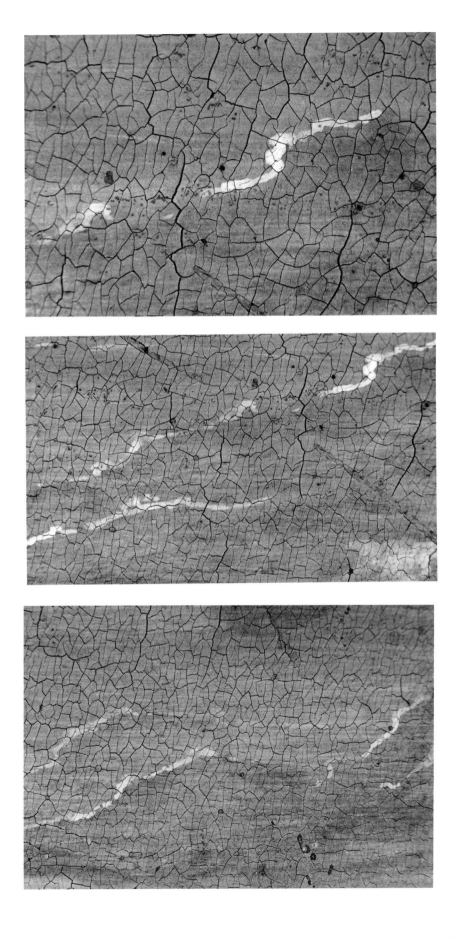

tion, and one organized around the regular volume of a centrally planned building, as is the case in the *Città ideale,* if allowances are made for differences of format and scale.

You don't pretend to be the first to have suggested this rapprochement. Kenneth Clarke, who attributed the Urbino panel to Piero della Francesca, thought the latter must have known Brunelleschi's *tavoletta* and "imitated" it as a tribute to Alberti and the conception of the "ideal city" as developed in his *De re aedificatoria,* but substituting resolutely "modern" buildings for Alberti's old or Gothic structures.[5] Piero Sanpaolesi posits the connection again, though without developing any of its implications, which is surprising given that he, along with Alessandro Parronchi, has understood the importance of Brunelleschi's experiments better than anyone. There's no need to imagine that the anonymous author or authors of the *Città ideale* had tried these experiments, although it would seem that the panels used by Brunelleschi in his demonstrations survived long after his death (we saw that Milanesi identified the two paintings mentioned by Vasari with two paintings on wood mentioned in the inventory of Lorenzo di Medici): Manetti's description of about 1465 indicated all the basic elements needed to reconstruct the prototype, at least approximately. A prototype lost to view soon after the appearance of this text, at least according to the myth, but not forgotten, as is indicated by Vasari's mention a century later.[6] But the lesson seems to have become obscure, for Vasari makes no mention of the hole piercing the first *tavoletta,* nor of the cutaway in the second. Either he chose to pass over the experimental intention in silence, retaining only the principle of construction to which they both conformed (perspective *con pianta e profilo*), thereby making them of greater interest to marquetry specialists than to painters. Or, as I've already hypothetically proposed, the hole had been filled up in the meantime, and the cutaway filled in, making these panels seem to be normal easel paintings. Vasari does not specifically state that he's seen them, nor does he claim, as does Manetti, to have held them in his hands and carried out the experiments in accordance with Brunelleschi's instructions; in all probability he simply lifted the argument from Manetti's text, subjecting it, typically, to a pro-

---

5.   Kenneth Clarke, *Piero della Francesca,* London, 1952, pp. 51 and 209.
6.   Cf. *supra,* chapter 4, pp. 68ff.

cess of reduction and simplification that stripped it of all theoretical connotations.

The reader will recall that a literal analysis of this text sanctions two hypotheses:[7] if it's conceded that the first of the two panels encompassed a view of only one array of facades bordering the piazza, that at its rear, to the complete exclusion of the buildings on its right and left sides, then the angle of vision must have been between 50° and 55°, the difference between this measure and that of 90° presupposed by the given of an observer situated at a distance of three *braccie* from a door six *braccie* wide being compensated by the partial closure of the two doors of the portal. This hypothesis, which is perfectly plausible, has the additional merit of an implicit connection with one of the most enigmatic features of the three panels in Urbino, Baltimore, and Berlin, one that's generally passed over in silence: the reiterate, multiple, ever-various play, to all appearances carefully calculated, of openings distributed over both sides of the scene, to say nothing of the *tempio* which, in the Urbino panel, is on the central axis of the painting, like the baptistry in Brunelleschi's *tavoletta*.

The other hypothesis, corresponding to Vasari's description, presupposes a much broader angle of vision, perhaps as wide as 90°, allowances being made once more for possible variations in the positioning of the portal doors. It is all the more remarkable, in light of this, that Vasari's description, while participating in a long-established tradition, mentioned above, of images in which the *istoria* unfolds around a centrally planned building in the center of a square whose lateral facades recede on either side of the scene, posits a configuration in every respect comparable to that of the *Città ideale*—save that the *view* proposed by the latter encompasses not only the receding facades but also the frontal ones, parallel to the picture plane, of the corner palaces. While the format of the Urbino panel—its dimensions, thickness, and weight—preclude its having been intended for manipulation, if not its having been viewed in a mirror, it should be pointed out that Vasari provides no indication as to the nature and measurements of the support used by Brunelleschi. Not to mention the other feature of Manetti's description he chose to ignore (supposing he knew it), just

---

7. Cf. *supra*, chapter 7, pp. 103ff.

as he'd done with the hole pierced through the *tavoletta,* so difficult to reconcile with the idea of a *painting* current at the time: the plaque of burnished silver which Brunelleschi had glued onto his panel in the place of the sky, intended to reflect "real" air and sky, specifically clouds passing by, driven by the wind. The same clouds and celestial blue sky visible *as painting* in the Urbino panel, the painter having had no need to resort to this specular artifice to introduce into his painting what's most impalpable, most resistant to geometric measure, least susceptible to reconstruction by the tools of linear perspective. Just as, in the form of two narrow *vedute,* he presents us with two fragments of landscape creating an effect of distance having nothing to do with metrics.

All of this suggests to you that the Urbino panel, while it clearly reworks the givens of the lost prototype, itself proposes a kind of experiment or demonstration—one in a repetitive mode, and one that intentionally exceeds the perspective proposition—that's focused on the powers of painting per se: the poetics specific to pictoriality resulting from a concerted effort to get beyond that ideological, or even metaphysical, opposition (one having nothing to do with theory) between the graphic component of painting and its chromatic component, between color and drawing, which Alberti saw as its fundamental rationale.[8] It will be recalled that, according to Manetti, Brunelleschi had represented the polychrome marble ornament of the baptistry with a miniaturist's precision: which indicates that in planar projection, this *rendering* conformed to a rigorous geometric schema, like that in the paving of the Urbino and Baltimore panels, standing out against the limitless, measureless sky and the clouds with no fixed contours. Such that the mirror of burnished silver took on the value of an emblem in the context of Brunelleschi's demonstration, functioning as both an optical relay and a symbolic element inserted into the configuration like some foreign body. An emblem of that which perspective excluded from its order, at least in principle, and at the same time, by contrast, of the logic on which it was based and from which it derived its coherence.[9]

Perspective, not necessarily painting. And perspective insofar as it has a privileged relation to architecture and is applicable to urban complexes

8.   Cf. my *Théorie du nuage,* op. cit., p. 162.
9.   Ibid., pp. 166–71.

of all kinds (*casamenti . . . e paesi d'ogni ragione*). Here it's necessary to cite Giulio-Carlo Argan's precious little book on Brunelleschi: "Brunelleschi doesn't paint the sky. . . . His interest is restricted to those things which, as Alberti would say, occupy 'a place.' The sky doesn't occupy 'a place.' Therefore it is not susceptible to measure, nor can it be comprehended 'by comparison.' Since the sky cannot be represented, in other words, included within a proportional system defining its form, the artist forgoes painting it. But however one interprets it, this renunciation is born of the architect's interests, not the painter's. If Filippo forgoes painting the sky, this is because he paints buildings, and these stand out against the real sky and not against painted backdrops. But it's also because buildings, by the perfection of their spatial relations, construct and define the atmospheric spatiality in which they're situated."[10] The first part of this argument is perfectly acceptable, it being understood that only bodies have places, themselves representable *through figures,* even if only in the negative, and as their container. But the proposition that architecture, in its harmonic structure, summons forth the idea of an *atmospheric* spatiality does not necessarily follow. Especially given that what's in question here is represented architecture: representation, which in this instance isn't so much intended to construct the surrounding space as to define, in Husserl's terms, *the spatiality of the thing* and of things that *cohere,* through reference, eventually to the ideal objects of geometry.

The full implications of the demonstration associated with Brunelleschi would be laid out for the first time only by Leonardo da Vinci: its implications with regard to pictorial qualities, to color, light, and "atmosphere," as well as to its graphic or geometric ones—which entails some contradictions. The "Urbino perspectives" must be re-situated within the context of this project which was ongoing for more than a century, regardless of whether one takes them to be contemporary with or immediately posterior to the circulation of Piero's *De prospectiva pingendi,* or sees them as echoing Leonardo's preoccupations, as does Alessandro Parronchi.[11] You favor the first hypothesis. For the central question defining the group is inscribed within the very title of Piero's treatise: What is it about perspec-

---

10. Giulio-Carlo Argan, *Brunelleschi,* op. cit., p. 18; French trans., Paris, 1981, p. 18.
11. Parronchi, "La prima rappresentazione . . .," op. cit., p. 38.

tive that's proper to painting, that owes its effectiveness completely to constraints imposed upon it by its two-dimensionality? And what are the consequences for painting when it surrenders to perspective, regulating itself in accordance with it—seeing as painting is not only a matter of points, lines, and surfaces but also of color and pigment? The power of attraction, and even of fascination, sometimes exerted by paintings constructed in perspective, is commensurate with the operation defining it as such, and that has, according to Brunelleschi, Piero, and Leonardo, the allure of a *demonstration*.

In this respect certainly the most striking feature, and the most immediately visible one, characteristic of all three of the panels, those in Baltimore and Berlin as well as that in Urbino, is their strictly symmetrical disposition. We've already seen that some have used this characteristic to argue for a connection between these panels and the many marquetry "perspectives" conforming to an analogous schema, whether intended to function as *cassone* frontals, overdoors, or decorative panels. "Perspectives" that, what's more, have comparable formats and are, as a general rule, devoid of all anecdote, if not of all figures. And yet the group constituting the three "Urbino perspectives" (and why not retain this convenient appellation without quotation marks, even if it's problematic, seeing that the problems in question have little bearing on the ones you're about to broach?) distinguishes itself decisively from the ensemble of this production by the rigor, extent, and unequaled complexity of the operations from which it takes its form, as well as its logical armature. And this is true of its manifestations of symmetry as well as of the other features already discussed.

You attach particular importance to these manifestations, given that symmetry, or rather *symmetries,* constitute, from a mathematical point of view, the model par excellence of a transformation group: to the point that they become a kind of foundation for the aforementioned operations, conferring on the group a descriptive power extending well beyond the strictly figurative register. U is characterized, in effect, by an overall bilateral symmetry organized around a central volume that is itself symmetrical, though allowance must be made for the irregularity represented by the opening, in the right background, onto a second square in front of the basilica. In BA the bilateral symmetry is also organized around a symmetrical central body, this time one pierced by three openings and itself flanked by two other regular volumes, one being an octagon, of which three sides are visible, and the other cylindrical, being an amphitheater with three superimposed orders surmounted by an attic and pierced by multiple openings; through three of these we can see the far side of the building and the three arches diametrically opposite them. In BE the bilateral symmetry is retained, in the absence of any central body—unless we consider (as you don't hesitate to do) the three-bayed portico framing the view to be a transformed equivalent of one. Thus BA functions as a mediating term between U and BE, simultaneously through the tripartite division of its central body, the prominence allotted in each of the latter cases to centrally planned buildings, and the major role played by the numbers three and five, at work in the paving design of, respectively, BA and U: a feature taken up by BE, where the tripartite configuration of the foreground portico interferes with the quintuple division of the paving.

(You note in passing that even within U itself the polychrome marble ornament figures in only three rows of the basic checkerboard. But the rule we've given ourselves—to pay attention only to syntagmatic content, at least initially—prohibits us from assigning absolute meanings to figurative functions, as is too often done in iconology. For example, from ascribing an intrinsic symbolic significance to the triple axes and formal and/or iconographic features in BA: in the group such as we're working to constitute it, this tripartite ordinance has no transcendental significance, only an operational, contextual value.)

Could it be, yet again, the emphatic bilateral symmetry, linked to a strictly central projection, that produces the archaic effect in these panels which we've discussed, even as it irresistibly prompts us to connect them with the "Italian" stage scene as it would take form in the sixteenth century? In his series of great reliefs for the *Santo* in Padua, Donatello had already employed an analogous principle of composition characterized by an open rectangular scenic area, quite wide and demarcated on three sides by structures more or less regularly aligned. But such a schema, as we've seen, was not without antecedents in painting of the fifteenth and even the fourteenth century; to say nothing of Roman painting, especially that from Pompeii, and certain depictions of the Hellenistic stage which could have been known to Renaissance artists through painted vases from southern Italy.[12] The novelty here—a relative novelty, if one holds that this feature first appeared in marquetry, but one to which, as Alessandro Conti understood so well, these panels still owe their manifest "theatrical" connotation[13]—this novelty consists in the scene's being empty but enlivened by all manner of stretches and violations of the purportedly constraining rule of symmetry, with some of the said violations being so subtle as to unequivocally set these works apart from more strictly decorative productions.

The Urbino panel is also characterized by a systematic deployment of different categories of symmetry, as defined by mathematics. Before we can assess this, we must establish a distinction between two modes of symmetry in painting: a formal one that's directly visible on the plane of projection and in the register of representation, and one that's indirect or referential, being deducible from the appearance of the represented object. Both modes come into play in U: its overall composition manifests a fully visible bilateral symmetry whose regimen appears to hold sway over all the objects within it, whether the two octagonal wells, the circular *tempio,* or the (truncated) facade of the basilica, or even those of the two corner palaces and the other structures succeeding them in the perspective order. As Hermann Weyl would put it, this symmetry corresponds to an inaccurate, or reflexive, congruence between the two blocks of buildings framing the square, as well as between the left and right halves of the volumes as they appear in planar projection: inaccurate congruence implying a transformation of the mirror image of any figure or body such that its dimensions are left intact.[14] Note that one can speak of bilateral symmetry even when this is indicated only by an (inaccurate) congruence of the overall volumetric contours, with symmetrical bodies occupying apparently commensurate portions of space, though in inverse positions, and without there being any need for perfect reciprocity in details of structure or internal organization: that amounts to saying that the idea of symmetry, at least bilateral symmetry, can manifest itself either in terms of figures (and volumes) or in terms

12. A. M. G. Little, "Scaenographia," op. cit., p. 416.
13. Conti, "Le prospettive urbinate . . .," op cit., p. 1195.
14. Hermann Weyl, *Symétrie et mathématique moderne,* French trans., Paris, 1964, p 50.

of space, and is applicable to bodies as well as to the space that contains them, to the place they occupy.

But other kinds of symmetry are in play here too. Rotational symmetry, for instance, which characterizes the circular edifice in the center of the composition. One can say of a figure that it possesses rotational symmetry around an axis if it can be rotated n times around this axis without perceptible alteration. That means, supposing it to have four identical doors at the extremities of a cross inscribed within it, that the circular *tempio* has a rotational symmetry of the fourth order, corresponding to the number of 90° shifts around its axis transforming it into itself.[15] You point out, however, that whereas the rule of bilateral symmetry comes into play directly in planar projection, rotational symmetry must have recourse to an imaginary trajectory into space.

A third category of symmetry included in the Urbino panel: rough mirror images of one another, for the corner palaces and those beyond them also conform, with their counterparts, to a translational symmetry linked to the principle of the classical orders, defined by the repetition at like intervals of an invariant figure (a window, for example, or a facade bay) which is itself reflexively symmetrical.[16]

These three categories of symmetry recur in the Baltimore panel: bilateral symmetry in the overall composition in relation to a vertical axis through the center of the panel, as well as in a monument (the triumphal arch) that's reflexively but not rotationally symmetrical (in contrast to the Urbino *tempio*). This last mode of symmetry is found, however, in the two buildings symmetrically disposed on either side of the piazza and occupying comparable ground surfaces. Both meet the criteria for rotational symmetry, of the fourth order in the case of the octagonal baptistry and of a much higher order for the cylindrical amphitheater. As for translational symmetry, this is found, again, in the facades of the two corner palaces: the construction lines of the palace on the right, their incisions visible beneath the painted surface, clearly indicate both the reflective and translational symmetry *vis-à-vis* the openings in the opposite and corresponding structure.

---

15. Ibid., p. 52.
16. Ibid., p. 54.

On the other hand, only two categories of symmetry seem to be in play in the Berlin panel: bilateral symmetry in the prosceniumlike portico as well as the overall view of the piazza framed by it, and translational symmetry in the facades of several palaces and, to a certain extent, in the portico, with its three regularly aligned bays. Unless one thinks of the tower in the background as comparable to the Castel Sant'Angelo, in which case it would constitute an example of rotational symmetry.

All these remarks also apply, a fortiori, to the designs in the paving. Insofar as its perspective schema is generated by the division of the baseline into equal segments (in conformity with Alberti's method), and the vanishing point is established on its vertical axis, the ground framework is in strict conformity with bilateral symmetry. But it also conforms, on the register of the represented, if not of the representor, to the rules of translational symmetry, in the like lateral displacement of the squares to either side. And even rotational symmetry appears in the figures of rhombuses and octagons, and that of the Maltese cross.

*

Among the three categories of symmetry at work in the transformation group composed of the Urbino perspectives—or perhaps more accurately, at work *through* them, for we shall see that the group is subject to and master of their law in equal degrees—bilateral symmetry is particularly significant with regard to the Brunelleschian prototype. If we adhere to Manetti's

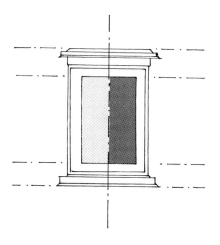

77   Baltimore panel, construction lines of the windows in the palace on the right.

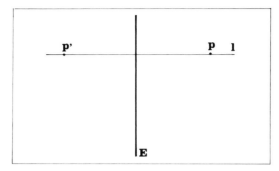

description of it, the image of a regular octagonal volume, standing out (according to the first hypothesis) against a background of facades parallel to the picture plane, was reflected in a mirror without the exchange of left for right having much consequence. But the Urbino panel was not conceived for insertion into a specular circuit, and neither were those in Baltimore and Berlin. And in each case any reversal would have significant effects: the facade of the basilica would appear to the left of the *tempio* and not to its right, the amphitheater and the baptistry would change places, etc. But reflection, while no longer in play between the panel and its specular double (with considerable theoretical consequences, as I've indicated, regarding the relation of the point of view and the vanishing point), still plays a role under the auspices of bilateral symmetry. We could say bodies or figures in space are symmetrical in relation to a given plane *E* if they coincide with their image as "reflected" in *E* considered as a mirror; and that an *application* occurs each time there's a straight line within which any point *P* of a line *l*, perpendicular to *E*, is associated with one point and one only *p'*, situated at a like distance from *E* but on its other side, with a corollary being that the point *p'* coincides with *p* only when *p* is situated on *E*. As Hermann Weyl writes, "the reflection in *E* is in sum the application ($S : p - p'$) of space onto itself, which transforms the arbitrary point *p* into its image *p'* through its relation with *E*, where *E* plays, I repeat, the role of a mirror."[17]

We will turn this idea of space being applied onto itself or, in the language of mathematics, of *automorphism*, in other words of a transformation that leaves the structure of space unaltered,[18] to our profit a bit further

---

17.   Ibid., pp. 12–13.
18.   Ibid., p. 49.

on. For the moment you'll make do with observing that the same result, the same image, the same symmetry, is obtainable through simple reflection as through rotation of point p around axis E. The definition stipulating that point p' is the image of p in relation to E nonetheless presupposes that E is assimilated to a mirror. Now the givens common to both the Urbino panel and the prototype determine that plane E be perpendicular to the picture plane, and that the intersection of these two elements correspond to the latter's vertical axis. And it's on this planar E, perpendicular to that of the painting, that's inscribed the line on which are established the point of view and the vanishing point, and on which these latter are geometrically located. The line serving as the support of what Alberti called the *centric ray* interpolates (as Manetti would put it) the picture plane at a point O, situated on E, which point will coincide with its own image E and will in turn represent, in planar projection, the geometric location of both the point of view and the vanishing point—a proposition of immense consequence for geometry (and not for it alone), but which was first demonstrated, in an experimental way, by Brunelleschi.

The Urbino panel thus constitutes a particularly interesting case because it makes direct play, without any intermediary, with the projective coincidence of the point of view and the vanishing point which Brunelleschi's experiment had revealed by means of the mirror: the eye—the point of the gaze—being established at the panel's back, at the very spot of the vanishing point as reflected in the mirror. Which has made some think, in the case of the San Giovanni configuration, of an optical experiment, while in matter of fact what was in question was something quite different: a performative passage from optics to geometry, and—from the beginning— to a projective geometry. But perspective, while it can dispense with mirrors, is nonetheless dependent, at least metaphorically, upon specularity (as is geometry too in its definition of application). The point of view and the vanishing point coincide by projection (but not, I stress, by symmetry), since they are situated on the same line of reflection, perpendicular to the painting, and are located, in terms of projection, at the point on which this line meets the picture plane, which is itself—this is the meaning of Brunelleschi's demonstration—the fulcrum for two axes running in opposite directions: one proceeding from the point of view to the vanishing point, and another from the vanishing point to the point of view.

*

You're not duped by such language. True, the preceding analysis makes use of a *geometric* concept of symmetry, a concept—in marked contrast to the vague notion of συμμετρια, in the Vitruvian sense of harmony among the parts of a whole—that is utterly precise.[19] But you don't pretend that Brunelleschi, or for that matter the anonymous author or authors of the Urbino perspectives, articulated it in these terms, any more than the painters of Pharaonic Egypt had at their command an instrument—the concept of the group—allowing them to analyze the ornamental motifs at which they so excelled, and their possible symmetries.[20] To analyze them but not to produce them, which they were quite capable of doing with the means at their disposal, which prompts us to ask just what kind of logic *did* preside over such work—one so rigorous that the results can only now, after many centuries or four millennia, be translated into structural or mathematical terms: but this question, if it has any relation at all to history, is not a matter of elapsed time, whether of long or short duration. On the basis of the work of the "perspectors" (as they would be dubbed by Abraham Bosse, a key figure because of his relation to Desargues), we might well ask ourselves if it's sufficient to posit an opposition between the mathematical *idea* and the artist's intuitive representation, as Hermann Weyl does for Egyptian ornament.[21] For this work constitutes, from an epistemological point of view, a singular mixture in which imagination contends with reason, and with idea—and also with intuition, which it carries beyond itself, though it's not always easy to distinguish, in the structures revealed by analysis, between the unconscious results of objective logical constraints and the products of deliberation or calculation. The operations worked on symmetry in the three panels in Urbino, Baltimore, and Berlin provide a good example of this.

You've indicated in passing that we can only speak of symmetry, in this instance, on condition that we come to terms with the many infractions and distortions to which it's susceptible. Infractions and distortions that, it's tempting to say, were intended to animate compositions that despite their strict frontality have a certain natural appearance, to which an overly

19. Ibid., p. 11.
20. Ibid., p. 59.
21. Ibid., p. 16.

79   The *Città ideale*, detail of the second square
in the background. Photo: Martino Oberto.

80   The *Città ideale*, the two wells. Photos: Martino Oberto.

81 The *Città ideale*,
roof of the rotunda and
its lantern. Photo: Mar-
tino Oberto.

rigid symmetry would have proved fatal, which, as Hermann Weyl reminds us, is the case in the organic world. But the deviations from the "perspectival" norm in Urbino owe nothing to the order of the living. And it could well be that they do more to confirm the perspective rule than to weaken it.

You cite two supporting examples. First, the opening to the right of the scene, already remarked, onto a second square beyond that of the circular temple in the center: which introduces, in plan as well as in volume, a marked dissymmetry into a composition that otherwise appears to be strictly symmetrical. This violation of symmetry is all the more remarkable in that it's accompanied, as we've seen, by an interruption in the square paving which is the foundation of the representation. The fragility of the configuration that's here exposed is further emphasized by the fact that the *veduta* to the right of the basilica, which opens onto a Mantegnesque landscape with a sinuous road climbing into the distance, cuts deeper into the line of background facades than does the one on the left, with this line being itself interrupted at this point to reveal a brick wall perpendicular to the facades, which indicates the limit of the scene without really closing it.

Another distortion, a bit more subtle and more difficult to describe, is linked to the lighting, which originates from a source outside the painting and to the left, slightly forward from the plane of intersection

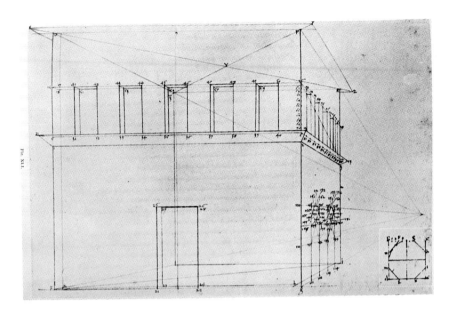

82　Method for constructing a palace in perspective. Piero della Francesca, *De prospectiva pingendi*, fig. XLI.

corresponding to the baseline. Careful examination of the distribution of light and shadow over the four visible sides of the two octagonal wells in the foreground reveals that the contrast of values is far less pronounced on the left than on the right, whereas one would expect the shadows there to be deeper; likewise for the corner palaces, but in reverse, with the facade of the one on the left being more brightly lit than that of the right palace, as only seems logical, given their respective placements with regard to the light source.

You'd also like to mention the distinct but symmetrical deformation visible in the *tempio,* whose lateral columns seem to incline inward, as has often been noted.[22] Reinforcing the impression, which you've previously remarked, that the triangle encompassing the perspective framework is somehow prolonged onto the building's conical roof, which is itself divided, like the paving, into five symmetrical sections, by bands of the same color culminating at a point on the same vertical axis as the vanishing point: all

22.　Saalman, op. cit., p. 376, note 2.

83 The *Città ideale*, the palaces on the left and
right. Photos: Martino Oberto.

of which can serve to remind us of the metaphorical assimilation of the
visual pyramid to a wicker cage, and of the straw caps worn by the women
of Florence, the ones to which Manetti referred in suggesting that the conical hole in the center of Brunelleschi's *tavoletta* had a similar form.[23]

But there's a distortion that's even more pronounced, though less
apparent, on the left of the painting, one that increases—and perhaps even
explains—the feeling of optical insecurity induced by prolonged study of
this painting, at the same time making it more difficult for the spectator to
remain focused on the point around which the perspective construction is
organized. No one has previously remarked on this distortion, and you
yourself only became aware of it recently: it's as though everything in the
painting conspired to ensure that it made only a subliminal impression. The
two corner palaces seem to occupy blocks of space that are more or less
equal and symmetrical. Judging from the five bays and small central pediment of their receding facades, and the occurrence of the same pediment

23. "E puoi considerare que questi razzi fanno una piramida della veduta superficie, piena di razzi,
e richiudendo in essa la detta cosa veduta, come dire una gabbia da uccegli fatta di vermene
sottilissime, o vero come uno capello fatto di giunchi, come fanno e'fanciugli." Filarete, *Trattato*,
book XXII, fol. 176 recto; op. cit., pp. 648–49; English trans., p. 300.

84 Botticelli, *History of Lucretia*, ca. 1490–1500.
Boston, Isabella Stewart Gardner Museum. Photo:
Museum.

above the third bay of both the facades paralleling the picture plane, neither
of which is fully visible, each of these palaces appears to be square in plan
and roughly cubical in volume, which is to say rotationally symmetrical.
But then how are we to explain that, while in the frontal facade of the
palace on the right four bays are visible as well as a portion of a fifth,
corresponding to the damaged area of the painting, in that of the left palace
we see only three bays, and only a portion of the pediment carrying the
inscription, whereas we have a full view of the one on the right?

One quickly becomes convinced that the palace on the left is, in
planar projection, slightly taller than that on the right, if only because its
pediments are closer to the edge of the painting than are those of the right
palace. But this assertion doesn't explain the anomaly you've noted. This
could only be justified by a dissymmetry in the disposition of the two
buildings on the ground, with the left palace being somewhat further forward than the palace on the right. Careful examination of the Berlin panel
lends support to this hypothesis: the slight difference in placement of its
two lateral palaces in plan[24] is coupled with an apparent disparity in the

---

24. Cf. *infra*, figure 104.

lighting of the facades and a marked difference in the height of the two structures. An analogous dissymmetry can be seen in a number of panels constructed along the same lines, for example, the *History of Lucretia* by Botticelli in Boston, with an extraordinary triumphal arch in its center, and in which the palace on the right is unmistakably further forward, its foundations touching the baseline, than that on the left. The Baltimore panel features a similar dissymmetry, even though its two corner palaces occupy exactly symmetrical positions in plan, if the plinth of the left one is ignored. On the one hand, the right palace is taller than that on the left, as indicated by the fact that its roof is closer to the edge of the painting than are the pediments of the left palace (an inversion of the arrangement in the Urbino and Berlin panels). On the other hand, whereas we see two bays and part of a third of the right facade paralleling the picture plane, we see only a bay and a half of that on the left. But this can be explained without resort to any kind of deformation, since the bays of the left palace are much wider than those of the right palace, whose facade has five bays as opposed to the left palace's three.

Thus our comparison of the three panels confirms, yet again, their participation in a single transformation group that has nothing to do with mathematics but that nonetheless is not without geometric consequences, since all three put into play the same set of divergences from bilateral symmetry. But this comparison leads us once again to assign the Urbino panel a special role within the group. For the deformation or aberration observable on the left of this panel cannot be explained through study of either elevation or ground plan: the two palaces, that on the left as well as its pendant on the right, rise from exactly symmetrical lines in the base checkerboard, their frontal facades being placed along the central axis of its third row, parallel to the baseline. How then are we to explain this seeming "error," this "aberration," within the context of a configuration that's so strictly controlled, so precisely calculated, so completely *rational*?

*

For some time now, on the basis of entirely subjective impressions, you've thought there was a slight discrepancy between the perspective and the composition proper: the same discrepancy that allowed for a deviation between the painted image and the incised tracings of the geometric construction, visible beneath the picture's surface. And I cherish the memory of the last day we spent with the restorers in their Urbino studio: the *Città ideale* was placed flat on a table, and over this panel on which Martino Oberto had all but completed his meticulous ministrations we set to work along with him, to the great alarm of his wife, equipped as we were with an array of rulers and squares, of compasses and protractors. Until the moment when, without having consulted one another, we pinpointed the spot within the opening of the *tempio* door where the vanishing point ought to be: not exactly, as it seemed to us, on the central axis, but slightly to its right, at the height of the eye of an imagined observer standing there, half hidden by the closed panel of the door and directing a Cyclopean gaze toward us.

Yes, I'll always remember the incredible gesture that Martino Oberto then allowed himself. Armed with a scalpel, he unhesitatingly removed a tiny bit of painting, revealing in precisely the spot I'd indicated to him a small conical hole doubtless marking the point of insertion of a needle or nail to which the painter had attached strings in order to trace the network of receding orthogonals. Seeing our astonishment, he showed us documents justifying this violation: among others, an X ray of the painting proving that this hole had been filled with a tiny bit of plaster, as had several others, smaller ones, situated along the same vertical axis. Subsequently the overseer of artworks in the Marches would give his approval for the hole to be left visible, and today it's remarked by visitors, visible evidence of the sole archaeological discovery with which I've been associated. To anyone made uncomfortable by such a violation of the painting's visual integrity, I'd answer as follows: the first effect produced by exposure of the point marked within the opening of the door, around which the perspective construction is organized, is to introduce into a configuration intended to create an illusion the point of the real. I can no longer prevent this point from appearing to me as other than it is, namely as the hole to which is affixed the "signifier" of the representation.

This hole, reduced as it is to a cavity one or two millimeters in diameter, has nothing to do with the one, wide as a lentil, in the center of Brunelleschi's *tavoletta,* on its painted side. The width of the wooden panel of the *Città ideale* precludes the possibility of such a piercing and thus of a mirror reflection like that in the experiment. What's more, this hole is not

Brunelleschi set out to demonstrate, in experimental terms. But such a
demonstration did nothing to resolve the question of the distance from
which the eye should view the painting, as the observer could determine
this only by looking at the image in the mirror, and from the point, again,
marked by a hole, inside the embrasure of the door.

*

The irregularities you've uncovered in the bilateral symmetry of the Baltimore and Berlin panels are explained by study of their elevations or ground
plans. This is not true of the one observable on the left of the Urbino
panel, which is made all the more apparent, once it's been pointed out, by
the otherwise rigorous application of the principle of symmetry. The violations of this principle, which comparison with the other panels suggests
were deliberate, take on particular relief when they seem to compromise the
economy of the perspective configuration itself, though it's not easy to
establish a clear distinction in this infringement between appearance and
reality, between "truth" and *appearance*. As Manetti said, à propos Brunelles-

chi's first experiment: *pareva che si vedessi 'i proprio vero*—"it *seemed* [my emphasis] that what one saw [literally: what was given to view] was *truth* itself, the *plain* truth.

You're tempted to seek out the rationale behind this particularly sophisticated turn of phrase in a passage from *De prospectiva pingendi* in which Piero addresses "those who understand nothing of the distance there should be between the eye and the boundary (*al termine*) where things are placed," in other words, the plane of projection, or of the angle at which the eye apprehends them: the result being that they're astonished by the aberrations which, according to them, are generated by perspective and thus have doubts about its "scientific character." Proposition XXX of the treatise's first book concerns the distance from the painting at which the eye should be situated or, what amounts to the same thing, the angle at which the painting must be viewed to avoid errors that, in a squared plane seen in perspective, result in receding quantities' appearing larger than nonreceding ones.[25]

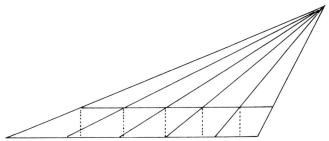

Here Piero is thinking of the aberrations arising at the lateral extremities of a checkerboard paving constructed in perspective, when the sides of the squares corresponding to the painting's baseline divide the latter into segments of equal length:[26] the further one moves away from the axis

25. "Per levare via l'errore ad alchuni, che non sono molto periti in questa scienza, quali dicono che molte volte nel devidere loro il piano degradato a bracci, li viene magiore lo scurto che non fa quello che non è scurto; e questo adiviene per non intendere la distantia che vole essere da l'occhio al termine dove se pongono le cose, nè quanto l'occhio può in sè ampliare l'angolo con li suoi raggi; si che stanno in dubitazione la prospectiva non essere vera scientia, giudicando il falso per ignoranza." Piero della Francesca, *De prospectiva pingendi*, book I, fol. 16 verso, proposition XXX; ed. G. Nicco-Fasola, Florence, 1942, vol. 1, pp. 96–97.
26. "E con queste braccia segno la linea di sotto qual giace nel quadrangolo in tante parti quanto ne riceva." Alberti, *Della pittura*, op. cit., p 70; English trans., p. 56.

on which the vanishing point is situated, the longer the foreshortened squares become in depth; beyond a certain limit, the sides of the receding squares will have, on the plane, a length greater than those of ones in less radical recession. *De prospectiva pingendi* offers an explanation of this aberration in the form of a demonstration, and also proposes a rule leading to its being remedied, which consists of assigning to the plane of projection, to Alberti's *intersegatione* or, in Piero's language, to "the boundary plane (*termine*) where things are placed," a double value as *limit:* limit in the sense of depth, since the plane must be situated at the appropriate distance from the eye, neither too close nor too far from it; but limit also in the sense of width: contrary to the widespread belief—a belief to which Panofsky himself-subscribed—holding that the "base plane" can be extended on either side as far as our imaginations might dictate, the "boundary" should not be situated beyond certain limits which, as we'll see, Piero did not confuse with those of the visual field.

Book I of *De prospectiva pingendi,* which is devoted to planar projections, concludes, strategically, with a proposition that seems to connect with the proposition, taken from Euclid, with which the book opens, asserting that "all quantities present themselves to the eye at a given

angle."[27] Its corollary being that different quantities viewed from the same angle will seem equivalent to the eye when they can be assimilated to as many bases, variously diposed and oriented, of the visual pyramid. Conversely, like quantities situated at different distances will present themselves to the eye at different angles. But this taking into account of the angle at which the thing is "represented" within the eye doesn't mean that Piero subscribed to the basic proposition of ancient and medieval optics, which held that apparent size is proportional to the visual angle. Contradicting

---

27. "Omne quantita se rapresenta socto angole nell'ochio." Piero della Francesca, op. cit., book I, fol. I verso, proposition I, cited ed., p. 66.

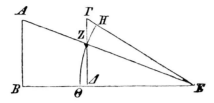

Euclid's *Optics*, proposition V of book I of *De prospectiva pingendi* implicitly establishes that apparent size is inversely proportional to the distance at which an object presents itself to the eye.[28] In other words:

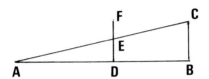

if $FD = CB$, then

$$EC : AE = FE : DE$$
$$ED : AD = FE : BD$$
$$AC : AE = CB : ED$$
$$FE : AD = ED : BD$$

which is explicitly confirmed by proposition XII of the same book, which holds that the recession of surfaces depicted in perspective is a function of their distance from the plane of intersection.

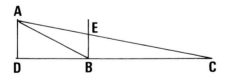

$$BC : DC = BE : DA$$

If Piero was able to continue speaking the language of classical optics while replacing its demonstrations with those of planar geometry, the reason is

---

28.   Op. cit., p 68. Cf. Euclid, *Optics*, proposition VIII: "Like and parallel sizes, at varying distances from the eye, are not seen in a way proportional to these distances."

that perspective presents particular difficulties because it appeals to the eye as well as the intellect, while being less closely related to what is "represented" inside the eye than to what's projected onto the plane, a circumstance that entails certain paradoxes and contradictions. Contrary to what Arthur Wheelock maintains in an otherwise excellent book,[29] the fact that the question of the angle at which a painting should be viewed plays a decisive role in *De prospectiva pingendi* doesn't indicate any conflict between the exigencies of geometric optics and those of physiological optics. For the aberrations produced at the edges of the checkerboard are not optical, by either nature or origin: they follow, rather, from the construction, in geometric planar projection, of the squared paving that grounds the perspective scene. And if any angle must be taken into account here, it's the one corresponding to the spread, on this plane, of the bundle of lines receding in the paving. It follows, and without entailing archaism of any sort, that Piero thought that construction schemas in which the vanishing point is centrally placed were those best suited to *making the work of perspective accessible to view,* as is confirmed by the Urbino *Città ideale* and, in general, by the group of so-called Urbino perspectives. Doubtless the painter was free to establish the vanishing point wherever he liked; but it had to be situated within certain limits, the ones defined by the final proposition of book I of the treatise and the demonstration on which it is based.[30]

A demonstration that, if fully grasped, is exceedingly strange. It presupposes in effect that a point *A,* marking the location of the eye, be inscribed in the center of a square crossed by diagonals dividing it into four equal parts. A curious point this, being subdivided into four quarters each of which can, in turn, be regarded as an independent organ. This corresponding, Piero notes, to the fact that while the globe of the eye is spherical, only a quarter of it is visible from the exterior; which authorizes us to consider "point" *A* as being made up of four "eyes." "For if four men were there [or, more accurately, four cyclops?], each looking in front of him, all

---

29. Arthur Wheelock, *Perspective, Optics and Delft Artists around 1650,* New York and London, 1977, pp. 72ff.

30. "Ma si tu dicesse: perchè mecti tu l'ochio nel mezzo? perchè me pare più conveniente a vedere il lavoro; nientedimeno se po mectare dove a l'omo piaci, non passando i termini che nell'ultima figura se mostrarà. . . ." Piero, op. cit., book I, folio 6 verso; cited ed., p. 77.

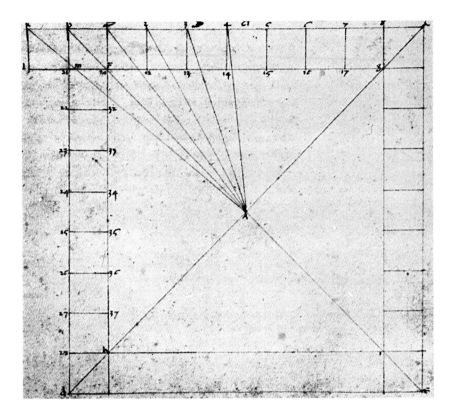

88 Demonstration of the limits of perspective
construction. Piero della Francesca, *De prospectiva
pingendi*, fig. XXX.

four would make up what I call eye *A,* which I declare to be round. And
from the intersection of the two nerves that cross one another the visual
faculty goes to the center of the crystalline humor, from which depart rays
extending in straight lines, dividing the four parts of the circle of the eye,
where they determine a right angle whose lines come to an end at *F* and *G:*
I say that the line *FG* will be the largest quantity that the eye opposite it
can see."[31]

---

31. "[Il] puncto A, il quale dico essere l'occhio, deviso da le diagonali BE et DC in quactro parti
equali, le quali quactro parti ciascuna per sè intendo essere uno occhio, perchè l'ochio nel capo è
tondo et di fuore se dimostra la quarta parte; si che dirò il puncto A essere quatro hocchi, uno dico
essere quella parte oposta a la linea FG, l'altro quella parte oposta a la linea HI; perchè se sono
quactro huomeni, ciascuno guardante a la sua faccia, farano quello medessimo che dico de l'occhio
A, il quale occhio dico essere tondo, et da la intersegatione de doi nervicini che se incrociano vene

Piero here refers to the eye, or the *chiasma,* as that part of the optic nerve in which vision was deemed to realize itself, but we should not be deceived by his use of this language borrowed from medieval optics: this is only an image, one consistent with a treatise offering no description, even elementary, of the functioning of the eye, and that makes no reference to it except "insofar as it's necessary to painting," and insofar as within it things seen present themselves (*s'apresentano*) at various angles, in conformity with the treatise's initial proposition.[32] Like *perspectiva naturalis, perspectiva artificialis* pretends only to knowledge of the visible. But to knowledge of it—a crucial difference—only insofar as it can be represented, insofar as it is part and parcel, from the beginning, of the circuit of representation. In this context the words used by Piero must be translated literally: quantity is a matter of an angle only to the extent that it's a matter of representation (*la cosa se rapresenta*), or of a-presentation (*le cose s'apresentano*), in the sense of an *Abbildung.* But what applies to things also applies, in turn, to the boundary or, to use Piero's word, the *termine* (from the Latin *terminus,* "the point at which an activity or process stops") on which things are placed: in other words, to the plane of projection, but a plane that has nothing indefinite about it, one that's strictly delimited, as is indicated by the Alberti's "window" metaphor.

Piero then made no pretense to having provided an optical explanation, much less a physiological one, for the aberrations produced, *beyond a certain boundary,* on the margins of the perspective configuration. And it is not sufficient to denounce the "falsity" of the argument attributed to him to resolve the difficulty he pointed out, or to eliminate the "errors" he set out to account for through a strictly geometrical demonstration. Specifically, with his point A in the center of two concentric squares *BCDE* and *FGHI,* the interval between them being regularly squared, as the figure indicates. This point A is joined to the divisions of lines *BC, AB, A*1, *A*2, *A*3, etc.

---

la virtù visiva al cintro de l'imore cristallino, et da quello se partano i raggi et stendonse derictamente, devidendo la quarta parte del circulo de l'occhio; sicommo o posto fanno nel cintro angolo recto, et perchè le linee uscenti da l'angolo recto terminano nel puncto F et nel puncto G, dico dunque che la linea FG sia la magiore quantità che l'occhio aposto a quella possa vedere." Ibid., fol. 16 verso, cited ed., pp. 97–98.

32. "La prima [parte] dissi essere il vedere . . . cioè l'ochio . . . del quale non intendo tractare se non quanto fie necessario a la pictura. Dunqua dico l'occhio essere la prima parte, perchè gli è quello in cui s'apresentano le cose vedute socto diversi angoli." Ibid., fol. 1 recto, cited ed., p. 64.

Line *AB* will correspond to the diagonal of the square *BA*1*F*21. If one then prolongs line *BC* by a length *BK* equal to *B*1, to construct a square *BKL*21, then line *KA* will intersect line *LG* at a point *M*; *KL* will be *represented* on *LG* by *LM* > *L*21, and the receding quantity will then appear, in planar projection, to be greater than the nonreceding quantity. To eliminate aberrations of this kind, strictly geometrical in nature and origin, one need only remain within the *termine* or boundary *FG* directly opposite the eye at *A*, without encroaching upon boundary *FH* perpendicular to it. Hence the rule proposed by Piero, who thinks the best way to avoid the aberrations resulting from transgressing these boundaries is to keep within an angle equal to two-thirds of a right one, its two sides forming an equilateral triangle with the picture plane, with the height of the summit of the angle of vision (which itself corresponds to the correct distance between the eye and the painting) being shorter than the side perpendicular to it, in other words, than the width of the painting.

It's worth repeating that this rule, contrary to appearances, is not based on the anatomy or physiology of the eye. And it won't do to simply refer to what we think we now know about the limits of the perceptual field (or about its lack of precise limits) to justify declaring "false" or "erroneous" a diagram that conforms to all other criteria of truth other than the perceptual one, and that's intended not so much to account for the appearance of things as they're accessible to vision as to indicate the limits of the validity of the representational configuration produced by perspective. It cannot a fortiori be concluded from the aberrations pointed out by Piero that he took binocular vision to be a deformed vision:[33] if there's any absurdity here, it's the confusion of the conditions of binocular vision, in which two eyes are situated on a single line, with the astonishing schema proposed by Piero, in which the field of vision available to one eye is perpendicular to that available to the adjacent one(s). Taken at face value, and this entails no anachronism, Piero's demonstration poses a problem similar to one that preoccupied a number of fine minds at the beginning of this century, among them Ernst Mach, Henri Poincaré, Bertrand Russell, and Rudolf Carnap, namely: What is the relation in our representations of space

33. Wheelock, op. cit., p. 178.

between what is *given* and what is *constructed?* Piero's usage here of geometry, intended to prepare the reader for his enunciation of the double limit to which paintings are subject, bears eloquent witness to a confusion analogous to the one between two languages, each with its own grammar and syntax, denounced by Ludwig Wittgenstein: that of visual or phenomenal space and that of geometric or physical space. Two languages distinguished from one another discursively by the clear distinction maintained between "being" and "appearing": considered from a given angle, two quantities can *appear* to be equal that *aren't*.[34]

Such a division is not necessarily self-evident, at least when what's presented to vision is the result of a *construction,* with the representation's coherence deriving from geometry and its figures. The aberrations revealed by Piero's diagram are real ones, and can be measured on the plane. But their "reality" nonetheless belongs to the register of "appearances," because they're generated by a disorderly functioning of the *projective* configuration, to once more use Wittgensteins terms. Hence it's not easy, within the perspective order, to maintain the distinction between these two languages, that of reality and that of appearances, of truth and semblance. And the paradox of perspective consists of the fact that the positions of the sensate and the conceptual can reverse themselves, that what appears to be an indeterminate factor with regard to geometry can be taken for a fact—not of the eye but of the understanding: for while the eye can *see* the boundary FG that presents itself at an angle of 90°, "the understanding doesn't grasp or comprehend the parts [the extremities] except as blurs seen from afar, which he cannot identify as either man or animal. Such is the case for points *F* and *G* in relation to *A:* for things whose parts cannot be clearly grasped cannot be made to recede systematically, only as blurs."[35] Now geometry as such has nothing to do with the *function of the blur,* which is—precisely—to make a blur in the painting, to introduce into its system a foreign element irreducible to its norms, as well as—initially—to resist being named. Even

---

34. Wittgenstein, *Philosophische Bemerkungen,* Frankfurt, 1964, chapter 10; Cf. Jacques Bouveresse, *Le Mythe de l'intériorité,* op. cit., pp. 338ff.
35. "Et perchè l'occhio veda FG, lo intellecto nol comprende nè intende le sue parti se non commo una machia veduta da lungo, che non sa giudicare se è homo o altro animale. Cosi è F e G al puncto A, et perchè le cose, che le loro parti non si possono intendere, non si possono con ragione degradare, se non per macchie." Piero della Francesca, op. cit., fol. 17 recto, cited ed., pp. 98–99.

so, geometry is once again of assistance here, demonstrating how it happens that at point *F* the foreshortened quantity *BM* presents itself as equal to the quantity *MF,* which is not so radically foreshortened. That is to say, the edges of the painting correspond to those of the field within which reality and appearance, truth and semblance, coincide. Beyond these frontiers, and on the boundary of this field, all kinds of aberrations will occur that can be avoided only by honoring a limit smaller than *FG.* "In order for the eye to more easily apprehend things in front of it, these must present themselves at an angle smaller than a right one, such that the three sides compose an equilateral triangle each of whose angles will be as strong as the others."[36]

*

The question of the angle of vision is not one to be passed over quickly when dealing with a painting like the *Città ideale:* a painting whose format makes it difficult, if not impossible, to see all of it without placing oneself at a distance inconsistent with close study. Hence the impression you've gotten that the "machinery" of the painting seems to have been conceived to preclude such detailed examination. But as for the image proposed by Piero's demonstration of a single eye divided into four quarters, each with its own field of vision, you unhesitatingly associate this with the configuration of the ground plan of the *tempio* in the center of the scene. Given its fourth-order rotational symmetry, an observer inside the building, and at its center, would have only to turn 90° on his heels four times in succession to see opening before him, through the four doors placed on two perpendicular axes, four extremely narrow perspectives (we shall see from the ground plan that this is precisely the arrangement in the Urbino panel, where the point corresponding to the center of the *tempio* is exactly symmetrical to the "point of view" in relation to the plane of projection).

The optical connotations of this configuration will be easier to grasp, and our field of comparison simultaneously enlarged, if we refer to Perugino's *Consignment* as well as Raphael's *Marriage of the Virgin* (dated

---

36. "Si che è necessario pigliare minore termini che la linea FG; ciò che l'occhio receva piu facilemente le cose a lui oposte bisogna che se rapresentino socto minore angolo che il recto, il quale dico essere doi terzi de angolo recto, perchè i tre [lati] compogono triangolo equilatero, che tanto a forza l'uno angolo quanto l'altro." Ibid.

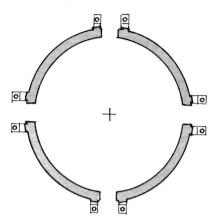

89 Reconstruction of the ground plan of the rotunda of the *Città ideale*.

1504) which reworks its basic elements, both of them featuring a centrally planned domed structure in the background of a composition of marked vertical extension: rising from stepped plinths, these buildings have central enclosures of relatively small diameter, Perugino's having porches which Raphael joined together to form a continuous portico, as well as aligned doors, framing the point of view toward which the orthogonals in the paving converge, through which one sees a view extending far into the distance. In both paintings this opening functions as a hole or "light" positioned on the composition's axis at the height of the horizon line that attracts one's gaze immediately, in a way that's become familiar to us but that here assumes particular prominence, carries a special punch. The horizon is much higher in the Raphael than in the Perugino, which increases the importance of the sacred building: it seems to preside over the scene and hover above its figures. The lack of connection between the group in the foreground and the temple in front of which the ceremony takes place, in conformity with iconographic tradition, is exacerbated by the duplication of the sightline imposed upon the gaze: scenographically the spectator is on a level with the foreground figures; but the perspective is falsified by the placement of the point of the eye within the opening of the temple door, at a height that would be totally incongruous, given the distance of the structure, if this weren't an altar painting originally intended to be viewed from below. This subtle play with the horizon of the scene and its tilt is particularly marked in Raphael's painting, where the fanlike spread of paved squares produces a radiating effect comparable to that of *da sotto in su* per-

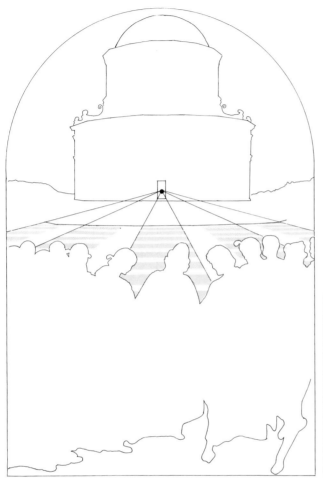

90   Raphael, *Marriage of the Virgin,* 1504. Milan,
Pinacoteca di Brera. Construction schema.

spectives, which this painter used elsewhere, for example—as already noted—in his *Ecstasy of Saint Cecilia*.[37]

The Urbino perspectives feature an analogous, though less spectacular, play with the horizon of the scene and its tilt. We've seen that the Urbino panel confirmed, a posteriori, the hypothesis endorsed above concerning the placement of the vanishing point, in the configuration of Brunelleschi's first experiment, within the baptistry door. But whereas the Florence baptistry is lower than the steps leading to the cathedral door, the *tempio* of the *Città ideale* rises from a plinth with several steps: it's as though the painter decided to compensate, after the fact, for the slight difference in level between the point of view and the vanishing point presupposed by the prototype, by reversing it, with the spectator's feet (as Serlio would say: ideally) situated on the base plane. The Berlin horizon line is somewhat higher than that in Urbino (at a height one-third that of the panel, as opposed to a little less than one-fourth in Urbino), while the disposition of the scene suggests, on the contrary, a slightly plunging perspective, with the plane of the water's surface being on a lower level than that of the square, which is in turn lower than the proscenium. The Baltimore horizon line is at an intermediate height (about two-fifths that of the panel), with its viewer occupying a position markedly higher than the foreground, and even above the plane from which the buildings rise, as is indicated by the fact that the figures' heads don't align with it. In the case of the Urbino and Berlin panels, the total absence of figures precludes us from determining with certainty the placement of the centric ray. But the presence of the two nesting doves in the *Città ideale* indicates that the real problem lies elsewhere: these fowl cannot help but bring to mind a bird's-eye view, the one that permitted us to verify the aberration you've described.[38]

*

The deformation you've uncovered on the left of the *Città ideale* is not, however, of the same order as the purported "errors" generated by perspective construction, demonstrated by Piero to derive from a disfunction of the

---

37. Cf. *supra*, chapter 2, pp. 25–26.

38. This would also apply to the flying birds visible in old photographs of the Baltimore panel (cf. Conti, "Le prospettive urbinate . . .," op. cit., p. 1195).

system when applied "outside the limits." In this instance the quantity to be foreshortened (the visible portion of the facade of the left palace paralleling the picture plane) and quantity as actually foreshortened (the receding facade of the same palace) are proportionate in both plan and elevation. If there's any aberration here, it manifests itself not within the geometric order but in a distension of the facade that becomes apparent from its smaller number of bays. In fact this aberration only becomes apparent if one compares the two facades of the corner palaces parallel to the picture plane. A task that can only be accomplished if the eyes turn within their orbits to consider them successively: if they remain motionless, these blocks will be perceived only as "blurs" enlivened by the "blinking" of the openings regularly distributed over them. The dissymmetry would then result from either a widening of the bays in the left palace (which would be consistent with its slightly greater height) or, conversely, from a narrowing of those in the palace on the right, which would be more consistent with the planimetrics: for this last facade seems to occupy only one square of the paving, whereas the receding facade of the same palace extends the length of a square and a half.

The comparison thus concerns two "transverse" quantities that should be equal. You don't doubt for an instant that this "error" is deliberate: the subtlety with which the transformations of the term-for-term oppositions between the two palaces have been effected provide, for you, sufficient proof of this. But you think it important to emphasize that it's only really apparent because it's been translated into architectural terms. As though the aberration, yet again, proceeded from the appearance of a tiny disparity between the geometric construction of the painting and its architectural ordinance, if not its composition.

What's important here is that the critical zones of the painting are those located, as indicated by *De prospectiva pingendi,* at its edges, and this tempts you to see these deformations, and the aberrations associated with them, as echoing Piero's treatment of the question of the angle at which a painting should present itself to the eye, or—what amounts to the same thing—that of the distance at which the spectator should stand in front of it: the fact that your attention was first drawn to the left side of the panel should be considered in tandem with the course followed by his demonstration. Of course the panel's format must be taken into account here: anyone

91 Reconstruction of the comic scene decor in the salon of the House of the Labyrinth in Pompeii (after A. M. G. Whyte, *Perspective and Scene Painting*, p. 409, fig. 2).

closely scrutinizing the *Città ideale* will feel like a viewer in the first row of a theater screening a film in cinemascope. Now there are a number of compositions that, while their scenic configurations are analogous, don't lend themselves to this experiment. You cite two examples: Botticelli's *History of Lucretia,* already mentioned, unfolds within a narrow scenic area contained by two lateral porticos and the triumphal arch in the background, and its dimensions (80 × 178 cm) preclude a "wide-angle" effect; and as for Domenico Ghirlandaio's fresco *Resuscitation of the Child* (Florence, Santa Trinita), while it depicts a scene whose plan is that of an upside-down *tau,* its central receding area between two rows of roughly symmetrical buildings seems more like a street leading into the background than a square of any significant width.

These two examples have not been chosen at random. While its dimensions are much more compact than those of the *Città ideale,* the *History of Lucretia* features a similar symmetrical scenic configuration bordered on three sides by architectural elements in an antique mode, with spatial extensions into the background effected by *vedute,* a pair of them disposed to either side of the triumphal arch, revealing two rows of rather prosaic buildings, and another through the arch, of a fortified gate: an arrangement similar to that in the Baltimore panel, though here the scenography interferes with the model of the Vitruvian *frons scaenae,* as indicated by the strange covered portico attached to the triumphal arch, somehow reminiscent of the architectural framework for the comic scene decor in the salon of the House of the Labyrinth in Pompeii. The lateral porticos in the Botticelli recede much further into depth while manifesting a dissymmetry analogous

92   Domenico Ghirlandaio, *Saint Francis Resuscitating a Child.* Florence, Santa Trinità, Sassetti Chapel, 1483–86. Photo: Alinari-Giraudon.

to that in the *Città ideale,* as the structure on the right begins much further forward than does the one on the left.

The components of Ghirlandaio's fresco are much less extravagant: a receding street, across which a large palace of archaic type faces a church which appears to be medieval, leading to a bridge beyond which are a few houses and a figure on which the composition's orthogonals converge (in fact it's the Piazza Santa Trinità, with the Palazzo Spini on the left and, on the right, the facade of Santa Trinità prior to the alterations effected by Buontalenti). But the *Confirmation of the Franciscan Rule* in the lunette immediately above the *Resuscitation of the Child* also attracts your attention, for several reasons: its markedly scenographic disposition (a proscenium frames the scene, in which we see, according to Aby Warburg,[39] Lorenzo di Medici, Antonio Pucci, and the donor Francesco Sassetti, while at their feet there opens like a stage trapdoor, in a gesture without parallel in contempo-

---

39.   Aby Warburg, "Bildkunst und Florentinisches Bürgentum. Domenico Ghirlandaio in Santa Trinita. Die Bildnisse des Lorenzo de' Medici und seiner Angehorigen" (1902), *Gesammelte Werke,* Leipzig, 1932, vol. 1, pp. 89–126.

rary painting, a stairway from which emerge Politian and Lorenzo's children), its program (which tightly weaves together religious, political, and personal themes), and its references: beyond the partition hung with brocade closing off the proscenium, a triple-arched portico opening onto the Piazza della Signoria frames a partial view, at left, of the Palazzo Vecchio, and in the center the skillfully truncated arches of the Loggia dei Lanzi, which echo those of the enframing portico. Which brings us back, yet again, to Brunelleschi, specifically his second experiment, which exploited this same site, though on the diagonal, while Ghirlandaio adopted a frontal view.

Panofsky cites a remark by Lessing to the effect that perspective is not a matter of genius. But you see evidence that there's a genius of perspective in these works, largely neglected by today's critics, which you think hold great interest for history as well as theory. These images, a bit too affable and anecdotal, interest you because of the evidence they provide, with regard to identifiable referents, of highly sophisticated scenographic research that's not unconnected with the disposition, in their case idealized, of our three panels. Notably the portico, an imaginary one, within which the "history" takes place, and which frames—as in the Berlin panel—a view of a square seen in perspective: proof that this idea was current when the Sassetti Chapel was painted (between 1483 and 1486), and that there's no need to refer to the much later example of Peruzzi. But you've isolated another feature here that's no less pertinent: the many doors and windows in the facades of the buildings bordering the scene in both images, some of which, especially in the *Resuscitation of the Child,* are distinguished by a remarkable darkness.

We are very far here, to be sure, from the imperious configuration, in the Urbino, Baltimore, and Berlin panels, of holes onto blackness, their openings varied infinitely by the play of their shutters. You want only to point out that the motif, treated in a quasi-emblematic way, of windows fitted with interior shutters, is quite frequently encountered in Florentine painting, and that it has no privileged connection to Cosimo Rosselli, whatever Howard Saalman may say.[40] Further evidence along these lines is provided by another fresco by Domenico Ghirlandaio: his *Annunciation* in the

---

40. Saalman, op. cit., p. 379.

93   Domenico Ghirlandaio, *Confirmation of the Franciscan Rule*. Florence, Santa Trinità, Sassetti Chapel, 1583–1586.

94   Domenico Ghirlandaio, *Confirmation of the Franciscan Rule*, detail.

95 and 96 Domenico Ghirlandaio, *Annunciation.*
San Gimignano, collegiate church, 1482. Photo:
Anderson-Giraudon. Construction schema.

collegiate church of San Gimignano. On the central axis of the painting, on
which the vanishing point is also situated, is a square window with a marble bracket, placed rather high. Of its two interior shutters, the one to the
left is closed; the other, swung backward, stands out against a dark ground.
To complete the analogy with the door of the Urbino *tempio,* a light point is
marked in the center of the window, slightly to the right of the closed
shutter. The function of this point is difficult to explain, but you note that
it's on the same horizontal line as the dove of the Holy Spirit and the fillets
of the capitals of the pilasters framing the scene.

Thus *pointed,* this window presents itself as a motif that proclaims
and reflects the work of the painting. As such, it is to be associated with

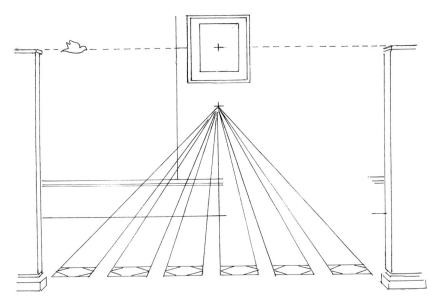

other windows with half-open shutters performing a similar function, such as those by Masaccio and Masolino in the Brancacci Chapel or that—once more in an *Annunciation*—in the upper right corner of Piero's *Annunciation* in Arezzo, whose three other compartments contain, respectively, figures of the Creator, an angel, and the Virgin. I designate as a painting's *ensign* or epigraph an iconic element which, without performing any syntactical or constructive function, broadcasts, as it were, its operations by miming them: in the same way a commercial sign indicates the business or profession of its owner (La Fontaine: "It is the sign that gets the client"), or an epigraph heading a volume or chapter indicates its essence: the syllable *graph* serving here—where inscriptions that might specify the meaning of the image are in fact illegible, when they're not altogether absent—as a reminder that painting sustains with writing, including the power of inscription (*in-signum*) proper to it, a relation that predates the articulation of characters. Thus Uccello's *mazocchio,* whose tubular, three-dimensional form assumes all the functions, in the perspective paradigm, of the checkerboard graph determining the paving squares. Thus in the Urbino, Baltimore, and Berlin panels, as well as earlier in the works of Masaccio and Piero, this proliferation of doors and windows, along with the insistent play of their variously positioned shutters, sepia against black, and with the field of vision of a postulated observer standing somewhat back, looking out

toward the exterior: painting here being as much a matter of *angle* as of *distance*.

Such ensigns (or epigraphs) can accrue the value of emblems where and when tradition consecrates them as such. But there's nothing arbitrary or conventional about them, however abstract the operations they echo and for which they propose, in terms of painting, visual metaphors. The motif of the window with interior shutters, or double doors, is emblematic in two respects. First, because of the link it posits with the art of marquetry, for which doors and shutters were privileged sites, and which itself used them prominently for illusionist purposes. Witness, in the palace at Urbino, the double doors, those—doubtless after designs by Botticelli—in the Sala degli Angeli as well as those in the Sala degli Arazzi, in the duchess's bedroom as well as the duke's, through which one must pass before reaching the room in which the *Città ideale* is now displayed: doors with marquetry inlay, their lower registers often featuring receding architectural perspectives apportioned over two facing panels. These "perspectives," completely devoid of figures and adhering to the same formula of a square or street bordered by two rows of buildings, are not strictly symmetrical: on the contrary, they seem to make play, within each "pair," with the same repertory of binary oppositions now familiar to us: palace facade with loggia and portico vs. a fortified wall (the duchess's bedroom); palace of Florentine type vs. porticoed corner palace (dressing room); arched portico on columns vs. columned portico with flat entablature (Sala degli Angeli), etc. The background generally being closed, beneath a sky scattered with clouds, by a crenelated wall, a fortification pierced by great doors surmounted by a tower opening onto the sea and its ships, or an open gallery resembling a two-tiered aqueduct, also affording a view of large sailing ships (the duke's bedroom); the sole trace, aside from the structures themselves, of human activity. But the essential point remains the use of a perspective construction with axial vanishing point, here situated on the join of the door's two wings: open them slowly, and the perspective will appear at first to distend itself and then to split up the middle, but without the notion of a vanishing point common to both panels, and the idea of their jointure, being completely abandoned, even though the angle at which they're viewed no longer allows them to be apprehended at a single glance.

98 Domenico Rosselli, marquetry door after
designs by Botticelli. Urbino, Palazzo Ducale, room
VIII. Photo: Anderson-Giraudon.

Conversely, it is in the marquetry decor of the *studiolo* that this angular play attains its maximum expression in an illusionist mode: the openwork doors of the trompe l'oeil cabinets reveal the objects, pieces of armor, books, musical instruments, armillary spheres, etc., placed inside as much as they obscure them, as is the case with veils. Which prompts you to observe (though the remark makes sense only within the context of the French language) that according to Littré's dictionary, *volet,* the French word for shutter, derives from the French verb "to fly," *voler,* by metonymic reference to the square of cardboard atop the sacred chalice of the host when it's covered by its veil (*voile*), which is said to "fly," just as in the language of heraldy we speak of a "flying" ribbon attached to top of a crest. If, following Littré, we understand a *volet* to be "a woodwork panel that can be opened or closed at will and serves to secure, from inside a room, the glazing of a window, as opposed to outside shutters (*contrevents*), which secure them from the outside," you note that here the windows fitted with shutters aren't glazed. This fact is all the more remarkable because in the Urbino panel both the *tempio* and the basilica feature, above their central doors, pedimented windows closed by *cul de bouteille* or medallion glazing (as are the spaces between the small columns of the lantern surmounting the *tempio*). In other words, these last openings cannot be considered transparent, in contrast to the openings whose appearance seems totally arbitrary, and in which you discern so many ensigns or epigraphs, as I've defined these terms, whether the shutterless windows, reduced to simple black holes, regularly distributed between the second-floor columns of the *tempio,* or the double-shuttered windows of the various palaces (to say nothing of those disposed in rows to either side of the square in which we can make out, here and there, outside shutters in the form of propped-open blinds and even, on the third floor of the second building beyond the left palace, a glazed window swung open toward the outside).

We've tried to discover the rule or law governing this distribution, whose variations seem to be systematic, but our efforts have proved vain. And then it's impossible to determine the relative dimensions of the windows (and doors) within the porticos, partially obscured by columns or piers, and of those partly hidden by other buildings. These remarks also apply to the Baltimore and Berlin panels, where the presence of this ensign

99 The *Città ideale*,
palace on the left, detail
of windows.

100 The *Città ideale*,
palace on the right, detail
of windows.

101 The *Città ideale*, detail, left portion of the panel.

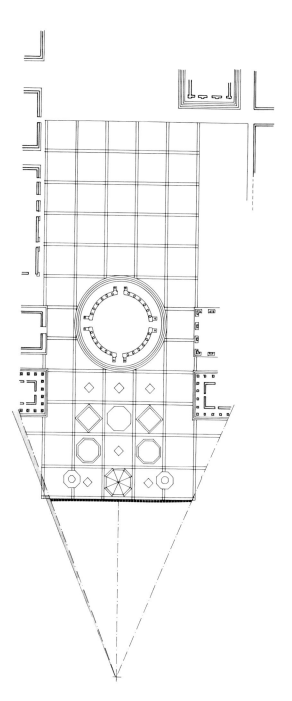

102 Ground plan of the
Città ideale (reconstruction by Jean Blécon).

is just as insistent. The shutters and door wings can only be there to signal the opening, its dimensions varying in function with the distance, corresponding to the view of an observer positioned behind the window and the door. Thus invoking the problem we've already encountered as it relates to Brunelleschi's first experiment, and which you yourself confronted as it concerns the Urbino perspectives, specifically the "aberrations" in the Urbino panel: aberrations one would be tempted to connect with the "wide-angle" effect generated by the painting's format—if, that is, this effect weren't illusory, totally deceptive.

The best way to convince oneself of this is to reconstruct, at least approximately, the ground plan of the scene. The results of this exercise are surprising. In Jean Blécon's reconstruction of the ground plan of the *Città ideale,* produced at my request, the piazza, or what passes for one, is reduced to a kind of corridor or passage that's quite narrow in relation to its depth, with the buildings in the foreground of the scene being concentrated at its entrance. And *scene* is decidedly the appropriate word, if we bear in mind that the Italian theater would exploit, much later, the same effects of foreshortening, of flattening, made possible by perspective. Whereas Serlio's scene still consisted of a rather wide proscenium that architectural elements made to seem deep, as can be seen in Peruzzi's drawings and Serlio's prints, whose proportions are quite different from those of the Urbino perspectives, the Baroque theater would not exploit the means of architecture, only those of painting: while sacrificing the classic taste for bilateral symmetry, this theater (which Georges Kernodle characterized as one of "pictorial illusion") would deploy its effects into depth by means of successive planes established by two rows of movable wings facing one another across a scene no less narrow than that of the *Città ideale.*

The two other panels, in Baltimore and Berlin, conform to the same schema: both are narrow scenes developed into depth—as best one can tell, given that in Baltimore the second level, higher than the forestage or proscenium area, is not squared, and that in Berlin it's rather difficult to determine the measurements of the transverse quantities. But this is not the essential point. More important for us would be the fact that the checkerboard construction of the paving is a function, in all three instances, of the same angle of vision. Now this is the case, roughly speaking, for the Urbino and Baltimore panels: in Urbino, the angle can be determined, with

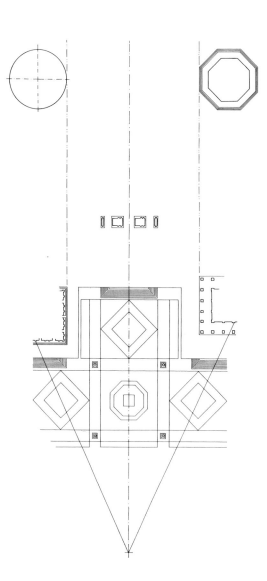

103 Ground plan of the
Baltimore panel (recon-
struction by Jean Blécon).

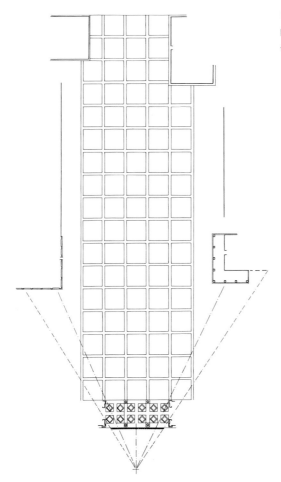

104 Ground plan of the
Berlin panel (reconstruc-
tion by Jean Blécon).

relative precision, to be a bit larger than 45°, while in Baltimore, where the point of view is difficult to situate with exactitude, it's somewhere between 40° and 50°.[41] The case presented by the Berlin panel is more complex: considered at its full width, the panorama of the piazza visible through the three bays of the portico as well as the two side doors corresponds to an angle of 70°. But if we limit ourselves to the view through the portico bays, we once more obtain an angle of vision of about 45°. The consistency of this feature, which runs counter to expectation, provides further confirmation, if such be needed, of the participation of all three panels in the same transformation group. But we must go further: the fact that the Urbino panel's vanishing point is exactly symmetrical to the one marked in the center of its *tempio* effectively constitutes an echo, admittedly a subtle one, of the fundamentals of Brunelleschi's first experiment, and is sufficient to identify the said group as a dependency of the prototype and simultaneously inscribe it within a history whose meaning is determined by the prototype. Within the same frame of reference, it's at least marginally possible that the variation in the angle of vision in the Berlin panel is a reference to the rule formulated by Piero della Francesca, who thought the only way to avoid the errors resulting, as he would have it, from *transgressing the limits* was to remain within an angle equal to two-thirds of a right one, its two sides composing with the line corresponding to the picture plane an equilateral triangle, with the length of the line inscribed within the peak of the angle being less than that of the side perpendicular to it. "I say that if your work is seven *braccia* long, you can view it from a distance of at least six *braccia*, and thus proportionately as its width increases. But if your work is narrower than seven *braccia*, you can view it from a distance of six or seven *braccia*, though you shouldn't get any closer to it than indicated by a proportion of six to seven. This is because, within these limits, the eye will see, without moving, all of your work, whereas if it's obliged to move, the areas (*termini*) beyond the limits of vision will appear false. Consequently, if

---

41. In his reconstruction of the ground plan of the *Città ideale*, Jean Blécon was obliged to introduce a slight dissymmetry in order to compensate for the discrepancy between the two facades of the corner palaces paralleling the picture plane. In fact the painting's measurements are perfectly symmetrical, and the angle of vision should be slightly wider on the left than he originally represented it as being.

you observe the reasons I've just enunciated, you will see that the defect results from them, and not from perspective."[42]

The formula has the virtue of being clear and without ambiguity: it could not be expressed better, or more simply, that contrary to received opinion the point at which the spectator should position himself is not identical with the one supposedly assigned him by the perspective construction. And this is so even when the subject necessarily has its place within the field of the work, but under auspices that are not exclusively geometrical—as we shall see.

---

42. "Dico che si il tuo lavoro è de larghezza secte braccia, che tu stia da lunghi a vedere sei braccia non meno, et cosi quando fusse più che ti stia a proportione. Ma quando il tuo lavoro fusse meno di secte braccia, tu puoi stara sei o secte braccia da lunga col vedere, ma non te puoi apressare con minore proportione che da 6. a 7., como è dicto perchè in quello termine l'occhio senza volgiarse vede tucto il tu lavoro, che se bisognasse volgere serieno falsi i termini perchè serieno piu vederi. Dunqua se tu osservarai le ragioni che se sono decte, cognoscerai che il difecto è de quelli tali, et non de la prospectiva. . . ." Piero della Francesca, op. cit., fol. 17 recto, cited ed., p. 99.

The view (*tertio*).

Diderot's telescope.

Rotation/ostension.

Quasi per sino in infinito.

The subject holds by a thread.

Serlio and the horizon of the theater.

Relief, style, and idea.

The theater of painting.

The contradictor.

Poetry and geometry.

Las Meninas, once again.

The geometry of the sentence.

The Loci of the Subject

That the perceiving eye is constrained, in the play of the perspective configuration, by a double limit, one in depth and one on the plane, had been
implicitly demonstrated by Brunelleschi's first experiment: Did this not
claim to reproduce, on the scale of a proportionately reduced "view," the
conditions under which the San Giovanni baptistry gave itself up to the
vision, framed by the central portal of Florence cathedral, of an observer
stationed inside at the prescribed distance? And wasn't its success predicated
on the use of a mirror, which from the beginning posited reflexivity or self-
reference as a constitutive property of the perspective configuration, and of
regulating configurations in general? A constitutive property of the perspective configuration and, through it, of painting itself, insofar as the latter
engendered it—to use Leonardo's term—as a means of reflecting upon and
regulating itself?

The apparatus conceived by Brunelleschi derived its demonstrative
value from the fact that it made repetition of the operation feasible. Anyone
could perform the experiment in turn: he had only to place his eye against
the hole at the panel's back and position the mirror at the proper distance,
and in it he would see reflected an image of the baptistry and its environs as
Brunelleschi had painted them in perspective. An image of the baptistry,
and not the baptistry itself, as the configuration was in no way comparable
to a camera or a *camera oscura* (though the mirror reflecting the sky was
another matter). The illusion—or, as Manetti put it, the effect of "truth"
(*e pareva che si vedessi 'l proprio vero*)—resulted, as did the information contained by the image, from the conditions of an experiment that, while
determined by the latter's structure, set out in part to isolate it from its
context by concentrating the gaze on it. Diderot did likewise when he
invited his reader to use a simple cardboard tube like a telescope in examining a painting by Joseph Vernet: "Look at the *Port of la Rochelle* with a

telescope encompassing the field of the painting but excluding its edges, and suddenly, forgetting that you're examining a painting, you'll cry out, as if you were situated high in the mountains, a spectator of nature herself: 'Oh! What a beautiful view!'"[1]

Though it took the form of a painting constructed in perspective, Brunelleschi's configuration exploited an effect comparable to that produced by Diderot's "telescope": for the image to forcefully register as "true," as "nature herself," it is best to prescribe limits to vision such that the observer no longer perceives an exterior reference point and must make do with those available to him in the painting. A consequence being that whereas trompe l'oeil necessarily operates in the dimension of the real, and thus need not concern itself with subtle, imperceptible shifts in scale, perspective, being a matter of proportions, can be made to accommodate frankly arbitrary scales. It matters little whether the scale in question takes the form of a reduction or an enlargement of the dimensions (as at the movies): the essential thing is that it function, phenomenologically, as the sole scale of reference.

But the configuration did not aim solely at allowing the spectator to consider the image of the baptistry with a minimum of distraction, like the viewer of a film in a darkened theater. As a "projection," this configuration (which only functioned in daylight) presupposed that, once the eye was pressed up against it, the hole in the panel would function as a *lens,* in other words as the origin or principle around which a construction was deployed that, while initiated from a point of view outside the picture plane, nonetheless was reinscribed there in the form—projective, specular, it's all the same—of the vanishing point. Such that the observer was summoned to experience both his exteriority in relation to a closed-circuit configuration (its only opening onto the exterior being this hole, which was blocked when the eye pressed against it), and his implication in the system, precisely as *origin,* but an origin that had to be deduced from the configuration itself, the primary goal of the experiment being to reveal, in a quasi-

---

1. Diderot, *Salon de 1763, Salons,* ed. by Seznec and Adhémar, vol. 1, Oxford, 1967, p. 229. Cf. also, in this same *Salon,* Diderot's remarks concerning Greuze's portrait of his wife: "Position yourself so the stairway's between you and the portrait, look at it with a telescope, and you'll see nature herself; I defy you to deny to me that this figure's looking at you, that she's alive" (ibid., p. 237).

photographic sense of the word, that in planar projection the image of it became confused with the vanishing point.

This paradox becomes clearer if we note that the 180° rotation of the panel on which the baptistry was painted, and the invitation that the spectator subsequently apply his eye against its central hole, is equivalent to the movement of objectification or *rotation* discussed by Ernst Bloch, in which the gaze tears itself away from the opacity of the given to establish itself opposite it—"like a hand grasping something at a certain distance and holding it up to view." In order for things and the world to become objects of perception, the subject must pull back from itself, having no vision that doesn't proceed, ultimately, from such a rotation as well as from the *elevation* or *ostension* of the object that is its corollary.[2] But this movement, even its theatrical aspect, remains subject to the law of representation: the distance established by the subject between itself and the object (Diderot: "Position yourself so the stairway's between you and the portrait") allows it to escape from the immediacy of lived experience; but only to discover that it itself is implicated, inescapably, in a spectacle whose truth is a function, precisely, of its being so implicated.

Drehung, Umgebung, "rotation," "ostension": these terms correspond, literally, to the two constitutive moments of Brunelleschi's experiment. Which is to say that the configuration responded to aims other than solely contemplative ones. Doubtless one of its necessary conditions was an image constructed in perspective, whatever method may have been used to generate it. It didn't teach how it itself had been constructed, but neither did it simply present itself to view. Anyone wishing to *see* it had to conform to the protocol stipulating first rotation of the panel, then ostension of the mirror in which the image was reflected, the effect of *truth* being dependent upon the mirror's being held, opposite the panel, at the appropriate height and distance. It matters little, in this connection, that Manetti's description may contain a misunderstanding:[3] the experiment aimed at nothing less than construction of a structure of objectivity in which the subject had its assigned position, indeed one that it could locate solely and exclusively by

2.   Ernst Bloch, *Experimentum Mundi: Frage, Kategorien des Herausbringens, Praxis, Gesammelte Werken,* Frankfurt, 1975; French trans. *Experimentum Mundi. Question, catégories de l'élaboration, praxis,* Paris, 1981, pp. 14ff.
3.   Cf. supra, chapter 8, pp. 134ff.

referring to a mirror, to specular reflection—which is to say, to a transformation, in the geometric sense.

*

The Urbino perspectives were certainly not made to be viewed in a mirror, nor to be held and manipulated. And as to the question of isolation from context, the one in Berlin makes so little pretense to this that it's on a wooden panel whose substantial lower portion is treated like trompe l'oeil woodwork. Moving from there to the assertion that this panel was conceived as part of a decorative ensemble might seem to entail no more than a small step, but it's a step you resist taking: for you're rather inclined to suspect some sort of ruse here, one perfectly consistent with an art attempting to discover what painting means to say, in the instance and under the constraints of perspective. A perspective, in this case, in which the subject—kept at a distance by the apparatus of a scene that's deserted but that nonetheless gazes at it with all its eyes, wary or not—has no specified place. The effect of theatricality generated by the suspension of the representation/performance is strengthened by the spectator's being prohibited from *entering into the painting* (as Diderot would say), from becoming absorbed into it, or putting it right in his imagination: for it's a very different thing to discover that one's implicated in it, but from a distance that's insurmountable.[4]

---

4.   Michael Fried has well described how the fiction of "entering into the picture" functions in Diderot's criticism, and particularly in the *Salon of 1767*. This fiction is best exemplified, *a contrario,* by Diderot's assessment in the same *Salon* of Hubert Robert's *The Port of Rome:* "This work is very beautiful, it's full of grandeur, of majesty; one admires it, but one isn't moved, it doesn't make one dream. . . . Ideal beauty strikes all men, beauty of handling attracts the attention only of connoisseurs; if it makes them dream, it's only of art and the artist and not of the thing itself, they remain outside the scene, *they never enter into it*" (*Salons,* op. cit., vol. 3, pp. 235–36, my emphasis). The fiction that the painting—to use Diderot's terms—draws the spectator into the scene ("A painting with which you become involved in this way, that draws you into the scene and gives the soul a delicious sensation, is never a bad painting," ibid., vol. 2 p. 173) is perfectly consistent with what Fried maintains is the "supreme fiction" of French painting in the second half of the eighteenth century, in accordance with which the artist sought out a means of neutralizing the spectator, such that the painting and its figures might create an impression consistent with there being no viewer in front of it who's looking at it. Indeed one way to deny the presence of the beholder is to induce him to enter into the painting, to draw him into it (as opposed to allowing him to keep his distance), thus delivering a fatal blow to pictorial theatricality at the same time as one clears the way for a new tradition, that of modernity (Michael Fried, *Absorption and Theatricality: Painting and Beholder in the Age of Diderot,* Berkeley, 1980, pp. 118–36). The series of the ports of France commissioned in 1753 of Carle-Joseph Vernet is a case in point: while these "views" were constructed in strict perspective, as specified by the contract between Marigny and the artist, they were

And yet the inconographic given, or rather, the symbolic given, the *imago* with which the Urbino panel renews contact, even rehearsing the point marked in the door opening of a round building in its center, in the same spot in which the hole was pierced in the prototype, this given suggests that here too the painting is as though traversed by a reflexive project, in this case one owing nothing to specularity. A reflexive project that, while not translated into experimental terms, nonetheless involves a kind of experiment, a strictly mental one. You maintain that an idea of this project can't be obtained from looking at the *Città ideale* alone. To fully understand it, one must follow the play of transformations that the group, in the course of its operations, is charged with producing, revealing, and putting to work: and this by means of a set of manipulations which, while abstract, are intimately linked with the functioning of the perspective paradigm, in its capacity as demonstrative and regulatory configuration. The fact that there can be no perspective unless it's "of something," and that the configuration has a privileged relationship with architecture, is something of an obstacle, but it also clears the way toward a work of idealization bearing less upon the referent than upon the play revealing, at the pivot between the real and the imaginary, the ascendency of the symbolic.

The height of the horizon line is one thing. The vanishing point's distance from it is another. In direct planar projection this point becomes confused, as we've seen, with the other one identified by the perspective configuration as its origin and which is called the point of view. Assimilation of the picture plane to a mirror or a transparent pane of glass changes nothing: both points would still be inscribed on a single perpendicular line on this plane. Hence the distress of the subject when it tries to get its bearings: "I" am there, at least in projection, at the point that's marked (*segnato,* Alberti would say) on the canvas; or rather, "I" have my geometric position there, even though I remain some distance from the painting—as any subject whose eye is situated on the same line will have its (geometric) place there, the positions of seer and seen being perfectly reversible, through rotation. Now it's at this point that the difficulties in play within

---

made to induce viewing from a certain distance and, what's more, from above, at least as much as to encourage in-depth exploration, in the form of an intimate traversal. Diderot's resort to his "telescope" argument proves this and establishes a connection with Brunelleschi's first experiment.

the Urbino perspectives' transformation group commence. Brunelleschi's experiment effectively presupposed a kind of symmetry between the position assigned the painter, inside the cathedral, and that of an observer standing on the jamb of the baptistry door. Manetti lacked the means to conceive of this symmetry (echoed in the construction schema of the *Città ideale*), since he had not fully grasped the principle of the *intersegatione* and its corollary, that of the distance point (unless, as already discussed, he deliberately ignored them). But this symmetry in no way addresses the question of the placement of the same vanishing point in depth, as opposed to on the plane.

While the constraint of the plane determines that the paving lines perpendicular to the painting's baseline will converge, in geometrical terms, toward a point inscribed on this plane corresponding in the *Città ideale* to the *tempio* door, these lines nonetheless extend, in figurative terms, beyond and behind this edifice. Does this mean that the point toward which they converge in depth would be *behind* an observer inside the *tempio* who's looking out at us? Just as any observer whose eye was situated on the same line perpendicular to the picture plane would have a similar point at a like distance *behind him,* one corresponding to Pascal's notion "of what's behind one's head"? This question of the vanishing point's position in depth is raised, if not explicitly articulated, by the transformation group using means proper to it, in this case the system of *vedute* and planar graduation which constitutes one of its basic structural features. While the Urbino panel's vanishing point appears to be inscribed within the interior of the *tempio,* the view on its right of a square that's much deeper than the proscenium reveals that the configuration is not closed at this point: the fact that the squared paving is interrupted some distance from the rotunda sustains a calculated ambiguity whose meaning we are now better equipped to grasp. In the Baltimore panel, on the other hand, the perspective has become multiple, so to speak: as you've already noted, the vanishing point is framed by the "door" represented by the central opening of the triumphal arch, only to be relayed into the background, where it's inscribed, again, within another door: an opening that's also a closure, since it corresponds to a fortified tower on the ramparts closing off the scene, beyond which we see a row of hills barring the horizon.

105   Bernardo Bellotto, *View of the Piazetta in Venice*. Rome, National Gallery. Photo: Ardo.

The Berlin panel is quite different. Here again the vanishing point is framed by a "door," in this case the central bay of the foreground portico. But the orthogonals in the paving, reduced to a bundle opening like a fan in the center of the scene, are interrupted before they reach the vanishing point, situated on the horizon. If their recession thus seems as though *suspended,* this is because, beyond the rupture parallel to the baseline corresponding to the edge of the quay, nothing is visible but a liquid expanse punctuated by the silhouettes of some ships, progressively smaller as they approach the horizon, and those of two islands or promontories which Parronchi identifies as Capria and Gorgona, dear to the inhabitants of Pisa as well as to Dante's fellow citizens.[5] Here it seems as though the vanishing point has been cast into infinity, there being no better image of infinite

5.   Parronchi, "La prima rappresentatione . . .," op. cit., p. 83.

distance than a marine horizon line, assuming this is framed by a clearly
delimited "view," in accordance with a schema still being used by Bellotto,
in the eighteenth century, in his *Views of the Piazzetta* in Venice. For as
Machiavelli has the naive Niccia say in his *Mandragola: e non si vede acqua,
acqua, acqua,* "one sees nothing but water, water, water." This remark
would indeed be naive, if watery expanses, unlike the sky, did not constitute a fine object for painting. As is indicated by Alberti's reference, in
Della Pittura, to the fable of Narcissus, whom he suggests was the inventor
of this art: "What else can you call painting but a similar embracing, with
art, of what is presented on the surface of the water of the spring?"[6] If we
momentarily disregard its function as a mirror, which is implied here, this
proposition about painting's origin only makes sense, in terms of perspective, because water necessarily gives itself up to view (though not, admittedly, to one's embrace) as a surface, enclosed within limits that can be
projected onto a plane. Regardless of whether it's a spring, a fountain, a
pool, or even a lake. But the sea? The sea that, once beyond the shore, is
subject to no limit other than that of the horizon—to such an extent that
Pascal resorted to the image of a boat gradually disappearing toward the
horizon to illustrate the paradox of the two infinities:

---

6.   "Che già, ove sia la pictura fiore d'ogni arte, ivi tutta la storia di Narcisso viene a prosposito.
Che dirai tu essere diginiere, altra cosa che simile abraciare con arte, quella ivi superficie del fonte?"
Alberti, op. cit., pp. 77–78; English trans., p. 64. I will return to this theme in a work-in-
progress, *D'un Narcisse l'autre.*

In space there is the same connection between these two contrary infinities: that is to say, it follows from the fact that a space can be indefinitely extended, that it can be indefinitely reduced, as appears in this example: if one looks through a glass directly at a boat disappearing into the distance, it is clear that the location of the transparency (*le lieu du diaphane*) where one remarks the point toward which the ship moves will consistently rise, in continuous flux, as the vessel proceeds. Thus if the vessel keeps to its course, even unto infinity, this point will still rise; and yet it will never reach the one upon which falls the horizontal ray coming from the eye through the glass, but will continuously approach it without ever arriving at it, ceaselessly dividing the space remaining beneath this horizontal point without ever arriving there. From which one can see that a necessary consequence following from the infinity of the expanse of the vessel's course is the infinite and infinitely small division of the tiny space remaining below this horizontal point.[7]

We should not be surprised that Pascal, in creating a *picture* of the relation between the two infinities, had recourse to language associated with *perspectiva artificialis:* even referring to the "glass" or *diaphane* slicing the visual pyramid, and to the centric ray striking at a perpendicular angle. And there's also a striking correspondence, over a gap of a century and a half, between this "demonstration" and the image presented by the Berlin panel, its ships approaching the horizon "without ever arriving there," the point signifying the most distant of them being inscribed on this line slightly to the left of the centric point of the perspective: as though, here again, it was

---

7.   "Dans l'espace le même rapport se voit entre ces deux infinis contraires: c'est-à-dire que, de ce qu'un espace peut être indéfiniment prolongé, il s'ensuit qu'il peut être indéfiniment diminué, comme il paraît en cet exemple: si on regarde au travers d'un verre un vaisseau qui s'éloigne toujours directement, il est clair que le lieu du diaphane où l'on remarque un point tel qu'on voudra du navire haussera toujours, par un flux continuel, à mesure que le vaisseau fuit. Donc, si la course du vaisseau est toujours allongée et jusqu'à l'infini, ce point haussera continuellement; et cependant il n'arrivera jamais à celui où tombera le rayon horizontal mené de l'oeil au verre, de sorte qu'il en approchera toujours sans y arriver jamais, divisant sans cesse l'espace qui restera sous ce point horizontal sans y arriver jamais. D'où l'on voit la consequence necessaire qui se tire de l'infinité de l'étendue du cours du vaisseau, à la division infinie et infiniment petite de ce petit espace restant au-dessous de ce point horizontal." Pascal, "De l'Esprit géométrique," *Oeuvres complètes,* Bibl. de la Pléiade, Paris, 1964, pp. 590–91.

important that there be an imperceptible discrepancy between the geometric construction and the disposition of the scene, as in the *Città ideale*.

Pascal's "demonstration" refers explicitly to the concrete practice of perspective, but it only convinces with regard to the infinitely small. As for the infinitely large, the visible horizon provides only a deceptive image of this when it functions as a limit, which of necessity must be finite—the same one governing *costruzione legittima*, which Alberti was able to conceptualize in perspectival terms two centuries before Pascal: "For me this line is a limit above which no visible quantity is allowed unless it is higher than the eye of the beholder [literally: the eye that sees]. Because this line passes through the centric point, I call it the centric line."[8] To convince his reader that this line indeed functioned as a limit, Alberti appealed to "natural" perspective, noting that in a temple we see the heads of all the faithful on one line, whereas the feet of those farthest away correspond to the knees of those closer to us.[9] But he could just as well have invoked *artificial* perspective, and the way intervals between the lines of the rows of squares paralleling the ground line progressively diminish toward the horizon, eventually becoming visually indistinguishable from it.

The fact remains that Pascal was able to broach the question of infinity as it relates not only to the "rise" of a ship toward the horizon but also to its endless flight toward what he designates as "the horizontal point," which it can never reach. But this "pointing" also has a predecessor in Alberti. Doubtless the latter never explicitly conceived the notion of a point "at infinity." But the centric point takes its place for the painter: if, beginning there, one traces straight lines intersecting the painting's baseline, this network that's supposedly perpendicular to the baseline will show or demonstrate (*dé-montrera*) how each transverse quantity (that is to say, in space, the deviation between two lines of the network) progressively diminishes, "as if to infinity."[10] It would fall to Desargues, Pascal's contemporary,

---

8.   "Io descrivo nel quadrangolo della pictura, ad traverso, una dritta linea dalle inferiori equidistante quale dal uno lato all'altro, passando su pel centrio punto, divida il quadrangolo. Questa linea amme tiene uno termine quale niuna feduta quantita, non piu alta che l'occhio che vede, puo sopra giudicare; et questa perche passa pel punto centrico dicesi linea centrica." Alberti, op. cit., p. 74; English trans., p. 58.
9.   Ibid. Cf. *supra,* chapter 8, p. 133, note 33.
10. "Adunque posto il punto centrico, come dissi, segno diritte linee da esso a ciascuna divisione posta nella linee del quadrangolo che giace, quali segnate linee a mi dimostrino in che modo, quasi

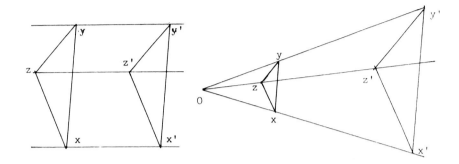

107 The theorem of Desargues.

to inscribe, in strict geometric terms, infinity within the finite and to contain it, literally, *within a point,* which would make Descartes uneasy.[11] The theorem bearing his name holds that given two triangles *xyz* and *x'y'z',* such that points *x, y,* and *z* are distinct from points *x', y',* and *z',* and lines *xy, yz,* and *zx* are parallel, respectively, to lines *x'y', y'z',* and *z'x',* then the lines *xx', yy',* and *zz'* can be either parallel or convergent. Now this theorem is presented as a derivation from results reported by Desargues in his *Méthode universelle de perspective* published in 1638, which Abraham Bosse subsequently republished with his own perspective treatise (1648), which used his master's methods. That is to say, he explicitly affiliated himself with the work of the perspectivists. Doubtless the implications of this theorem, which was long neglected, were fully developed for the first time by Poncelet, in the framework of so-called projective geometry—that is, a geometry in which a postulate asserting that two parallel lines meet at infinity is verifiable. But this verification was already implied by perspective, as can be seen in the Urbino perspectives, which demonstrate by painterly means alone that a bundle of parallel lines amount, on the plane of projection, to a bundle of converging lines, and that one can pass without a break from one to the other by introducing a point that's infinitely distant or, as Desargue

per sino in infinito, ciascune traversa quantità segua alterandosi." Alberti, op. cit., p. 71; English trans., p. 56.

11. "As for your way of considering parallel lines as eventually joining at an infinite distance, in order to comprehend them in the same way as those converging on a point, that's all very well, provided that you make use of it, as I assure myself you do, as a way of explaining what's obscure in one of these examples by means of the other in which it's clearer, and not the other way around." Descartes to Desargues, June 16, 1639, *Correspondance,* ed. by Adam and Tannery, vol. 2, p. 555.

would say, an "infinitely distant goal," common to all straight parallel lines and situated on a straight line at infinity, itself common to all parallel planes: Desargues' "infinitely distant axle"[12] being nothing other than what Alberti (and Pascal after him) called the "horizon."

The question of infinity consistently preoccupied Renaissance culture, just as it has unceasingly preoccupied geometry, *from the origin.* Finding itself inscribed, within the perspective context, in a position marked by a hole in the center of the prototype, this *original* feature (in all senses of the word) took on an emblematic value. For it is here, at this point that absented itself, so to speak, from its place, that was decided the destiny of a system that would have been unable to escape its own closure if it hadn't resorted to it. In this process, theoretical as well as historical, which attained its logical conclusion with Desargues and Poncelet, the transformation group constituted by the Urbino perspectives occupies—in ideal terms—an absolutely decisive position. For, examined as a series, the three panels in Urbino, Baltimore, and Berlin demonstrate that if the horizon is established and posited as a limit on the plane of projection, the apparent distance at which the vanishing point is established (even if this be at "infinity") will change nothing in the projective space of the representation: in all cases the volumes caught in the net of the perspective construction will become smaller on the plane in accordance with an analogous rule of transformation, which transformations affect, in proportion to distance, a body seen in perspective constituting a group of similarities or automorphisms, which is to say, according to Herman Weyl's Leibniz-influenced definition, spatial transformations that leave the structure unaltered.[13]

This is the language of geometry, but it certainly doesn't indicate that the "subject" implied by the painting—and which, to use Lacan's phrase, should get its bearings through it—is any the more stable. Going beyond Brunelleschi's experiment, our transformation group attests that the subject of perspective, which is said to be "dominant" because it's established in a position of mastery, *this subject holds only by a thread,* however

---

12. "Essieu à distance infinie." Cf. Gérard Desargues, *Brouillon project d'une atteinte aux événements des rencontres du cône avec un plan* (1639).
13. Weyl, op. cit., p. 49.

tightly stretched this might be. The demonstration of this is all the more blindingly clear because the Urbino perspectives conform strictly to Piero's rule holding that if an eye is placed in the center of the painting, then the *work* of perspective—the work of a tightrope walker as much as that of a painter or architect, or even a geometer—is made that much more visible.[14] The subject interpellating the painting, and interpellated by it from the point marked at its center, this subject can only get its bearings within the configuration by being reabsorbed into it, by becoming lost in it. In the sense not of a walk through it, but rather of a *traversal* of it, manifested externally by a point or hole: in ideal terms, the one through which would pass a string, perpendicular to the painting, stretched from the observer's eye to the vanishing point. So it's not a point that perspective designates, but rather a line, one corresponding in projection to the plane marked as that of the eye, or the subject. A line of approach, an Ariadne's thread, if you will, but one that's indistinguishable from the labyrinth in which it traps the subject:[15] a labyrinth—if I dare say it—that's perfectly rectangular, and from which (thanks to the law of the two infinities) there can be no escape. But also an errant line, as this straight line supports two axes in opposed directions as well as vectors of various lengths, always reversible, its being understood that they're between two points, each of which has infinity *behind it*.

*

According to Serlio, the strength of painter's perspective depends upon three main lines: the baseline corresponding to the groundline of the perspective construction, the one "lying beneath the painting," as Alberti put it, from which everything is born;[16] the second, "that of the point which some call the view, and others the horizon," which is a more appropriate

---

14. Cf. *supra*, chapter 15, p. 348, note 30. Linked as it is to the position of the eye, the point at which the ray emanating from it pierces the picture plane at a perpendicular angle can vary. Piero agrees with Alberti in preferring that it be situated within the limits of the painting.

15. On the model of "Ariadne's thread" and its importance for contemporary mathematics, cf. Pierre Rosenstiehl, "Les Mots du labyrinth," in the exh. cat. *Cartes et figures de la terre*, Centre George Pompidou, Paris, 1980.

16. "Al prima e la linea piana, dalla quale nascono tutte le cose." Serlio, *Il secundo libro*, folio 25a; English facs. ed., "The Second Booke," opening statement.

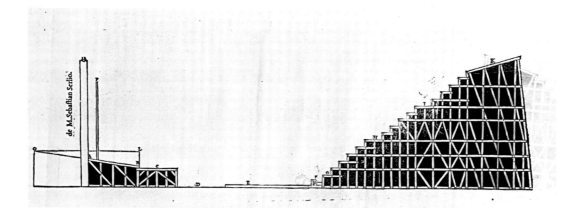

108 Serlio's theater,
profile section. *Il secondo
libro . . .*, fol. 64 recto.
Photo: Bibliothèque
Nationale, Paris.

term "given that the horizon is there where our view, in all respects, comes to an end;"[17] and the third, finally, which Serlio calls that of "distance," which can vary at the will of the *architect* (my emphasis: the problem here, at least for the moment, being that of representation or scenography, in Vitruvius's sense). Its being understood that, the painting's baseline being indistinguishable from the line at which the (vertical) plane of projection intersects the (horizontal) ground plane over which move the observers (*i riguardente*), whether they're approaching or moving away, distances should always be determined from eye height.[18] All of which definitions correspond to those of descriptive geometry, but nonetheless present a problem to which I will return on another occasion, namely that of the constitution or genesis of history from the "distance point," which Parronchi has correctly identified as the *punctum dolens* of *construzione legittima*.[19]

Let's state immediately that the theater described by Serlio has nothing to do with antiquity, or even with Vitruvius in the sense we've specified. The descriptions and reconstructions of antique scenes are found

---

17. "La seconda linea e quella che va al punto, altri lo dicono il vedere, altri l'orizonte, ma l'orizonte e il suo proprio nome, imperho che l'orizonte e per tutto dove termina la veduta nostra." Ibid.

18. "La terza linea e quella della distantia, al quale e sempre a livello de l'orizonte, ma piu apresso o piu lontano secondo che accadera . . .. L'architteto vorra domostrare un casamento in un pariete, il quale havera lo suo nascimento dal piano, dove posarano li giedi de i riguardenti, in questo caso sara ragione de l'orizonte sia di tanta altezza, quanto l'occhio nostro, et sia posta la distantia nel piu commodo loco di quella." Ibid.

19. Parronchi, "Il 'punctum dolens' della costruzione legittima,'" *Studi . . .*, op. cit., pp. 296–312.

in book III of the *Treatise on Architecture,* which is devoted to the antiquities in Rome and elsewhere in Italy.[20] As for book II, it sticks to scenes "that are now in use," notably in the wooden theater built by Serlio, in 1539, in the Palazzo Da Porto in Vicenza, which was the largest of his time,[21] consisting of a platform in front of the painted scene that was about 20 meters wide and 4 deep on which most of the action unfolded (and which was thus consistent with our stipulation of a scene that's broad and shallow). But you think much the most important thing here is that Serlio, to make certain he was properly understood, used both a ground plan and a longitudinal section showing both the stage and the auditorium, and that he expected his reader to study the plan in conjunction with the section, which he thought spoke for itself,[22] whereas the perspective construction schemas in book II make do, as was customary in the period, with ground plans: a move that justifies the assimilation of the horizon to a point, but at the cost of a kind of rotation that entails considering the perspective configuration not in frontal projection but in profile, which had already been encouraged by Brunelleschi's experiment, it's apparatus being most easily described in longitudinal section.

As is customary with perspective, the description begins at the ground, at the "foreground plane."[23] But one quickly discerns, in comparing plan and section, that there was nothing "cubic" or "unitary" about this stage. It began with a horizontal platform established at eye height (marked *C*) and separated from the public by the space of the proscenium. After which came an inclined plane (from *B* to *A*) in perspective, apparently rising at an angle of about 10°, sturdy enough to support heavy and agitated loads: parades of chariots and elephants, "Arabian" ballets, etc. This section terminated, at *M,* with the back wall of the theater. But it was first interrupted by a backdrop corresponding to the vertical marked *P,* which

---

20. Serlio, *Il terzo libro . . . nel quale si figurano e descrivano le Antichità di Roma e le altre cose che sono in Italia,* Venice, 1540; English facs. ed., op. cit., 1611/1970.

21. "La Maggiore che a nostri tempi sia fatta." Serlio, *Il secundo libro,* op. cit., fol. 64 verso; English facs. ed., fol. 24 recto.

22. "Ho voluto far prima questo profilo accio, che la pianta insieme col profilo l'un per l'altro si possino intendere, ma sara perho bene a studiare prima su la pianta, e se quelle cose non si intenderanno ne la pianta, recorrere al profilo dove meglio s'intendera." Ibid., fol. 63 recto; English facs. ed., fol. 23 verso.

23. Primieramente donque io comminciaro dal suolo davanti: la quale sara a l'altezza del occhio." Ibid.

was treated as a "flat painting," the constructed space of the second portion of the stage exploiting only some of the resources of illusionist perspective, with the use of foreshortening making it seem larger than it was.

If, Serlio now says, one takes the point O to be the horizon, the line going from L to O will intersect plane P at a point that will serve in turn as its horizon; which we should take to mean that it will serve as the vanishing point for the planar perspective on the backdrop but not for the scenic apparatus itself. As for the facades parallel to the backdrop, these would be organized—insofar as they had any thickness, if only apparent—in accordance with a vanishing point indicated on the drop. But the foreshortened lateral facades could only be constructed in relation to a "horizon" (a vanishing point) situated beyond the back wall. This is consistent with the fact, says Serlio, that when we see two facades of a building simultaneously, they have two different vanishing points.[24] If one considers only planar projection this is easy to understand: one need only cite the schema of "horned" perspective introduced by Pélerin Viator to show that two sides of a prism viewed from any given perspective will have two different vanishing points aligned on a single horizon, which has nothing to do with "bifocal" perspective, *contra* Robert Klein. But Serlio says something very different here, something that's not based upon descriptive geometry, nor even upon *perspectiva artificialis* in the strict sense. If reason dictates that the various constructions in the theater have different horizons, different vanishing points, this is with respect to the section or profile of the scene (*e questo e quanto al profilo della scena*). This will be easier to grasp if we focus on the latter's floor grid. For it's there, in the theater as in painting, that perspective's lessons are localized: in the construction of a site in which the apparatus and the actors of the *istoria* will find their places, on the checkerboard paving that's the ground of *costruzione legittima*. No difficulties arise with respect to the horizontal portion of the scene: as the paving is not governed by a horizon (in other words, is not foreshortened), its components will be perfect squares.[25] But such is not the case for the inclined plane beyond it: if Serlio

---

24. "Et e ben ragione se i casamenti in effetto han due faccie: le quali spettino a dua lati: che ancore habinno due orizonti, e questo e quanto al profilo della Scena." Ibid.
25. "Questo primo suolo essendo piano lo suo pavimento non ubidiva a l'orzonte, ma le suoi quadri furono perfetti." Ibid., fol. 64 verso; English facs. ed., fol. 24 recto.

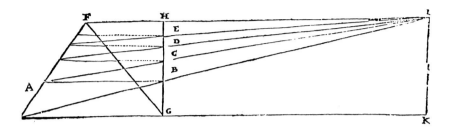

109 Schema for perspective construction of the distance point. *Il secondo libro . . . .*

chose to foreshorten the grid, taking O as the distance measure, this is—as he himself says—to avoid the error committed by many architects who, wanting to place the horizon on the backdrop, feel obliged to establish it on the groundline and thus to make the orthogonals in the paving and the built elements converge there, in a brutal foreshortening. Hence the solution he supports, which he feels works very well: he advises the reader to place the horizon beyond the wall of the theater, at a distance twice that between the beginning of the inclined plane and the said wall, which will result in the houses, and the entire scenic apparatus, receding more gradually.[26]

You have not neglected to note, in all the preceding, that there's been no question of the *point of view,* since the effect of distance in the theater was a function of the position of the horizon, not of the eye. In the theater, but not in painting: the horizon line being set at eye height, the painter is obliged to have recourse to a "third point," its position corresponding to the distance between the eye and the picture plane, to determine the relative disposition of the base checkerboard (in conformity with the schema provided by Serlio in his second book, the model for which is to be found in Alberti), whereas the architect can place the vanishing point wherever he likes, its displacements resulting in an increase or decrease of the steepness of the incline, as well as affecting the acuteness with which

26. "Et perche alcuni han posto l'ộizonte a l'ultimo pariete che termina la scena, il quale e necessario metterlo sul'proprio suolo an nascimento di esso pariete dove dimostra che tutti li casamenti se adunano; io mi sano imaginato di trapassare piu la con l'orizonte, la quale cosa mi a cose ben reuscita; che a fare tal cose ho sempre tenuto questa strada, et cosi consiglio coloro che di tal arte si dileterano . . . et cosi tutti li casamenti et altre cose haveranno piu dolcezza ne i scurci." Ibid.

the vanishing lines converge.[27] To do this, says Serlio, there's no need to demolish or even pierce the back wall of the theater: one need only construct a reduced model of it, in wood and cardboard, that can then be used to determine the proper measurements for the actual building. Which is the proposal of a "perspector," if ever there was one: for it implies that the solution can be found by resorting to models and experiments.[28]

If I've felt it worthwhile to review Serlio's argument with you in detail, this is because the various problems it addresses parallel those central to the transformation group including the Urbino perspectives. It's clear that the transformations playing over the group have a privileged relation to the horizon, as Serlio understood it: the horizon, whose point sometimes seems very close (as in the *Città ideale*) and sometimes seems to be situated somewhere near infinity, as in the Berlin panel, but can also appear to be positioned, as in Baltimore, at an intermediary distance, thanks to a series of calculated visual relays. Such that the question, mathematical in nature, seems to fuse with that of the theater, at least as Serlio formulated it, thus adding support to the position of George Kernodle, who maintained that what he called theaters of "pictorial illusion" derive from painting, as the architects did nothing more than reproduce a scenic type perfected earlier by Italian painters of the quattrocento.[29]

In your view, however, the question must be posed in different terms, ones that would allow us to clear away the equivocation that's so pervasive in studies treating the relation between painting and the theater as well as those between art and science. The problem is not to determine whether, and how, the work (*travail*) of painters was able to prepare the way for or "anticipate" that of architects and geometers, and whether or not we should discern in certain quattrocento paintings models for the Italian stage as well as intimations of the theorems of projective geometry. It would be

---

27. It should be noted, however, that Serlio says nothing about how one should determine, in the theater, the transverse quantities and the corresponding foreshortening of the squares of the basic grid in relation to the distance separating them from the horizon (*il che con la sua debita distantia sminui*), a function performed in painting, precisely, by the distance point.

28. "Un modello piccolo di cartoni et lagnami, ben misurato et trasportato poi in grande di cosa in cosa giustissimamente con facilitia. Ma questa lettione farsi al alcuno sara difficile, nondimena sara necessario faticarsi nel far di modelli et esperientie, che studiando trovara la via." Ibid., fol. 65 verso; English facs. ed., fol. 24 recto.

29. George R. Kernodle, *From Art to Theater . . .*, op. cit., pp. 174ff.

better to follow an exactly opposite course, and ask, retrospectively, what there was about painters' work that could have led to such a dialectical advance—in the Hegelian sense of an *Aufhebung* or sublation—in areas as seemingly disparate as the theater and mathematics. Though the distance between these areas is not—in historical terms—as great as it might seem, as is shown by the treatise on perspective by Guidobaldo dal Monte: in this publication, which appeared in 1600, the first to treat perspective in purely mathematical terms, an entire chapter is devoted to the problem of theatrical scenery.[30] What, then, was the nature of this work (*travail*), and what were the forms it took that facilitated such an advance? The speculation on the notion of the *horizon* stimulated by the group of Urbino perspectives offers a particularly interesting case in point, as it's situated at the pivot of the above-cited areas, mathematics and the theater.

In the context of the theater, the limit of Krautheimer's hypothesis, and of all those who would see in the Urbino perspectives models for scenery, derives from their having restricted themselves to iconographic arguments, whereas the question demands to be posed in technical, even constructive terms. It's not so much a matter of determining whether painting did or did not have ties to the theater as of understanding how the work of painting was able to proceed in the same direction as theatrical work per se, of which Serlio's *Treatise on Scenes* was an early compendium. Serlio's text offers proof that scenographers of the early sixteenth century worked with givens analogous to those that had earlier preoccupied painters, but with the intention of transforming them. If this text is used to reactivate the group of Urbino perspectives, the difference between the constraints governing painting and those shaping scenic constructions in the theater is striking. Scenes appealing not only to the imagination, which were not conceived only to "create an image" (as Kernodle says, somewhat hastily), but which were, in part, three-dimensional and had to be sufficiently solid to support moving actors and animals, though admittedly these last were often artificial. Which is to say that the scenographers must have had recourse to rules other than those applying to "flat painting." As is proved by the fact that, whereas in painting the apparent distance at which the vanishing point is established has no effect on the spatial structure, this

---

30. *Guidibaldi e' Marchionibus Montis Perspectivae, libri sex*, Pesaro, 1600.

is not necessarily true in the theater: the Serlian scene is not a homogeneous euclidean space whose structure is describable by measured relations between points, or again—in Leibnizian terms—on the sole basis of the notion of similitude. Considered in terms of both geometry and measurement, there's nothing unitary or isomorphic about it. While the checkered ground of its horizontal section is made up of "perfect" and thus identical squares, such is not he case on the inclined plane. But the intervening transformation of space (to say nothing of the projective space of the backdrop) is still more apparent if we think in volumetric rather than figurative terms. For instance, a scenic element consisting of two facades forming a right angle could not be moved from one portion of the scene to the other. And in a change of scenery involving mechanisms similar to ancient *periaktoi,* it would be impossible to have volumes constructed in perspective pivot on their own axes, with one side facing the front and another receding. Hence the necessity, emphasized in all the treatises, from Serlio to Bibiena by way of Barbaro, Vignola, and Furttenbach, of constructing these volumes partly of canvas, with their receding lines being painted, as also should be those portions of the corner standing out against the floor or the sky.[31] Prior to the so-called baroque era, architects ceded precedence to painters and, in an evolution which Kernodle pronounced to be "natural," the three-dimensional elements of the Renaissance stage gradually gave way to a series of planes incrementally disposed in depth and handled illusionistically.[32]

Strictly speaking, it's only in that period that one can speak of a theater of "pictorial illusion" in Kernodle's sense: a theater whose apparatus facilitated changes of scenery and spectacular effects, all the while satisfying, in an illusionist mode, the principle of unitary organization of the scenic space. But it's important in this connection to make another observation consistent with the notion of an "advance," even though it runs counter to a view that's widely held. One can maintain that this form of theater corresponded in allegorical terms to the ideal of an aristocratic society, centered on the figure of the prince, and that it implied a radical transformation of the scenic conception of the Middle Ages: while the medieval theater

---

31. Serlio, *Il secundo libro,* op. cit., fol. 65 verso; English facs. ed., fol. 25 recto.
32. Kernodle, *From Art to Theater . . .,* op. cit., p. 186.

addressed a popular or "democratic" public, to use Kernodle's term,[33] its scenic elements consisting of facing "houses" so disposed that spectators could move to keep track of the unfolding action, the Italian theater conformed to another conception. But does this mean that the perspective scene was able to prevail only in the age of absolutism, when architects were charged with the task of conceiving theaters for the few, and primarily for the pleasure of the prince, who was to be placed in a privileged position?[34]

This argument, which Kernodle has defended with considerable erudition (though some of the latter tends to contradict his view), and which has often been reduced to its most patently ideological content, is mistaken in several key respects. From the point of view of performance practice, it's surprising that such a theater, so well suited to the ideal of a court society, established itself in England and France only at a relatively late date, and after many ups and downs like those entailed by the competition between "French" and "Italian" acting companies. And it's also surprising, as Kernodle himself admits, that this kind of stage persisted through the nineteenth century and into the twentieth, when one would have expected the bourgeois theater to develop its own theatrical forms.[35] But where the evolution of technical conceptions shaping the development of modern scenography is concerned, this is just ideological twaddle: for it is mistaken to say that the Italian scene was initially prompted by the imposition of central, dominant point of view corresponding to that of the prince. On the contrary, absolutist discourse discovered the advantages deriving from such a configuration only belatedly.

What's been said about the construction of the Serlian scene indicates that the first question confronting the architect was that of the proper distance at which to establish the vanishing point. This question, to which Serlio gave a precise answer, was still being discussed in the eighteenth century. Thus Fernando Bibiena proposed placing the horizon sixty-seven *braccia* (about ten feet) behind the backdrop,[36] while other authors made

33.   Ibid., p. 179.
34.   Ibid., p. 178.
35.   Ibid., p. 186.
36.   Ferdinando Galli da Bibiena, *L'architettura civile, perparata sù la geometria, e ridotta alle prospettive*, Parma, 1711, p. 129; as cited by Kernodle, op. cit.

other recommendations, not all of which entailed situating it at eye level.[37] According to Serlio's text, this problem was quite distinct from that of the point of view, even that of the painter. What exactly does Serlio say? That the horizon should be placed at a height corresponding to that of point L, indicated by the vertical rising above the groundline from the point at which the inclined plane begins to rise. Judging from the sectional view of his theater, this point should be situated at a height equal to that of the forestage from the floor of the auditorium, that is to say, at eye height, which is consistent with the rules of *costruzione legittima*. The dotted line running horizontally from this point L to the point named the "horizon" intersects the backdrop at a point that will be, as we've seen, that of this plane's horizon, though the latter cannot be used as a reference point for the construction of the foreshortened lateral facades, which should conform with the horizon marked O, beyond the theater's back wall. On the other hand, to construct the facade fronts of the stage's two lateral wings, one should stretch a cord from point L to the horizon on the drop, which would allow one to decide how high their relief should appear to be, and how deep their doors and windows.[38]

So far, we've seen nothing that would allow us to connect the scenic construction with a point of view outside it. The point L corresponds to the position of an actor whose feet are on the edge of the inclined plane, which should allow for construction of the scenic apparatus to the measure of man, as Alberti wanted. But if we examine the disposition of the audience on risers facing the stage, we're quickly convinced that the most privileged position would seem to be that reserved for women of quality, who were in the rows rising from G, the less noble among them being far from the worst off, for they occupied the upper rows.[39] And as for the "orchestra"

---

37. François Aguilon, *Opticorum libri sex,* Antwerp, 1613; as cited by Kernodle, op. cit.
38. "Dipoi quanto si trovera alto l'orizonte, sia tanto alzato in termino al principio del piano B che sara L a da li a l'orizonte sia tirata una linea chi e di punti, laquale sera allivello, et dove questa erira nel ultimo pariete: ivi sara l'orizonte di esso pariete: et non servira perho ad altro gelaro: ma la detta linea sia una cosa stabile, perche questa servira a tutti quei telari che saranno in majesta, per trovare le grossezze di alcune cose; ma lo primo orizonte dila dal muro servira a tutti le scurcii de i casamenti." Serlio, op. cit., fol. 65 verso; English facs. ed., fol. 24 recto.
39. "Per le donne piu nobili, et salando piu alto le men nobili vi si metterano." Ibid., fol. 63 recto; English facs. ed., fol. 24 verso.

(marked E) intended for "senators," raised only about .16 meter above the ground level, with the noblest of them to be seated in its first row, the most to be said is that the view it offered of the stage was scarcely enviable: those stationed toward its front, just below the stage, could doubtless hear very well but they'd see no more of the actors than their heads, and their view of anything happening on the inclined plane would be almost totally blocked.

In theater as in painting, then, it's up to the "subject," even if the prince himself, to get its bearings within the configuration of the scene, as within that of a painting; and this, by means of an "advance" requiring more than a century to reach fruition, and that without princes, dukes, cardinals, or kings deriving even the slightest benefit from it, aside from having their post designated in the center of the auditorium; but this certainly didn't guarantee them the best perspective of the stage. Kernodle, despite himself, provides proof of this when he evokes the lengthy campaign waged by theoreticians to determine the best position for the princely box. Even in the seventeenth century, Sabattini set out to formulate a method, rather like Brunelleschi's first experiment, for determining the proper distance between this box and the stage, which involved looking at the stage through a square frame and positioning oneself until its edges seemed to form a right angle.[40]

Here again, close technical study has led us to question a number of received ideas. If these seem to be justified by the configuration in accordance with which painting regulates itself, we must remember that the scene as constructed by quattrocento painters, which by rights ought to find its fullest expression in the Urbino perspectives, seems to have been conceived first and foremost as a function of the *istoria* to take place and be represented within it, to be *enunciated* within it. The symmetry—as you insist, too ostentatious, too emphatic not to be suspect—governing perspective construction, including the point marked at the composition's center, had, according to Piero, a purely demonstrative goal, one that allowed the subject but a single privilege: that of finding its bearings as such within it.

---

40. Nicola Sabattini, *Pratica di fabricar scene e machine ne teatri*, Pesaro, 1637; new ed. Rome, 1953, vol. 1, chapter 8.

If the work of painting was, in the theater, really the object of such an advance, the reasons are to be found not only in the economy of representation but in its very structure. By which I mean that the eventual dialogue between quattrocento painting and contemporary forms of theatrical presentation, as well as the lessons learned by theatrical architects from painters in the sixteenth century, weren't limited to the transposition from one field to the other of a few principles of assemblage, or narrative, syntactical procedures better suited to represent a story. As Alberti said, *istoria* is the painter's supreme task.[41] But there are different ways of conveying a narrative using the means of painting: just as there are different modes of performance, diverse kinds of theater," some of which don't necessarily imply the construction of a *scene,* much less the production—even to strictly demonstrative ends—of a configuration in which the representation would be obliged to reflect upon its own operation, as well as upon its constitutive role in the positioning of the subject.

If there was any such dialectical advance, it took place through history by means of a series of relays and mediations, of interferences and transformations, if not deformations, which don't fall into a neat, linear sequence like the links of a chain. Krautheimer's contention that he'd found proof in Peruzzi's drawings and productions of a continual process leading from the Urbino perspectives to Serlio's description of the comic and tragic scenes has convinced no one, even among those who have eyes only for what a painting signifies, and above all for what it *represents*. If his thesis still intrigues, this is because, through description of iconographic features, his analysis outlines a structural project even as it suggests one that would be this side of the representation, as is indicated by the very idea of a "scene" that's independent of any specific use.[42] One consequence of this being that the works in question appear to belong to a transformation group that takes

---

41. "La istoria è summa opera del pittore." Alberti, op. cit., book III, p. 111; English trans., p. 95. I will discuss on another occasion the incipient contradiction between Alberti's reduction of painting to a register of pure visibility and the narrative functions he assigns it; for the moment I will say only that the perspective model proposed in *Della pittura* is in no way a "humanist" one.
42. The idea that the "scene" existed apart from its deployment to tragic, comic, or satyric ends is implied by Vitruvius, who uses the verb *deformare* in describing these applications; cf. *supra,* chapter 12, p. 201, note 3.

its place, in turn, within a much larger series, one that's far from homogeneous with regard to either "genre" or "substance," since it includes paintings as well as sculpture, cassone frontals as well as marquetry panels, and even designs for the theater.

Among the productions situated, for one reason or another, within the orbit of the Urbino perspectives, we've already mentioned, aside from the decor of the *studiolo* and the marquetry doors in the palace in Urbino, the so-called Barberini panels in New York and Boston, the *Miracles of Saint Bernardino* series in Perugia, frescoes by Botticelli and Perugino in the Sistine Chapel, the *History of Lucretia* also by Botticelli, the *Consignment of the Keys* by Perugino, the *Marriage of the Virgin* by Raphael, etc. This short list should be enough to convince us that this inquiry could end by encompassing the largest possible number of works somehow belonging to this same nebula, with the open-ended ensemble constituted in this way having no genuine reality, and no pertinence to anything save the initiating analysis. But this pertinence would nonetheless encompass such-and-such a relief by Donatello, to say nothing of contemporary productions (by Ghiberti, for example), and others still earlier that somehow broach the question of the scene, though in completely nonreflexive ways, and that tend to have certain iconographic features in common, beginning with a centrally planned building placed in the middle of the composition. The example of Donatello is all the more apposite here, as his dates correspond perfectly with the probable timetable of Brunelleschi's "invention" having influenced the sculptor: the relief of the *Feast of Herod* (Siena Cathedral) has two vanishing points, one for the orthogonals of the paving and another for the deep triple-arched arcade in the background which dominates the scene.[43] But two reliefs for the altar of San Antonio in Padua, the *Miracle of the Miser's Heart* and the *Miracle of the Irascible Son,* are still more consistent, in their oblong formats as well as the symmetrical disposition of their perspective scenes, with the set of givens that would be taken up by the Urbino perspectives for systematic elaboration, in a mode totally and deliberately antithetical to the representational *pathos* with which Donatello instills them.

---

43. Cf. Edgerton, "Alberti's Perspective . . .," p. 374, note 8.

110 Donatello, *Feast of Herod,* ca. 1425. Siena, baptismal font, cathedral baptistry. Photo: Alinari-Giraudon.

It's not insignificant that in the *Santo* in Padua Donatello introduced for the first time, in the place traditionally occupied by the classic predella, the formula—to use Alessandro Parronchi's term—of the *sgabello,* an altar frontal composed of panels of much larger dimensions, like those in Mantegna's San Zeno triptych in Verona.[44] In the same line of argument, Parronchi pointed out to me a marble relief (2.16 × 53 cm, excluding its elaborate frame) in Santa Maria dell'Impruneta, near Florence, which has been attributed to Filarete and which served as *sgabello* for the altar of one of the two aediculae built by Michelozzo at the entrance to the choir. This relief is free of all reference to urban perspective: the *Story of the Miraculous Image,* which recounts how the said image was disinterred by the cultivators of a field, takes place in a mountainous landscape, its sole element treated in perspective being a porticoed church, whose precipitously receding mass seems grafted onto the background. In addition to the analogy with the Berlin panel, as well as with numerous cassone panels, suggested by the

---

44. Alessandro Parronchi, "Per la ricostruzione dell'altare del Santo," *Arte antica e moderna,* no. 22 (1963), p. 116. According to Parronchi, the Barberini panels and Piero's *Flagellation* also adhere to the *sgabello*formula. Cf. A. P., "Ricostruzione della Pala dei Montefeltro," *Storia dell'arte,* no. 28 (1978), pp. 235–48.

111 Donatello, *Miracle of the Miser's Heart,* 1446–
50. Padua, San Antonio. Photo: Alinari-Giraudon.

112 Donatello, *Miracle of the Irascible Son.* Padua,
San Antonio. Photo: Alinari-Giraudon.

113 Filarete (?), *Story of the Miraculous Image*.
Impruneta, Santa Maria (dimensions of the panel,
without framing elements: 216.5 × 53 cm). Photo:
Soprintendenza, Florence.

cornice that was added after the fact, the format of the composition merits
comment. While such formats are quite well suited to the simultaneous
representation of several episodes of a given story, as in the Impruneta *sgabello* and countless decorative panels, it's as though, in the Urbino perspectives as well as in the marquetry work that may have influenced them
(notably the "emptiness" of their scenes) as well as the much earlier ones
(decidedly peopled) by Donatello, the perspective configuration had affected
to submit to this constraint all the better to demonstrate its power in the
representational order: making it all the more noteworthy that Francesco di
Giorgio, to whom the Berlin panel has been attributed by some, painted in
his youth, before going to Urbino, a considerable number of cassone frontals
coupling a wealth of architectural elements with extremely approximate perspective constructions.[45]

  So much is clear: painting's work is not solely a matter of variations or transformations. The same possibility of an *advance* we've discussed
with regard to the pictorial and theatrical series, as well as with respect to
the relation of the artistic register to that of science, and to that of thought
in general, is available to the painter, in the field that is his own. An

---

45. Cf., for example, the *Triumph of Chastity* (Getty Museum, Malibu), or *Solomon and the Queen of
Sheba* (Victoria and Albert Museum, London), or the *Meeting of Dido and Aeneas* (Kress Collection,
Portland). Cf. Burton B. Fredericksen, *The Cassone Paintings of Francesco di Giorgio,* J. Paul Getty
Museum, Los Angeles, 1969.

115 Carpaccio, *Reception of the Ambassadors*, from
the Saint Ursula cycle, 1490–96. Venice, Accademia. Photo: Cameraphoto.

cation outside the lagoon.[48] This clearly implicates Piero. But what about
the author of the *Città ideale*, whoever he might be? What about the "perspectives" in Baltimore and Berlin? Without drawing any conclusions, I
simply note that the fact the Venetian painter was hired by the Dalmatians
or *schiavoni*, as he would be some years later by the Albanians for their
scuola, resonates curiously with Bernardino Baldi's mention, in his description of the palace in Urbino, of inscriptions in "slavic" characters he'd read
on some scenes "traced in perspective" and purportedly signed by Laurana,
who was himself from Dalmatia.[49] But other arguments deriving from the
works themselves merit discussion. In particular, from the apparently fantastic architectural elements in the backgrounds of the Saint Ursula and Saint
George cycles, which prompt the same questions about their "referents" as
did corresponding elements in the Urbino perspectives: in both instances,
the problem is that of determining the extent to which these pictured struc-

48.   Carlo Ginzburg, *The Enigma of Piero*, pp. 144–45. Cf. Guido Perocco ed., *Tutta la pittura del Carpaccio*, Milan, 1960, p. 15.

49.   The Dalmation *scuola* was officially recognized by the Republic of Venice in 1541; the decree of the Council of Ten approving its *mariegola* (the *Regola Madre*) would further increase the importance of the role played by the Dalmatian colony in Venice (cf. G. Perocco, *Carpaccio. Le pitture alla scuola di S. Giorgio degli Schiavoni*, Treviso, 1975, pp. 10ff).

tures have some basis in reality. Even if Carpaccio started out by consulting the woodcuts by Erhardum de Reuwich illustrating the edition of the *Peregrinatio* to the Holy Land by Bernard von Breydenbach, published in Mayence in 1486,[50] the Bramante-like inflection of these passages, especially the use made of buildings in cylindrical or prismatic form and of centrally planned temples with domes, both as motifs and as poles of attraction in the scenic organization, and this in a period—it would be impossible to overemphasize this point—when such monuments essentially existed only as projects, all these elements suggest that despite Carpaccio's penchant for the anecdotal, these representations are controlled by an *idea* very close to that being worked out in the Urbino, Baltimore, and Berlin panels, even as they reveal the need for a serious reconsideration of the standard art historical profile of Carpaccio.

Michelangelo Muraro has studied the analogies between Carpaccio's handling of the Saint Ursula cycle, which was based on images from the *Golden Legend* (a translation of which appeared in Venice in 1475), and the rules governing the *sacra conversazione,* in the peculiar form this assumed in Venice, after a long hiatus, in performances mounted by the *compagni della calza,* the associations of young men to whom the Serenissima had confided the responsibility of organizing the popular festivals and entertainments so characteristic of Venetian culture in this period.[51] Muraro is all the less vulnerable to charges of having confused a properly pictorial mode of representation, as current at the end of the quattrocento, with one that would prevail in theatrical productions a few decades later,[52] for having stressed the originality of the painter's synthesis of forms drawn from both the sacred and the secular theater, also emphasizing Carpaccio's attentiveness to the ceremonial aspects of representation. The fact that in signing several of his works Carpaccio placed before his name the verb *finxit* or *fingebat* (as opposed to *pinxit* or *pingebat*) further supports Muraro's view of his art: though surely it's preferable to speak of a theater of painting than of a theater *in* painting,

50. Bernhard von Breydenbach, *Sanctorum peregrinatiorum in montem Syon ad venerandum Christi sepulchrum in Jerusalem . . . opusculum,* Maydence, 1486; this pamphlet was republished and translated many times, and was rapidly disseminated throughout Europe (cf. Hugh M. Davies, *Bernhard von Breydenbach and His Journey to the Holy Land, a Bibliography,* London, 1911).

51. Michelangelo Muraro, "Vittore Carpaccio o il teatro in pittura," M. -T. Muraro, op. cit., pp. 7–19.

52. Chastel, "'Vues urbaines peintes' et théâtre," op. cit., pp. 501–502, note 12.

a phrase that might suggest to a hurried reader (or one of bad faith) that Carpaccio did nothing but translate *into painting* spectacles that he clearly could not have seen, at least not in this form.

Commissioned from the painter for the *scuola* of San Giovanni Evangelista a bit before the Saint Ursula cycle, the *Miracle of the Relic of the True Cross* is nonetheless an iconographic document of some importance, a work that somewhat resembles a Canaletto *avant la lettre*:[53] it provides us with a precious record of the partially "dramatized" ceremonies that took place in Venice in palace courtyards, the cloisters of churches and monasteries, the *campi,* and even—as here—in front of the loggia of the Rialto. But while the Saint Ursula cycle itself uses numerous elements taken from the Venetian context, including the ceremony of the reception of ambassadors (which occasioned particular pomp), the agitation of crowds witnessing such spectacles, and even the presence in exterior scenes of young members of the *calzi,* identifiable by their multicolored hose as well as by their clothing and insignias, to say nothing of countless other typically picturesque Venetian details, these components were deployed in view of realizing a representational project whose aims were quite distinct from documentary ones and which in this period could only have been carried out in painting. The articulation of different narrative moments might seem consistent with a principle fundamental to the *sacra conversazione:* that of *luoghi deputati,* or distinct places between which performances successively moved, each of them being identified by a number of characteristic emblems (in the *Arrival of the Saint and His Suite in Rome,* for instance, a building resembling the same Castel Sant'Angelo which Piero Sanpaolesi recognizes in the Berlin panel[54]). It nonetheless remains that the later scenes, those which the painter executed last and whose subjects are in fact the earliest in the story, evidence an extremely sophisticated study of the possibilities, both scenic and symbolic, in the strongest sense of this word, afforded by the perspective configuration, and directly engage the problematic central to the group of Urbino perspectives.

Some of them having proportions analogous to those of the said perspectives, but of much larger dimensions, the more imposing composi-

---

53. Jean Lauts, *Carpaccio: Paintings and Drawings,* London, 1962, p. 28.
54. Sanpaolesi, "Le prospettive . . .," op. cit., p. 328.

tions of the Saint Ursula cycle were conceived for placement along the oratory walls, such that the story would unfold in a continuous horizontal band encompassing the entire perimeter of the room, in accordance with the schema still observable today in the Scuola di San Giorgio degli Schiavoni. That is to say, these *quadri riportati,* or canvases painted in the studio and subsequently attached to the wall, have an ambiguous aspect, being halfway between fresco (which was physically ill-suited to the Venetian climate, as Giorgione and Titian were to discover) and painting. Paradoxically this ambiguity—which the circumstances of their present museum exhibition tends to obscure—increases the pertinence of a comparison of the first great narrative composition in the Saint Ursula cycle to the Urbino perspectives, the status of which is equally equivocal, and most particularly to the Berlin panel, in which the painting is joined to a bit of feigned paneling.

Unlike the other canvases of the cycle, the *Reception of the Ambassadors* (they'd been sent to ask the king of Brittany for his daughter's hand) is inscribed within an architectural framework evidencing the painting's subordination to the order of the wall to which it was attached, on which it opened up the perspective of a "scene." In this respect it recalls Giotto's frescoes in Assisi: the painting "pierces" the wall all the more effectively because it concedes its presence, incorporating mural elements into its own field. But in the Giotto the images have no connection to the feigned cornices and pilasters framing them, whereas Carpaccio managed to make singular (though not unprecedented) and typically "scenographic" play with elements of the *frons scaenae,* seizing the opportunity to articulate the decorative elements with the architecture of the scene proper: while the cornice recurs here, supported on the left by the arched end bay of a portico and on the right by a pilaster, the candelabralike column separating the loggia at the painting's left from the *sala reggia* in its center, where the ceremony unfolds, is situated in front of the *frons scaenae* on a kind of narrow proscenium on which are also situated the narrator, the *nunzio* whose presence is here established at the beginning of the story, in the corner of the painting, and the old woman seated at the foot of the steps in front of the room in which the king listens to his daughter specify the conditions under which she would agree to marry the English prince—specifically, the latter's conversion to the Christian faith and the organization of the pilgrimage that constitutes the ensuing narrative. The three moments of the action, which are articulated in architectural terms, are themselves inscribed within a very narrow space, slightly elevated in relation to the proscenium, beyond which opens, on a lower level, a wide *veduta* deployed like a backdrop, of which we see, at left, through the loggia's arcades, only two narrow fragments, one of which is a famous view of the lagoon. Open on the side of the spectator, the king's room which is its pendant on the right is closed at the rear by a wall: but there's an open window shutter at the right edge of the painting which suggests that this closure is relative.

There are obvious analogies between this composition and the Berlin panel. In both cases the fanlike perspective array is framed by two parts of an architectural structure occupying the foreground—though Carpaccio has placed the horizon much higher than that in the Berlin panel and its line is all but obliterated by building facades and port structures, as well as by the masts of the ambassadors' ship moored at the quay and by the sail of a felucca, taking a full head of wind, positioned precisely at the vanishing point, which it screens off.[55] In the matter of transformations, if we take the Berlin panel as our painting of reference, then the *Reception of the Ambassadors* proposes at least two, both equally singular, the one linked with the other in both principle and effect. Whereas in the Berlin panel the scene offers itself to view in depth, the eye being led by the red brick lines of the paving (which recur, less emphatically, in the Carpaccio) toward the horizon and toward a boat that seems to approach, without being able to reach, the composition's vanishing point, in the Carpaccio there's a tension between the perspective construction of the scene and the longitudinal, procession-like development of the narrative. While in both cases the scenic apparatus features a transparent *frons scaenae*, it's almost as though the portico extending into depth at the left of Carpaccio's painting were the exact equivalent of the portico in Berlin but had been rotated 90° in its relation to the picture plane. And this, in order to introduce into the painting a perspective other than the geometric, illusionist one of the scene: the perspective of a narration, its origin being the figure of the narrator at the painting's left edge, who seems to listen to the young men of the *calza* standing under the portico, in the antechamber of the palace, waiting for the presentation cere-

---

55. This same motif is found in Bellotto's *View of the Piazzetta*, which has already been discussed in connection with the Berlin panel. Cf. figure 105.

116 Carpaccio, *Reception of the Ambassadors*, left portion: the *nunzio* and young members of the *calza*. Photo: Scala.

mony, and who finds in this loggia opening directly onto the lagoon his preamble,[56] if not—literally—his *preambulatio:* some of the young men turn toward the narrator, while others face the other way and move through the colonnade separating them from the *sala regia* in which the story proper begins. This narrative, lateral perspective is compensated by the presence, immediately above and beyond the spot where the ambassadors consign their message directly into the king's hands, of a tiny, frontally positioned page who looks right into the eyes of the spectator: a key figure, one hitherto dissimulated in painting, which the recent cleaning has made more prominent, re-establishing its balance with another one, the leaning sailor who also faces the spectator, directly beneath the most important point in the *Leave-taking of the Betrothed Couple,* that at which their hands meet for

---

56. Muraro, op. cit., p. 9.

117 Carpaccio, *Reception of the Ambassadors:* geometric pole. Photo: Scala.

118 Carpaccio, *Reception of the Ambassadors:* the
symbolic pole. Photo: Scala.

119 Carpaccio, *Leave-taking of the Betrothed
Couple,* from the Saint Ursula cycle, detail.
Photo: Scala.

the first time. In both cases the painter makes a direct appeal to the
beholder, in an allocutionary mode and in the first person, so to speak, to
emphasize an articulation essential to the narrative.

But there's more: in Berlin the vanishing point that the sail of the
felucca screens out (like a stain intended to dissimulate the hole used to
generate the configuration) is on the central axis of the composition, but
here it has been shifted to the left: which is not immediately apparent,
thanks to the tripartite division, itself seemingly symmetrical, of the scene,
and to the introduction at its center, more or less, as part of the background panorama, of a large, domed octagonal building into which opens a
door (another kind of "hole") within which stand two figures, one on its
threshold and the other slightly inside, as in the image of the two witnesses

120 Carpaccio, *Triumph of Saint George,* from the
Saint George cycle, 1502–1507. Venice, Scuola San
Giorgio dei Schiavoni. Photo: Scala.

121 Temple of Solomon, detail of a woodcut by
E. Reuwich for Breydenbach's *Peregrinatio* (1486).
Photo: Bibliothèque Nationale, Paris.

reflected in the mirror of the *Arnolfini Wedding.* Which again sets up an
equivalent, in the iconographic register as well as in that of the imaginary,
of the rotunda in the *Città ideale* in Urbino, referring us, through it, to the
imago dominating Brunelleschi's first experiment: the San Giovanni baptistry, as depicted on a small panel pierced by a hole at the spot which Viator
would designate as the subject point, the tension between the economy of
the scene and that of the narrative being thus exacerbated by the discrepancy between these two compositional poles—one of them geometric, and
the other imaginary.[57]

---

57. Omar Calabrese correctly pointed out to me that the importance in the cycle of the motif of
the centrally planned building is reinforced by the great mural octagon in marble revetment in the
Departure of the Ambassadors, which Carpaccio positioned directly above the two figures of the writing scribe and the narrator dictating to him.

122 Carpaccio, *Triumph of Saint George,* preparatory drawing. Florence, Uffizi, Department of
Drawings. Photo: Museum.

If we should require proof that we're dealing with a calculated,
perfectly conscious transformation, this can be found in another, slightly
later work by Carpaccio, the *Triumph of Saint George* in San Giorgio dei
Schiavoni. Several of the incidents in the Dalmation cycle are set within
unitary perspective scenes, such as the monastary yard, delimited on three
sides, in which Saint Jerome introduces his lion, frightening the monks, or
the other courtyard in which Jerome's funeral is set (disposed longitudinally
like the *Reception of the Ambassadors,* and equally shallow), or the cubic volume of the room in which Saint Augustine is visited by an otherworldly
light. And as for *Saint George Baptizing the Pagans* and *The Miracle of Saint
Tryphon,* these episodes unfold on platforms or stepped porticoes that are
themselves oriented lengthwise, with squares bordered by diverse buildings
spread out behind them like drops, each featuring a cylindrical monument,
a temple or turret, displaced to the right of its central vanishing point. But
it's in the *Triumph of Saint George* that the scene, in the theatrical sense of
the word, attains its full amplitude, with the disposition of the figures into
two symmetrical groups, on either side of the saint and the dragon in the
center, doubling that of the buildings distributed around its perimeter on

three sides,[58] among which is recognizable the minaret of the mosque of Rama as represented in Breydenbach's *Peregrinatio,* but placed atop an arcaded cubic structure which has reminded some of the Holy Sepulchre, also pictured in this pamphlet. It's difficult to determine the precise location of this painting's vanishing point, though it is clearly somewhere along the vertical axis corresponding to the minaret of the mosque and thus has been shifted, once again, to the left. But the preparatory drawing in the Uffizi shows that Carpaccio had first intended to place it on the symmetrical axis of the composition, which he carefully traced (though this is difficult to see in reproduction): more specifically, within the central portal of a large domed octagonal building suggestive of Bramante but whose overall form recalls the image of the *Templum salomonis* in Reuwich's woodcut for the *Peregrinatio:* Solomon's temple, that is to say, due to a confusion prevalent at the time, the Dome of the Rock, symbolically situated on the hill of the Temple of Jerusalem, whose precise location is unknown, and whose distance from the spot in question can thus not be determined. The same Dome of the Rock that Reuwich represented as we still see it today, preceded by a mameluke portico erected at the top of a flight of stairs leading from the Haram al Sheriff to the upper esplanade. This building is a recension of the temple in the *Reception of the Ambassadors,* as is indicated by its general form and by the fact that on the threshold of its central door there stands a figure dressed in black followed by two others in white, as well as by its also having itself been shifted to the right in the final composition, creating a tension analogous to that exhibited in the earlier painting, the result of a deliberate, marked discrepancy between a scenic arrangement that's rigorously symmetrical and an architectural framework that's decen-

---

58.   Pierre Provoyeur has seen in the *Triumph of Saint George* "a final *Città ideale*" in the sequence including the "Urbino perspectives," the Perugino *Consignment,* and the Raphael *Sposalizio.* And he has correctly drawn attention to the way Carpaccio was able to deploy both the architecture and the numerous figures so as to open up the scenic space (*Le Temple. Représentations de l'architecture sacrée,* exh. cat., Nice, 1982, pp. 103, 107–108). Among the Venetian antecedents for Carpaccio's work with the representational configuration, the drawing books of Jacopo Bellini must be cited, especially if one accepts Marcel Röthlisberger's thesis that Bellini, after having depicted an *istoria* on the right-hand page, often set it within an unexpected context on the left one, with its natural or architectural elements disposed like a perspective scene, either restoring symmetry to the scene or making it dissymmetrical, as is the case in the *Combat of Saint George and the Dragon* (cf. Victor Goloubeq, *Les Dessins de Jacopo Bellini au Louvre et au British Museum,* vol. 1, *Le Livre d'esquisses du British Museum,* Paris, 1912, plate VIII, and Marcel Röthlisberger, "Notes on the Drawing Books of Jacopo Bellini," *Burlington Magazine,* vol. 97, no. 643 (October 1956), pp. 358–64.

tered: a discrepancy between the geometric and imaginary orders that is further intensified, perhaps, by an implied opposition between the temple of the old law and that of the new.

In the face of operations like these, whose remarkable subtlety is inconsistent with the prevalent view of Carpaccio as little more than a prodigious storyteller, tainted with a condescension registering a failure to take account of what it means to tell stories *in painting,* should we conclude that the theater of Carpaccio was at the origin of a number of trends preoccupying sixteenth-century scenographers, going so far as to find its echo in the Urbino perspectives, and so embracing the relatively late dating for them proposed by Parronchi?[59] This would be to fall into the same old rut usually followed by art history, and would lead us to ignore the questions, of a very different nature, raised by this *rapprochement* of works whose agendas are in fact quite different. For while we do well to approach the Urbino perspectives as paintings or *tableaux* in Lacan's sense, namely as configurations through which the subject constitutes itself as such, Carpaccio's "theater" is an altogether different matter, the problem here being focused not so much on the "subject" as on the *istoria:* a story, however, deriving much of its meaning and energy from the discrepancy it introduces, with the intention of eventually surmounting it, between the geometric point of the subject and the latter's imaginary position.

Certain characteristics of sixteenth-century Venetian painting suggest, contrary to the prevailing consensus, that problems, or *thoughts,* of this kind did not cease to preoccupy the imagination of painters, particularly—which might seem surprising—Venetian painters. Titian's *Presentation of the Virgin in the Temple* in the Accademia conforms to a schema analogous to that of the *Reception of the Ambassadors* (the presence here of an old woman sitting at the foot of some stairs, like a citation from the Carpaccio, is no accident): here too the emphasis placed on the longitudinal advance of the figures, notably the Virgin on the right, conflicts with the architectural perspective opening into depth on the left. Tintoretto, in his version of this subject in the Madonna dell'Orto, seems to have used a more classic compositional formula; indeed the stairway seen in perspective allows him to create the impression not of a horizontal progression but of a veritable

---

59. Cf. Zorzi, in Muraro, op. cit., p. 38.

ascension, while the receding lines of the architectural elements converge upon the figure of the Virgin, in which the symbolic charge of the image is concentrated. Likewise in his *Wedding at Cana* in the Salute, where the compositional arrangement, far from entering into conflict with the perspective construction, readily conforms to it. Here we find once again, deployed like a kind of backdrop, the traditional motif of the three-arched loggia; but whereas in Veronese's version this motif serves to establish a scenography that's rigorously symmetrical, with the dining table placed parallel to the picture plane, Tintoretto has set it perpendicular to this plane, on axis with the vanishing point, which is again shifted to the left, the greater part of the scene remaining empty, while the figure of Christ, seated at the far end of the table (also an important transformation), is inscribed within the outline of the left arcade instead of occupying, as was conventional, the center of the scene. A careful, systematic study of the transformation group consisting of Tintoretto's versions of the *Last Supper* (which exploit a maximum number of the possible ways of placing a rectangular table within the perspective scene, to say nothing of the distribution of the guests) would doubtless reveal that the divergence—in the optical sense of the word— between the work's thematic "subject" and the one orienting its geometric organization like a compass, that the element of calculation, of intentionality in this divergence perhaps constituted the best way of preventing the

123 Titian, *Presentation of the Virgin in the Temple,*
1534–1538. Venice, Accademia. Photo: Alinari-
Giraudon.

124 Tintoretto, *Presentation of the Virgin in the
Temple,* ca. 1552. Venice, Madonna dell'Orto.
Photo: Anderson-Giraudon.

125 Tintoretto, *Wedding in Cana*. Venice, Santa
Maria della Salute. Photo: Anderson-Giraudon.

system from succumbing to a generalized, totally uncontrollable drift fostered by the expressive and dramatic qualities inherent in the "theater of painting."

*

As we're approaching our conclusion, it might seem a bit late to give voice to a "contradictor," as was customary in old treatises, a gesture that was not merely an empty rhetorical exercise. As though a two-way dialogue was inadequate to full development of the debate, it's being necessary to summon a third party to place it in proper perspective. The conceit might seem crude; but it is important, near the end of this overextended two-voice invention, that someone stand up for the rights of "poetry," so at odds with all this talk of the "work" of painting. Hearing it suggested that an excess of theory has blinded us to what is most central to the Urbino perspectives

126 Tintoretto, *Last Supper,* 1594. Venice, San
Giorgio Maggiore. Photo: Anderson-Giraudon.

and that this is closer to the world of dreams than to that of geometry, one
first wants to respond that dreams also have laws, that dreams *work* (and
everyone knows that dreams, like myths, like paintings, think among
themselves). And then there's the fact that the *Città ideale* has lost much of
its purported dreamlike quality since the conservators have delivered it from
the shadows into the diurnal light which is its own. If the comparison with
dreams has a certain pertinence, this is not because of something in these
paintings that's approximate or indecisive (as Valéry said, there's nothing
approximate about poetry), but rather because of their characteristic excess
of clarity and precision. Paradoxically, if there's any question of poetry here,
it's less a function of what's played out in the scenes of our three panels
than of the very production, the very establishment of these scenes: the
fascination these paintings exert over the viewer results from their bringing
into full, brightly lit view the space of dreams, the scene where they
unfold, even as they subject it to the norms of representation.

But there's another response one might make to the contradictor's objection (which you certainly don't take lightly): the seeming constraints of the perspective paradigm are precisely the determinants of the "poetry" of these paintings. At the end of the fifteenth century, painters had to come to terms with it: every question relating to a painting's geometry had to be translated into its terms, beginning with that of symmetry, which constitutes, as we've seen, a remarkable tool for rendering the work of perspective *visible.* Thereafter artists faced a choice: they could either raise the stakes of the perspective rule, or they could take exception to it—but they couldn't pretend to be ignorant of it. Hence the historically grounded analogy drawn by Jakobson between the role of grammar in poetry and, in the art of painting, that of compositional rules based upon a latent or manifest geometric order. In poetry as in painting, technique can be grammatical or nongrammatical; but in no case can it be agrammatical. According to Jakobson this functional analogy was first proposed in the thirteenth century, at a time when pictorial grammar took its measure from a paradigm other than that offered by the perspective model; and much later it led Spinoza to treat Hebrew grammar in terms of *more geometrico.* But its field of application could be extended even further, according to certain contemporary linguists who've gone so far as to speak of a "geometry" of the formal principles characteristic of a given language.[60] And this field would seem to have no a priori limits if it's true, as Wittgenstein claimed, speaking nonmetaphorically, that color itself is a matter of geometry.[61]

The geometry to which *perspectiva artificialis* was linked, and to which it's supposed to have given a new stimulus in the early fifteenth century, for painters this geometry was not, and could not be, on a level of abstraction appropriate for mathematicians. As Alberti was to write, the painter should use "a more sensate wisdom," along with points on a specific surface, lines of a certain thickness, and figures everyone can see.[62] How

60. Roman Jakobson, "Poésie de la grammaire et grammaire de la poésie," French trans., *Questions de poétique,* Paris, 1973, pp. 227–28; English trans. by R. J. Rudy and Stephen Rudy in R. J., *Language in Literature,* Cambridge and London, 1987, pp. 132–33.

61. Ludwig Wittgenstein, *Bemerkungen über die Farben,* 1956; English trans., *Remarks on Color,* Berkeley, 1977.

62. "Noi, perche vogliamo le cose essere poste da vedere, per questo useremo quanto dicono piu grassa Minerva . . .," Alberti, *Della pittura,* op. cit., p. 55; English trans., p. 43.

could it have been otherwise, if the analogy with grammar is well founded? Considered as a grammatical rule applicable to painting, a geometric principle can only be accepted if it makes sense; and if something is to make sense in painting, it must first of all be visible. And this sense condition, as formulated in terms of visibility, might still have been a factor in the advance effected in perspective, in the field of mathematics, two centuries after Alberti. In which case Brunelleschi's experiments would have prepared, and not "anticipated," the advent of both descriptive and projective geometry, insofar as they put in place a configuration of visibility in which the subject, the one to become that of modern science, had its assigned place from the beginning (and at the origin) of the system, in the form of a point: Desargues' revolution rose on this foundation or—to use Husserlian language—on this ground of significant experience. Did the passage to geometry presuppose that the operations constituting the system had been purged of all phenomenological or subjective connotations, and that there was now a permanent disjunction between the point of view and the point said to be that "of the subject"? This is not the place to answer such a question. But we've seen that an analogous operation had long been underway in the field of art: Carpaccio's work (*travail*) attests to the subsequently acknowledged necessity of a division, in painting (insofar as it conforms to the perspective paradigm) between that which is a matter of geometry, in the strictly mathematical sense of the word, and that which has to do with another kind of geometry, one that's imaginary—or symbolic.

The most probing example of such an extension of the idea of "geometry," the work that explores it in the fullest, most spectacular, most systematic—and most enigmatic—way is incontestably Velázquez's *Las Meninas*. And it was not by accident that Michel Foucault's analysis of this painting was cited at the beginning of this volume, and that we now return to it at the end of our journey. In my opening remarks I expressed regret that this analysis had had no discernable influence, and that far from opening the way toward investigations—seemingly crucial ones in the context of the "archaeology of knowledge"—into the role of art in the genesis of the classic system of representation, it had been received as little more than a fable or conceit. At least in France, it must be said. For things worked out rather differently in the United States, where after an initial incubation period the literature on *Las Meninas* has proliferated to such an extent that

127 Velázquez, *Las Meninas,* 1656. Madrid, Prado. Photo: Bulloz.

one must now make excuses before adding to it. Leo Steinberg has made a particularly elegant contribution to the debate: in his view, any description of Velázquez's masterpiece must be inadequate, *Las Meninas* being comparable to a musical composition lending itself to multiple interpretations, none of which can be definitive.[63] The dodge is skillful, but it avoids the question as to whether there's such a thing as a history of description and interpretation, and whether this might somehow or other pretend to truth, or at least to pertinence—to put this another way: whether advance or progress is

---

63. Leo Steinberg, "Velazquez' 'Las Meninas'," *October,* no. 19 (winter 1981), pp. 45–54.

possible in this matter, without which critical activity would be reduced to an interminable series of performances, more or less successful or spectacular, with a failure to clearly define the specific competence required of interpreters making the entire exercise all the more dubious. It goes without saying that one must know how to read music to make it heard and understood. But in the case of painting?

Of what relevant competence can the philosopher boast here? Foucault's analysis, while it immediately took on classic status, to the great annoyance of many historians, is concerned primarily, if indirectly, with classicism: Does it not claim to give us access, by means of Velázquez's painting, to the most constant ground of the classic *episteme,* the theory of representation? *Las Meninas* is presented as being, "perhaps" (it is Foucault who hedges), a representation of classic representation and of the space it opens up. But a representation that is—as is only proper—itself *suspended,* like the brush of the painter depicted on the canvas, such that one can't decide whether he's about to add a final touch to his painting or has yet to make the first brushstroke.[64] A representation of representation, and not of *a* representation, as the philosopher John Searle would say, in the course of denying its very possibility. That representation whose various forms and signs are enumerated in the painting: images (the paintings within the painting, though their function is thwarted, insofar as they're illegible save to knowledgeable specialists[65]), portraits, looks, gestures, etc.—while the scene he describes sustains itself, in its scenic existence, only by means of the references it imposes to another scene, facing it and thus invisible, but whose trace or echo is found in the painting's center, in the form of the mirror and the two figures reflected in it. The consequence being, between these facing scenes, an unending series of relays or dodges, as a result of which the spectator is simultaneously implicated in the painting and excluded from the circuit of representation, or rather conducted to its back: a back for which that of the canvas within the painting, the one at which the painter works, is a literal metaphor. To use Foucault's own term, the spectator's attention "flutters" (*papillote*), being simultaneously solicited by

---

64. Michel Foucault, *Les Mots et les choses,* op. cit., p. 19; English trans., p. 3.
65. Cf. Charles de Tolnay, "Velasquez' 'Las Hilanderas' and 'Las Meninas' (an Interpretation)," *Gazette des Beaux-Arts,* vol. 35 (January 1949), pp. 21–38.

128 Velázquez, *Las Meninas:* the "other" Velazquez. Photo: Giraudon.

the painter's gaze at him, by the mirror facing him, and by the open door at the rear of the painting, similar to a "light" (though it illuminates only itself), at whose threshold, a bit inside it, there stands another spectator, this one too partially turned away, and who sees only the back of the scene as presented to us by the painter, and yet whose view encompasses all of it, including the *other* painting, the one we can't see, to which no one in the scene pays any attention, not even the painter himself in this suspended moment. To say nothing of all those eyes looking out at us from most places in the canvas where there are figures, or of the dog in the foreground who neither looks nor moves, and who is present, as Leo Steinberg observes, as a figure of *apathes* or tranquility.[66]

Thus the spectator is linked to the representation taking place within this scene by a network of lines leading from the painting, traversing the viewer and apparently converging on a point which Foucault qualifies as "uncertain" (*douteux*), because invisible (but then what is the precise role of visibility in this inquiry?). An ideal point, and also a functional one. An "inevitable" point, in Foucault's words. And a necessary one, since it's a prerequisite for the representation that's ordered and deployed from it,[67] and to which corresponds, in the painting, the image of the three functions of which it is by turns the site: the figures of the "models" reflected in the mirror, who are purportedly situated there; that of the painter, who has had to place himself, at least ideally, at this point (which is, I repeat, uncertain) in order to paint the painting we're examining; and that, finally, of the spectator, who in principle would be superfluous to the configuration, unless he took it in from the back, opening his own "light" into it, guided by the position assigned him in Brunelleschi's first experiment. Which makes the conclusion inevitable: "The entire painting is looking out at a scene for which it is itself a scene."[68] The space opened by representation is, in principle, *split:* for there to be a painting or *tableau* in the classic sense of the word, it is necessary, simultaneously, for the position it sets up to be developed in front of the plane of projection, in the direction of the spectator, who will thus find himself on an equal footing with the figures within it

---

66. Steinberg, op. cit., p. 50.
67. Foucault, *Les Mots et les choses,* op. cit., p. 29; English trans., p. 13.
68. Ibid.; English trans., p. 14.

(and on an equal footing as well with both the master who represents and the sovereigns who are represented—which summarizes the meaning that art historical consensus has seen fit to ascribe to Velázquez's masterpiece), and for the painted scene to be a slice through this "face-off." The painting is both the instrument and the product of this caesura, and corresponds—quite literally—to what perspective theory designated as the "section," the *intersegazione*.

The subject is thus elided from the configuration set up by *Las Meninas*. Triply so, because "subject" should be understood here in all three senses of the word, each of them classic: that of the thematic subject of the painting only visible to the spectator from the back; that of the author of *Las Meninas*, who could only have executed it by removing himself from the place he occupies within it; and that of the spectator himself, before whom the scene deploys itself without his being able to discern, initially, any way to situate himself as a subject within it. According to Foucault this elision was necessary in order for the representation to present itself as being pure, liberated from this relation that impeded it:[69] which doesn't preclude the possibility that, once disconnected from the subject, points of view or focus can multiply within the limits of the painting. It is this aspect of Foucault's description that has met with the greatest resistance. Leo Steinberg insists upon the feeling of reciprocal implications generated by the play of the mirrored encounters that Velázquez proposes to us: no one looking at *Las Meninas* is excluded from the scene; he is part of the family, part of the event.[70] As for John Searle, he holds to what appears to be a commonsense argument: for there to be any such elision, the object elided must initially have been posited as such; how can we speak of representation if its fundamental condition is absent? Or to put it somewhat differently, in the terms of "speech act" theory: every pictorial proposition must necessarily be coupled with an implicit active verb such as "I see," just as every statement implies an "I say."

Svetlana Alpers has rightly expressed concern over the fact that the most thorough, penetrating description of *Las Meninas* to appear for some time was penned by a philosopher, which she takes to indicate that the

---

69. Ibid., p. 31; English trans., p. 16.
70. Steinberg, op. cit., pp. 48, 54.

standard interpretive methods of art history are *structurally* inadequate to deal with such a painting.[71] So it's not surprising that it is another philosopher, and not an art historian, who has most closely scrutinized Foucault's analysis. According to John Searle, *Las Meninas,* far from being a representation of classic representation, is a veritable challenge issued to the theory of representation. His argument can be summarized as follows: given that in classic painting illusion is based upon resemblance, and that all resemblance must be relative to a point of view,[72] the fact that the point from which *Las Meninas* is supposed to be contemplated is already occupied by the royal couple amounts to an aporia that can only be adjusted if we concede that the point of view from which Velazquez painted his picture is not the one assigned by perspective (and is not in fact where Searle thinks it is) but rather the one *shown* by the painting: which amounts to saying that the painting on which the painter works is none other than the one we see, in which case we're no longer dealing with a representation of a representation, and there's no scene in question other than the one we actually see on the canvas. But the paradox here is not the one Searle articulates: in the totally closed, self-referential configuration he posits, the mirror is superfluous, and yet the sense of his argument depends upon it; unless, that is, we are to suppose that Velázquez depicted himself in the course of painting *Las Meninas* under the eyes of his masters, which in fact brings us back to Foucault's description.[73]

Las Meninas is the only example in Velázquez's work of a painting constructed in strict perspective. As often happens, the apparent rigor of its construction obscures a trap—an especially perverse one in this case because it exploits the constitutive prejudice of the system, namely the assumption that perspective assigns the spectator a place at the start, or rather at the origin of the "view" proposed by the painting, directly in front of the point toward which its receding lines converge. In thrall to this assumption, Searle has not escaped the trap set for him by *Las Meninas:* his misadventure

71. Svetlana Alpers, "Interpretation without Representation, or the Viewing of *Las Meninas,*" *Representations,* no. 1 (February 1983), pp. 31–42.

72. John Searle, "*Las Meninas* and the Paradoxes of Pictorial Representation," *Critical Inquiry,* vol. 6, no. 3 (spring 1980), pp. 447–88.

73. The idea that the painter in *Las Meninas* is painting *Las Meninas* was first proposed by Elizabeth du Gué Trapier in her book *Velázquez,* New York, 1948, p. 339.

is all the more piquant—and revelatory—because he thought, having read Foucault a bit too quickly (like many others), that the vanishing point was inscribed within the mirror of *Las Meninas,* perpendicular to the figures of the two sovereigns, whereas in fact, if one looks closely, it appears to be situated somewhere along the forearm, or on the hand, of the figure at the threshold of the open door to the rear of the scene. It's on this axis then that the spectator should be placed, such that he senses the royal couple to be to his left.[74] But here again, *optical* analysis of the painting reveals that this cannot be so, and that the mirror cannot present a direct reflection of the figures of the king and queen. Which prompts us to allow that the image reflected in the mirror might correspond to the central portion of the canvas on which the painter works.[75] If such were the case, the analysis would not further our understanding of the workings of a painting whose perspective scheme seems to have been devised with ends in view other than illusionist ones: if there's any illusion in question here, it passes by way of the mirror before—if the reader will indulge me—heading out the door.

Another way of approaching *Las Meninas,* one that we might by rights have expected an adherent of speech act theory to propose, would be to focus not on what the painting *represents* but rather on what it *does,* and primarily on what it *transforms.* In this connection we have at our disposal a document that's virtually unique: the series of studies painted by Picasso in his studio in Cannes, between August and December of 1957, using material from Velázquez's masterpiece. The set of transformations they propose constitute without doubt the best introduction to the operations of which *Las Meninas* is the theater. What did Picasso choose to work with? Among other things, the relation between the mirror reflecting the figures of the royal couple (which Foucault situated in the painting's center) and the nearby door within which is framed, at the beginning of a flight of stairs, the silhouette of a third figure. As for this last motif (and the figure in a doorway is definitely a motif, one that appears frequently in painting of the

---

74. Steinberg, op. cit., p. 52.

75. Cf. Joel Snyder and Ted Cohen, "Critical Response. Reflections on *Las Meninas:* Paradox Lost," *Critical Inquiry,* vol. 7, no. 2 (winter 1980), pp. 429–47. George Kubler proposed the same reading in 1966 ("Three Remarks on *Las Meninas,*" *Art Bulletin,* vol. 48, 1966, p. 213). More recently, Kubler has advanced an even subtler reading, namely that the mirror in *Las Meninas* is a *false* mirror, a painting executed to look like a mirror, which would redouble its imaginary valence.

period, and must be considered as such[76]), Foucault is far from regarding it as secondary, for he views it as manifesting one of the three functions concentrated in the point supposedly assigned by the painting (note: the painting, not the perspective scheme). But he does not accord it an importance equal to that of the mirror, whose function it is to draw into the painting, in the form of a reflection, something that's essentially foreign to it, namely the gaze that has organized it and to which it presents itself.[77] In this respect, but in this one only, the mirror indeed occupies the center of the composition, at least its *imaginary* center. As for its geometric one, that—as we've seen—is quite another matter. Curiously, part of Picasso's work seems to have involved reducing this mirror to its bare minimum: to such an extent that it was no longer anything but a sign lacking all appearance of specularity, a kind of blind painting, a simple frame, a white rectangle—in other words, totally eliminating it so as to allow the motif of the door and the silhouette framing it, suggestive of a shadow theater, to assume a place smack in the painting's center. This displacement (this transformation) corresponds to the opening in the painting of a white gap, a fissure that in some cases is quite small but is all the more visible for having been stripped of all geometric connotation, and all the more active for being inscribed within a more compact and densely charged composition (see the two "general views" of October 2 and 3, 1957[78]).

To be sure, the context of Picasso's transformation is very different from that of the picture from which he took his material: in 1957 painting was no longer in the age of representation, its characteristic game of mirrors having come to an end. But what then are we to make of the prominence he accorded this opening to which, within the painting, no one pays even the slightest attention? In Velázquez's canvas the mirror and the door are plainly in direct competition with one another, and Foucault saw this quite clearly: Does he not say of this light (a light—I must stress this point again—that illuminates only itself) that its brightness challenges the reflection, in the mirror, of the two doll-like figures as would the flame of a

---

76. Cf. André Chastel, "La Figure dans l'encadrement de la porte chez Velázquez," *Fables, Formes, Figures,* op. cit., vol. 2, pp. 145–54.

77. Foucault, *Les Mots et les choses,* op. cit., p. 30; English trans., pp. 14–15.

78. Museo Picasso, *Catalogo I,* Barcelona, 1975, nos. 70.465 and 70.466.

129 Picasso, *Las Meninas* (after Velázquez), dated
August 17, 1957. Barcelona, Picasso Museum.
Photo: Museum.

130 Picasso, *Las Meninas,* September 18, 1957.
Barcelona, Picasso Museum. Photo: Museum.

131 Picasso, *Las Meninas,* September 19, 1957.
Barcelona, Picasso Museum. Photo: Museum.

132 Picasso, *Las Meni-
nas,* October 2, 1957.
Barcelona, Picasso
Museum. Photo: Museum.

candle? But this competition is all the more apparent for being strictly
programmed, with the mirror and the door being placed on either side of
the painting's vertical axis, which passes through the latter's left frame. The
very curtain held open by the figure at its threshold responds, symmetrically, to that hanging above the royal couple. But the indefinitely suspended gesture of the hand on which the painting's vanishing point is
situated, or very nearly, echoes that on the other side of the canvas of the
hand holding the brush. There's nothing surprising in this: without taking

133 Picasso, *Las Meninas,* November 15, 1957.
Barcelona, Picasso Museum. Photo: Museum.

proper names to be anything other, as Foucault notes, than deictic artifices allowing us to pass from the space where one looks to that where one speaks,[79] we cannot ignore the fact that this figure, this *witness,* bore the same name as the painter, for he is don José Nieto Velázquez, *aposentador* or steward of the palace, in the service of the queen and responsible for the royal tapestry collection, as was the king's painter for the picture collection.[80] The fact that their names correspond, in the case of the painter, to that of his father and, in the case of the *aposentador,* to that of his mother should be linked to the symmetry of the functions they perform, one for the king and the other for the queen. Allowances being made for this exception, the like proper names only serve to exacerbate the disjunction of the two figures between which the mirror (and the image of the royal couple) takes its place: in *Las Meninas* there is not one Velázquez but *two,* the self and the other. And the other is situated, as if by chance, within the painting, and takes it in, so to speak, from the back, from the spot at which the spectator, the "observer," finds through projection his geometric position.

The strength of Foucault's account, its analytic pertinence, derives from his having managed to avoid privileging any of the three functions of which the painting is the site. Some have claimed his description takes its measure from the painting's perspective organization, but this is hardly the case, as Foucault's reference to a network of lines deemed to emanate *perpendicularly* from the canvas, its "end point" (*pointillé*) corresponding to the locus assigned by perspective, is in the end metaphorical. In this sense Foucault is perfectly right to see the mirror as the painting's "center," though—as I've said—its *imaginary* center. Hence it is incorrect to say that the perspective paradigm provides us with the most appropriate model of the classic system of representation. If there is any representation in painting, the configuration of *Las Meninas* reveals it to consist of a calculated discrepancy between a painting's geometric organization and its imaginary structure. It is this that Foucault's critics have failed to see, as a result of their having adhered to a strictly optical, conventional definition of the perspective paradigm. But to fully comprehend the operation of the paint-

---

79. Foucault, *Les Mots et les choses,* op. cit., p. 25; English trans., p. 9.
80. Cf. F. J. Sánchez-Cantón, *"Las Meninas" y su personajes,* Barcelona, 1943, pp. 14–27.

ing, we must still examine the material transformed by it and work this into the interpretation.

It is true that the operations of *Las Meninas* are not without precedent in the history of painting. But their difference from those in such-and-such a self-portrait in a mirror,[81] their greater complexity and subtlety, can be demonstrated with a single example. With regard to the mirror/door pairing with which Picasso worked, I'd observe that Velázquez severed two terms or motifs that had been conjoined, even encased in one another, in a painting that seems to be directly connected with *Las Meninas,* as Searle has suggested. A painting executed more than two centuries before the masterpiece by Velázquez, one that he must have seen and could easily have studied, as it then figured in the collection of the king of Spain, for which the artist was responsible. This painting, whose basic elements are incorporated into *Las Meninas* and transformed there, is none other than the *Arnolfini Wedding* by Jan van Eyck—already mentioned in connection with Brunelleschi's first experiment—in which we see, framed by the circular convex mirror in which they're reflected, two witnesses (two, like the king and queen in *Las Meninas,* or the two "Velázquezes") slightly beyond the threshold of a door. In this play of closed-circuit relays giving the painting its testamentary force, the written inscription ("I was there") would seem redundant if it didn't perform the function of leading the painting from the space of visibility to that of legibility, and of transforming an implicit proposition into an explicit statement. But this configuration, which we might say was one of implication as well as one of proof, was itself not unprecedented. A decade or two before the *Arnolfini Wedding,* Brunelleschi's first experiment had already made use of a door and a mirror. And it was within the frame of this door, according to my hypothesis (a bit forced, I'll concede, but now justified a posteriori by an entire history[82]), that was inscribed the point which, by means of the mirror reflection, became confused with that of the eye. This door which opened, atop a short flight of stairs, into a centrally planned temple, into the baptistry which would serve as *imago* for the Urbino *Città ideale* and, after it, for a number of quite different compositions, the Perugino *Consignment* and Raphael *Sposalizio* being among the

---

81. Steinberg, op. cit., p. 46.
82. Cf. *supra,* chapter 15.

134 Jan van Eyck, *Arnolfini Wedding*, 1434. London, National Gallery. Photo: Museum.

most famous. Which is to say a symbolically connoted locus, one confounded, in Brunelleschi's demonstration, with the geometric locus of the subject, as is also the case in the *Arnolfini* mirror.

If in *Las Meninas* Velázquez severed the two terms, or the two loci, he effected this by means of an operation in a direct line with that of Carpaccio, which can now, retrospectively, be seen in all its nonanecdotal significance. Likewise, in another context, the point marked in the window of Ghirlandaio's *Annunciation:*[83] a point that's tangent to the closed shutter, just as the vanishing point in the *Città ideale* is contiguous with the closed wing of the door. But a point that's strictly symbolic, that's stripped of all geometric connotation, even though it's situated on the same vertical axis as the vanishing point, where it intersects with the horizontal line passing through the dove of the Holy Spirit, which line thus comes to figure as a horizon line, itself imaginary. This fundamentally metonymic play takes on still greater relief in *Las Meninas,* in light of the painting's self-referentiality, which Searle has correctly stressed. We will never know what the artist in *Las Meninas* is painting: but the turned canvas is an emblem or ensign of the founding operation of modern painting, which consisted of Brunelleschi's piercing a hole in his panel and turning it around to view it in a mirror.

Which is to say that if the perspective paradigm is inadequate to define the system of classic representation, it nonetheless remains a condition of it. The discrepancy between a painting's geometric organization and its imaginary structure is conceivable only if the latter can get its measure from the former, miming its operation, as Foucault's analysis implicitly reveals. Is *Las Meninas* constructed in perspective? The answer seems so obvious as to render the question pointless. And yet there are very few indicators, and these far from clear, to help us situate the vanishing point: the oblique line where the ceiling meets the right wall, and another one, on the same wall, passing through the window lintels, and the ceiling brackets from which chandeliers can be hung, etc. If the perspectival illusion is totally convincing, it convinces in the imaginary register by the accumulation of features that animate the representation, all of them linked to the visual order: the mirror, the glances, the gestures, the paintings within the

---

83. Cf. *supra*, chapter 15, pp. 360–62.

painting, and even the turned canvas, placed obliquely such that it forms a right angle with the open door. The point most conspicuously assigned by the painting is not the geometric point, which must be induced or inferred, but an uncertain point, as Foucault properly puts it, a point that's not invisible but rather unassignable, and that flutters, that darts about, establishing itself first in the painter's gaze, then in the mirror, and then (as indicated by the perspective construction) to the right of the arm of the other Velázquez, the one drawing back the curtain, metonymously miming the unveiling of the painting and the scene with which it presents us. A point, if we take Foucault literally, that will fluctuate into infinity. A point, in any case, no surer of its position than is the painter, who must pull back to get a proper view of his model, or the lady-in-waiting leaning toward the infanta, not out of deference (she has eyes only for "us") but to move as close as possible to the painting's axis, like those annoying bystanders who try, despite a cameraman's protests, to force their way into the field of his viewfinder.

The operation of the painting, then, can be translated into the analytic register in terms of a competition, to the point of interference, between two language games—one that's technical (geometric or perspectival) and another that's phenomenological. In the one case, the subject is, so to speak, produced by the system in which it has its designated place (as in language); in the other, it manifests itself through a goal defining it as a subject, but not without allowing itself to become captivated by the mirror in which it vainly seeks its own reflection. It's common knowledge that there's a bit of Narcissus in every spectator, in every lover of painting. The great dealer Duveen took care to heavily varnish the paintings in his shop, for he had observed that his clients enjoyed seeing their own images reflected in the works presented to them.[84] Classic representation appeals to a similar desire, but in a form that's perverse in another way: to understand it properly, we must ourselves be careful not to confuse elision of the subject with its absence, its suppression, or its exclusion. The subject is "elided" in *Las Meninas,* but it is presupposed by it, as it was in the specular circuit put in place by Brunelleschi, which appealed to it as its condition, or its origin, precise and instantaneous, as would be Descartes's *cogito.* In painting, the point is the sign of the elision of the subject. A sign that is placed, as it must be, under the aegis of an *apostrophe,* a direct address, but that has meaning and existence as this sign only within the space of the visible.

*

If resistance to Foucault's description of *Las Meninas* has far outweighed its positive influence on subsequent research into the role of art in the genesis of the economy of the classical *episteme,* the author himself is partly to blame: in the context of his book this analysis functions only as a kind of emblem, like a frontispiece. As is often the case in works of history, in

---

84. N. S. Berman, *Duveen,* New York, 1951, p. 134.

Words and Things painting is called into play only to serve illustrative or allegorical ends. And if there is one primary lesson to be learned from all of the preceding, it is that painting is a distinct object of historical study and must be dealt with as such: which means paradoxically that one must adopt a deliberately structuralist point of view, which only throws the historical dimension of phenomena into greater relief. In contrast to the operations studied by mythology, those of which art is the theater belong to a history that is anything but continuous, one that's marked by all kinds of advances, retreats, and detours and can unfold over several centuries. A history that cannot a priori be assigned any chronological or geographic limits. Four centuries after Velázquez, Picasso would undertake to reactivate the question posed by *Las Meninas,* just as Velázquez used the apparatus put in place by Jan van Eyck two hundred years before him. It is known that Velázquez, especially in his most important canvases, frequently reworked elements drawn from paintings of the preceding century, transforming and enriching them.[85] But we must go further: through the *Arnolfini* mirror, *Las Meninas* renews, objectively, with Brunelleschi's configuration, adapting it to the context of its own time. I've further suggested that the Urbino perspectives have their "own" history: a plural history, and perhaps a collective one, with which men of quite diverse backgrounds may have been associated, which would be in keeping with what we know of the period and of the Urbino court in particular. A history encompassing several years, if not several decades, for which the *Città ideale* opened the way by renewing with elements of the prototype that were subsequently transformed in the two other panels, resulting in the constitution of the group we've been discussing.

Leading from Brunelleschi's experiments to Velázquez's *Las Meninas* by way of the *Arnolfini Wedding,* the Urbino perspectives, Raphael's *Spozalizio,* and the great narrative cycles of Carpaccio, this structural analysis has traced a historical trajectory that will strike many historians as improbable, but it is consistent with the image of art itself. Conversely, history confers meaning upon moves it's tempting to regard as strictly formal and redundant, as has been said (a bit hastily) of the Lévi-Straussian conception of

---

85. Cf. Diego Angulo, *Velázquez, como compuso sus principales cuadros,* Seville, 1947.

myth:[86] if a language spoke only of itself, it would still have much to say. We have just seen proof of this: when painting turns in on itself and reflects upon its own operations, the results affect the position of the subject, the emergence of a science, and the status of representation.

Émile Benveniste maintained that language alone has the power to interpret itself and is also the unique interpreter of all other semiotic systems—this *interpretive* relation furnishing the criterion, according to him, for a division between systems manifesting their own semiotic and those whose semiotic becomes manifest only by means of another mode of expression. And yet he acknowledged that the distinction between interpretive and interpreted systems, between those that "articulate" and those that "are articulated," has meaning only "from the point of view of language."[87] Picasso's work with *Las Meninas,* and Velázquez's masterpiece itself, if its operations are taken to be self-referential, attest to the fact that painting, while it cannot interpret other systems, disposes of all the means necessary for it to turn back on itself, from the point of view and in terms of the forms that belong to it. The perspective configuration demonstrates this, in that it reflects, in the course of its own regulated operation, the operators at work in it, without being obliged to introduce any arbitrary or imported categories. The contradictor (the same one or another) will say that these categories are nonetheless linguistic ones and that, because of this, they must be applied through language. But this is true *only from the point of view of language,* within the space in which we speak, and is not true from the point of view of painting, within the space in which we look. For the painter, the "horizon" is first of all the line described by Alberti, on which are aligned the heads of the figures populating a canvas, the limit, though he was under no obligation to name it, toward which a painting's receding lines converge: the site of points at the infinity of a plane, as Poncelet would put it in another language, a conceptual one, but one that's also founded on a primordial intuition. And as for the "point of view," it falls to perspective (so it's said), and not to language, to assign this in painting.

---

86. Dan Sperber, *Le Symbolisme en général,* Paris, 1974, p. 19; English trans. by Alice L. Morton, *Rethinking Symbolism,* Cambridge, 1975, p. 12.

87. Benveniste, "Sémiologie de la langue," *Problèmes de linguistique générale,* op. cit., vol. 2, p. 61; English trans. in *Semiotics,* op. cit., pp. 241–42.

Index

Numbers in italics refer to illustrations

Accoramboni da Gubbio, Ottavio, 183
Aguilon, François, 398n
Alberti, Leon-Battista, xxiii, 36, 59–61, 66, 68, 71, 123, 173
    on ancient theater, 218, 223–224, 237, 237n
    and Brunelleschi, 59–61, 75, 90–91, 102n, 119, 119n, 130, 134, 138, 139,
        139n, 155, 163, 164, 447
    centric ray of, 120, 332
    and distance point, 107–108, *108*
    and Filarete, 62, 65, 65n
    Filodosso (comedy), 224
    on geometric perspective, 37, 107–108, *108,* 124, 124n, 133, 133n, 136,
        346, 381, 385–386, 387n, 388, 389, 389n, 424, 424n, 445
    and horizon, 133, 133n, 385–386, 386n, 388, 445
    and *intersegatione,* 136, 346
    on painting, 83, 102, 212, 239, 324, 383, 383n, 400, 400n
    Palazzo Rucellai, *206,* 206–207, 208, 209, *240,* 243, 244, 307
    on perspective scene, 35, 95, 97n, 267, 330, 398, 447, 447n
    and Pliny, xxiv, xxiv(n)
    and Serlio, 393
    two-person form of address of, 447, 447n
    and Urbino perspectives, 175, 180n, 202, 212n
    window metaphor of, 102, 136, 301, 301n, 350
Alexander VI (pope), 308
Alpers, Svetlana, 430, 431n
Angelis, L. de, 179n
Angulo, Diego, 444n
Annunciation (Ghirlandaio), 360, 362, *362,* 441

Annunciation (Lorenzetti), *80*

Annunciation (Piero), 363, *364*

Antique (herringbone) perspective, xvi, 12, 15–16, 63–64, 161–162, 184

Architectural perspective, 271

Architectural Perspective (Peruzzi), 203, *203*

Architectural Perspective (Baltimore). *See* Baltimore panel

Architectural Perspective (Berlin). *See* Berlin panel

Argan, Giulio-Carlo, 64n, 118n, 325

Ariosto, 215

Aristotle, 16, 153, 270

Arnolfini Wedding (Van Eyck), 43, 130–131, 416, 439, *440,* 441, *442,* 444

Ashby, Genette, 263n

Atget, Eugène, 265

Austin, J. L., 258

Automorphism, 331, 388

"Autopsy," 132, 138

Baker, H. F., 50n

Baldi, Bernardino, 182n, 273, 274, 407

Baltimore panel, 173, *174–175,* 182–183, *191,* 193–194, 202, *241,* 242, 258, 289, *290,* 291–294, 297, 299, 300–312. *See also* Urbino perspectives

    amphitheater and "sun" in, 239, 243, *304*

    attribution of, 196, 200, 279

    and Baccio d'Agnolo, 208

    Berlin panel compared with, 280

    and Cancelleria, 223

    and epigraph, 275

    ground plan of, 371, *372,* 374

    and History of Lucretia, 358

    horizon in, 356, 394

    images in, 188

    Krautheimer study of, 199, 253

    multiple perspectives in, 382

    and "New Rome" dream, 190

    palace windows in, *330*

    paving design in, 293, *296,* 297, 324, 327

    perspective hole in, 343

    and Perugino/Botticelli frescoes, 276–277

and Rome-Florence marriage, 244

Sanpaolesi on, 211n

symmetry of, 326–327, 329, 331, 340, 344

and theater, 213–214, 217, 218, 219, 254, 257–258, 259

triumphal arch in, 301, *303*

Urbino panel compared with, 255–257, 281

windows and doors in, 360, 363, 367, 371

Baltrušaitis, Jurgis, xxii

Barbaro, Daniele, 223, 396

Barberini panels, *178,* 179, 401, 402n

Barthes, Roland, 29, 29n, 259

Battisti, Eugenio, 217n, 224, 224n, 244, 244n, 281

Bellini, Gentile, 226

Bellini, Jacopo, 417n

Bellotto, Bernardo, *152,* 153n, 383, *384,* 411n

Beltrame, R., 101n

Benjamin, Walter, 160, 185, 185n, 187, 187n, 225, 225n, 226, 226n, 262, 263, 263n, 265

Benveniste, Émile, 4, 5, 5n, 8, 20n, 132n, 263, 263n, 285, 286n, 445, 445n

Berenson, Bernard, 181, 194n

Berkeley, George, 269, 446

Berlin panel, 175, *176–177,* 183, *240,* 280–281, 289, *290,* 291–293, 294, 297, 299, *300, 301,* 301–302, 305, 307–312. *See also* Urbino perspectives

angle of vision in, 374

attribution of, 196, 279, 308n, 404

boats in, 267

detail of central portion of, *386*

feigned wooden paneling under, 316

and *Filodosso,* 224

framing in, 360

ground plan of, 371, *373,* 374

horizon in, 356, 394

images in, 188

and infinities, 385

and isolation from context, 380

paving design in, 294, *296,* 327

perspective hole in, 343

and *Reception of the Ambassadors,* 411

Berlin panel (cont.)

    right portion of, *300*

    and *Story of the Miraculous Image,* 402

    symmetry of, 327, 330, 331, 339–340, *340,* 344

    and theater, 218, 219

    vanishing point of, 383, 414

    windows or doors in, 360, 363, 367, 371

Berman, N. S., 443n

Bernard, Émile, 160n

Bernini, Dante and Grazia, 179n, 181n, 182, 182n, 183n, 184n, 212n, 272n, 311, 311n

Berruguete, Pedro, 179

Bettie, E., 281n

Bibiena, Fernando (cardinal), 214n, 216, 396, 397

Bifocal system, 79, 108, *110,* 228, 392

Birth of the Virgin, 178, 179

Blécon, Jean, xxv, 371, *372, 373,* 374n

Bloch, Ernst, 379, 379n

Boscovics, M., 67n

Bosse, Abraham, 36, *37,* 50, 150, 150n, 333, 387

Botticelli, 275, *276,* 277, 312n, *339, 340,* 358, 365, *365,* 401

Bouveresse, Jacques, 33–35, 34n, 39, 39n, 352n

Bramante, 173, 179, 179n, 180, 180n, 181, 182, 186, 217, 217n, 243, 246, 252, 271, 307, 408, 418

Braque, Georges, 144, 148

Bregno, Andrea, 242

Breydenbach, Bernhard von, 408, 408n, 417

Brion-Guerry, Liliane, 43n, 121n, 133n

Brunelleschi, Filippo, 59, 61, 68, 75, 76, 77, 127, 378

    and Alberti, 59–61, 75, 90–91, 447 (*see also under* Alberti, Leon-Battista)

    and ancient perspectivists, 161–162

    and coverings of buildings, 95

    and discovery of perspective, 162

    and Filarete, 63, 64–65, 70, 75, 92 (*see also under* Filarete)

    as inventor of Renaissance, 157, 163–164

    and Masaccio, 70, 233

    and Newtonian physics, 27

    and *Novella del Grasso,* 72n

perspective demonstration of, 84, 85, 89, 101–112, *116,* 126, 134–137, 155, 205, 232, 323, 326, 377, 425

and *Arnolfini Wedding,* 131, 439

and Donatello, 401

and geometry, 157–159, 333, 382, 425

and *Las Meninas,* 429, 444, 446

and Leonardo, 325

and mirror, 63, 92, 94, 97, 98, 115–118, 119–122, 125–126, 127–128, 129–130, 131–133, 137–140, 146, 155, 332, 377, 379–380, 439

and modern painting, 441

and reduction to point, 121, 132, 382, 446

and Sabattini's theater method, 399

second experiment, 143–155

and Serlio's theater, 391

and space, 227, 324–325

and truth value, 159

and Urbino perspectives, 319, 322–325, 338, 342, *343,* 344, 371, 374, 380, 382, 416

Vasari vs. Manetti on, 118–119

and window, 102, 136, 152

procedures prior to, 79

and symmetry, 333, 382

Thales compared with, 76, 77, 83, 85, 164

and Toscanelli, 71

Vasari on, 68–72, 92, 93 (*see also under* Vasari, Giorgio)

Bruno, Giordano, 18, 48, 49

Bruschi, Arnaldo, 186, 186n, 190n, *221,* 246, 247n

Bryson, Norman, 261n

Budinich, Kornelije, 273

Buontalenti, Bernardo, 282n

Byzantine art, 13

Calabrese, Omar, 416n

Campori, G., 215n

Canaletto, 138, 409

Capitoline Theater, Rome (Rosselli), *221*

Carnap, Rudolf, 351

Carnevale, Fra, 179, 179n, 181, 184

Carpaccio, Vittore, 226, 405–411, 411–412, *412, 413,* 414, *414, 416,* 417–419, *419,* 425, 441, 444, 447

Cassirer, Ernst, 6–9, 7n, 8n, 10, 10n, 11–12, 13, 15, 17, 19, 23, 25, 81, 82n, 123, 446

Castel Sant'Angelo, 330

Castiglione, Baldassare, 26, 181, 185, 186n, 187, 187n, 189, 215, 216, 216n, 217, 255, 255n, 305, 318, 319n

Cavalcaselle, Giovanni Battista, 181

Cavallini, Pietro, *251*

Cegia, Francesco di Agostino, 72n

Centric ray, 120, 128, 146–147, 332

Cesariano, Cesare, 217n

Cézanne, Paul, 29, 31, 35, 86, 160, 160n

Chastel, André, 79, 79n, 182n, 191n, 218, 218n, 219, 225, 225n, 227, 228n, 229, 229n, 232, 232n, 233, 233n, 234n, 237, 237n, 252, 254, 257n, 268, 268n, 408n, 433n

Cheles, Luciano, 232n

Chirico, Giorgio De, 265

Christian art, early, 13

Città ideale ("Ideal City"). *See* Urbino panel

City space, and perspectives, 225

Clarke, Kenneth, 322, 322n

Cocteau, Jean, 172, 172n, 265, 266

Code, and perspective, xvi, 23, 53, 233

Cohen, Ted, 432n

Comic Scene (Serlio), 200

Condillac, Étienne de, 269

Confirmation of the Franciscan Rule (Ghirlandaio), 359, *361*

Consignment of the Keys to Saint Peter (Perugino), 248, 275, *277,* 353, 401, 417n

Construction distance, 136–137
    in Brunelleschi's perspective demonstration, 135

Conti, Alessandro, 179n, 181n, 212n, 309n, 328, 328n

Crombie, A. C., 228n

Cronaca, 207, 208

Cruciani, Fabrizio, 222n

Cubism, 28–29, 39, 86

Cusin, Fabio, 186, 186n, 188, 188n, 190n

Daedalus, 61

d'Agnolo, Baccio, 191, 207, *207,* 208, 211n, 241, 243

Dalai, Marisa, 25, 26, 26n

Dante, 179n

Degenhardt, Bernard, 211n

Delacroix, Eugène, xiv-xvi, 166

Deleuze, Gilles, 47, 47n

Demoiselles d'Avignon (Picasso), 29, 30

De prospectiva pingendi (Piero), xxii–xxiii, 11, *256,* 325, *337,* 345–352, 357

Derrida, Jacques, 76n, 78, 78n, 82n, 85n, 132n

Desanti, Jean T., 159n

Desargues, Gérard

    and Bosse, 36, 333

    Brouillon project of, 159

    on Brunelleschi's demonstration, 108

    and geometry, 51, 83, 425

    infinitist geometry of, 49–50

    on painting, 150–151

    and plane geometry, 11

    print by, 37n

    renewal of perspective by, 227

    theorem of, 386–387, 387, 387–388, 388n

Descartes, René, xv, xvii, 18, 39, 45, 46, 48, 52, 95, 130, 130n, 132n, 149, 151, 269, 387, 387n, 443

Descriptive illusion, 238–239, 245–246, 258, 263. *See also* Representation

d'Este, Lionello, 224

Diderot, Denis, 45, 137, 137n, 261, 262, 262n, 377–378, 378n, 379, 380, 380n, 381n

Dilthey, Wilhelm, 16

Diogenes Laertius, 76

Distance point, 15, 107–108, *108,* 382, 390, *393,* 446

Distancing maneuvers, 199, 228, 237

    by Krautheimer, 202

    and Uccello, 234

Donatello, 59, 60, 66, 72n, 233, 327, 401, 402, *402, 403,* 404

Duccio, 79, 81n, 106, 106

Dürer, Albrecht, 126

    "gate" of, 36, 45

Duveen, 443

Dvořák, Antón, 17

Ecstasy of Saint Cecilia (Raphael), *24,* 25–26, 356

Edgerton, Samuel Y., xvii(n), xxiv(n), 27, 27n, 28, 84

Einstein, Albert, 16n, 19

Einstein, Carl, 29n

Ensign, of painting, 363, 367, 441

Ettlinger, Leopold D., 276n

Euclid, 30, 66, 162, 270, 346–347, 347n, *347*

Feast of Herod (Donatello), 401, *402*

Federico, Duke. *See* Montefeltre, Federico da

Feltria, Elizabeth, 182

Fenton, Roger, 265

Ferretti, Massimo, 234n

Filarete, 61, 63–64, 64n, 65, 66n, 67n
    and ancients, 161, 161n
    and Brunelleschi, 61, 61n, 63, 64–65, 70, 75, 92, 98, 102n, 120–121, 130,
        130n, 157–158, 164, 338n
    and deception in painting, 150, 150n
    marble relief attributed to, 402
    on paradox of square, 149
    on perspective as "scabrous," 146, 146n
    and *scenographia,* 62, 62n
    Story of the Miraculous Image, 404

Filodosso (Alberti), 224

Fixed point, 48, 50, 52

Flagellation (Piero), 171, 179, 191, 256, *294,* 318, 402n, 406

Florence
    architectural motifs in, 207, 209
    Baptistry of San Giovanni in, 70, 89, 91, *104, 105,* 131, 133, 152, 225,
        260, 307
    and Brunelleschi, 75
    Palazzo Cocchi, 206–207, *207, 241,* 243
    Palazzo Guadagni, 207, 208, *208,* 209
    Palazzo Rucellai, *206,* 206–207, 208, 209, 240, 243, 244, 307
    Piazza della Signoria, 143, 144, *145,* 152, *152,* 153

and Rome, 190, 244

and Urbino perspectives, 191, 192, 196, 279

Florentine Renaissance, 202

Foucault, Michel, xiii, xiv, 45, 45n, 132, 132n, 149, 149n, 269, 425, 427, 427n, 429, 429n, 430, 431, 432, 433, 433n, 438, 438n, 441, 442, 443

Francastel, Pierre, 3, 139n, 218, 218n, 232, 244, 244n, 254, 298n

Franciabigio, 192, 193, 193n, 194, 194n, 196, 216

Fredericksen, Burton B., 404n

Frege, Gottlob, 130, 130n, 147, 147n

Freud, Sigmund, xiv, 54, 123, 123n, 124n, 125n

Fried, Michael, 380n

Frommel, C. L., 222n

Fucci, 143

Fuchs, Edward, 185n, 187n

Furttenbach, Joseph, 396

Galileo, 19, 29, 118, 158

Galuppi, B., 29

Gauricus, Pomponius, xvii(n), 228

Gaye, G., 181n

Gaze, of painter/spectator, 103, 126, 128, 140, 261, 266, 332, 379, 433

Genga, Girolamo, 182, 215, 216, 217, 227, 243, 254, 271, 283

Gentile da Fabriano, 251, *252*

Geometric figures, *295, 296*

Geometry, xvi, xxiii, 232, 238, 332, 424–425

    conical vs. spherical, 51

    of Desargues, 49–50

    as discovered vs. invented, 163

    Greek or euclidean, xvii, 18

    origin of, 75–78, 82, 83, 135

    and parallel vs. converging lines, 387–388

    and perspective, 78–79, 232, 238

    of the sentence, 446

    and space, 154 (*see also* Space)

    vs. phenomenal space, 352

    and writing, 162

Geometry of visibility, 132, 134

Gesta romanum (romanorum), 249, 251

Ghiberti, Lorenzo, 35, 59, 60, 60n, 401

Ghirlandaio, Domenico, 358, 359, *359*, 360, *361*, 362, *362*, 441

Ghirlandaio, Ridolfo, 192, 192n, 193, 194, 196, 216

Ginzburg, Carlo, 184n, 191n, 194n, 406, 407n

Giorgio, Francesco di Martini, 174, 181, 181n, 182, 186, 189, 211, 279–280, 404

Giorgione, 410

Gioseffi, Decio, 4, 4n, 84, 84n, 92, 92n, 138, 138n

Giotto, 66, 410

Giusto, Andrea di, 194n, *195*

Gleizes, Albert, 36n

Godel, Robert, 36n

Gombrich, Ernst, 6n, 16n, 32–33, 33n, 138, 138n, 282n

Granger, Gilles-Gaston, 269n

Gronau, G., 183n

Guardians at the Tomb, 250

Guidobaldo dal Monte, 227, 395

Hall of Columns, Villa Farnese (Peruzzi), *245*

Healing of the Lame Man (Giusto?), 195

Hegel and Hegelianism, 7, 13, 16, 27, 395

Heidegger, Martin, 18n

History, xviii–xx, 4, 27–28, 38–39, 77, 123, 157, 263

 of geometry, 82

 and perspective as revolution, 83

 of science, 78, 82

 and spatial relations, 13–14

History of art, 184–185

 analytical reconstruction in, 194

 and attribution, 199

 positivist and factual, 197

 and textual proofs, 218, 281

 textual proofs in, 281

History of Lucretia (Botticelli), *339*, 340, 358, 401

History of perspective, xiv, xxii–xxiii, 13, 38, 47

Horizon, 133, 381, 385, 388, 445

 Husserl's notion of, 82

 in Serlio's theater, 391–394

 and Urbino perspectives, 356, 394, 395

Horned perspective, *133,* 147, 392

Hubert, Henri, 139n

Huelsen, C., 210n

Humanism, xvii

Husserl, Edmund, 31

    on "blinders," 151, 151n

    on Brunelleschi's demonstration, 95, 95n

    on contemporary psychology, 6, 6n

    and cultural products, 160

    and Derrida, 78, 78n

    and "European" thought, 157

    and "field of work," 79

    on geometry, 94, 163n, 164

    on geometry (origin), 76, 76n, 82, 82n, 85, 86, 161n

    on "horizon of open-ended infinity," 155, 155n

    and intersubjectivity, 132, 132n

    on "limit-shape," 149

    on mathematicization of nature, xix

    on "perdurable presence," 162

    on practice and theory, 83, 83n

    on science after Galileo, 158, 158n

    and "significant experience," 425

    and spatiality, 325

    on substratum of perceptual experience, 159

    on "unity of ground and horizon," 152

"I," 9, 20, 123–125, 125, 381. *See also* Self; Subject

"Ideal City," 169. *See also* Urbino panel

Ideology, xv, xvi, 52

Imago, 117, 319

Infinity(ies), xviii, 121–122, 122, 384–389

Innis, Robert, 262n

Intarsia, 229

Interpretation, contextual approach to, 186

Jakobson, Roman, 319n, 424, 424n

Jammer, Max, 16, 16n, 18, 18n

Julius II (pope), 181

Kant, Emmanual, 7, 18, 18n, 47, 54, 76, 76n, 92, 158

Keller, Gottfried, 185n

Kemp, Martin, 35n, 85n, 93n, 101, 101n, 103, 105, 107, 107n

Kepler, Johannes, xviii, 48, 50, 50n

Kernodle, Georges R., 215n, 222n, 371, 394, 394n, 395, 396, 397, 399

Kimball, Fiske, 173, 173n, 174, 181, 184, 191, 200, 202, 203n, 211–212, 213, 237, 239, 243n, 246, 257, 273n, 274, 279, 306, 307, 308, 308n, 315

Klages, Ludwig, 10, 10n

Klein, Robert, xvii, xvii(n), 3, 79
    on bifocal system, 79n, 108, *110,* 392
    on Brunelleschi's demonstration, 135, 135n, 136
    on *De sculptura* (Gauricus), 228
    on scenography, 222, 224, 225n, 255, 255n
    on scientific perspective, 233–234
    on Toscanelli treatise, 71n
    on Urbino perspectives, 191, 191n
    on Vitruvius, 222n

Knowledge, 52, 287
    and truth, 82

Koyré, Alexandre, 19, 154, 154n, 228, 228n

Krautheimer, Richard
    on architecture and scenography, 203n
    and Brunelleschi's demonstration, 84, 84n, 118n
    on Serlio's view of theater, 253
    and Urbino perspectives, 199, 199n, 200, 202, 211–212, 252–253, 255–256, 257, 258–260, 279, 282, 315, 400
        and Chastel, 218
        and cleaning of "Ideal City," 213
        inscriptions, 274
        and *macellum,* 202, 259, 282, 284
        paving, 293
        and referential prejudice, 283–284
        and Sulpizio, 223
        and theater, 201, 253n, 264, 395
        and Vitruvian interpretation, 254, 281

Kubler, George, 432n

Kuhn, Thomas S., 26, 26n, 27

Lacan, Jacques, xiii, xiv, xiv(n), 19, 20, 33, 44–45, 45n, 46, 46n, 54, 54n, 56, 97, 97n, 103, 117, 117n, 123, 126, 126n, 128, 129, 129n, 284–285, 287, 388, 419

La Fontaine, Jean de, 163, 363

Language, 5, 9, 23, 25, 53, 233, 445

    and subject, 126

    and symbolism, 127

Laplanche, J., 123n

Last Supper (Tintoretto), 420–422, *423*

Laurana, Luciano, 173n, 173–174, 181, 182, 186, 189, 200, 206, *209*, 211, 243, 273, 274, 279, 307, 308, 308n, 407

Lauts, Jean, 409n

Leave-taking of the Betrothed Couple (Carpaccio), 412, 414, *415*

Leavey, John P., 78n

Lefort, Claude, 31

Lehmann, Heinze, 317n

Leibniz, Gottfried, 8, 39, 46, 47, 51, 55, 388, 396

Leonardo da Vinci, xvii(n), 55

    and atmospheric perspective, 194

    and "brake" on representation, 233

    on Brunelleschi's demonstration, 122, 122n, 127, 325, 326

    on clouds, 93

    on common place of geometric optics, 128

    and distance point, *109*

    and history, 123

    and horizon, 133n

    on images in mirrors, 125, 125n

    and Palazzo Medici, 192–193

    on perspective, 11, 25, 25n, 124, 232, 239, 239n

    on spectators' positions, 136

    and subject as cyclops, 35

Leo X (pope), 193, 214n

Lessing, Gotthold, 262, 360

Lévi-Strauss, Claude, 127, 282, 282n, 284–285, 286, 286n, 288n, 306, 306n, 444

Lichtenberg, Georg, 125

Linear perspective, 32, 153

Mirror (cont.)

    in Brunelleschi's demonstration, 63, 92, 94, 97, 98, 115–118, 119–122, 125–126, 127–128, 129–130, 131–133, 137–140, 146, 155, 377, 379–80, 439

    as demonstrative aid, 62–63, 65–66

    Diderot's blind man on, 137

    in *Las Meninas,* 427, 429, 431, 432, 433, 438

Modern (central) perspective, xvii, 12, 18–19

Monge, Gaspard, 132n

Montefeltre, Elizabeth, 182

Montefeltre, Federico da, 173, 179, 181, 182, 185, 186, 187, 187n, 188, *189, 189*–190, 231, 246, 247n, 318

Montefeltre, Guidobaldo da, 247n, 318

Montefeltre family, 181

Morelli, Giovanni, 181

Muraro, Michelangelo, 408, 408n

Myth, 9, 444–445

Narcissus fable, 46, 383, 443

Newman, Barnett, 311

Newton, Sir Isaac, 18, 27, 29

Nicolas of Cusa, xxii, xxii(n), 18, 48, 49

Nietzsche, Friedrich, 47, 52, 173

Novotny, Fritz, 31, 31n

Oberto, Anna, 179n, 274, 318

Oberto, Martino, 179n, 274, 318, 341

Offner, Richard, 274

Optics, 5–6, 238, 346–353

Pacioli, Luca, 182, 406

Painting

    and language, 287, 445

    and perspective, 325–326

    and representation, 262–263

    significance of, 285–286, 287

    spectator neutralized in, 380n

    thinking in, 446

Palazzo Cocchi (d'Agnolo?), 206–207, *207, 241, 243*

Palazzo della Cancelleria, *242, 243*

Palazzo Ducale, Urbino, *209, 230*

    marquetry door in, *366*

    studiolo in, 231, *231*

Palazzo Guadagni, 207, 208, *208,* 209

Palazzo Piccolomini, 208–209, *209*

Palazzo Rucellai, *206,* 206–207, 208, 209, *240,* 243, 244, 307

Palladio, 223, 225

Panofsky, Erwin, 3–4, 4n, 5, 13n, 14–15, 15n, 18n, 19, 26, 26n, 27, 29, 29n, 43n, 82, 234n

    on Alberti and distance point, 107, 108, *108,* 108n

    and anachronism, 44–45

    and antique perspective, 12, 16, 16n

        vs. modern, 12–13

    and *Arnolfini Wedding,* 131, 131n

    and art as conversing, 285, 285n

    and base plane, 346

    and Brunelleschi, 145n, 154

    and Cassirer, 6–7, 11–12, 15

    on center of projection, 62n

    and Cézanne, 31

    and curvilinear perspective, 6

    on discovery of vanishing point, 126

    on effects of perspective, 11

    and "imaginary space," 30

    Lessing remark cited by, 360

    and linear perspective, 32

    and Mannheim, 17

    on medieval painting, 14

    and Merleau-Ponty, 31, 82n

    and noneuclidean geometries, 28

    and origin of perspective, 79, 80n, 84

    on painting and space, 82–83, 83n

    and perspectives of other periods and regions, 63

    on perspective and style, 10, 10n

    Perspective as Symbolic Form, xix, 3–4, 5, 14, 19, 31, 234n

    on projective geometry, 81–82

    on quarrels about perspective, 38, 38n

Panofsky, Erwin (cont.)

    and *scenographia,* 219

    and signification, 17, 17n

    and space, xvii(n), 154n

    and symbolic form, 6–7, 11–12

    on two levels of signification, 259

    and vanishing point, 23, 82

Paradigm, xxi–xxii, 25–28, 90

    perspective, xxi–xxii, 28, 47, 90, 287

Parronchi, Alessandro, xxii

    on Barberini panels, 179–180n

    Brunelleschi-Galileo comparison by, 118, 118n

    and Brunelleschi's demonstration, *110,* 111–112, 322

    and descriptive illusion, 245

    on distance point, 390

    on measurement in perspective, 134, 134n

    and optics, 151

    research by, 84, 84n

    review of, xxiv, xxiv(n)

    and *sgabello,* 402, 402n

    and Toscanelli treatise, 71n

    and Urbino perspectives, 192, 192n, 193, 193n, 194, 194n, 196, 196n, 200,
        200n, 214, 246, 246n, 279, 307n, 308, 308n, 325, 383, 383n, 419

Pascal, Blaise, 47, 49, 51, 52–53, 53n, 54, 54n, 121, 162, 217, 269, 382, 384–
    386, 388

Passavant, Johann David, 175, 179n, 181n, 273, 273n

Paulhan, Jean, 39, 39n, 144, 144n

Pedretti, Carlo, 193n

Peirce, Charles S., 90, 255

Péladan, Joséphin (the Sâr), 36n

Pélerin, Jean, 43, 133, *133*

Pelicani, Biagio, 71, 71n

Pentecost (Signorelli), 171

Perocco, Guido, 406

Perrault, Charles, 189, 189n, 202, 223n, 270, 270n

Perspecteurs, Les (Bosse print), 37

Perspectival meditation, 49, 51

Perspective

    antique (herringbone), xvi, 12, 15–16, 63–64, 161–162, 184

    architectural, 271

    axonometric, 30

    bifocal, 392

    and demonstrative operation, 263–264

    and geometry, 78–79, 232, 238 (*see also* Geometry)

    and history, xviii–xx, xxii–xxiii (*see also* History; History of art)

    horned, *133,* 147, 392

    and language or code, xvi, 23, 25, 53, 233

    mechanical construction of, 35–37

    modern (central), 12, 18–19

    origin of, xviii, 75–78, 79, 83–84, 95, 152, 270, 447

    and painting, 325–326

    as paradigm, xxi-xxii, 19–20, 28, 47, 90, 287

    and perception, 31–32

    and *perspectiva naturalis,* 67–68

    and photography, xiv–xvi, 125–126, 139, 265, 266

    scientific, 160–161, 233

    as symbolic form, 3–4, 5, 9–12, 14, 23, 44

    and vision, 45–46

    and *Weltanschauung,* 16–17, 47, 84

Perspective subject, 132. *See also* Subject

Perspective as Symbolic Form (Panofsky), xix, 3–4, 5, 14, 19, 31, 234n

Perugino, 248, 251, 275–276, *277,* 312n, 353–354, 401, 418n, 439

Peruzzi, Baldassare, 201, 203, *203,* 214n, 220, 221, 222, 227, *245,* 246, 271, 308, 360, 371, 400

Philip, Lotte Brand, 215n

Philosophy of Symbolic Forms (Cassirer), 7, 23

Photography, xiv–xvi, 125–126, 139, 265, 266

Piaget, Jean, 32

Piazza della Signoria, 143, 144, *145,* 152, 153

Piazza della Signoria in Florence (Bellotto), *152*

Picasso, Pablo, 29, 154n, 432–433, *434, 435, 436, 437,* 439, 444, 445

Piccaluga, Gabriella Ferri, 217n

Piero della Francesca, xxi, 68, 68n, 186, 325–326

    Annunciation, 363, 364

Piero della Francesca (cont.)

and Berlin panel, 183

Brera Altarpiece, 184

and Carpaccio, 406, 407

on constructing bodies in elevation, 255–256, 256n

De prospectiva pingendi, xxii–xxiii, 11, *256,* 325, *337,* 345–352, 357

Flagellation, 171, 179, 191, 256, *294,* 318, 402n, 406

on force of perspective, 121

on limits of viewing, 345–346, 356–357, 357, 374–375, 375n

Madonna of Senigallia, 179

Montefeltro dyptich by, 188, *189*

and optics, 346–352

on overtones of "perspective," 69

and Pacioli, 182

and perspectival paradigm, 67n

and planar geometry figures, 293

and plane geometry, 11

and production of volumes, 267

on spectators' positions, 136

on subject-painting relation, 389, 389n

on symmetry in theater, 399

and Urbino panel, 174–175, 181, 181n, 279, 322

and windows or doors, 363

Pinelli, A., 181n

Pinturicchio, 182

Pisano, Bonanno, *250*

Plato, 9, 16, 52

Plautus, 222

Pliny, xxiv, xxiv(n)

Poetry, 422–424

Poincaré, Henri, 238, 238n, 264, 351

Point of view, 48, 49–50, 54–55, 121, 126, 332, 381, 445, 446

in Brunelleschi's demonstration, 103, 120, 134, 136, 164

and *Las Meninas,* 431

and Serlio's theater, 393

Pollux, Julius, 281

Pompeii, xvi, 327, 358, *358*

Pomponius Laetus, 222

Poncelet, Jean, 29, 50, 133, 387, 388, 445

Pontalis, J. -B., 123n

Pontelli, Baccio, 181, 186

Port-Royal, 52, 269

Poussin, Nicolas, 171, 318

Pozzo, Andrea, 218

Presentation in the Temple (Barberini Panel), *178, 179*

Presentation in the Temple (Cavallini), *251, 251–252*

Presentation in the Temple (Fabriano), *252*

Presentation in the Temple (Pisano), *250*

Presentation of the Virgin in the Temple (Tintoretto), *421*

Presentation of the Virgin in the Temple (Titian), 419, *420*

Prigogine, Ilya, 47n

Procession of the Banners of San Giovanni, 111

Projection, 123, 124

Prosperi, Bernardino, 215n

Prototype, 90, 92, 322

Provoyeur, Pierre, 417n

Ptolemy, 28

Pucci, Antonio, 359

Punishment of Corah (Botticelli), 275, *276*

Pythagoras, 160

Raphael, *24,* 25, 173, 175, 181n, 186, 243, 251, 271, 307, 353, *355,* 401,
    417n, 439, 444

Reading metaphor, 261–262

Reber, Franz von, 173

Recanati, François, 239n, 258n, 269n

Reception of the Ambassadors (Carpaccio), *407,* 410, 411–412, *412, 413, 414,* 417,
    418, 419

"Reception" theorists, 185

Reichenbach, Hans, 39n

Reichenbach, Maria, 39

Renaissance, 19, 160, 163, 173, 184, 202, 205, 224, 267
    and Brunelleschi, 59
    and infinity, 388
    representational system of, 14, 27, 86, 224–225, 227

Representation, xvi, xviii, 9, 226, 238–239, 269
    in *âge classique,* xi, 47–49, 52
    and *Las Meninas, 426,* 427, 429, 430–431, 438
    and Narcissus, 443
    and perspective paradigm, 438, 441
    and self-reflection of painting, 445
    and Urbino perspectives, 226, 239, 259, 264, 268
Representationalist hypothesis or principle, 239, 258, 263, 267–268
Resuscitation of the Child (Ghirlandaio), 358, 359, *359,* 360
Reuwich, Erhardum de, 408, 416, 418
Riario, Alfonso (cardinal), 222
Richter, George Martin, 179n, 180n
Richter, Jean-Paul, 25n, 122n
Ridolfi, Roberto, 192n
Riegl, Aloïs, 16, 79n
Robbia, Luca della, 59
Robert, Hubert, 380n
Robertis, Domenico, 66n
Romanesque art, 13
Rome, 190
    and Florence, 244
Rosenstiehl, Pierre, 389n
Rosselli, Cosimo, 191n, 311, 311n, 360
Rosselli, Domenico, *230, 231, 231, 365*
Rosselli, Pietro, 221, *221*
Rossellino, Bernardo, 206, 208–209, *209,* 243
Rossi, O., 181n
Rothlisberger, Marcel, 418n
Roussel, Raymond, 127
Rovere, Francesco Maria II della, 183, 193, 217, 271
Russell, Bertrand, 351
Russio, Adelaide, 263n
Rykwert, Josef, 283n

Saalman, Howard, 191, 244n, 245, 261n, 308, 308n, 311, 311n, 337n, 360
Sabattini, Nicola, 399, 399n
Sacchetti, Francesco, 101n
Sagolacheni plaque, 252n

Saint Francis Resuscitating a Child (Ghirlandaio), 358, *359, 359*–360

Saint George Baptizing the Pagans (Carpaccio), 417

Saint George cycle, 407

Saint Ursula cycle, 405, 407, 408, 409–410, 447

Salmi, Mario, 246, 246n

Sanchez-Canton, F. J., 438n

San Daniele, Pellegrino di, 215

Sangallo, Antonio da, 243, 307n

Sangallo, Battista da, 282n

Sangallo, Giuliano da, 191, 191n, 196, 210, 211, 211n, 221, 280, 308

Sangiorgi, F., 179n

San Giorgio dei Schiavoni cycle, 405

San Giovanni, Baptistry of, 70, 89, 91, *104, 105,* 131, 133, 152, 225, 307

Sanpaolesi, Piero, 84n, 191, 191n, 207n, 211n, 245, 279, 308, 308n, 322, 409, 409n

San Romolo, church of, 143

Santa Chiara convent, 175, 181–182

Santa Maria dei Fiori, 89, 102

Santa Maria presso San Satiro, 217, 217n

Sartre, Jean-Paul, 17, 271

Sassetti, Francesco, 359

Satyric Scene (Serlio), *284*

Saussure, Ferdinand de, xxi, 5, 23, 36

Saussurian linguistics, 286

Scenic apparatus, 193, 214–216, 392, 396–400

Scenography *(scenographia),* 62, 93, 203, 213, 218–219, 224–225, 245, 270, 271, 395, 397

Shapiro, Meyer, 262n

Schefer, Jean-Louis, 261n, 262n, 285, 285n

Schoenberg, Arnold, 405, 405n

Schubring, Paul, 317, 317n

Searle, John, 427, 430, 431, 431n, 439, 441

Serlio, Sebastiano, 201, 203, 271, 396, 447
    on architect-perspective relation, 217, 217n, 270–271, 271n
    and Baltimore panel, 254
    on constructing bodies in elevation, 255–256, 256n
    and geometric perspective, 267, 293, *295,* 389–390
    and scenography, 201, 208, 208n, 213, 220, 253, 253n

Serlio, Sebastiano (cont.)

    and theater (comic, tragic, satyric scene), 200, *200, 201,* 212, 215, 215n, 218, 219, *220,* 253, 254, 256n, 257, 257n, 260, 283, 283n, *284, 390,* 391–394, 394n, 395–396, 397–398, 400

    and Urbino panel ("Ideal City"), 169, 169n, 213–214, 214n, 291, 305, 305n, 371

    and Urbino perspectives, 283

Serres, Michel, 48, 48n, 49, 50, 52n, 79n, 95n

Seurat, Georges Pierre, 35

Sforza, Battista, 188, *189*

Signorelli, Luca, 171

Simmel, Georg, 13, 14n

Simon, Gérard, xviii(n)

Sistine Chapel, 248, 275–276, 276n, 401

Site, for drawing, 64–65

Sky

    in Brunelleschi's demonstration, 89, 93–95, 98, 139, 148, 153, 155, 324–325

    in Urbino panel *(città ideale),* 320–321, 324

Snyder, Joel, 432n

Sophocles, 270

Space, xvii, 10, 39–40, 49, 83, 95, 149. *See also* Geometry

    and art (Panofsky), 154n

    geometric, 154

    in geometry of Desargues, 49

    given vs. constructed in, 351–352

    Kant's definition of, 18

    and modern perspective, 18–19

    subjective vs. objective, 39

Spencer, J. R., 161n

Sperber, Dan, 445n

Spinoza, Baruch, 424

Steinberg, Leo, 426, 426n, 429, 429n, 430, 430n, 432n, 439n

Stengers, Isabelle, 47n

Stereoscope, 127–128

Story of the Miraculous Image (Filarete?), 402, *404*

Strozzi, Lorenzo, 193, 196

Structuralism and structural analysis, xviii, 197, 281, 306

Studiolo (Rosselli), *231*

Studiolo in Urbino, 229, 231, 266–267

Subject, xiii–xvi, xviii, xxi, 9–10, 19, 20, 46, 53, 126, 126–127, 132, 446

    cartesian, 45

    and conical geometry, 51

    and eye, 124

    and geometry, 425

    implied by painting, 388–389

    Kantian view of, 47

    in *Las Meninas,* 430, 443

    perspective, 132

    and perspective construction, 122

    and point in painting, 443

    and point of view, 48

    in theater, 399

    and Wittgenstein, 34

Sulpizio da Veroli, Giovanni, 219, 222, 223, 223n

Surrealism, 265

Symbolism

    and language, 127

    Lévi-Strauss on, 282

    in painting, 3–4, 5, 9, 12, 14, 23, 44, 446

Symmetry, 289, 424

    in Brunelleschi's demonstration, 382

    direct vs. indirect, 328

    in theater art, 399

    and Urbino perspectives, 326–333, 336–340, 344

Tanturli, Giovanni, 66n, 72n

Temple of Saint George (Carpaccio), *416*

Temple of Solomon (Reuwich), *416, 418*

Temptation of Christ (Duccio), *106*

Terence, 222

Thales, 76, 77, 79n, 83, 85, 92, 95n, 135, 164

Theater, 214–216, 371, 394–399

    and Renaissance culture, 224

    and Serlio, *200, 201,* 215, 215n, 218, 219, 220, 253, 254, *390,* 391–394, 394n, 395–396, 397–398, 400

    and Urbino perspectives, 201–203, 212–227, 253, 254, 257–258, 259, 279, 305, 395, 399

Thinking, in painting, 446. *See also* Knowledge

Tintoretto, 419, 420, *421, 422, 423*

Tisseron, Claude, 50n

Titian, 410, 419, *421*

Tolnay, Charles de, 427n

Toscanelli, Paolo, 71, 72n

Tour d'Auvergne, Madeleine de la, 192

Tragic Scene (Serlio), 201

Trapier, Elizabeth du Gué, 431n

Trinity, The (Masaccio), *96, 233*

Triumph of Saint George (Carpaccio), *416,* 417–418, *419*

Trompe l'oeil, 217–218, 229, 271

Truth, 53–55, 148, 158, 159

    in painting, 150–151, 159–160

    and science, 82

Uccello, Paolo, 44, 66, 68, 68n, 69, 70, 143, 153, 179, 231, 233, 234, 267, 363

Urbino panel ("Ideal City," *città ideale),* 169–173, 181–182, 191–192, 202, *204, 205, 206*–207, 238, 243, 258, 289, *290,* 291–294, 297–299, 300–302, 305–312, 318, 444. *See also* Urbino perspectives

    "aberrations" in, 356–358, 371

    and angle of vision, 353

    attribution of, 175, 179, 181, 196, 200, 322

    Baltimore panel compared with, 255–257, 281

    and Baptistry of San Giovanni, 225

    "basilica" of, *210*

    Berlin panel compared with, 280

    and Brunelleschi's demonstration, 319, 322, 323, 338, 344–345, 374, 416, 439

    and comic scene, 260

    and date of painting, 211, 227

  details of sky in, *320–321*

  display room for, 179, 366

  and distancing maneuvers, 237

  and gaze, 265–266

  and Ghirlandaio's *Annunciation,* 362

  ground plan of, *370, 371*

  hole at vanishing point of, 341–344, 348, 382, 441

  horizon in, 356, 394

  images in, 188

  inscriptions in, 272, 273–275

  Krautheimer study of, 199, 213 (*see also* Krautheimer, Richard)

  and Leonardo, 194

  palaces in, *338, 338–339, 334, 335, 369*

  paving design in, 295, 324, 327

  rotunda in, 217, 246, 247, 252, 282, *336,* 354

  and Sangallo, 210–211, 211n

  symmetry of, 326, 327, 328, 329, 331, 332, 340, 344

  and theater, 212, 218, 219, 252–53, 259

  two wells in, 335, 337

  vanishing point of, 348, 381–382, 441

  windows or doors in, 360, 363, 367, 368

Urbino perspectives, 175, 181, 183–184, 185–197, 205, 225, 227, 233, 279–284, 287–312, 315–318, 400, 401, 404–405, 444. *See also* Baltimore panel; Berlin panel; Urbino panel

  attribution of, 181, 196, 200, 246, 279, 316

  and Brunelleschi's demonstration, 319, 322–325, 371, 380, 382

  and Carpaccio, 407, 408, 409, 410, 418

  dating of, 191, 194, 196, 227, 274, 279, 319

  and linear perspective, 234, 237, 252, 356, 387–389, 394, 395, 446

  and *Miracles of Saint Bernardino,* 180

  and representational principle, 226, 259, 268

  and Serlio's theater, 394

  symmetry in, 326–333, 336–340

  and theater, 201–203, 212–227, 253, 254, 257–258, 259, 279, 305, 395, 399

  and *Triumph of Saint George,* 417n

  and utopia, 264

  and vanishing point (Piero), 348

Urbino *studiolo,* 229, 231, 266–267

Utopia, 239, 244, 264

Valéry, Paul, 423

van Eyck, Jan, 444

    Arnolfini Wedding, 43, 130–131, 416, 439, 440, 441, 442, 444

    Virgin in the Church, 15n

Van Eyck brothers, 43

Vanishing point, 23, 51, 80, 81, 82, 121, 157, 332, 381, 388, 446

    and Brunelleschi's demonstration, 111, 120, 134, 136, 157–158, 164

    in *Las Meninas,* 436, 441

    Piero on, 348

    and Serlio's theater, 392, 393, 397–398

    in *Triumph of Saint George,* 417–418

    in Urbino perspectives, 170, 374, 382–383, 441

        and hole in Urbino panel, 341, 344

Vasari, Giorgio xvii, 44

    and bifocal method, 79

    on Bramante, 179, 179n

    and Brunelleschi, 68–72, 86, 92, 93, 103, 109, 118, 134, 135, 151, 151n, 153, 159, 164, 229n, 322, 323–324

    and *Calandria,* 214n

    and Franciabigio, 192, 192n, 193, 193n, 194n

    and Ghiberti's *Commentari,* 60, 60n

    on *intarsia,* 229, 229n

    on Manetti, 66, 66n

    and scenic apparatus, 216, 222

    and tradition of perspective, 76

    on two types of artist, 233

    and Urbino perspectives, 196

Velázquez, Jose Nieto, 425–432, 433, 438, 439, 441, 442, 444, 445

Velluti, Agostino, 183

Venturi, Adolfo, 179n, 181

Vernarecci, A., 183n

Vernet, Joseph, 377, 380n

Veronese, Paolo, 420

Versailles, 189

Viator, Pélerin, 19, 121, 392

View of the Piazetta in Venice (Bellotto), *384*

Vignola, 50, 396

Villon, Jacques, 36n

Vision, 45–46

    and blur, 352–353, 357

    and conical geometry, 51

Vitruvius and Vitruvian interpretation, 62, 62n, 63, 201, 212, 218, 219, 222, 223, 223n, 227, 244, 253, 254, 257, 257n, 270, 279, 281, 282, 283, 283n, 312, 333, 390, 400n

Void, 267–268

Voyeurism, 128–129, 146

Warburg, Aby, 359, 359n

Warhol, Andy, 126

Wedding at Cana (Tintoretto), 420, *422*

Weltanschauung, and perspective, 16–17, 47, 84

Westheim, Paul, 29n

Weyl, Hermann, 328, 328n, 331, 333, 336, 388, 388n

Wheelock, Arthur, 348, 348n, 351n

White, John, 3, 84, 84n, 102n, 108, 119, 119n

Window(s)

    in Brunelleschi's demonstration, 102, 136, 152

    in Florentine painting, 360

    in Urbino perspectives, 363, 367, *368, 371*

    vs. perspectival paradigm, 67n

Window metaphor, 102, 136, 350

Wittgenstein, Ludwig, 33–35, 39, 45–46, 46n, 52, 268–269, 352, 352n, 424, 424n, 446, 446n

Wittkower, Rudolf, xxi(n), 94, 95n

Zeri, Federico, 179n, 181n, 190, 190n, 243n, 244, 274, 274n, 309, 309n

Zerner, Henri, 191n, 203n, 222n, 225n

Zorzi, Ludovico, 406n, 419n